C000126025

"Gregory Shaffer has written a superb analysis of the
world trade. The core of the book consists of co-author
the trading system of China, most significantly, but
decisive actor now turns out to be the US, which has inc
created. In the future, suggests Shaffer, international r
room to act and also to react to the actions of others.
systems is also vital if the world is to enjoy a measure oɪ ɔtɑʋiɪity and peace."

Martin Wolf, *Financial Times*

"For decades, international trade has been at the heart of globalization. And as Shaffer
brilliantly illuminates in this book, trade — and the way countries like China, India and
Brazil have used the laws and regulations that govern it to promote their own interests
— has very much shaped the world we live in today. But globalization is now changing
trajectory, and the way trade laws and regulations evolve from here will shape tomor-
row's world. Which makes Emerging Powers and the World Trading System essential
reading for policymakers and academics alike. A book written exactly for our current
moment."

Ian Bremmer, President of Eurasia Group, founder of GZERO Media

"A monumental achievement! Not only does Shaffer provide a comprehensive elucida-
tion of how we got to where we are on trade law, but he also lays out a broader framework
and methodology for understanding how the international system changes over time. A
superb example of work that is both theory-generating and empirically grounded, with
implications for multiple disciplines."

Tom Ginsburg, Leo Spitz Professor of International Law and Professor of
Political Science, University of Chicago

"Gregory Shaffer has researched the global diffusion of international trade rules for over
two decades. This unique book synthesizes developments across China, Brazil, and India
- as well as the United States – putting this critical moment for the multilateral trading
system into fascinating historical context."

Chad P. Bown, Reginald Jones Senior Fellow, Peterson Institute
for International Economics

"Shaffer broadens our gaze, deepens our knowledge, and connects the micro to the
macro in explaining how the international trade regime works. In doing so, he not only
furnishes us with critical knowledge of Brazil, India, and China, and their relation to the
trade law system; he also provides a masterclass in how to undertake transnational
research."

Anthea Roberts, Professor at the School of Regulation and
Global Governance, Australia National University

"Professor Shaffer's work eloquently illuminates a complex but vital subject – the law's power
to shape a more inclusive model of transnational trade. By examining how and by whom the
rules have been written and rewritten, he details the ways in which emerging economies like
Brazil, China, and India can spur the creation of capabilities needed to help reform and
rebuild the multilateral trading system, so that the benefits of trade accrue to all. This is an
important contribution to our understanding of recent geopolitical history and the forces that
will continue to define our future."

Roberto Azevêdo, Director-General of the World Trade Organization (2013–2020);
Ambassador of Brazil to the WTO (2008–2013)

"Greg Shaffer's dogged and exhaustive research provides an unparalleled and realistic insider's guide to how the WTO dispute settlement system has operated behind the headlines in the first 25 years of its existence. Professor Shaffer has properly put his focus on the three emerging giants in the world economy – China, India, and Brazil – and their ability to make strategic use of the dispute settlement system to advance their trading interests. His analysis will be invaluable for WTO Members and the broader trade community to make the necessary mid-course corrections to the WTO dispute settlement system that must continue to provide an invaluable resource for countries to settle their trade-related differences in the decades ahead."

Scott Andersen, former Managing Partner of the Geneva office
of Sidley & Austin, and former member of the U.S. Mission to the WTO

"International economic law can only be understood from a holistic view of law, economics, and politics. Here we finally have a study that offers sophisticated analysis of legal constraints and their economic impact while attending to political context within countries and the power politics between them. In a masterful study, Shaffer explores how Brazil, China, and India interact with the World Trade Organization. The book compellingly portrays how emerging powers were changed by engagement in the international trade system and, in turn, forced responses and adaptation to those rules, including in the states that originally drove their formation. From rich details based on local knowledge to larger questions about the survival of the trade regime, this book should be required reading for scholars, trade officials and practitioners."

Christina L. Davis, Professor of Government, Harvard University, and Susan S. and
Kenneth L. Wallach Professor, Radcliffe Institute

"This brilliant and artfully narrated comparative assessment from the inside, of the strategies by which three ascendant member states within the WTO have gained power through legal capacity has been achieved by a sustained, collaborative practice of the fieldwork method which ethnographers of elite cultures in the changing international system would be proud of, might be envious of, but most importantly, can learn from."

George E. Marcus, Distinguished Professor, University of California, Irvine,
member of French-funded collaborative anthropological team study of the
WTO, 2008–2013, and co-editor of *Writing Culture: The Poetics and
Politics of Ethnography*

"At a time when the world is struggling to understand the trade policies of the Trump Administration and what motivated them, Greg Shaffer has provided compelling answers grounded in decades of research along with case studies of the shifts in economic power and legal capacity in China, India and Brazil. If you want to understand the past and the future of the transnational legal order for trade, read this book!"

Jennifer Hillman, Senior Fellow, Council on Foreign Relations; former member
of WTO Appellate Body, Commissioner of the U.S. International
Trade Commission, and USTR General Counsel

"Changes in international trade and the legal economic order cannot be understood without taking into account the impact of emerging economies such as China, Brazil and India. Any analysis is incomplete without considering their legal capacity and practice. Professor Gregory Shaffer's book provides the story that fill in a vacuum in the literature and becomes an obligatory reference."

Alejandro Jara, former WTO Deputy Director-General and Ambassador
of Chile to WTO

EMERGING POWERS AND THE WORLD TRADING SYSTEM

Victorious after World War II and the Cold War, the United States and its allies largely wrote the rules for international trade and investment. Yet, by 2020, it was the United States that became the great disrupter – disenchanted with the rules' constraints. Paradoxically, China, India, Brazil, and other emerging economies became stakeholders in and, at times, defenders of economic globalization and the rules regulating it. *Emerging Powers and the World Trading System* explains how this came to be and addresses the micropolitics of trade law – what has been developing under the surface of the business of trade through the practice of law, which has broad macro implications. This book provides a necessary complement to political and economic accounts for understanding why, at a time of hegemonic transition where economic security and geopolitics assume greater roles, the United States challenged, and emerging powers became defenders of, the legal order that the United States created.

Gregory Shaffer is Chancellor's Professor at the University of California, Irvine School of Law. His publications include 9 books and over 100 articles and book chapters, including *Constitution-Making and Transnational Legal Order* (with Ginsburg and Halliday, 2019), *Transnational Legal Orders* (with Halliday, 2015), and *Transnational Legal Ordering and State Change* (2013).

Emerging Powers and the World Trading System

THE PAST AND FUTURE OF INTERNATIONAL ECONOMIC LAW

GREGORY SHAFFER

CAMBRIDGE
UNIVERSITY PRESS

University Printing House, Cambridge CB2 8BS, United Kingdom

One Liberty Plaza, 20th Floor, New York, NY 10006, USA

477 Williamstown Road, Port Melbourne, VIC 3207, Australia

314–321, 3rd Floor, Plot 3, Splendor Forum, Jasola District Centre, New Delhi – 110025, India

79 Anson Road, #06–04/06, Singapore 079906

Cambridge University Press is part of the University of Cambridge.

It furthers the University's mission by disseminating knowledge in the pursuit of education, learning, and research at the highest international levels of excellence.

www.cambridge.org
Information on this title: www.cambridge.org/9781108495196
DOI: 10.1017/9781108861342

First published 2021

A catalogue record for this publication is available from the British Library.

Library of Congress Cataloging-in-Publication Data
NAMES: Shaffer, Gregory, 1958– author.
TITLE: Emerging powers and the world trading system : the past and future of international economic law / Gregory Shaffer, University of California, Irvine.
DESCRIPTION: Cambridge, United Kingdom ; New York, NY : Cambridge University Press, 2021. | Includes index.
IDENTIFIERS: LCCN 2020051783 | ISBN 9781108495196 (hardback) | ISBN 9781108817127 (paperback) | ISBN 9781108861342 (ebook)
SUBJECTS: LCSH: Foreign trade regulation. | Commercial treaties.
CLASSIFICATION: LCC K4600 .S53 2021 | DDC 343.08/7–dc23
LC record available at https://lccn.loc.gov/2020051783

ISBN 978-1-108-49519-6 Hardback
ISBN 978-1-108-81712-7 Paperback

To Michele, Brooks, and Sage

Contents

Figures

Tables

Preface: The Project and Its Methodology

This project started from the question of how developing countries could build trade law capacity to defend their interests in a system largely developed by the United States and Europe. Its focus evolved over time as it became apparent that by building legal capacity and engaging with the trade system, the three emerging economies, Brazil, India, and China, were transforming themselves. It became further evident that, when successful, they were also affecting the trade legal order itself. It is through the study of these intermeshed processes that we can better understand the central conundrum and paradox that this book addresses: how it is that the United States now calls into question the trade law system it created, while emerging economies that long criticized that system for its bias in favor of US interests defend it.[1] This shift preceded the election of President Trump, but that election accentuated and accelerated it. The world changed dramatically as I conducted this research, to which the research questions responded. The book thus addresses the broader ecosystem of trade law involving not only the World Trade Organization (WTO) but also bilateral and regional trade and investment agreements and domestic law, legal practice, and legal capacity building. Most importantly, it addresses the critical links between changes within states and changes in international regimes, which the book theorizes in terms of "transnational legal ordering." Together these changes constitute the dynamic making and unmaking, settlement and unsettlement, and fragmentation of what the book calls the "transnational legal order" for trade.

The book's methodology is a multi-method qualitative approach involving three extended case studies – those of Brazil, India, and China, and their links with the transnational legal order for trade. This work was conducted over two decades involving elite interviews (a term of art referring to those in positions of authority) and fieldwork on trade policy making and dispute settlement in Brazil, India, China, the United States, and Europe – including Geneva, the WTO's home – combined

---

[1]   In the words of a Brazilian official, "It is a paradoxical moment because you have the hegemon that wants to reform and the target country that wants to keep the system as is." Interview, July 11, 2019.

with a survey, descriptive statistics, participant observation, and a review of primary and secondary materials. The analysis is both longitudinal and cross-sectional. It is longitudinal in that it tracks changes over time, including both before and after the 2007–2008 financial crisis, which accelerated a shift in global economic power away from the United States and Europe and catalyzed the rise of anti-trade populist politicians in the United States. It is cross-sectional in that the study closely analyzes changes in three different emerging powers regarding an array of trade and trade-related issues (such as intellectual property and investment law), and addresses parallels, congruences, and differences among them.

THE INTERVIEWS AND PARA-ETHNOGRAPHY

For the study, I conducted over two hundred in-depth, semi-structured, elite interviews in Beijing, Brasília, Brussels, Geneva, Kerala, Mumbai, New Delhi, Rio de Janeiro, São Paulo, Shanghai, Shenzhen, Washington, DC, and other locations where I was granted considerable access to meet with informants, including at the highest levels. The interviewees included officials at the WTO across all levels from the director general and members of the Appellate Body to high- and mid-level secretariat staff across multiple divisions; officials at the United Nations Conference on Trade and Development (UNCTAD); current and former ambassadors to the WTO; officials at WTO Missions in Geneva; government officials in the national capital; private lawyers engaged in trade law practice (both domestic lawyers and foreign lawyers working for and against these countries); company, trade, and industry association representatives (working with and against these countries); heads of think tanks and researchers within them; academics in law, political science, and economics within them; representatives of nongovernmental organizations; and news reporters writing on trade law from these countries. Most of the interviews were with one interviewee, but some interviews included small groups of colleagues, whether in government, law firms, academia, and think tanks. The interviews generally lasted from one to two hours. They were held most frequently in the interviewee's office, but also in neutral venues such as restaurants and coffee shops.

For each of the three country studies, I worked with one or more leading academics from the country, Michelle Ratton Sanchez Badin (on Brazil), James Nedumpara and Aseema Sinha (on India), and Henry Gao (on China). This provided an important entry point into the trade policy world in these countries, and helped me bridge language challenges, particularly in China. We conducted many interviews together and shared interview notes when we did not. Each of my collaborators is part of the trade law network in these countries and themselves engaged in participant observation.

My approach can be viewed as having an ethnographic dimension when ethnography is viewed in a broad (but nontraditional) sense of participant observation of a field.[2] The object of this study is the flow of norms and institutional practices in the field of international trade law, and, to a lesser extent, the related field of investment law. It is not a traditional ethnography rooted in a specific location, but rather the place of study is multisited and "deterritorialized."[3] My approach entails sustained engagement with practitioners in multiple locations in different states over time. Within the case studies of Brazil, India, and China, the sites are likewise multiple and include government offices, lawyer offices, trade association offices, think tanks, law schools, and embassies.

My method can be viewed as a form of "para-ethnography" given that many of my informants were equally interested in understanding the processes that I was studying. Para-ethnography entails the study of social processes through interviewing, and even working with, practitioners "who are themselves engaged in quasi-social scientific 'studies' of the same processes" in an effort to understand and respond to them.[4] In this way, the interviews, in part, can be viewed as "collaborations" in the sense of forays into "making sense" of developments in the trade world. These actors must respond to a continuously unfolding present on partial information in real time.

My interviews began with questions concerning the interviewee's background and experiences, both in relation to the trade regime and more generally. I then asked open-ended questions regarding the challenges and opportunities that the WTO system posed. My aim was to first obtain the interviewee's general perspectives without being steered by my questions. I wanted the interviewee to be in the position

[2] Compare Michael Burawoy, "The Extended Case Method," *Sociological Theory* 16 (March 1998): 1 ("by ethnography I mean writing about the world from the standpoint of participant observation"); Mathew Desmond, "Relational Ethnography," *Theory and Society* 43 no. 5 (2014): 547–579 ("studying fields rather than places"); and Julian Go and Monika Krause, "Fielding Transnationalism: An Introduction," *The Sociological Review Monographs* 64, no. 2 (2016): 6–30.

[3] Sally Merry, "Ethnography of the Global," Workshop on Empirical Research Methods: Center for the Study of Law and Society, 2013. For an application to human rights, Sally Merry, *Human Rights and Gender Violence: Translating International Law into Local Justice* (Chicago: University of Chicago Press, 2006). For an earlier application to global economic governance that includes trade, John Braithwaite and Peter Drahos, *Global Business Regulation* (Cambridge: Cambridge University Press, 2000).

[4] Douglas R. Holmes and George E. Marcus, "Para-Ethnography," in *The Sage Encyclopedia of Qualitative Research Methods: M-W*; Vol. II, ed. Lisa M. Given (Thousand Oaks: SAGE, 2008), 595 ("By treating our subjects as collaborators, as epistemic partners, our analytical interests and theirs can be pursued simultaneously, and we can share insights and thus develop a common analytical exchange"); Douglas R. Holmes and George E. Marcus, "Collaboration Today and the Re-Imagination of the Classic Scene of Fieldwork Encounter," *Collaborative Anthropologies* (2008): 81–101, 83 ("'key informants,' who as epistemic partners, instead define the imaginary and plot of our own inquiries"); George E. Marcus, "The Uses of Complicity in the Changing Mise-En-Scène of Anthropological Fieldwork," in *Ethnography Through Thick & Thin*, ed. George E. Marcus (Princeton: Princeton University Press, 1998), 105–131; Douglas R. Holmes and George E. Marcus, "Fast Capitalism: Para-Ethnography and the Rise of the Symbolic Analyst," in *Frontiers of Capitalism: Ethnographic Reflections on the New Economy*, eds. Melissa S. Fisher and Greg Downey 33–57 (Durham: Duke University Press, 2006), 33. The quote is from Mathew Erie, "The New Legal Hubs: The Emergent Landscape of International Commercial Dispute Resolution," *Virginia Journal of International Law* 60 (2019): 225–298.

of teaching me what the challenges were, and what had been and could be done over time.[5] I wanted to see the challenges of the trade law world from their eyes. The conversation was open and informal. My aim was to develop a rapport with the interviewee to understand the challenges they faced. In this way, I established ease before transitioning to more direct questions. Often the best information I received was their description and explanation of events and experiences recently encountered. Because of the inside knowledge that I built, I was able to gain confidence in discussing the challenges faced and strategies used in comparative perspective and over time.

I made sure during the course of the interview to ask each interviewee a set of prepared questions, which I tailored to their specific position and the flow of the interview. For example, for government officials, I asked how the bureaucracy was structured; the number of lawyers committed to WTO and other trade dispute settlements; interagency processes; the relation of the Geneva mission to the capital; and the difficulty of retaining expertise, and how this changed over time. I asked how they gathered information, developed negotiating proposals, developed cases, and worked with private lawyers and affected businesses. I asked about forming negotiating coalitions and other strategies, domestic input processes, and external pressures in trade negotiations. Over time, I discussed all the dispute settlement cases that the country litigated as a party, as well as important examples of its acting as a third party in WTO disputes. I asked as well about cases that were not litigated and that led to settlements, and the processes used in these situations. I also asked for them to identify cases that were not brought, and why they were not brought – the proverbial dogs that do not bark. For lawyers, I asked about the cases on which they worked and their experiences with government officials and the international trade dispute settlement process. For trade association representatives, I asked about their organization; the trade challenges they face; their views of and experiences with trade law, negotiations, and dispute settlement; the ways they interact with the government and lawyers; and how that changed over time.

Much of the interviewing was problem-focused. It often was apparent that the interviewees were actively thinking in light of their experience, reflecting upon it, and making sense of it. For many of them, the process provided a space for someone to hear and take seriously their stories and reflections, exploring the complexities of the trade system, and the commonalities and differences in the challenges they faced compared to others. It offered them an opportunity to step back and put the demands and challenges of their daily work into broader focus. They often were interested in

---

[5] "In elite interviewing ... the investigator is willing, and often eager to let the interviewee teach him what the problem, the question, the situation is – to the limits, of course, of the interviewer's ability to perceive relationships to his basic problems, whatever they may be .... [I]n an elite interview, an exception, a deviation, an unusual interpretation may suggest a revision, a reinterpretation, an extension, a new approach." Lewis Anthony Dexter, *Elite and Specialized Interviewing* (Colchester, UK: ECPR Press, 1970), 5–6.

hearing my views, and, in the process, I obtained their responses to my working ideas, theories, and hypotheses. Many of them welcomed this form of engagement. Invariably, I learned from it, a knowledge that accrued and deepened over time. The interviews snowballed into further interviews, such as with other government officials within the same or different ministries and departments, with private lawyers who worked on cases, with think tanks and trade associations, and with academics training students and interacting with the government.

PARTICIPANT OBSERVATION

Through this fieldwork, I and the coauthors of the case studies also engaged in participant observation over years. For example, in the spring of 2012, I was an academic scholar in the WTO's research division on a research grant. That visit complemented annual visits to the WTO in Geneva over twenty years. For a number of years, I worked with International Center on Trade and Sustainable Development (ICTSD), a Geneva-based, nongovernmental organization, to create a project on developing countries in WTO dispute settlement that received outside funding. We held dialogues in Beijing, Geneva, Jakarta, Mombasa, Moscow, and São Paulo; conducted and published the results of a survey of WTO members regarding the impact of legal capacity building in trade dispute settlement[6]; and published a book on *Dispute Settlement at the WTO: The Developing Country Experience* (2010).[7] This work enabled me to observe dialogues among stakeholders and to engage in informal conversations that complemented the formal interviews.

My country collaborators (Sanchez Badin, Nedumpara, and Gao) went further in collaborating, formally or informally, with national officials to assess particular issues. James Nedumpara worked in a major project of the UNCTAD to help develop Indian trade-related capacity and later led a Department of Commerce–sponsored think tank, the Centre on Trade and Investment Law. Michelle Ratton Sanchez Badin consulted with the Brazilian government and was central to the formation of Brazilian trade and investment law networks. Henry Gao worked in the WTO Appellate Body and participated in closed online discussions of China's trade policy with members of the Chinese trade bureaucracy, private lawyers, and Chinese academics, who also worked on investment law. In contrast, I only worked within my own research agenda, one that was constantly informed by, and (at times) adapted through these encounters.

---

[6] Marc L. Busch, Eric Reinhardt and Gregory Shaffer, "Does Legal Capacity Matter? Explaining Patterns of Protectionism in the Shadow of WTO Litigation," Issue Paper no. 4, *International Centre for Trade and Sustainable Development,* Geneva, Switzerland (2008); Marc L. Busch, Eric Reinhardt and Gregory Shaffer, "Does Legal Capacity Matter? A Survey of WTO Members," *World Trade Review* 8, no. 4 (2009): 559–578.

[7] The project gave rise to the book *Dispute Settlement at the WTO: The Developing Country Experience,* eds. Gregory Shaffer and Ricardo Meléndez-Ortiz (Cambridge: Cambridge University Press, 2010).

PROCESS TRACING THROUGH CASE STUDIES

To address the role of these countries' investments in trade-related legal capacity and its relation to the paradox lying at the center of this book – the switch in the US and emerging powers' views and approaches to the trade law regime – I also engaged in process tracing.[8] This book traces the processes through which these countries developed legal capacity to constrain US options against them under the international trade law system. In this way, it studies the link between these legal capacity-building efforts, changes within these countries, and changes in the ecology of the international trade law system. It shows how building legal capacity to take on the United States and Europe at the WTO was a *critical reason* – if not a *necessary condition* – for the United States becoming disenchanted with the system. Counterfactually, why else would the United States attempt to neutralize it? The book does not contend that legal capacity development is the sole cause of US disenchantment with the WTO and the decline of WTO judicial authority. Rather, the book aims to provide a complementary (and necessary) "legal" explanation of such US disenchantment, which has given rise to a more pluralist ecology of international trade legal ordering. It is a legal account that meshes with economic and political accounts and, in doing so, both reshapes and reinforces them.

By assessing the impact of transnational processes in three large, emerging powers through extended case studies, I could compare and contrast dynamics, capturing similarities and differences among them. In particular, the similarities were quite striking despite the significant differences in these countries' political structures and legal heritages. From a methodological perspective, these countries are similar in terms of economic size in relation to their respective regions.[9] Their relative power mattered both in incentivizing their development of legal capacity and in their ability to harness it effectively. Each of these countries became central to the WTO's functioning, forming part of a new core of WTO members that shape the contours of negotiations and decision-making. Moreover, while all three had strong bureaucratic traditions, none

---

[8] Alexander L. George and Andrew Bennett, *Case Studies and Theory Development in the Social Sciences* (Cambridge: MIT Press, 2005).

[9] The book does not cover Russia, the fourth of the original BRICS, which only joined the WTO in August 2012, but is already an active participant in negotiations and dispute settlement, nor South Africa, which joined the BRICS in 2010. In the first five years after the Russian Federation joined the WTO on August 22, 2012, it worked hard to develop trade-related legal capacity, and I was invited to participate in a meeting in Moscow on this issue shortly after it joined, together with China's ambassador, as part of an ICTSD project. As of January 1, 2020, Russia already had been a complainant in eight cases and a respondent in nine cases, primarily against the European Union and Ukraine. It also had been a third party in seventy-nine cases, replicating China's earlier strategy of learning by observing. The book also does not cover South Africa, which is a much smaller economy (roughly one-seventh the size of Brazil's), and which has never filed a complaint before the WTO and has generally aimed to curtail further WTO rulemaking. On South Africa, see Gustav Brink, "South Africa's Experience with International Trade Dispute Settlement," in *Dispute Settlement at the WTO: The Developing Country Experience*, eds. Gregory Shaffer and Ricardo Meléndez-Ortiz (Cambridge: Cambridge University Press, 2010), 251–274.

had any organization for trade disputes prior to the WTO's creation and none had traditions of legalism in bureaucratic governance, unlike the United States. While these countries had these attributes in common, they are significantly different cases in terms of a large range of other characteristics.[10] China is an authoritarian government, while Brazil and India are democracies with independent legal systems. Brazil has a corporatist tradition with well-organized, independent, engaged trade associations, while China's centralized trade associations are largely government controlled, and India's became engaged in trade negotiations, but were much less engaged on dispute settlement. India's legal system is common law-based and is in English, unlike the other two. As a result, the state–society interface differed in these three countries, giving rise to different trajectories in their formation of "public-private partnerships" for trade governance. Despite these differences, the resemblances are remarkable in these countries' building of trade law capacity and its implications within them, illustrating the importance of transnational legal ordering in the field of trade, including its spillover effects.

METHODOLOGICAL LIMITATIONS AND ADVANTAGES

This type of empirical work is subject to limitations. The people interviewed were not randomly selected and they predominantly came from the trade law and policy field. The interview questions were not standardized. The challenge of bias with such fieldwork and interviews lies both in the interviewee (who may have an agenda and who is just a data point) and in the author (who comes with assumptions, including those from the discipline in which the author is embedded).[11] To address potential bias, I cross-checked what I learned with further interviewees, not letting them know the source. I also asked my questions to a diverse range of informants with different interests – such as in government, in the private sector, in civil society, and from outside the country – to check statements for consistency, complementarity, and contradiction. In a number of cases, I interviewed the same individual more than once, which allowed me to corroborate information, assess trends, and evaluate ideas raised over the project's course.[12] I also cross-checked such information through a review of primary and secondary sources in Chinese, Portuguese, and

[10] George and Bennett, *Case Studies*; Katerina Linos, "How to Select and Develop International Law Case Studies: Lessons from Comparative Law and Comparative Politics,"*American Journal of International Law* 109, no. 3 (2015): 475–485.

[11] The author's background brings experiences and presuppositions to the interview, which calls for self-reflexivity throughout the process. Pierre Bourdieu, "Participant Objectivation," *Journal of the Royal Anthropological Institute* 9 (2003): 283 ("What needs to be objectivized is . . . the social world that has made both the anthropologist and the conscious or unconscious anthropology that he (or she) engages in her anthropological practice").

[12] As Dexter writes, "[F]ield research, that is, always ought to be and frequently is a process of continuing discovery. One is learning how to reformulate or at least modify one's formulation of a problem; one is locating new data. So, the decision as to whom to see depends largely upon one's on-going reflection about the issues, upon new data and hypotheses that come to one's attention, from whatever source – often from earlier interviews." Dexter, *Elite Interviewing*, 43.

English, including with the help of my local collaborators and research assistants. I complemented this work with statistics, including regarding each country's use of the WTO dispute settlement system. In this way, I gathered and assessed information from multiple sources to provide robustness and confidence. I documented these sources in the footnotes. In parallel, I presented the work and received comments from reviewers from different disciplinary fields in different countries.

Because I focus on the process of building trade law capacity, I talked predominantly with those engaged in these processes. The information I present thus foregrounds parts of the governments I study more than others, which are those parts involved directly in trade and trade-related policy. It also predominantly captures the views and experiences of a group of stakeholders whose professions and businesses are linked to international trade. The interviews reflect their views grounded in their particular situations and experiences. Nonetheless, I always asked my sources about the limits of their positions in the broader field of policy making, and they frequently stressed those limits in the context of internal contests over the role of trade law and the directions of their country's economic policy, as the case studies show. The interviewees reflected a range of ideological and material positions and interests, with some having a more developmentalist and others a more trade-liberal orientation.

When sustained over time with a large number of informants, this type of work offers unique advantages that cannot be gained from any other research method given the access that I was granted and maintained over time. My background as a trade law specialist greatly facilitated such access.[13] There is a growing amount of statistical work on trade and investment flows, the WTO, and WTO dispute settlement, including some that I have conducted with others. That statistical work is important, but also has limits as it depends on reducing large amounts of information into discrete variables that are then correlated. Control variables are used to isolate inferences, but the variables themselves involve difficult choices of reducing, categorizing, and collating complex social facts, and they thus face limits in what they inform, particularly for questions of process that this book addresses.[14]

I engaged in one quantitative study of WTO legal capacity described in Chapter 2. NSF grant SES0351192 (on "WTO Dispute Settlement and Legal Capacity") provided me with the means to work with political scientists Marc Busch and Eric

---

[13] Access is critical but not always easily obtained. *Gaining Access: A Practical and Theoretical Guide for Qualitative Researchers*, eds., Martha Feldman, Jeannine Bell, and Michele Tracy Bergers (Walnut Creek: Altamira Press, 2003). My knowledge and training in law, including years of practice, combined with my building of contacts over time, facilitated access across countries, institutions, and levels of organization.

[14] Lukas Linsi and Daniel Mugge, "Globalization and the Growing Defects of International Economic Statistics," *Review of International Political Economy* 26, no. 3 (2019): 361–383 ("reported figures are far less accurate than they are typically imagined to be and often do not correspond to the theoretical concepts with which users associate them"); Victoria Nourse and Gregory Shaffer, "Empiricism, Experimentalism, and Conditional Theory," *SMU Law Review* 67 (2014): 141–186.

Reinhardt and to create and conduct a survey of WTO members, from which we developed a new trade law capacity index based on their responses.[15] We then correlated this index against outcomes in domestic antidumping investigations and use of the WTO system to challenge antidumping awards, subject to a series of controls, in particular for market power. We provided quantitative evidence that legal capacity matters to protect a country's exports from import protection, at least as much as market power. It was important original work, but it too is subject to limitations. Although we pretested the survey, it was completed in a limited time and only by government officials. It thus did not include the views of stakeholders and participants in the system from the private sector. It nonetheless complements the other methods used in this book.

In the process of working on this study, I often had my assumptions challenged and my understandings changed and evolved. The power of engaging in such work is "to push us beyond our personal politics or situations, to enforce a form of humility in which we must listen to voices other than our own."[16] This is particularly important in the world of international trade scholarship that is so often dominated by normative and prescriptive perspectives promoted by those born, reared, living, and advancing their careers in the United States, Europe, and other richer countries, and whose views are thus informed by those countries' contexts and prevailing concerns. An additional benefit of this book is to chronicle and compare the experiences and perspectives of those outside the United States and Europe whose views are less frequently heard. Indeed, in developing their "new independence theory," with which this book has many parallels, political scientists Henry Farrell and Abraham Newman stress the need for work that extends beyond the United States and Europe.[17]

This book provides the most thorough, empirically grounded analysis of Brazil's, India's, and China's development of legal capacity in trade, and the implications both within these countries and for the changing ecology of the trade and broader economic legal order. From such ethnographic *microanalysis*, it provides a unique view of the processes that gave rise to the extraordinary *macro*structural development in which the United States now calls into question the very trade law regime it built.[18] This book shows the processes through which the transnational legal order

---

[15] Busch, Reinhardt and Shaffer, "Does Legal Capacity Matter?: A Survey of WTO Members"; Busch, Reinhardt and Shaffer, "Does Legal Capacity Matter?: Explaining Patterns of Protectionism in the Shadow of WTO Litigation."

[16] Elizabeth Mertz, "Challenging Translations: New Legal Realist Methods," *Wisconsin Law Review* 2 (2005): 483.

[17] Henry Farrell and Abraham Newman, "Domestic Institutions Beyond the Nation-State: Charting the New Independence Approach," *World Politics* 66 (April 2014): 331–363, 354 ("scholars of the new interdependence have focused almost exclusively on the US and the EU").

[18] Braithwaite and Drahos, *Global Business Regulation*, 14 ("Micro-macro theory" attempts to build theory "by comprehending micro processes that constitute structural change, just as those micro processes are constituted and contained by the structural.").

for trade has so dramatically changed. In a field in which US policymakers and scholars increasingly attend to the question of what to do about China, this book aims to assess these developments in a neutral manner since meaningful normative and policy prescription depends on clear analysis.[19]

Finally, this book's extended case method raises broader inferences regarding the role of legal capacity in transnational legal ordering generally, which involves the interaction of states, societies, and international institutions. The book's qualitative methodology applies a theoretical framework – that of transnational legal orders – to assess particular empirical developments in the world. In parallel, as a qualitative study, it aims to generate further theorizing regarding the role of law and legal capacity in assessments of state capacity, state institutional change, state–society relations, economic and political development, and the international order. What the book shows regarding the trading system extends beyond it.

---

[19] As a US national in Geneva in the trade field quips, "now if you are not a China basher, you are called a 'China dove'." Interview, July 11, 2019.

PART I

Legal Capacity and Transnational Legal Orders

1

Introduction

Emerging Powers and the Transnational Legal Ordering of Trade

Where there is globalization, there are rules. What they are, who imposes them, and how – those are the only real questions.[1]

    – Dani Rodrik, *The Globalization Paradox*

We are in the history. We are making the history.[2]

    – Peng Jun, Jincheng Tongda, and Neal (JT&N, Beijing)

Victorious after World War II and the Cold War, the United States and its allies largely wrote the rules for international trade and investment. Critically, the United States and European Union drove the creation of the World Trade Organization (WTO) in 1995 with the aim of opening trade in goods and services for their products, ramping up protection for their intellectual property, and transforming national trade-related law and institutions within countries around the world to look more like American and European law and institutions. Developing countries joined the WTO but often complained that its rules were skewed. As a result, it was argued that the United States and European Union could rule the global economy through rules. They were incredibly successful, as WTO norms transformed laws and institutions within emerging economies.

 Yet by 2020, twenty-five years after the WTO's creation, it was the United States that had become the great disrupter – disenchanted with the rules' constraints, including on its ability to create new rules. It was the United States that flouted WTO rules in the name of "national security" and the national interest – even to protect American producers of aluminum siding and to pressure countries to block migration from Mexico and Central America. It was the United States that neutered trade dispute

---

[1] Dani Rodrik, *The Globalization Paradox: Democracy and the Future of the World Economy* (New York: W.W. Norton & Company, Inc., 2011), 9.

[2] Peng Jun, "Wo yu WTO de Jige Shunjian [Glimpses of WTO and I]," in *Wo yu WTO: Falvren de Shijiao [Me and WTO: Lawyer's Perspectives]*, eds. Yang Guohua and Shi Xiaoli (Beijing: Zhishi Chanquan Chubanshe [Intellectual Property Publishing House], 2015), 222.

settlement and threatened to withdraw from the organization.[3] Meanwhile, the United Kingdom – the European Union's second largest economy – voted by referendum to leave the European Union. As nationalist parties rose in prominence throughout Europe, the European Union was pressed to turn inward to protect its very existence, curtailing its role on the global stage. It continues to defend multilateralism, but it is in a much weaker position following the Euro crisis, internal divisions over migration, Brexit, and the ravages of the COVID-19 virus, than it was in the 1990s.

Paradoxically, China, India, Brazil, and other emerging economies became stakeholders and (at times) defenders of economic globalization and the rules regulating it, even while they too have taken nationalist turns. Before the World Economic Forum in Davos, the paragon of global institutions, China's President Xi declared in his 2016 keynote address, "We must remain committed to developing global free trade and investment, promote trade and investment liberalization and facilitation through opening-up and say no to protectionism."[4] How did this come to be? How did the emerging powers invest in trade law to defend their interests? What has this meant for their own internal economic governance? And what does it mean for the future of the trade legal order in light of intensified rivalry between the United States and China, triggering a new economic cold war?

Many economists write of China's rise in terms of *efficiency* – a combination of Western know-how and Chinese wages that triggered a "manufacturing miracle" where China became producer for the world. In his book *The Great Convergence*, Richard Baldwin explained how the revolution in information and communications technology in the 1990s led Western firms to outsource production of goods and services to countries like China and India, creating a new unbundling of production through global supply chains. This unbundling "created a new style of industrial competitiveness – one that combined G7 know-how with developing-nation labor."[5] China became the manufacturer for the world. Its share of world manufacturing surged from three percent in 1990 to nineteen percent in 2015.[6] Western firms outsourced services to India, whose services

---

[3] President Trump threatened to pull the United States out of the WTO if the WTO ruled against his plan to massively increase tariffs on Chinese products. Geoff Dyer, "Donald Trump Threatens to Pull US Out of WTO," *Financial Times*, July 24, 2016 ("It doesn't matter. Then we're going to renegotiate or we're going to pull out. These trade deals are a disaster, the World Trade Organization is a disaster."); Scott Lanman, "IMF Panel Drops Anti-Protectionist Pledge in Nod to Trump View," *Bloomberg*, April 22, 2017.

[4] He further stated, "There was a time when China also had doubts about economic globalization, and was not sure whether it should join the World Trade Organization. But we came to the conclusion that integration into the global economy is a historical trend." "Opening Plenary with Xi Jinping, President of the People's Republic of China," *World Economic Forum*, January 17, 2017, www.weforum.org /events/world-economic-forum-annual-meeting-2017/sessions/opening-plenary-davos-2017.

[5] Richard Baldwin, *The Great Convergence: Information Technology and the New Globalization* (Cambridge: Harvard University Press, 2016), 6.

[6] Compare "Trade in Manufactures," *World Trade Organization*, 2016, www.wto.org/english/res_e/statis_e/ world_commodity_profiles16_e.pdf; Brookings Institute, *Global Manufacturing Scorecard*, www.brook ings.edu/research/global-manufacturing-scorecard-how-the-us-compares-to-18-other-nations/. Its share fell slightly to eighteen percent in 2018.

exports increased over twenty-two-fold from US$ 8.9 billion in 1997 to US$ 204 billion in 2018, while its manufacturing grew in parallel.[7] Such growth triggered a commodity boom for Brazil's highly competitive agribusiness and mining sectors.

These economic shifts catalyzed dramatic changes in shares of global gross domestic product (GDP). In just twenty-nine years, the share of the G7 (the United States, Japan, Germany, the United Kingdom, France, Canada, and Italy) plummeted eighteen percentage points, from sixty-four percent (in 1990) to forty-six percent (in 2019) in nominal terms, and to thirty percent measured by purchasing power parity (PPP).[8] In contrast, China's and India's share soared. At the start of 2020, the share of global GDP of China, India, and Brazil approached that of the United States in nominal terms (twenty-one percent compared to twenty-four percent) and almost doubled it in terms of purchasing power (twenty-nine percent to fifteen percent).[9] Within a decade, China should become – once more – the world's largest economy, as Figures 1.1 and 1.2 capture.[10]

These changes in the share of global GDP gave rise to shifts in *power*, as political scientists stress. While the United States and Europe turned inward, emerging powers like China, India, and Brazil gained confidence and became central players in the global economy. The creation of the G20 for global economic governance first reflected this transition. Growing US–China rivalry now dramatizes it. China, India, and Brazil each play a leadership role in regional economic governance, and they aim to play a growing role globally. Although the United States wishes to halt China's rise, the reality is that two-thirds of countries trade more goods with China than the United States, compared to just one-fifth in 2001, the year China

---

[7]   Compare "Trade Profiles 2016," *World Trade Organization*, 2016, 169, www.wto.org/english/res_e/booksp_e/trade_profiles16_e.pdf; "Commercial services exports by sector and partner – annual (2005-onwards) (Million US dollar) for India," *World Trade Organization*, https://data.wto.org/.

[8]   Purchasing power parity (PPP) sets a hypothetical exchange rate based on a basket of consumables to equalize the purchasing power of different currencies, such that a person could buy the same amount of goods and services at the PPP exchange rate. Calculations are based on IMF Data Mapper, World Economic Outlook (April 2019), www.imf.org/external/datamapper/PPPSH@WEO/CAN/FRA/DEU/ITA/JPN/GBR/USA.

[9]   Stated differently, the combined GDP of China, India, and Brazil in 2018 jumped to 88 percent of US GDP in nominal terms, and to almost double US GDP measured by purchasing power parity. The author's calculations of Share of Global GDP are based on IMF Data Mapper, World Economic Outlook (October 2019), www.imf.org/external/datamapper/NGDPD@WEO/USA/IND/CHN/BRA/WEOWORLD. Purchasing Power Parity is based on IMF Data Mapper, World Economic Outlook (October 2019), www.imf.org/external/datamapper/PPPSH@WEO/USA/IND/CHN/BRA. Compare the highly-cited Goldman Sachs study, which predicted that by 2025, four economies – Brazil, Russia, India, and China, which it famously labeled the BRICs – would account for over half the size of the G6 countries (United States, Japan, Germany, United Kingdom, France, and Italy). Dominic Wilson and Roopa Purushothaman, "Dreaming With BRICs: The Path to 2050," Global Economics Paper No: 99 (Goldman Sachs, 2003). China vastly outperformed Goldman Sachs's predictions, and India and Brazil outperformed them as well.

[10] IMF, "China's Economic Outlook in Six Charts," July 26, 2018, www.imf.org/en/News/Articles/2018/07/25/na072618-chinas-economic-outlook-in-six-charts.

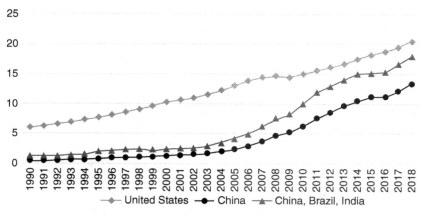

FIGURE 1.1 Nominal GDP 1990–2018 (US$ trillion)[11]

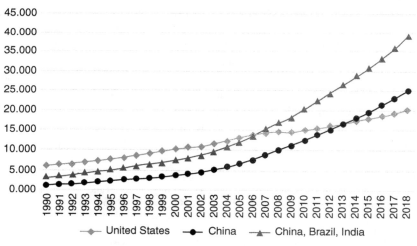

FIGURE 1.2 GDP by PPP 1990–2018 (current international $ trillion)[12]

joined the WTO.[13] Simply put, the economies and market size of China, India, and Brazil matter, which provide them with negotiating leverage, constituting a form of power.

So what about *law*? This book, written by a lawyer who has coauthored work with political scientists, economists, and sociologists, tells *a complementary and indispensable story that focuses on law* and the critical development of *legal capacity* to

---

[11] Ibid.

[12] Ibid.

[13] Alyssa Leng and Roland Rajah, "Global Trade Through a US-China Lens," *The Intercept*, December 18, 2019.

use, make, shape, and apply the law. The book aims to build bridges across disciplines with those who are interested in understanding change in international law and legal ordering – the rules of the game – and its implications for governance not only between but also within states. I develop the concept of legal capacity in Chapters 2 and 3, which I define as *the ability of a country, through harnessing resources, to use law to defend and advance its international and domestic trade and trade-implicated policies*. The concept has equivalents in other disciplines, as it constitutes a form of power (for political scientists) and an incentive-driven investment (for economists).[14]

This book addresses law's two-sided nature. On one side, law serves as *a medium* (or instrument) to exercise and reflect power (the dominant variable in political science) and to advance efficiency and social welfare (the dominant variable in economics). On the other side, law can serve as a *constitutive force* that implicates institutions, professions, norms, and practices within countries and transnationally as part of ongoing, dynamic, and recursive processes.[15] Law helps constitute markets and policy, shaping who gets what.[16] In both cases, law can be viewed as a form of politics. However, law cannot be reduced to material or structural power.[17] Law, although an instrument for the institutionalization of power, is also a set of rules and practices that parties use to provide order, pursue justice, and solve problems. Weaker parties can invoke and harness these rules in ways that press stronger parties to justify their actions in legal terms. Where the legal order provides for neutral third-party dispute settlement, as in trade, law and legal institutions can empower weaker parties even when the rules and institutions are slanted against them. It is the idea of law's neutrality and universality that permits weaker parties, as well as stronger parties, to deploy it successfully.[18] It is for these reasons that actors invest resources in it.

This book adopts a legal realist perspective on international trade law, which differs from international relations realism's view of law as epiphenomenal.[19] Legal

---

[14]   I thank Krzysztof Pelc for this point.

[15]   Gregory Shaffer, *Transnational Legal Ordering and State Change* (Cambridge: Cambridge University Press, 2013); Terence Halliday and Gregory Shaffer, *Transnational Legal Orders* (Cambridge: Cambridge University Press, 2015).

[16]   Katharina Pistor, *The Code of Capital: How Law Creates Wealth and Inequality* (Princeton: Princeton University Press, 2019).

[17]   As Barbara Koremenos writes, "Powerful states want their asymmetric power reflected in the terms of the agreement, but desire is not synonymous with having complete control." Barbara Koremenos, *The Continent of International Law: Explaining Agreement Design* (Cambridge: Cambridge University Press, 2016). Compare Michael Barnett and Raymond Duvall, "Power in International Politics," *International Organization* 59 (2005): 59 (on different facets of power).

[18]   Judith Shklar, *Legalism: Law, Morals, and Political Trials* (Cambridge: Harvard University Press, 1964), 1–4 (legality as a form of ideology); E. P. Thompson, *Whigs and Hunters: The Origin of the Black Act* (London: Breviary Stuff Publications, 1975).

[19]   This approach differs from international relations realism in highlighting not only the role of power, but also the role of norms in global economic governance, including their flow, settlement, and unsettlement. It differs also in its attention to the role of competing actors within states, both public and private, as well as international organizations. Gregory Shaffer, "Legal Realism and International

realists contend that law is constituted by both power and reason.[20] For those working in the legal realist tradition, law is a semiautonomous field comprised of rules and mechanisms to induce compliance that operate in broader social and political contexts.[21] On the one hand, international trade law's meaning and operation *reflect external factors* involving particular actors pursuing their conceptions of their interests who use particular legal and extralegal resources to shape it in light of the distributional consequences. Commentators often refer to such instrumental use of international law as *"lawfare."*[22] On the other hand, reasoning through law (in drafting, litigation, and bargaining in the shadow of law) *can affect the normative understanding* of both "problems" and "commitments," shaping expectations, communication, and behavior within and between states.[23] Such reasoning can provide a *"public good"* in helping resolve conflicts, especially where parties resort to neutral, third-party decision-makers applying institutionalized rules and procedures. International trade law is constituted by the interaction of power and interest, on the one hand, and institutionalized rules and reasoning practices, on the other hand. It involves both *interests* and *legal reasoning*. Ultimately, from a legal realist perspective, one cannot understand international trade law without empirical study of how it operates and develops in practice, which this book illustrates.[24]

Stated simply, it is not just structural and material power that govern the world but also law, legal institutions, and their practices. *They are complementary, and they affect each other.* Law and legal institutions provide normative resources that actors harness to advance their interests. They simultaneously affect the normative environment in which actors operate, which shapes their understanding and pursuit of interests. The story of emerging powers' rise and the implications for global trade

---

Law," in *International Legal Theory: Foundations and Frontiers,* eds. Jeffrey Dunoff and Mark Pollack (Cambridge: Cambridge University Press, 2021); Gregory Shaffer, "The New Legal Realist Approach to International Law," *Leiden Journal of International Law* 28 (2015): 189–210 (addressing the difference between legal realism and international relations realism).

[20]   Hanoch Dagan, "The Realist Concept of Law," *University of Toronto Law Journal* 57 (2007): 607; Shaffer, "Legal Realism and International Law."

[21]   In the words of Sally Falk Moore, the legal field is comprised of "rule-making capacities, and the means to induce or coerce compliance" while being "simultaneously set in a larger social matrix which can, and does, affect and invade it, sometimes at the invitation of persons inside it, sometimes at its own instance." Sally Falk Moore, "Law and Social Change: The Semi-Autonomous Social Field as an Appropriate Subject of Study," *Law & Society Review* 7 (1973): 719–746.

[22]   Ian Hurd, *How to Do Things with International Law* (Princeton: Princeton University Press, 2017), 11 ("lawfare is better seen as the typical condition of international law," but reaching this conclusion from case studies of the law of the use of force, nukes, drones, and torture).

[23]   Halliday and Shaffer, *Transnational Legal Orders,* 7–8 (on the political and social construction of behavior as a "problem" as part of transnational legal ordering); Hurd, *How to Do Things with International Law,* 131 ("By presenting acts as lawful, governments seek the political legitimation that comes from behaving legally in a rule-of-law setting").

[24]   Gregory Shaffer and Tom Ginsburg, "The Empirical Turn in International Legal Scholarship," *American Journal of International Law* 106 (2012): 1; Howard Erlanger et al., "Is it Time for a New Legal Realism?," *Wisconsin Law Review* 2005, no. 2 (2005): 335–363; Shaffer, "The New Legal Realist Approach."

governance requires a complementary story about law and their deployment of it. This book provides that story. It tells the *past* story of trade law's impact within large, emerging powers and their response to trade law, which, in turn, helps us understand the current context and responses to this context that will shape international trade and economic law's *future*. In a vein related to Katharina Pistor's assessment of the legal organization of finance,[25] this book addresses the legal organization of trade. It illustrates how international trade law shapes regulation, institutions, professions, normative understandings, and accountability mechanisms within countries, as well as the role that legal capacity plays in dynamically shaping such law over time. It shows how emerging powers changed internally to engage better externally, thereby domestically embedding and recursively affecting what the book calls the transnational legal order for trade.

I. THE BOOK'S THREE QUESTIONS

This book addresses the following question:

> *How has the international trade and broader economic legal order changed since the WTO's creation because of Brazil's, India's, and China's rise and their development of trade law capacity?*

It breaks down this broad question into three interlinked questions regarding the relation of these emerging powers and the international economic law order, focusing on trade law while covering its expanding scope:

(i) *How did Brazil, India, and China invest in trade law capacity to take on the United States and European Union at the WTO and defend their interests?*

(ii) *In doing so, how did these emerging powers change internally?*

(iii) *What are the implications of these developments for the transnational legal order for trade and broader economic governance?*

Critically, as this book shows, law making and practice at the international and national levels mutually implicate each other in complex processes of transnational legal ordering and disordering. Developments in one cannot be understood without attending to the other. International trade law has deeply implicated Brazil, India, and China – the world's three largest emerging economies. Their rise, in turn, is deeply implicating international trade law's future. The book explains these changes within the theoretical framework of *transnational legal orders*, introduced in Chapter 2.

Regarding the first question, building *trade law capacity* to engage with the international trading system is not easy. The scope of coverage and implications of the WTO and broader trade and economic law system are broad, deep, and

---

[25] Pistor, *The Code of Capital*.

substantive. To engage with the WTO and other trade agreements, and to defend their interests, these countries had to change themselves internally. They did so to mediate their development goals in view of WTO requirements, tailoring their laws, regulations, and practices. They also did so to enhance their capacity to gather information, monitor foreign behavior, and investigate, develop, and bring WTO cases to gain access to foreign markets for their exports, on which their development strategies increasingly focused.

Regarding the second question, these countries' engagement with the international trade legal order drove *institutional change* within them. They affected the relation of the state to domestic and global markets, allocations of power between and within state institutions (such as the role of agencies and courts), and business and individual investments in knowledge and professional development (such as the role of lawyers). The international trading system also affected the normative frames in which policy was debated, including by creating new transnational accountability mechanisms for officials, involving peer review, consultations, and litigation. To operate effectively, officials needed to work more transparently with other stakeholders, affecting state–private sector relations. When challenged, they needed to justify their decisions and practices in legal terms. In short, this book empirically assesses how the WTO and its dispute settlement system spurred these countries to enhance their legal infrastructure in relation to international economic law by reorganizing their bureaucracy and expanding coordinated linkages with the private business sector and with private professionals that offer expertise.

Actors deeply contested these processes within these countries. The trade regime provided opportunities, constraints, and leverage for them to do so, as they defended and advanced their interests and priorities. Over time, actors became more sophisticated in understanding the importance of investing in expertise not only for the negotiation of international rules but also for their interpretation, including in terms of what "compliance" means. It is a multilevel game that involves not only international lawmaking, including through the export of domestic rules and practices to the international level.[26] It also involves the importation of rules through domestic enactment, which engages rival factions. It is a multilevel game not only in the shaping of the meaning of rules through international litigation. It is also one through domestic implementation and practice, which creates new models that can be exported and diffused. In sum, political contests in the United States, European Union, Brazil, India, and China have external spillover effects. The internal contests in one power affect the contests in others.

These countries' institutional changes and investments in legal capacity *recursively shaped the international trade legal order*. The third question again brings

---

[26] This approach complements "two-level game" theory, but it is broader in its dynamic, multilevel focus on transnational legal ordering. For a comparison of the theory of "transnational legal orders" (in which this book is grounded) and "regime theory," Halliday and Shaffer, *Transnational Legal Orders*, 21–24.

domestic and international developments dynamically together in a single frame. These countries, as well as actors within them, learned how to play the legal game to thwart US and European dominance of the trade regime, both in negotiations and in litigation over the meaning of legal texts. This dynamic, in turn, constrained US and EU policymaking, ranging from agricultural subsidies to industrial protection through import relief law. When the United States and European Union turned away from the WTO to create new rules through bilateral and regional trade and investment agreements, these emerging powers developed their own initiatives and models as well. Paradoxically, now the United States has neutered and significantly constrained the WTO and its dispute settlement system. This book empirically tells the legal side of this story as a necessary complement to the better known economic and political ones, explaining how this came to be.

The challenges for the future of the transnational legal order for trade are clearly material, structural, and ideological, as well as legal. On the one hand, they reflect the growing economic power of China, and the impact of trade from China and other emerging economies within the United States. On the other hand, traditional narratives of the benefits of free trade that ignore the impact on the economically vulnerable have been destabilized, especially in the United States, as Chapter 8 shows.

Yet, law and the development of legal capacity to use, make, shape, and apply law are a critical part of this story and will continue to shape the evolving ecology of the trade order. By defining the trade order in terms of rules and judicialized dispute settlement, the WTO system created an opening for emerging economies to invest in trade law capacity and take on the United States and Europe at their own legal game. As a system of law purportedly in service of fairness and equal treatment, weaker players could also win. Law's ideology of rationality and fairness could constrain the powerful, shape the interpretation of norms, and affect their strategies. The transnational legal order for trade, although slanted in favor of the powerful, offered opportunities to weaker parties who could compete through building legal capacity. China's, Brazil's, and India's investments in legal capacity help explain the *paradox* of the United States abandoning the legal order that it created.[27]

In sum, this book addresses the *micropolitics* of the WTO – what has been developing under the surface of the business of trade through the practice of law, which has broader *macro* implications. The subterrane of developing legal capacity is where important shifts have been occurring. Much has been written on trade politics, but that work has not mined the politics and long-term shifts within the trade legal order itself, which is recursively linked to institutional changes within emerging powers.[28] This book provides a necessary complement for understanding why,

---

[27] The book examines these three countries largely in relation to the United States and European Union, and not with other WTO members, so as not to lose focus on the major power shifts within the trade legal order and the paradox at the heart of this book. It goes without saying that other countries also are part of these transnational legal ordering processes.

[28] I thank George Marcus for some of this phrasing.

at a time of hegemonic transition where economic security and geopolitics assume greater roles, emerging powers became defenders of the legal order that the United States created.

II. SOME BACKGROUND: POWER AND THE LEGALIZATION OF THE TRADE REGIME, FROM THE GATT TO THE WTO

The United States and Europe long dominated the design and drafting of international trade rules. They did so first with the formation of the General Agreement on Tariffs and Trade (GATT) in 1948 after World War II, and then again with the creation of the WTO in 1995 after their victory in the Cold War.[29] They were times of American triumphalism. The United States had become the world's hegemon, its "hyperpower."

Beginning in the 1950s, European nations pooled sovereignty over decades through a series of treaties to eventually create the European Union in 1993 with its vast, single market – a supranational bloc that (until Brexit) was roughly the size of, and even a bit larger than, the US economy. That was just two years before the WTO's creation and the same year that the United States first deployed a major trade agreement to require binding rules on services, intellectual property, and investment – the North American Free Trade Agreement (NAFTA). Given the European Union's economic weight, it too exercised immense leverage in trade negotiations. Together, the United States and European Union drove the initiation and conclusion of negotiations that created the WTO, the world's most legalized and judicialized multilateral regime.[30] The WTO effectively became a constitution for global capitalism that provided the rules for trade, rules that the United States and European Union largely wrote.[31]

The United States and European Union also had the world's leading specialized lawyers in government and in the private sector – based in Washington, DC and Brussels – to bring and defend cases under these rules. Their private sectors and professionals provided them with significant advantages. Working though public–private partnerships with industry and industry's lawyers, not only could the United States and European Union prevail in WTO litigation and bargaining

---

[29]   The United States and the United Kingdom took the lead in the formation of the GATT in 1948, and the United States and European Union in the formation of the WTO in 1995. Other countries of course played roles and the United States and European Union could not simply dictate rules. Nonetheless, the United States and European Union were by far the two most important protagonists and drivers of the process.

[30]   Hugo Paemen and Alexandra Bensch, *From the GATT to the WTO: The European Community in the Uruguay Round* (Leuven: Leuven University Press, 1995); John Croome, *Reshaping the World Trading System: A History of the Uruguay Round* (Boston: Kluwer Law International, 1998).

[31]   They had to compromise, but WTO rules reflect US and EU preferences and domestic law more than those of anyone else, as Chapter 3 further notes. John Jackson, *The World Trade Organization: Constitution and Jurisprudence* (London: Royal Institute of International Affairs, 1998); Deborah Cass, *The Constitutionalization of the World Trade Organization* (Oxford: Oxford University Press, 2005).

in its shadow, but through litigation they could shape the interpretation of the rules.[32] In the WTO system, they were the "haves" and they were well-positioned "to come out ahead."[33] In WTO litigation, the United States first took the lead, litigating high-profile cases against longstanding EU policies. However, the European Union soon followed suit. It too played the WTO legal game, although it did so uniquely in light of the European Union's political, administrative, and cultural context.

This was a time of triumphalism for liberalism and its view of the "rule of law." The year of the WTO's creation marked the fiftieth anniversary of the United Nations Charter and the 200th anniversary of the publication of Immanuel Kant's *Toward Perpetual Peace*, where Kant advocated the creation of a "league of nations" grounded in law.[34] For the first time in 1995, trade law panels formed automatically following the filing of a WTO complaint.[35] For the first time, these panels' decisions were binding, subject to appeal before a new Appellate Body, whose decisions, in turn, were binding.[36] This dispute settlement system, touted as the WTO's "crown jewel," would establish a coherent and sophisticated jurisprudence. New casebooks and journals specialized in WTO law. A plethora of articles and books circulated. WTO moot court competitions emerged. Countries hired and worked with law firms, which were often paid by businesses and trade associations. The press reported the decisions on their front pages. Politicians referenced them in their campaigns. In short, the trading system became judicialized under the rule of lawyers.[37] The Appellate Body became the world's most authoritative, multilateral (de facto) court.[38] The eminent trade law scholar John Jackson described the creation of this

[32]   Gregory Shaffer, *Defending Interests: Public-Private Partnerships in WTO Litigation* (Washington, DC: The Brookings Institution, 2003).

[33]   Marc Galanter, "Why the 'Haves' Come Out Ahead: Speculations on the Limits of Legal Change," *Law & Society Review* 9 (1974–1975): 95, 96, 107. In the WTO context, Joseph Conti, "Learning to Dispute: Repeat Participation, Expertise, and Reputation at the World Trade Organization," *Law & Social Inquiry* 35 (2010): 625–662.

[34]   James Bohman and Matthias Lutz-Bachmann, "Introduction," in *Perpetual Peace: Essays on Kant's Cosmopolitan Ideal*, eds. James Bohman and Matthias Lutz Bachmann (Cambridge: MIT Press, 1997), 2. According to Kant, "The spirit of commerce, which is incompatible with war, sooner or later gains the upper hand in every state." Immanuel Kant, *Perpetual Peace: A Philosophical Essay*, ed. Lewis White Beck (Indianapolis: Bobbs-Merrill, 1957), 32.

[35]   Formally, the panel is formed upon a party's second request, which can be a month after the first request. At that time, its formation is automatic. "Understanding on Rules and Procedures Governing the Settlement of Disputes," in *Marrakesh Agreement Establishing the World Trade Organization* (April 15, 1994), art. 6, art. 16, Annex 2, 1869 U.N.T.S. 401 [hereinafter DSU].

[36]   In each case, they could be blocked by consensus of the entire membership, but that would never occur in practice since there would always be a winning party. DSU, art. 14.

[37]   J. H. H. Weiler, "The Rule of Lawyers and the Ethos of Diplomats: Reflections on the Internal and External Legitimacy of WTO Dispute Settlement," *Journal of World Trade* 35, no. 2 (2001): 201 ("[T]he Appellate Body is a court in all but name.").

[38]   I write "(de facto) court" because the United States vociferously contests that the Appellate Body is a court and nowhere do WTO texts reference it as a court. Gregory Shaffer et al., "The Extensive (but Fragile) Authority of the WTO Appellate Body," *Law & Contemporary Problems* 79 (2016): 237.

dispute settlement system as a move from a "power-oriented technique" to a "rule-oriented" one, which, in the words of other commentators, had led to the triumph of "right over might."[39]

In response to Jackson, many trade scholars argued that law is always mixed with politics, so power would simply manifest itself in new ways. International relations realists stressed that the United States should have little to fear.[40] Politics should constrain WTO judicial interpretation so that it would heed the interests of powerful states. Institutionalist-oriented scholars emphasized that the United States and European Union wielded vast legal resources, combining experienced government attorneys with private lawyers hired by US and European companies for WTO dispute settlement. As a result, the United States and European Union were in the best position to shape WTO jurisprudence.[41] In addition, the enforcement of WTO judicial decisions depended on WTO authorized retaliation of an equivalent amount of trade concessions, pursuant to the WTO Dispute Settlement Understanding. This remedy structure favored members with large markets – that is, those whose markets mattered and thus gave them leverage. For developing countries and development activists, not only were the substantive rules tilted; they feared that the costly dispute settlement system's procedures and remedies were structurally biased against them.[42]

III. EMERGING ECONOMIES AND THE TRADE REGIME

In contrast to the United States and European Union, India, Brazil, and China were economically weak during the half century from the end of World War II through the WTO's creation. Indian economists long complained of the "Hindu rate of growth," which totaled just 3.5 percent per year between 1960 and 1985, keeping

---

[39] John Jackson, *The World Trading System*, 2nd ed. (Cambridge: MIT Press, 1997), 111 ("One way to explore the questions raised above is to compare two techniques of modern diplomacy: a 'rule-oriented' technique and a 'power-oriented technique'."); *see also*, J. Lacarte-Muró and P. Gappah, "Developing Countries and the WTO Legal and Dispute Settlement System: A View from the Bench," *Journal of International Economic Law* 3 (2000): 401 (arguing that "right perseveres over might"); James Bacchus, "Might Unmakes Right: The American Assault on the Role of Law in World Trade," *CIGI Papers*, no. 173 (2018).

[40] Richard H. Steinberg, "Judicial Lawmaking at the WTO: Discursive, Constitutional and Political Constraints," *American Journal of International Law* 98 (2004): 247 ("Politics, however, constrains both discursive and constitutional latitude, which should alleviate concerns that WTO judicial lawmaking is so expansive as to undermine the sovereignty of powerful states, create a serious democratic deficit for their citizens, or catalyze withdrawal of their support for the organization").

[41] Shaffer, *Defending Interests*.

[42] As Hudec wrote, "Larger and more powerful countries – those accustomed to living by rules slanted in their favor – are likely to aim for a somewhat less balanced result. For them, the optimal remedy package will be one that works well against others but not so well against themselves. This tendency also has to be considered in explaining why WTO remedies are as they are." Robert Hudec, "Broadening the Scope of Remedies in WTO Dispute Settlement," in *Improving WTO Dispute Settlement Procedures: Issues and Lessons from the Practice of other International Courts and Tribunals*, ed. Friedl Weiss (London: Cameron May, 2000): 369–400, 377.

rough pace with its growing population and leaving a significant proportion of Indians in extreme poverty. The phrase captured a sense of inevitability, predestination, a mix of sober acceptance and incapacitating despair.[43] Commentators saw large, inward-looking Brazil in slightly better terms, but still found it never lived up to its expectations, captured in the quip "Brazil is the country of the future – and always will be."[44] During the thirty years of Mao's rein, China turned even further inward with its authoritarian, centrally planned, command economy that led to economic disaster, from the 1959–1961 famine in which over thirty million people died to the Cultural Revolution of 1966–1976 with its economic and social chaos.[45]

The three countries played little role in drafting the GATT rules and, although Brazil and India were more active in the Doha Round negotiations, they were primarily on the defensive.[46] India was an original member of the GATT, but the country was only a few months old following its grant of independence and emergence from Britain's colonial yoke in 1947. Brazil joined the GATT six months after the GATT was formed. Their representatives did participate in the negotiations, but the United States prevailed in structuring it.[47] Although China was an original GATT member under the nationalist regime of Chiang Kai-Shek, the regime withdrew after the Communist revolution in 1949. Both India and Brazil were original WTO members, but they vigorously opposed and unsuccessfully resisted US and EU pressures to expand the trade regime to incorporate intellectual property protection, investment, and trade in services.[48] Under Deng Xiaoping, China sought to rejoin the GATT in 1986 and later the WTO as an original member, but it was blocked. The United States and other members only accepted China into the WTO in December 2001, almost seven years after the WTO's creation and fifteen years after China's request to join the GATT.[49] At the time, China appeared to get the worst deal of all WTO members.[50] It had to agree to China-specific rules that

---

[43] Jagdish Bhagwati, *India in Transition: Freeing the Economy* (Oxford: Clarendon Press, 1993).

[44] The phrase originated from a book by Stefan Zweig, *Brazil: Land of the Future*, but is also attributed to a statement of French President Charles de Gaulle. Simon Romero, "Fresh Look for Author, and for Land He Lauded," *New York Times*, November 21, 2011.

[45] Maurice Meisner, *Mao's China and after: A History of the People's Republic* (New York: Simon & Schuster, Inc., 1977), 119; Jonathan D. Spence, *The Search for Modern China* (New York: W.W. Norton & Company, Inc., 1991), 606.

[46] The main exception is Brazil's participation in the Cairns group which worked with the United States to press for greater liberalization and disciplines in agricultural trade.

[47] Robert Hudec, *The GATT Legal System and World Trade Diplomacy* (Salem: Butterworth Legal Publishers, 1990); Nicolas Lamp, "The Club Approach to Multilateral Trade Lawmaking," *Vanderbilt Journal of Transnational Law* 49 (2016): 107–190.

[48] Silvia Ostry, "The Uruguay Round North-South Grand Bargain: Implications for Future Negotiations," in *The Political Economy of International Trade Law*, eds. Daniel L. M. Kennedy and James D. Southwick (Cambridge: Cambridge University Press, 2002), 285.

[49] Henry Gao, "China's Participation in the WTO: A Lawyer's Perspective," *Singapore Year Book of International Law* 11 (2007): 41–48.

[50] As a developing country (as measured in terms of per capita income), China's bound tariff rates were higher than those of the United States and European Union, but they were much lower than those of Brazil, India, and all other emerging economies.

granted other WTO members greater rights against China, and China fewer rights against them. It was – once more – an "unequal treaty," one which, for some Chinese, reverberated with China's colonial history.[51]

International relations scholars stress the importance of who designs and drafts international rules to place constraints on others. After wars, the prevailing powers (such as the United States after World War II and the Cold War) create "constitutional settlements" that "specify the rules of the game – that is, the parameters within which states will compete and settle disputes over specific issues."[52] Through defining the rules and supporting institutions, a powerful state "can constrain other states well into the future."[53] Lloyd Gruber shows how such institutional power can cause countries to join an international organization that they never wanted formed in the first place. In his words,

> Institutionalized cooperation by one group of actors (the winners) can have the effect of restricting the options available to another group of actors (the losers), altering the rules of the game such that members of the latter group are better off playing by the new rules despite their strong preference for the original, pre-cooperative status quo.[54]

The WTO, in Gruber's terms, was an example of weaker states facing an institutional choice where they were "damned if they do," but "doubly damned if they don't."[55] Indeed, when the WTO was formed, the United States and European Union withdrew from the GATT so that countries desiring market access to the world's largest markets on most-favored-nation terms had to join the WTO with its new rules on trade in services, intellectual property rights, and other regulation.[56] As Robert Zoellick, former USTR, stated, "Our intention was to create institutions,

---

[51]   Julia Qin, "WTO-Plus Obligations and their Implications for the World Trade Organization Legal System – An Appraisal of the China Accession Protocol," *Journal of World Trade* 37 (2003): 483.

[52]   John Ikenberry, "Constitutional Politics in International Relations," *European Journal of International Relations* 4 (1998): 147, 156; John Ikenberry, *After Victory: Institutions, Strategic Restraint, and the Rebuilding of Order after Major Wars* (Princeton: Princeton University Press, 2000).

[53]   Ikenberry, "Constitutional Politics."

[54]   Lloyd Gruber, *Ruling the World: Power Politics and the Rise of Supranational Institutions* (Princeton: Princeton University Press, 2000), 7. Similarly, George Soros wrote in terms of the international financial system, "Periphery countries may find it painful to belong to the system, but opting out may be even more painful." George Soros, *On Globalization* (New York: Public Affairs, 2002). Compare Peter Bachrach and Morton Baratz, "Two Faces of Power," *American Political Science Review* 56 (1962): 948 (institutional power "limit[s] the scope of the political process to public consideration of only those issues" of interest to the powerful).

[55]   Michael Barnett and Raymond Duvall, "Power in International Politics," *International Organization* 59 (2005): 59. Compare Robert Hudec, "GATT and Developing Countries," 1992 *Columbia Business Law Review* (1992): 67–80, 76 (the WTO single undertaking "completely restructures the developed-developing country bargain, proposing to pay for all the new developing country concessions simply by agreeing not to destroy the market access they already have").

[56]   Richard Steinberg, "In the Shadow of Law or Power? Consensus-Based Bargaining and Outcomes in the GATT/WTO," *International Organization* 56 (2002): 339–374.

habits, and inclinations that would bias policy in these countries in our direction."[57] Since law constitutes legitimized coercion that creates normative expectations – such as regarding the proper treatment of intellectual property and the place of industrial policy – the United States was highly successful in "biasing" policy in directions it wanted.

One would thus expect the United States and Europe, as the creators of WTO rules, to be the WTO's champions, and emerging economies to be the complainers. Indeed, this was the case in the WTO's first decade when developing countries and their allies objected that "the rules were rigged."[58] These countries' push for a New International Economic Order (from the 1970s) was long dead, and their preferred institution – the United Nations Conference on Trade and Development (UNCTAD) – was a toothless talking shop. In contrast, the WTO intruded deeply into their developmental and regulatory policy space. India's Commerce Minister was "outspoken and often hostile . . . about the WTO," and other countries' officials accused him "of whipping up anti-WTO sentiment in order to win political support at home."[59] A senior Brazilian diplomat complained of structural bias in the WTO, noting: "It's a question of power. We don't have the power to call for a high-level meeting on matters important to us, such as tariff escalation or agricultural protection in the E.C. We would simply be ignored. Only the U.S. and E.C. have the power to pressure other countries into holding high level meetings of ministers on specific matters of interest."[60] China contended that "the lack of human and financial resources as well as capacities and experiences of developing-country Members results in de facto imbalance in the participation in the dispute settlement mechanism."[61] It unsuccessfully proposed to limit to two the number of complaints that a developed country could bring against a developing-country member in a calendar year.

Yet, through these countries' significant investments in trade law capacity, understood broadly as a key part of state capacity, they became formidable players in the WTO system and eventually rivals to the United States and Europe in WTO negotiations and dispute settlement. They blocked US and EU initiatives at WTO ministerial meetings, allying with each other to exercise effective veto power. In litigation, Brazil and India were the first to win important cases against the United States and European Union, which received front-page media coverage. By 2006,

---

57 Ikenberry, *After Victory*, 246, citing interview with Robert B. Zoellick, May 28, 1999.
58 Chakravarthi Rahgavan, *Recolonization: GATT, the Uruguay Round & the Third World* (Penang: Third World Network, 1990) Kevin Watkins and Penny Fowler, *Rigged Rules and Double Standards: Trade, Globalization and the Fight Against Poverty* (Oxford: Oxfam International, 2002).
59 Daniel Pruzin, "Indian Commerce Minister Maran Takes Hard Stance in WTO Talks on New Round," *WTO Reporter* (2001): 219.
60 Interview with Carlos A. da Rocha Paranhos, Brazil's Deputy Permanent Representative to the WTO, June 1998.
61 Communication from China, "Responses to Questions on the Specific Input of China," WTO Doc. TN/DS/W/57 (May 19, 2003).

China began to assert itself by vigorously using WTO rules to defend its domestic policies, and then (afterward) by bringing cases against the United States and European Union. As an EU official related, "China now knows how the WTO works. It does not hesitate to threaten bringing a WTO case ... . For the Commission, it creates more challenges in the relationship. They know, and they know we know they know."[62] All three emerging economies moved from being "rule takers" under the GATT and WTO to become "rule shakers" and (potentially) "rule makers."[63] To take from the influential work of socio-legal scholar Marc Galanter, these countries illustrate how to develop legal capacity to take on the "haves" in dispute settlement, and help shape the rules of the game.[64] It is a remarkable story. This book explains how it came to be.

IV. THE EXPANSION OF TRADE LAW: INVESTMENT AND INTELLECTUAL PROPERTY LAW

Although this book is predominantly about trade law, trade law has expanded to incorporate services, intellectual property, and (increasingly) investment, thus enlarging the boundaries of the field. During the 1990s and 2000s, the United States and capital-exporting European nations took the lead in developing a transnational legal order for investment law – just as in trade – again triggering charges of unequal bargaining power and rigged rules.[65] Investment law was not centralized like the trade legal order with the WTO at its core but was composed of around three thousand bilateral investment treaties, complemented by customary international law, and enforced by investor–state dispute settlement. It too became transnationalized as a body of law and jurisprudence, since it is based on relatively common substantive law protecting foreign investors and a common framework for investor–state arbitration to settle disputes.[66] The regime is backed by the International Centre for the Settlement of Investment Disputes at the (US-dominated) World Bank that administers the arbitrations, complemented by other public and private institutions that offer such services.[67] Private investor claims drive the jurisprudence,

[62]   Interview, Beijing, July 30, 2017.

[63]   Henry Gao, "China's Ascent in Global Trade Governance: From Rule Taker to Rule Shaker, and Maybe Rule Maker?," in *Making Global Trade Governance Work for Development*, ed. Carolyn Deere-Birkbeck (Cambridge: Cambridge University Press, 2011), 153.

[64]   Galanter, "Why the 'Haves' Come Out Ahead," 95.

[65]   M. Sornarajah, *The International Law on Foreign Investment*, 4th ed. (Cambridge: Cambridge University Press, 2017) (chapter 1); David Schneiderman, *Constitutionalizing Economic Globalization: Investment Rules and Democracy's Promise* (New York: Cambridge University Press, 2008).

[66]   Stephan Schill, *The Multilateralization of International Investment Law* (2009).

[67]   Under the system, the investor and state generally each select one of the three arbitrators. The agreement establishing the International Centre for Settlement of Investment Disputes (ICSID) has 163 signatories and 154 contracting parties. ICSID also offers an Additional Facility that

which builds from the work of an intertwined community of academic experts, lawyers, and arbitrators who, in practice, may assume all three roles.[68]

As an increasingly judicialized investment law threatened huge claims against them, implicating their domestic policy space, emerging economies began developing their own investment law models. Although this book's central chapters on Brazil, India, and China focus predominantly on trade law, they also address investment law because of its increasing enmeshment with trade law in international economic law governance. The two legal orders were initially distinct, but they became increasingly intermeshed in at least four ways. First, materially, over two-thirds of international trade has been conducted through global value chains.[69] Although we lack global statistics regarding trade among corporate affiliates, the WTO estimates "that upwards of 80 per cent of global trade now takes place within the international production networks of multinational companies."[70] Thus, investment and trade are closely linked in the private sector's production decisions, which, in turn, incentivized the private sector to push for investment protection's inclusion in trade agreements. Second, governments increasingly incorporated investment and trade rules in international economic partnership agreements. This occurred in NAFTA in 1994, and then in investment-related provisions of the WTO's General Agreement on Trade in Services in 1995. Since around 2002, investment chapters were increasingly included in trade agreements, reflected in the new mega-regional negotiations for a Regional Comprehensive Economic Partnership in Asia, the signed Trans-Pacific Partnership, and the ratified Comprehensive and Progressive Agreement on Trans-Pacific Partnership in 2018.[71] Third, the jurisprudence of trade and investment law includes many overlapping concepts, in particular regarding the defense of a state's "legitimate" regulatory objectives.[72] Investment tribunals cited and built from WTO jurisprudence, and former WTO Appellate Body members

non-ICSID members can use, including through investment agreements with ICSID members, as was the case with Mexico under NAFTA until Mexico joined ICSID in August 2018. In addition, the Permanent Court of Arbitration in the Hague offers administrative services for arbitrations, as do many private bodies such as the International Chamber of Commerce.

[68]   Thomas Schultz and Niccolò Ridi, "Arbitration Literature," in *Oxford Handbook of International Arbitration*, eds. Thomas Schultz and Federico Ortino (Oxford: Oxford University Press, 2020) (on systemic and self-interest in the literature); Malcolm Langford, Daniel Behn, and Runar Hilleren Lie, "The Revolving Door in International Investment Arbitration," *Journal of International Economic Law* 20 (2017): 301 (on double hatting of lawyers and arbitrators).

[69]   WTO, *Global Value Chain Development Report 2019* (Geneva: WTO, 2019), 1.

[70]   World Trade Organization, *World Trade Report 2018: The Future of World Trade: How Digital Technologies Are Transforming Global Commerce* (2018), 19; WTO, *World Trade Statistical Review* (2018), 54; Sarah Stutzman, Activities of U.S. Affiliates of Foreign Multinational Enterprises in 2015, Survey of Current Business, 97: 8, August 2017 (on US affiliate trade).

[71]   A study found investment provisions in 111 of 230 preferential trade agreements, with the bulk of them being since 2002. About 77 percent of these provide access to ISDS. Jo-Ann Crawford and Barbara Kotschwar, "Investment Provisions in Preferential Trade Agreements: Evolution and Current Trends," *WTO Staff Working Paper*, December 14, 2018, 28.

[72]   Jurgen Kurtz, *The WTO and International Investment Law: Converging Systems* (2016).

served on investment arbitral tribunals, which highlighted the potential of bringing a more public law focus to them. Fourth, and critically for this book, emerging economies developed legal capacity in trade law that they subsequently used to develop investment law models. Brazil, India, and China invested in creating their own models for the transnational legal ordering of investment facilitation and protection that are linked to their trade objectives.

As the United States and Europe became wary of being subject to investment law claims, and as nationalists in the United States wished to renationalize global supply chains, each of Brazil, India, and China began playing more entrepreneurial roles in developing the legal order for investment. The enmeshment of finance, investment, and trade are key to the governance of China's ambitious Belt and Road Initiative (Chapter 7). Although China gradually moved toward more conventional bilateral investment treaties with investor–state arbitration to protect its foreign investments abroad, it borrowed from Western models but repurposed them in ways that are more respectful of state sovereignty and place greater focus on mediation. Concurrently, India terminated its existing bilateral investment treaties and created a new model treaty for its future negotiations. And Brazil created its own unique model based on investment facilitation and signed a dozen Cooperation and Facilitation Investment Agreements that focus on dispute avoidance rather than on extensive investor protection backed by investor–state arbitration. In turn, Brazil advocated the multilateralization of its model in the WTO (Chapter 4). In developing their investment law models, these countries tapped into the trade-related expertise they developed earlier.

Similarly, with the WTO's creation, intellectual property law became a core part of the trade regime, which has since been further developed through bilateral and regional trade agreements. The GATT regime did not include intellectual property protection, and the Paris Convention for the Protection of Industrial Property provided no minimum substantive standards. Under these treaties, each country could create its own patent regime so long as it did so on a nondiscriminatory basis. All this changed with the WTO Agreement on Trade-Related Aspects of Intellectual Property Rights (TRIPS). Against the protest of developing countries, and in particular Brazil and India, it mandated minimum standards for intellectual property protection modeled after those applied in developed countries.[73]

Intellectual property became central to the international trade legal order not only because of its formal inclusion in WTO, NAFTA, and other bilateral trade agreements. It also did so because of intensified competition over the commanding heights of the economy protected by intellectual property, and because of the implications intellectual property laws have for the pursuit of other social goals. Societies face multiple problems, from encouraging innovation to assuring public

---

[73] TRIPS sets forth minimum intellectual property standards for WTO members in the following seven areas: copyright; trademarks; geographical indications; industrial designs; patents; layout designs of integrated circuits; and trade secrets.

health and inclusive access to public goods. These goals often conflict, involving tradeoffs. There are thus diagnostic struggles over the construction and framing of the social problem at stake, reflecting both conflicting material interests and conflicting ideological approaches to intellectual property. These conflicts occur both between countries and within them.

V. THE BOOK'S ORGANIZATION

Building from over two decades of intensive fieldwork and interviews in these three countries and other global capitals, this book shows the enmeshment of international and national trade law in three emerging powers (China, India, and Brazil) and the implications of these developments for the international trade legal order itself. It is in nine chapters. Chapter 2 presents the book's theoretical framework of "transnational legal ordering" and "transnational legal orders," together with the book's three central questions regarding the building of trade law capacity, accompanying internal institutional change in emerging powers, and the ensuing settlement, unsettlement, and splintering of the transnational legal order for trade. Chapter 3 presents the considerable challenges that these countries faced in building legal capacity for international trade negotiations, monitoring, implementation, and disputes with the United States and Europe. Chapters 4, 5, and 6, respectively, tell the stories of how Brazil, India, and China (i) developed trade law capacity, including to take on and go lawyer-to-lawyer with the United States, Europe, and others before the WTO, (ii) in the process, changed themselves institutionally, and (iii) now are deploying that legal capacity for their own trade and economic law initiatives. Because of China's centrality for the trade legal order's future, the book includes a separate chapter assessing China's new initiatives in Chapter 7. It examines China's development of a potential Sino-centric legal order through the combination of its Belt and Road Initiative, a complementary web of trade and investment agreements, and an indigenous innovation policy with transnational ambitions where intellectual property (paradoxically) is playing a key supporting role. Chapter 8 turns from these three emerging powers to the impact of their rise and successful deployment of trade law capacity on trade politics and narratives within the United States. It assesses what is at stake for the future of the trade order and the need for a new interface – the rules of the game – between these countries' economic systems. Chapter 9 concludes, addressing the role of legal capacity going forward for the transnational ordering of trade, while assessing the implications of these case studies for theorizing transnational legal orders.

2

The Theory: Building Trade Law Capacity in Emerging Powers and Its Implications

We live in a pivotal time for international economic law. Emerging powers have ascended in prominence and the United States and Europe declined as economic and trading powers. China has become a rival to the United States. Economists tend to explain the shift from the angle of *efficiency* and innovation, while political scientists in terms of *power*, and more precisely market and economic power. This book provides a necessary complement to these analyses by assessing changes in *law* and legal institutions, and, in particular, these countries' development of *trade law capacity*, which is linked to broader policy capacity, to interpret, apply, develop, and shape the rules of the game.

Some international relations scholars posit that the "emerging nations are intent on altering existing rules," believing they will "reshape international arrangements to suit them," reflective of a power transition.[1] Some critical theorists, building from dependency theory and world systems theory, assess how the new powers can radically change the existing international economic order.[2] Yet, ironically, emerging powers have defended the existing trade legal order that the United States created from US attack while simultaneously building their own bilateral and regional trade and investment law initiatives.

This book explains this paradox by evaluating the responses of the three most important emerging economies – China, India, and Brazil – to the international trade legal order. Although these three countries are similar in being regional economic powers, they vary significantly in other characteristics, such as their form of government, their legal tradition, their system of business organization, and state–society relations. Despite these differences, the resemblances in their

---

[1] Stewart Patrick, "Irresponsible Stakeholders? The Difficulty of Integrating Rising Powers," *Foreign Affairs* 89, no. 6 (November/December 2010): 47.

[2] Giovanni Arrighi and Lu Zhang, "Beyond the Washington Consensus: A New Bandung?," in *Globalization and Beyond: New Examinations of Global Power and Its Alternatives*, eds. Jon Shefner and Patricia Fernández-Kelly (University Park, PA: Penn State University Press, 2011), 25. Relatedly, Hopewell asks, "How changes in the distribution of power among states are affecting the governance of neoliberal globalization." Kristen Hopewell, *Breaking the WTO: How Emerging Powers Disrupted the Neoliberal Project* (Stanford: Stanford University Press, 2016), 2.

building of trade law capacity, their internal institutional changes, and their engagement with the international trade regime are striking, illustrating transnational legal ordering at work. Building from multisited fieldwork in both international and national settings, the book investigates how the legalization and judicialization of international trade relations spurred institutional transformations within government, business, and civil society in these countries. They adapted internally to meet international trade law's institutional demands and, in turn, assumed critical roles in the changing trade legal order.

I. THEORETICAL APPROACH: THE SETTLEMENT AND UNSETTLEMENT OF TRANSNATIONAL LEGAL ORDERS

Before examining the book's three questions regarding legal capacity, state transformation, and their implications for trade law's future, this section explains its theoretical approach. The book builds from a socio-legal analytic framework for studying transnational legal ordering and the settlement and unsettlement of what Terence Halliday and I call "transnational legal orders."[3] The framework assesses the recursive linkages between international and national law and practice within a given field, which can give rise to a transnational legal order, or coexisting or competing transnational legal orders.

By *transnational legal ordering*, I refer to the processes through which legal norms are constructed, flow, settle, and unsettle transnationally across levels of social organization.[4] These processes involve the recursive interaction of lawmaking, interpretation, implementation, and practice at the international, national, and local levels. They can be bottom-up, top-down, horizontal, and transversal. They often involve networked intermediaries operating at multiple levels. The impact of these transnational processes implicate more than just positive law, but also institutions, professions, and normative frames through which policy is made and implemented.

The result of these processes can give rise to one or more *transnational legal orders*. The concept of a *transnational legal order* refers to a collection of formalized legal norms and associated organizations and actors that authoritatively order the understanding and practice of law across national jurisdictions.[5] Through a transnational legal order, actors aim to produce order in an issue area that they construe as a problem and use law to address the problem. When successful, they create shared norms and institutions regarding regulation and practice in an issue area that orients social expectations, communication, and behavior within and between states. It is a *transnational*

---

[3]   Gregory Shaffer, *Transnational Legal Ordering and State Change* (Cambridge: Cambridge University Press, 2013); Terence Halliday and Gregory Shaffer, *Transnational Legal Orders* (Cambridge: Cambridge University Press, 2015).

[4]   Shaffer, *Transnational Legal Ordering* (defining "transnational law" as the process of the "Transnational Construction and Flow of Legal Norms," as opposed to a body of law); Gregory Shaffer, "Theorizing Transnational Legal Ordering," *Annual Review of Law and Social Science* 12 (2016): 231–253.

[5]   Halliday and Shaffer, *Transnational Legal Orders*, 5.

order in that it not only transcends but also permeates national boundaries. And it is *legal* in that it adopts legal form to address the problems and because the norms directly and indirectly engage international and national legal institutions. The norms may be negotiated at the international level, but they are often derived from some states' national laws and practices, and they are directed at and engage national legal institutions and practices.

In a transnational legal order, norms "settle" when they comprise new working equilibria regarding the appropriate legal norms and institutions to order particular issues.[6] They become "cognitively taken for granted by actors," attain "a high level of normative consensus," or otherwise are accepted as the rules of the game.[7] It is such settlement that constitutes *order* through law, which both provides certainty and predictability for economic operators (as stressed by economists) and provides leverage for certain constituencies in relation to others (as emphasized by political scientists). To constitute a transnational legal order, settlement involves more than formal international law and national codifications of such law. Such normative settlement rather comprises the habits and mindsets of executives, parliamentarians, administrators, and private practitioners. It encompasses the day-to-day practices of officials and professionals, whether they be customs officials, import relief practitioners, patent processors, attorneys, or otherwise.

Norms can settle differently in multiple issue areas that overlap, raising the question of how legal norms "align" with an issue.[8] Legal norms closely align with an issue where a single transnational legal order (such as for trade) corresponds in its legal and geographic scope to an underlying problem or issue area. Alignment also can involve partition among transnational legal orders that address different subsets of an issue, such as between the International Monetary Fund (IMF) and World Trade Organization (WTO) regarding balance-of-payment issues, which affected India. Alternatively, a transnational legal order can apply to only part of an issue, creating gaps, such as WTO and IMF rules in relation to Chinese exchange rate policy. Finally, different transnational legal orders can compete in the framing of an issue, as instantiated in contests over the framing of the regulation of genetically modified foods and of pharmaceutical patents.[9] In this latter case, these competing framings engage different stakeholders as well as different ministries within states.

---

[6] Ibid., 42–44.

[7] Niklas Luhman, *A Sociological Theory of Law* (London: Routledge & Kegan Paul, 1985), 77 (law as creating "generalized normative behavioral expectations" for communication and interaction); Ryken Grattet and Valerie Jenness, "The Birth and Maturation of Hate Crime Policy in the United States,"*American Behavioral Scientist* 45 (2001): 668–696, 670.

[8] Work on "regime complexes" addresses this issue, but not from the multilevel and recursive perspective of transnational legal order theory. Compare Kal Raustiala and David Victor, "The Regime Complex for Plant Genetic Resources," *International Organization* 58, no. 2 (2004): 277–309.

[9] Laurence Helfer, "Pharmaceutical Patents and the Human Right to Health: The Contested Evolution of the Transnational Legal Order on Access to Medicines," in *Transnational Legal Orders*, eds. Terence Halliday and Gregory Shaffer (Cambridge: Cambridge University Press, 2015), 311;

When legal norms settle *concordantly* across levels of social organization and align with an issue, the transnational legal order becomes institutionalized.[10] In the terms of sociological field theory, the norms can become "habitual, patterned ways of understanding, judging, and acting," constituting a "habitus."[11] To translate this term into the vernacular of political science, such normative settlement gives rise to "path dependencies," as actors adapt to the institutional rules of the game.

This form of ordering differs from other alternatives. Most prominently, it differs from balance-of-power politics in international relations.[12] It also differs from economic ordering through systems of barter or impersonal markets,[13] as well as from religious, cultural, and other forms of social ordering, which also can extend transnationally.[14] In practice, these types of ordering will interact in different ways in different historical contexts, but the legal field, as empirically studied in this book, is semiautonomous from them.

These transnational processes are often highly contested, involving considerable resistance. They encompass both strategic action and social interaction within structured contexts. In the language of political science, they entail the interaction of interests, ideas, and institutions. Prevailing ideas and institutions shape interests, while interests strategically create, exploit, and promote particular ideas and institutions to advance their goals.[15] Such strategic action and social interaction affect each other, and in this way are mutually constitutive. On the one hand, strategic action takes place within social and institutional contexts where norms matter. On the other hand, powerful actors shape these social and institutional contexts. "Structure," in the words of Anthony Giddens, "is both medium and outcome."[16]

The concepts of transnational legal ordering and transnational legal order highlight the interpenetration and dynamic interaction among international, national,

---

Mark Pollack and Gregory Shaffer, *When Regulation Fails: The International Law and Politics of Genetically Modified Foods* (Oxford: Oxford University Press, 2009).

[10] Halliday and Shaffer, *Transnational Legal Orders*, 44–55 (on concordance and alignment).

[11] Richard Terdiman, Translator's Introduction, Pierre Bourdieu, "Force of Law: Toward a Sociology of the Juridical Field," *Hastings Law Journal* 38 (1986): 805, 811.

[12] Compare Kenneth Waltz, *Theory of International Politics* (New York: Random House, 1979).

[13] Compare F. A. Hayek, *Studies in Philosophy, Politics and Economics* (London: Taylor & Francis, 1967), 97 (defining spontaneous order as "the result of human actions, not of human design").

[14] Compare David Kang, *East Asia Before the West: Five Centuries of Trade and Tribute* (New York: Columbia University Press, 2010) (on the role of Confucianism and the tribute system in international relations in East Asia).

[15] Some social scientists call this approach "strategic constructivism." For relevant works in this vein, see Mark Blyth, *Great Transformations: Economic Ideas and Institutional Change in the Twentieth Century* (New York: Cambridge University Press, 2002); Cornelia Woll, "Firm Interests in Uncertain Times: Business Lobbying in Multilateral Service Liberalization," in *Constructing the International Economy*, eds. Rawi Abdelal, Mark Blyth, and Craig Parsons (Ithaca: Cornell University Press, 2010), 137–154.

[16] In social theory, Anthony Giddens's concept of structuration addresses the relation of structure and practice. Anthony Giddens, *Central Problems in Social Theory: Action, Structure, and Contradiction in Social Analysis* (Berkeley: University of California Press, 1979), 5. Different theoretical approaches to social theory view these structures as ecologies, fields, or institutions.

and local law and practice. Importantly, the lens of transnational legal ordering differs from a conventional international law approach because it focuses simultaneously on changes in law, institutions, professions, networks, norms, and practices *within* countries and at the international level, and it does so within a single analytic frame.[17] Theory and research in this vein do not look solely at the international level – the traditional approaches of positivist law, law and economics, and international relations scholarship on the WTO.[18] Rather, they assess how legal norm-making by actors at the international, national, and local levels coexists, overlaps, interacts, coordinates, competes, and conflicts recursively over time. From the perspective of theorizing transnational legal ordering, states participate in their own transformations in engaging with international institutions. State, business, and civil society responses to international rules and standards feed back into revisions and revised understandings of them, including through formal interpretation and informal practice.

This book's unit of analysis is thus the rise and fall, settlement, unsettlement, and change of a transnational legal order. Such a transnational legal order develops through the growing interface between what were once (and are still often formally) viewed as autonomous spaces (such as international and national legal systems), as they adapt and change through *recursive* processes. Put negatively, one errs by approaching a transnational system only by analyzing its component parts, however autonomous each part is formally from a legal point of view, such as in terms of legal sources and jurisdiction.[19]

For those working in other disciplines and theoretical traditions, this book's approach has close analogues. In international relations, Henry Farrell and Abraham Newman's "new interdependence" and Thomas Oatley's complexity theories apply analogous approaches for political analysis, as they too theorize endogenous change within global and transnational systems.[20] Similarly, Alec

---

[17]   Gregory Shaffer and Carlos Coye, "From International Law to Jessup's Transnational Law, From Transnational Law to Transnational Legal Orders," in *The Many Lives of Transnational Law: Critical Engagements with Jessup's Bold Proposal*, ed. Peer Zumbansen (Cambridge: Cambridge University Press, 2020), 126–152.

[18]   Some approaches assess the impact of domestic politics in key countries on international politics, and others assess the impact of international politics on domestic politics, but they do not address these processes recursively in a single frame. Compare Andrew Moravcsik, "Taking Preferences Seriously: A Liberal Theory of International Politics," *International Organization* 51, no. 4 (1997): 513–553 and Peter Gourevitch, "The International Sources of Domestic Politics," *International Organization* 32, no. 4 (1978): 881–912.

[19]   I thank Alec Stone Sweet for this formulation.

[20]   Henry Farrell and Abraham Newman, "The New Interdependence Approach: Theoretical Development and Empirical Demonstration," *Review of International Political Economy* 23 (2016): 713–736 (viewing globalization as an "endogenous process rather than an exogenous shock"); Henry Farrell and Abraham Newman, *Of Privacy and Power: The Transatlantic Struggle over Freedom and Security* (Princeton: Princeton University Press, 2019); Thomas Oatley, "Toward a Political Economy of Complex Interdependence," *European Journal of International Relations* 24 (2019): 957–978 (system as unit of analysis, building from complexity theory).

Stone Sweet earlier theorized courts – including international courts – as a form of triadic dispute settlement that shapes the "normative structure" in which actors operate, constituting a field.[21] When applied to international courts, such as those in Europe, he showed how these structures can catalyze dynamic, multilevel governance systems.[22] More generally, this book's approach aligns with institutionalist-oriented scholars across disciplines. Historical institutionalists in political science assess how institutions are sticky and structure outcomes, including by creating "path dependencies" such that institutional change often occurs through "layering" upon what came before.[23] Sociological institutionalists stress the importance of framing, paradigms, and the hybridization of norms in different cultural contexts,[24] which give rise to fields.[25] For institutional economists, such as Douglas North, institutions represent the "rules of the game" under which economic activity occurs within a given society, which helps to explain why certain societies experience greater economic growth than others.[26] Critically, this book theorizes, empirically documents, and explains institutional change, in this case of a transnational legal order.

This analytic approach raises key questions as to how legal norms settle and unsettle transnationally, and when and why do transnational legal orders rise, fall, or fragment? Changes can be explained in terms of exogenous events, endogenous

[21] Alec Stone Sweet, "Judicialization and the Construction of Governance," in *On Law, Politics, & Judicialization*, eds. Martin Shapiro and Alec Stone Sweet (Oxford: Oxford University Press, 2002), 55–89.

[22] Alec Stone Sweet, *The Judicial Construction of Europe* (Oxford: Oxford University Press, 2004); Alec Stone Sweet, Wayne Sandholtz, and Neil Fligstein, eds., *The Institutionalization of Europe* (Oxford: Oxford University Press, 2001).

[23] James Mahoney and Kathleen Thelen, Preface to *Explaining Institutional Change: Ambiguity, Agency and Power*, eds. James Mahoney and Kathleen Thelen (Cambridge: Cambridge University Press, 2010), xi, xii (providing a historical institutionalist perspective); Paul Pierson, *Politics in Time* (Princeton: Princeton University Press, 2004); Thomas Rixen and Lora Anne Viola, "Historical Institutionalism and International Relations: Towards Explaining Change and Stability in International Institutions," in *Historical Institutionalism & International Relations: Explaining Institutional Development in World Politics*, eds. Thomas Rixen, Lora Anne Viola, and Michael Zürn (Oxford: Oxford University Press, 2016).

[24] John Campbell, *Institutional Change and Globalization* (Princeton: Princeton University Press, 2004).

[25] Within field theory, there is variation between those who place greater emphasis on structural constraint and reproduction, and those who provide a greater role for agency and change. Neil Fligstein and Doug McAdam advance a variant of field theory in terms of "strategic action fields," which provides a greater role for agency and institutional change, with which this book more closely aligns. Daniel N. Kluttz and Neil Fligstein, "Varieties of Sociological Field Theory," in *Handbook of Contemporary Sociological Theory*, ed. Seth Abrutyn (Switzerland: Springer, 2016), 185–204; Neil Fligstein and Doug McAdam, *A Theory of Fields* (Oxford: Oxford University Press, 2012).

[26] Douglass C. North, *Institutions, Institutional Change and Economic Performance* (Cambridge: Cambridge University Press, 1990), 3. Compare Masahiko Aoki, *Toward a Comparative Institutional Analysis* (Cambridge: MIT Press, 2001), 2–3, 377; Avner Greif, *Institutions and Path to the Modern Economy: Lessons from Medieval Trade* (Cambridge: Cambridge University Press, 2006), 4–5.

processes, and the interaction between them. Transnational legal order theory explains exogenous change in terms of facilitating circumstances and precipitating events,[27] which has parallels across disciplines. *Facilitating circumstances* that contribute to the rise and fall of transnational legal orders include the following:

- inventions and technological changes, such as container ships and communication technologies. New communication technologies today facilitate the outsourcing of tasks, on the one hand, and raise security concerns about "connectivity" wars, such as over 5G telecommunications infrastructure and the Internet of Things, on the other hand;
- changes in corporate organizations and networks, such as the rise and restructuring of global supply chains;
- increases and decreases in interdependence and the conceptualization of problems as "transnational" that were once viewed as local, such as in light of regulatory policy spillovers;
- shifts in the relative power of states and other actors, such as the rise of China and emerging powers, and the decline of the United States and Europe; and
- shifts in ideas and conceptualizations of "problems," such as increases in security and inequality concerns regarding trade, and challenges to neoliberal ideology for privileging market mechanisms.

In addition, transnational legal order theory notes how the *unintended consequences* of a transnational legal order themselves may generate facilitating circumstances. In this study, for example, the trade legal order facilitated the economic rise of China and other emerging powers, and the United States lost control of lawmaking and legal interpretation within it. By supporting economic globalization, the WTO legal order also contributed to a shift in bargaining power between capital and labor, and the ensuing rise of inequality within the United States and elsewhere. The distributive effects of a transnational legal order can trigger legitimacy challenges to its authority, such as by creating underlying conditions for a populist reaction in a major power, as Chapter 8 explores.

The slow buildup of such pressures can reach a tipping point where *precipitating conditions* catalyze major changes. These precipitating conditions include the following:

- a financial crisis, one whose impact may be delayed as it works its way through social and political processes;
- a geopolitical crisis, such as between the United States and China;
- a health or ecological crisis, such as the COVID-19 pandemic or developments in global warming; or
- a policy change in a key state, such as in the United States following the election of President Trump.

---

[27] Halliday and Shaffer, *Transnational Legal Orders*, 32–37.

Importantly, because the theoretical framework of transnational legal ordering and transnational legal orders places international and national institutional development within a single analytic frame as its unit of analysis, it also permits one to trace *endogenous*, continuous, and gradual changes in such legal ordering. The concept of *transnational recursivity* helps to explain these endogenous processes. It refers to the links between global, national, and local legal and normative change through feedback loops regarding the production, diffusion, and implementation of norms.[28] In law, such recursive processes are driven by diagnostic struggles over the problem that the texts aim to address, the indeterminacy of legal texts, ideological contradictions within texts, and actor mismatch between those that adopt global norms (such as at the WTO) and those that implement them, including through practice.

First, there are *diagnostic struggles* over the problems that trade norms are intended to resolve. Those who negotiate the norms are different than those who implement and practice them at the national level, and these different actors may have very different conceptions of the "problems" that the norms should address. Likewise, there can be contests within states, including among ministries, regarding the framing of the "problem" at issue and how the norms should be interpreted and applied in light of such framing. For example, should pharmaceutical patenting issues be seen in terms of their implications for innovation or for access to medicines? Officials in different ministries and branches of government, pressed by different private and civil society actors, will frame differently the problem that legal texts are to resolve.

Second, there is often *actor mismatch* between those who negotiate and those who implement the legal norms. If those who implement them were not represented in the international process that created the texts, they may use different techniques to thwart and reorient the norms' domestic application. Issues that were not apparent (or that were resolved) at the negotiation stage may appear for the first time (or reappear) at the implementation stage.

Third, there may be *internal contradictions* within the texts. They may result from vague compromises between negotiators who represent different interests and ideological orientations, such as regarding free trade and developmentalism, or free trade and other regulatory concerns. Texts, for example, tend to include both requirements and "exceptions," both commitments and "flexibilities." At the implementation stage, different ministries may emphasize different aspects of such texts.

Fourth, the meaning of texts is often *indeterminate*, not only because of the multiplicity of rules and exceptions, and conflicting doctrinal canons for interpreting them, but also because of the limits of language as applied to different and changing factual contexts. For example, WTO rules are now applied to a data-driven

---

[28]   Terence Halliday and Bruce Carruthers, "The Recursivity of Law: Global Normmaking and National Lawmaking in the Globalization of Bankruptcy Regimes," *American Journal of Sociology* 112 (2007): 1135–1202; Halliday and Shaffer, *Transnational Legal Orders*, 37–42.

economy where products and services are mixed in the so-called Internet of Things, which was not imagined when the texts were negotiated.[29] Similarly, questions arise as to how the legal norms should apply to China's new variety of state capitalism after the country reorganized its economic model under President Xi Jinping.[30]

This book applies the concept of recursivity not only to assess changes in legal norms over time but also in a broader sense regarding *the interaction of legal norms with social and political forces* within states and their ensuing implications for international institutions and relations between states. As Chapter 1 noted, from a legal realist perspective, law is not just a mode of reasoning that actors use to pursue goals and to resolve problems. It also reflects and implicates power, in particular because of law's distributive implications. Developments in trade law thus spur social and political responses that, in turn, shape it. The concept of recursivity places law's production, interpretation, and application within a single *processual* frame. As a result, this book not only traces the implications of international trade law for law and institutions within states in light of contests among domestic factions (such as in Brazil, India, and China) but also how these processes operate recursively to affect international trade law and institutions (such as the WTO and other trade agreements), which, in turn, recursively shapes contests among factions within third states (such as the United States), which, in turn, implicates further change in the international trade legal order. The recursivity concept specifies the mechanisms through which legal norms dynamically change through transnational legal ordering processes, thus highlighting the political economy of law and its interpretation. Law is an ongoing institution. Viewed in transnational terms, it is through these recursive processes that transnational legal orders settle and unsettle, stabilize and destabilize. It is through these processes that a transnational legal order not only institutionalizes but also becomes destabilized and potentially falls.

These recursive processes occur within states, between states, and across international regimes. Within states, different ministries and interest groups coordinate and clash. Between states, mutual concerns and conflicts generate bilateral negotiations, such as between the United States and China, India, and Brazil. Within regions, legal norms develop through negotiations, dispute settlement, and practice, such as under NAFTA (now USMCA), Mercosur in South America, and the Regional Comprehensive Economic Partnership in Asia. Between the international and national levels, national norms may be uploaded, or international ones downloaded, in each case often involving hybridization. At the international level, interactions recur between the WTO and other international organizations, such as the International Monetary Fund (regarding trade and balance-of-payments

---

[29] Gregory Shaffer, "Trade Law in a Data-Driven Economy: A Call for Modesty and Resilience," in *Reconfiguring International Economic Law in an AI Era*, eds. Shin-yi Peng, Ching-Fu Lin, and Thomas Streinz (Cambridge: Cambridge University Press, forthcoming 2021).

[30] Mark Wu, "The 'China, Inc.' Challenge to Global Trade Governance," *Harvard International Law Journal* 57 (2016): 1001–1063.

restrictions), Codex Alimentarius (regarding food standards), the International Labor Organization (regarding trade and labor rights), and human rights and health organizations (such as regarding access to medicines).

These recursive processes involve feedback loops that parallel studies in historical institutionalism in political science and neo-institutionalism in sociology, as they encompass path dependencies, hybridization, isomorphism, and the layering of new norms and institutions on existing ones. Yet, the theorizing of transnational recursivity and transnational legal ordering also significantly advances and contributes to institutional theory. An international or transnational legal order is not simply "designed." In practice, it emerges from ongoing interactions over legal norms that, given law's characteristics, can lead to stabilizing and destabilizing outcomes. They can lead to the settlement and unsettlement of the legal norms' meaning and application. Put in economic terms, the resulting "equilibrium" is never permanent because it has distributional consequences that favor some over others, which can catalyze ongoing and new challenges to legal rules and (potentially) the broader legal order.[31]

Earlier empirical work showed how actors in developing countries adapt, hybridize, and localize international legal norms, assessing these actors' agency in light of local contexts, including local cultures and power dynamics.[32] This book too addresses such adaptation, contestation, and localization in Brazil, India, and China. However, the book also shows how these countries' actions *recursively affected the transnational legal order for trade* itself. In short, law and societies should not be viewed in purely national terms combined with their inter-state (or international) counterpart, but rather should be viewed transnationally.[33] It is this recursive relationship between international legal ordering and national law and institutions in the field of trade that this book theorizes and empirically investigates.

These countries' initiatives are often not completely new, but they build from earlier models of the United States and Europe. Emerging powers repurpose those models to advance their own priorities and interests. In this way, their initiatives can be viewed as "layering" on existing international economic law institutions as part of

---

[31] I thank Krzysztof Pelc for this point.

[32] Amitav Acharya, "How Ideas Spread: Whose Norms Matter? Norm Localization and Institutional Change in Asian Regionalism," *International Organization* (2004); Yves Dezalay and Bryant G. Garth, *The Internationalization of Palace Wars: Lawyers, Economists, and the Contest to Transform Latin American States* (Chicago: University of Chicago Press, 2002); Sally Merry, *Human Rights and Gender Violence: Translating International Law into Local Justice* (Chicago: University of Chicago Press, 2006).

[33] Dezalay and Garth, *Palace Wars*; Boaventura de Sousa Santos, *Toward a New Legal Common Sense: Law, Science and Politics in the Paradigmatic Transition* (Cambridge: Cambridge University Press, 2002); Saskia Sassen, *Territory, Authority, Rights: From Medieval to Global Assemblages* (Princeton: Princeton University Press, 2006); William Twining, *General Jurisprudence: Understanding Law from a Global Perspective* (Cambridge: Cambridge University Press, 2009); Eve Darian-Smith, *Laws and Societies in Global Context: Contemporary Approaches* (Cambridge: Cambridge University Press, 2013); Shaffer, *Transnational Legal Ordering*; Halliday and Shaffer, *Transnational Legal Orders*.

an "ecology" of global and transnational lawmaking and practice. The concept of *layering* involves the building of new elements and structures on existing ones.[34] The concept of *ecology* captures how actors interact, coexist, cooperate, and compete in complex processes within and between institutions that shape institutional development over time.[35] As Susan Block-Lieb and Terence Halliday write:

> An ecology is a form of *bounded* social space. Like any space, some actors are inside its often invisible boundaries and other actors are outside. For our purposes, any international lawmaking ecology is constituted by actors who construe a behavioral phenomenon as a problem that can be resolved through law. Lawmakers in the ecology seek to construct transnational legal orders that span frontiers, whether bilaterally, multilaterally, regionally, or globally.[36]

As we will see, this book's study of China's initiatives in Chapter 7 supplements accounts in international relations. China's transnational legal initiatives, which include its Belt and Road Initiative, now form a critical part of the ecology of the transnational legal ordering of trade, constituting both a complementary and a competitive legal order to those that the United States and Europe built.

Over time, a sort of tipping point can be reached in which major changes in the transnational legal order occur. In the case of this book, Brazil, India, and China built legal capacity and transformed their institutions and economies in the process, enhancing their sway within the transnational legal order for trade. They began to shape it in ways that reverberated within its original sponsor, the United States, catalyzing US responses that challenged the legitimacy of the WTO and its dispute settlement system, and that undermined their authority. In parallel, these reactions spurred the emergence of competitive processes of transnational legal ordering through bilateral and regional initiatives, potentially splintering the system into overlapping, coexisting, and competing transnational legal orders. To the extent this change represents a paradigm shift such that the world now faces a critical

---

[34] Kathleen Thelen, *How Institutions Evolve: The Political Economy of Skills in Germany, Britain, the United States and Japan* (Cambridge: Cambridge University Press, 2004), 35 ("layering ... involves the grafting of new elements onto an otherwise stable institutional framework"); Jeroen van der Heijden, "Institutional Layering: A Review of the Use of the Concept," *Politics* 31, no. 9 (2011): 9–18.

[35] Susan Block-Lieb and Terence Halliday, *Global Lawmakers: International Organizations in the Crafting of World Markets* (Cambridge: Cambridge University Press, 2017). This view of "ecology theory" intersects with Bourdieusian "field theory." Sida Liu and Mustafa Emirbayer, "Field and Ecology," *Sociological Theory* 34 (2016): 62–79. Joseph Conti applies field theory to international trade law, where he explains the links between international and domestic law in terms of "legitimacy chains" in which actors compete to frame processes of legitimation, involving brokering and translation. Joseph Conti, "Legitimacy Chains: Legitimation of Compliance with International Courts Across Social Fields," *Law & Society Review* 50 (2016): 154–188 ("fields ... are socially constructed arenas of action, where interaction is oriented towards shaping the 'purpose of the field, relationships to others in the field (including who has power and why), and the rules governing legitimate action in the field'"), 161. Compare Kenneth Abbott, Jessica Green, and Robert Keohane, "Organizational Ecology and Institutional Change in Global Governance," *International Organization* 70, no. 2 (2016): 247–277.

[36] Block-Lieb and Halliday, *Global Lawmakers*, 33.

juncture, it was made possible, in large part, through the gradual, continuous developments that this book explains.[37] In sum, transnational legal ordering is not static but dynamic. It changes through social interaction and strategic maneuvering in light of ongoing technological, organizational, economic, social, and political developments.

II. BUILDING TRADE LAW CAPACITY

Analyses of law, from whatever academic discipline, risk reifying law as a relatively seamless, cost-free system, not subject to the effects of asymmetric information and resources, interpretation and manipulation, implying that once the "rule of law" is created, rights will be neutrally enforced. Substantive law – however neutral, and whether it operates directly or diffusely – is of limited neutrality if parties cannot mobilize legal resources in a cost-effective manner to interpret law for policy application, negotiate in the law's shadow, pursue their claims, and defend claims against them. This book focuses on the concept of legal capacity, which is linked to policy-making capacity, and which became a key element of broader state capacity when international trade relations were legalized and judicialized.

I define *trade law capacity* broadly as *the ability of a country, through harnessing resources, to use law to defend and advance its international and domestic trade and trade-implicated policies.* From a "field theory" perspective, trade law capacity represents *a form of capital (or power)* to advance interests in a contested trans-national legal field – that of trade law.[38] Countries can only take advantage of international trade law if they develop mechanisms to effectively define duties and pursue and defend their rights. When countries lack legal capacity, they cannot participate fully in negotiations, monitoring, and dispute settlement, so that the trading system will be slanted against them. In parallel, constituencies within countries develop such legal capacity for the implementation and application of trade law domestically, whether to defend or advance their particular interests or careers, including within state agencies and private practice.

Trade law capacity is the *medium* through which public and private actors advance their goals through trade law, thereby shaping the legal field. By developing it, they can exercise agency in transnational legal ordering to establish, apply,

---

[37] On tipping points and critical junctures in historical institutionalism, Giovanni Capoccia and Daniel Keleman, "The Study of Critical Junctures: Theory, Narrative, and Counterfactuals in Historical Institutionalism," *World Politics* 59 (2007): 341–369; Rahul Mukherji, *Globalization and Deregulation: Ideas, Interests and Institutional Change in India* (Oxford: Oxford University Press, 2014), 23–33.

[38] Yves Dezalay and Mikael Madsen, "The Force of Law and Lawyers: Pierre Bourdieu and the Reflexive Sociology of Law," *Annual Review of Law and Social Science* 8 (2012): 433–452; Jacob Holtermann and Mikael Madsen, "European New Legal Realism and International Law: How to Make International Law Intelligible," *Leiden Journal of International Law* 28 (2015): 211–230; Joseph Conti, *The Juridification of International Affairs: Legal Idealists, World Government and the Emergence of Transnational Stateness* (draft on file).

interpret, and shape the rules of the game. Following the WTO's creation, trade law capacity became an important component of *state capacity*. The domestic development of it complements other forms of technical capacity, including economic policy analysis, such as economic modeling for trade negotiations. These different forms of technical capacity serve to enhance state capacity. This approach contrasts with a neoliberal conception that questions the need for domestic legal capacity for international trade relations since legal counsel can be purchased more efficiently through hiring the best lawyers from the United States and Europe. In contrast, this book's approach takes a broader view of the role of trade law capacity, as Chapter 3 further develops. To participate effectively in the transnational legal ordering of trade, legal capacity needs to be embedded within the state and society. It will be developed differently in light of a state's institutional heritage, as the book's case studies illustrate.

Some dub the deployment of legal capacity to defend trade interests as "lawfare" in a political game for economic dominance.[39] Some write of capture by transnational capital of national and global governance,[40] and others view these investments as contributions to a public good – "the rule of law."[41] It is not that one of these stories alone is correct. They operate simultaneously. Understanding countries' investments in legal capacity is critical for each of these analyses. In terms of the paradox animating this book, it provides the legal component to the story of why the United States has become disenchanted with the trade legal order that it created.

A. *Eight Ways That Legal Capacity Matters*

In a project with political scientists Marc Busch and Eric Reinhardt, we surveyed the delegations of members of the WTO, and composed an index measuring the members' trade law capacity. The index captured the country's experience, continuity of representation, institutional specialization, and assistance from private sector coordination.[42] We drew on Chad Bown's Global Antidumping Database and

[39] Ian Hurd, *How to Do Things with International Law* (Princeton: Princeton University Press, 2017), 11 ("lawfare is better seen as the typical condition of international law"); Anthea Roberts, Henrique Choer Moraes, and Victor Ferguson, "The Geoeconomic World Order," *Lawfare*, November 19, 2018.

[40] B. S. Chimni, "International Institutions Today: An Imperial Global State in the Making," *European Journal of International Law* 15 (2004): 1–37; B. S. Chimni, "Prolegomena to a Class Approach to International Law," *European Journal of International Law* 21 (2010): 57–82; B. S. Chimni, "Power and Inequality in Megaregulation: The TPP Model," in *Megaregulation Contested: The Global Economic Order after TPP*, eds. Benedict Kingsbury David Malone, Paul Mertenskotter, Richard Stewart, Thomas Streinz, and Atsuhi Sunami (Oxford: Oxford University Press, 2017), 124–139.

[41] James Bacchus, *The Willing World: Shaping and Sharing a Sustainable Global Prosperity* (Cambridge: Cambridge University Press, 2018).

[42] The legal capacity score was compiled based on the number of professional staff dedicated to WTO dispute settlement, the cumulative amount of years of a staff member, turnover as a problem, private assistance in funding litigation, and attendance at WTO meetings. Marc L. Busch, Eric Reinhardt, and Gregory Shaffer, "Does Legal Capacity Matter?: A Survey of WTO Members," *World Trade*

examined 1,321 antidumping investigations over ten years by seventeen WTO members against firms from thirty-three members. Using multivariate analysis that controlled explicitly for market power, we assessed whether countries with greater WTO legal capacity are less likely to be subjected to antidumping actions at the end of investigations, and whether they are more likely to challenge resulting measures before the WTO. We found that those countries with significant WTO legal capacity were more likely to challenge antidumping duties brought against them before the WTO, and that their exports were less likely to be targeted by antidumping duties in the first place. The study provided evidence that legal capacity matters at least as much as market power in explaining the use of the WTO legal system, as well as outcomes in US domestic antidumping investigations that can raise tariffs and block a country's exports.[43] We concluded that "countries that invest in developing professional staff who retain expertise in WTO matters over time, that develop specialised WTO dispute settlement units, and that work with their private sectors are better-positioned to roll back and deter barriers to their exports."[44]

Trade law capacity is linked with and part of broader trade policy-making capacity. It matters in at least eight ways, which is why understanding it is a necessary complement to geopolitical and economic analysis. First, it is critical for the drafting and *negotiation* of international trade rules, whether in multilateral, regional, or bilateral fora. To make proposals suited to their situations that can win allies, countries need to develop modalities based on solid economic analysis. Their governments can work with think tanks and consultants. As we will see, Brazil and India – two countries with very different interests in WTO agricultural negotiations – created new proposals that reoriented the Doha round negotiations over agriculture, starting at the 2003 WTO Ministerial Meeting in Cancun, which was a watershed event, ending US and EU negotiating dominance in the WTO.[45]

Second, such capacity is necessary for the *monitoring* of foreign compliance with commitments under trade agreements. One must first "name" a problem and link it to someone to "blame" before one can begin analyzing and building a trade law "claim."[46] Countries can expand their Geneva missions and build trade units in their capitals and

Review 8 (2009): 559–577; Marc L. Busch, Eric Reinhardt, and Gregory Shaffer, "Does Legal Capacity Matter?: Explaining Patterns of Protectionism in the Shadow of WTO Litigation," Issue Paper #4 *International Centre on Trade and Sustainable Development* (2008), www.ictsd.org/themes/trade-law/research/does-legal-capacity-matter-explaining-dispute-initiation-and-anti-dumping.

43 Busch, Reinhardt, and Shaffer, "Explaining Patterns of Protectionism," 14. Compare Chad Bown, "Participation in WTO Dispute Settlement: Complainants, Interested Parties and Free Riders," *World Bank Economic Review* 19 (2005): 287–310, and Andrew T. Guzman and Beth A. Simmons, "Power Plays and Capacity Constraints: The Selection of Defendants in World Trade Organization Disputes," *The Journal of Legal Studies* 34 (2005): 557–598.

44 Ibid., 14.

45 Amrita Narlikar, "New Powers in the Club: The Challenges of Global Trade Governance," *International Affairs* 86, no. 3 (2010): 717–728; Hopewell, *Breaking the WTO*.

46 William L. F. Felstiner, Richard L. Abel, and Austin Sarat, "The Emergence and Transformation of Disputes: Naming, Blaming and Claiming," *Law & Society Review* 15 (1980–1981): 631.

embassies to better monitor the implementation of trade agreements. They can consult with the private sector and private professionals, including to compile annual trade reports of trade barriers and to develop legal complaints. These mechanisms multiply the number of eyes cast on trade practices affecting the country's exporters.

Third, legal capacity is essential for *bringing complaints* successfully in specific cases to defend market access rights. Legal decisions can affect specific economic outcomes, as the study with Busch and Reinhardt evidenced. Bown and Reynolds similarly found that compliance with WTO rulings and settlements following complaints mattered economically.[47] Bechtel and Sattler further found that "sectoral exports from complainant countries to the defendant increase by about $7.7 billion in the three years after a panel ruling."[48] In parallel, Busch and Reinhardt showed how around two-thirds of WTO complaints "ending prior to a ruling (whether before or after the establishment of a panel) exhibited full or partial concessions by the defendant."[49] In other words, trade dispute settlement can have tangible effects by providing greater market access for individual companies and entire industries.

Fourth, more technically, but importantly, the failure to participate in trade dispute settlement can have *terms-of-trade effects* that adversely affect a country's social welfare. A country's "terms of trade" refers to the value of products that it must export to receive a given value of imports. If a country exercises market power and raises a trade barrier that induces another country's exporters to lower their prices to sell in that market, then such other country must export more products to obtain the same amount of imports, adversely affecting its terms of trade.[50] As Bagwell and Staiger write, "The terms-of-trade consequences of trade-policy choices can be expressed equivalently in the language of market access, and so the terms-of-trade consequences and the market-access implications of trade-policy choices are different ways of expressing the same thing."[51] Yet, while market access benefits an

---

[47] Chad P. Bown, "On the Economic Success of GATT/WTO Dispute Settlement," *The Review of Economics and Statistics* 86, no. 3 (August 2004): 811; Chad P. Bown and Kara M. Reynolds, "Trade Agreements and Enforcement: Evidence from WTO Dispute Settlement," *American Economic Journal: Economic Policy* 9 (2017): 64–100. Compare Stephen Chaudoin, Jeffrey Kucik, and Krzysztof Pelc, "Do WTO Disputes Actually Increase Trade?,"*International Studies Quarterly* 60, no. 2: 294–306 (finding only very specific effects of disputes based on the dispute outcome and issue-area), and Christina Davis, *Why Adjudicate? Enforcing Trade Rules in the WTO* (Princeton: Princeton University Press, 2012) (finding that adjudication leads to greater progress in the removal of trade barriers compared to the alternative of negotiation).

[48] Michael M. Bechtel and Thomas Sattler, "What is Litigation in the World Trade Organization Worth?," *International Organization* 69, no. 2 (2015): 375–403, 375.

[49] Marc Busch and Eric Reinhardt, "Bargaining in the Shadow of the Law: Early Settlement in GATT/WTO Disputes," *Fordham International Law Journal* 24 (2000): 162.

[50] Christian Broda, Nuno Limão, and David E. Weinstein, "Optimal Tariffs and Market Power: The Evidence," *American Economic Review* 98, no. 5 (2008): 2032–2065.

[51] Kyle Bagwell and Robert W. Staiger, *The Economics of the World Trading System* (Cambridge: MIT Press, 2002), 5. Bagwell and Staiger's theory accounts for both economic and political motivations since member governments implicitly make commitments of greater market access to these industries in return for their political support during the negotiation and ratification of trade agreements.

individual industry, the terms of trade affect the welfare of a country as a whole. Bown and Reynolds find empirical evidence showing positive terms-of-trade effects from use of the WTO dispute settlement system.[52]

Fifth, trade jurisprudence affects the interpretation, application, and social understanding of the "law" over time, thus *shaping the meaning of obligations*. A text's meaning is not simply natural, but it is a social construction developed within a contested community of interpreters.[53] Legal actors contest to take "control of the legal text."[54] Participation in dispute settlement determines the arguments that judges hear. If they predominantly hear only one side, they are more likely to read texts in that way. Legal texts are applied to different contexts and they assume different shades of meaning through their application. Those who participate in cases help define legal meaning through case law by propounding arguments about how the texts should be read and applied to relevant factual scenarios.[55] A central reason that the United States attacked and neutered the WTO Appellate Body was because of the systemic implications of the Appellate Body's interpretation of WTO provisions regarding US antidumping and countervailing duty practices. These decisions curtailed the US ability to raise tariffs on imports, such as from China, in accordance with WTO rules.

Sixth, effective participation in litigation affects *bargaining in the shadow of the law*, both as regards future negotiations and the strategic pursuit of settlement in discrete cases.[56] On the one hand, shaping jurisprudence affects the "status quo" around which future bargaining organizes. By interpreting the law, Appellate Body decisions, such as regarding US and European agricultural subsidies, or antidumping and countervailing duty practices, effectively create new bargaining chips in negotiations to develop and change the law. On the other hand, if one has established oneself as a "repeat player" in litigation, one is more likely to have shaped judicial interpretations and social understandings useful for bargaining in future disputes. Countries with lawyers conversant in trade law are thus better positioned to use precedent to negotiate favorable settlements. In contrast, countries that lack such lawyers are less able to mobilize legal resources cost-effectively to threaten to invoke legal procedures to gain favorable settlements or to ward off such threats from others. Even when formal complaints are brought, there is often

---

52 Bown and Reynolds, "Trade Agreements and Enforcement."

53 Stanley Fish, *Is There a Text in This Class?: The Authority of Interpretive Communities* (Cambridge: Harvard University Press, 1982).

54 Bourdieu, "Force of Law," 818.

55 Mark Daku and Krzysztof J. Pelc, "Who Holds Influence Over WTO Jurisprudence?," *Journal of International Economic Law* 20, no. 2 (2017): 233–255.

56 Robert Mnookin and Lewis Kornhauser, "Bargaining in the Shadow of the Law: The Case of Divorce," *Yale Law Journal* 88 (1979); Marc Galanter, "Contract in Court; or Almost Everything You May or May Not Want to Know about Contract Litigation," *Wisconsin Law Review* 2001 (2001): 579 (Contracts Symposium 2001). Marc L. Busch and Eric Reinhardt, "Bargaining in the Shadow of the Law: Early Settlement. In GATT/WTO Disputes," *Fordham International Law Journal* (2000): 162.

negotiation in their shadow, including after the ruling, constituting what Marc Galanter calls "litigotiation."[57]

Seventh, legal capacity is critical both for *protecting domestic policy space* for developmental and regulatory initiatives and *to ward off capture* by protectionist sectors. On the one hand, understanding flexibilities in WTO law is crucial for retaining policy space for development initiatives – what Alvaro Santos calls "developmental legal capacity."[58] It is important for using industrial policy to create comparative advantage in high-value industries, an area where China has excelled. It is needed to safeguard vulnerable sectors and populations, such as to ensure access to medicines through intellectual property exceptions, and to assist peasant farmers through agricultural policy, which are pressing issues for emerging economies.[59] It helps them fend off legal claims against these policies. On the other hand, the international trading system gives governments leverage over economic sectors that demand protection, especially where it would not advance a development policy objective. Governments can argue that such protection is costly because it will result in authorized trade retaliation.[60] State legal capacity is thus critical for compliance with international trade rules. Given the contested nature of these policy decisions, actors make use of international trade law arguments and broader normative frames in the formation of domestic policy, such that interpretive contests at the international and national levels interact. They inform, constrain, and aid each other.

Eighth, building international trade law capacity in the private sector can trigger spillover effects and *catalyze a greater role for a country's lawyers in international private law settings.*[61] Cross-border contracts are negotiated in the shadow of international trade law. They are thus not disconnected from trade law norms, as a formalist segregation of public and private international law suggests. Private lawyers are involved in cross-border intellectual property, investment, customs, standard setting, and other transactions and disputes, which can give rise to transnational arbitration, litigation, and other forms of dispute resolution. The role of Chinese corporate lawyers in China's Belt and Road Initiative and in its innovation policies, covered in Chapter 7, illustrates the links. As a general counsel

---

57 Galanter, "Contract in Court," 579; Marc Galanter, "Why the 'Haves' Come Out Ahead: Speculations on the Limits of Legal Change," *Law & Society Review* 9 (1974–1975): 95–160 (on "repeat players" vs. "one shotters").

58 Alvaro Santos, "Carving Out Policy Autonomy for Developing Countries in the World Trade Organization: The Experience of Brazil and Mexico," *Virginia Journal of International Law* 52 (2012): 551–632.

59 Gregory Shaffer, "Recognizing Public Goods in WTO Dispute Settlement: Who Participates? Who Decides?," *Journal of International Economic Law* 7 (2004): 459–482.

60 Robert Staiger and Guido Tabellini, "Do GATT Rules Help Governments Make Domestic Commitments?," *Economics and Politics* 11 (1999): 109–144; Helen Milner, *Interests, Institutions and Information: Domestic Politics and International Relations* (Princeton: Princeton University Press, 1997).

61 I thank Tom Ginsburg for this last point.

for a major Chinese state-owned enterprise stressed, "the WTO changed every side of our life," including "our habits and practices."[62] These habits and practices can now be used for the development of special economic zones and other transnational projects.

In sum, legal capacity provides public and private actors with arguments they may deploy in both international and domestic policy contexts. At times, actors harness international trade law norms as leverage in domestic political contests to facilitate domestic policy reforms. In parallel, officials can seek to shape and modify the understanding of the rules' constraints and flexibilities at the international level, whether regarding industrial goods, agriculture, services, or intellectual property. To do so, they must build significant trade law capacity. For this reason, officials may open the state bureaucracy to engage with the private sector and private lawyers. They may build mechanisms of public–private coordination to deploy, resist, and shape international trade rules, and assess implementation alternatives to protect policy space, adopt domestic reforms, and mediate the tensions between development strategies and these rules.

One need not be a lawyer to develop and use such trade law capacity. At times, policymakers will work with lawyers, such as in trade litigation, but litigation is just a small part of how legal capacity is deployed. Law plays important roles in normative ordering outside of disputes, such that basic legal capacity is critical for policymaking generally. Even as regards disputes, most of them do not reach litigation, but are bargained around, as socio-legal scholars stress.

From a historical institutionalist perspective, the development of trade law capacity illustrates the role of path dependency. These emerging powers were not central to the WTO's creation, but once it was formed, and given its implications for their development, they responded to it by developing broadbased trade law capacity. While some commentators stress how these processes helped to permeate WTO norms into states, giving rise to an "embedded neoliberalism," these states and stakeholders also built legal capacity to advance and defend their interests and, in turn, potentially shape the transnational legal order for trade.

III. TRANSNATIONAL LEGAL ORDERING AND INTERNAL CHANGES IN EMERGING ECONOMIES

The second question this book addresses is the effect of the international trade regime within these countries, and more specifically, on these countries' domestic laws, institutions, professions, and government–business and government–civil society relations. In earlier work, I typologized five dimensions of state change that

---

[62] Telephone interview, March 30, 2020.

TABLE 2.1 *The dimensions of state change*

Dimensions of state change	Associated disciplines
(1) Changes in national law and practice	Focus of Legal Studies
(2) Changes in the boundary of the state, the market, and other forms of social ordering	Focus of Institutional Economics & Economic Sociology
(3) Changes in the allocation of authority among state institutions	Focus of Comparative Institutional Analysis in Comparative Politics
(4) Changes in expertise and the role of expertise in governance	Focus of Sociology of the Professions
(5) Changes in associational patterns, institutionalized through transnational mechanisms of accountability and their accompanying normative frames	Focus of Organizational Sociology

transnational legal ordering implicates.[63] Table 2.1 summarizes these dimensions, together with academic disciplines associated with their study.[64]

Most legal studies focus on the first dimension – *changes in national law and practice*. However, this dimension implicates the other four, which raise deeper structural and normative issues and thus highlight the stakes of transnationally induced legal change. The second and third dimensions involve shifts in the architecture and authority of state institutions, while the fourth and fifth involve developments in professional expertise and associational patterns institutionalized within particular normative frames. These dimensions are interlinked, as changes in one dimension can catalyze changes in others. For example, transnational legal processes can create new demands on the state by enhancing the authority of certain forms of expertise, which, in turn, creates pressure for shifts in the allocation of authority among state institutions or in the boundary of the state and the market. The book's case studies are not specifically organized around these dimensions, although they cover each of them. It is nonetheless useful to disaggregate these dimensions to illustrate the broader implications of the transnational legal ordering of trade that the case studies illustrate.

A. Five Dimensions of State Change

New Laws and Regulations

The implementation of transnational legal norms in a national legal system can be viewed as a two-stage process. Formal domestic enactment of international trade

---

[63] This section draws from Shaffer, *Transnational Legal Ordering and State Change* (Chapter 2); and Gregory Shaffer, "How the WTO Shapes Regulatory Governance," *Regulation & Governance* 9 (2015): 1.

[64] These associated disciplines are not meant to be exclusive, only indicative. The table's aim is to highlight the breadth of what is at stake with transnational legal ordering.

commitments (the focus of positivist legal scholars) is followed by actual legal practice, the law-in-action (the focus of empirical scholars). As Chapter 3 notes, accession to the WTO required few changes in US and European law but massive changes in other countries. China, for example, changed over 3,000 laws and regulations after it joined the WTO, arguably constituting the largest law reform in history. Yet, although formal legal change can provide tools for domestic actors to change regulatory practice, they do not necessarily do so. As legal skeptics warn, countries can enact WTO requirements as binding national law, but these formal changes may have little practical impact. This book's case studies thus focus on the law's domestic application, where the development and harnessing of trade law capacity can play a critical role.

Reshaping the Boundary between the Market and the State

Second, and more broadly, international trade law *affects the boundary between the market and the state*. It involves market liberalization, such as through the reduction of tariffs and elimination of quotas, as well as the growth of the administrative state, such as for standard setting, intellectual property, and import relief. Externally and internally, governments are pressured to bolster or constrain domestic regulation in light of WTO rules. Externally, states face claims against them, which can give rise to WTO rulings. Internally, rival groups and factions clash over policymaking, some of which reference WTO rules as leverage to advance their agendas.[65] Trade law can shift the balance of power among interest groups within states, both in relation to each other and in relation to government regulators. For example, the WTO enhanced leverage of export-oriented businesses over protectionist ones.[66]

Liberalized trade heightens global product competition, which can trigger domestic producer interests to demand less government regulation in order to increase their competitiveness, potentially leading to reduced regulation and taxation of business. Yet, the WTO also can trigger more regulation in multiple ways. For example, the WTO helped invigorate international standard setting, implicating states that otherwise might impose no regulatory standards governing an issue.[67] Moreover, in response to imports, states may enhance their customs, quarantine, and other inspection services at the border, creating an expanded import regulatory apparatus. They may concomitantly raise internal regulatory standards, and create

---

[65] Paul Mertenskötter and Tim Dorlach, "Interpreters of International Economic Law: Corporations and Bureaucrats in Contest over Chile's Nutrition Label," *Law & Society Review* 54, no. 3 (2020): 571–606.

[66] Nitsan Chorev, *Remaking U.S. Trade Policy: From Protectionism to Globalization* (Ithaca, New York: Cornell University Press, 2007).

[67] Tim Büthe, "The Politics of Food Safety in the Age of Global Trade: The Codex-Alimentarius Commission in the SPS Agreement of the WTO," in *Import Safety: Regulatory Governance in the Global Economy*, eds. Cary Coglianese, Adam Finkel, and David Zaring (Philadelphia: University of Pennsylvania Press, 2009), 88–109.

new requirements on the private sector, such as regards food safety.[68] Exporting states, in turn, may augment their inspection standards for their products to be accepted in global markets. For example, India tightened its inspection and certification standards and procedures in response to US and EU rejections of Indian food products.[69] Similarly, toys made in China tend to bear the CE (*Communauté européenne*) mark, signifying that they conform with the European Union's regulatory requirements, even when they are sold in the Chinese or other non-EU markets.[70]

Reshaping the Institutional Architecture of the State

The WTO legal order not only shapes the boundary between the market and state regulation but also shapes the *institutional architecture of the state*, affecting the allocation of power among state institutions.[71] It implicates the relative authority of state institutions, such as the executive, legislature, agencies, and courts, as well as the federal government in relation to sub-state governments. For example, the WTO constrains the role of legislatures to provide protectionism, catalyzes the creation and professionalization of bureaucratic agencies, and promotes the strengthening of judiciaries.

International trade law tends to enhance the power of the federal government in federalist systems. It creates a focal point for negotiation, monitoring, deliberation, and dispute settlement in which sub-state actors do not participate. With expertise concentrated at the national level, sub-state governments may cede authority toward the center. In India, for example, Indian states unsuccessfully challenged the central government before the Indian Supreme Court regarding its power to make trade commitments on agriculture in which state governments have competence.[72] Indian state governments similarly revised their internal tax systems under pressure from the central government in light of the WTO case *India – Additional Duties*.[73] In response, sub-state actors often develop some international trade law expertise,

---

[68] Kenneth Bamberger and Andrew Guzman, "Importers as Regulators: Product Safety in a Globalized World," in *Import Safety: Regulatory Governance in the Global Economy*, eds. Cary Coglianese, Adam Finkel, and David Zaring (Philadelphia: University of Pennsylvania Press, 2009), 193–214.

[69] Thomas Bollyky, *Global Health Interventions for U.S. Food and Drug Safety* (Washington, DC: CSIS Global Health Policy Center, 2009).

[70] Francis Snyder, "Governing Globalisation," in *Transnational Legal Processes: Globalization and Power Disparities*, ed. Michael Likosky (London: Butterworths Tolley, 2002), 65–97.

[71] Terence Halliday, "Architects of the State: International Financial Institutions and the Reconstruction of States in East Asia," in *Transnational Legal Ordering and State Change*.

[72] Aseema Sinha, "The Changing Political Economy of Federalism in India: A Historical Institutionalist Approach," in *Globalization and Politics in India*, ed. Nayar Baldev (New Delhi: Oxford University Press, 2007), 477–515.

[73] Panel Report, *India – Additional Duties on Imports from the United States*, WT/DS 360/R (June 9, 2008).

both to support local exporters in relation to export markets and to protect themselves from challenge to their own policies.

International trade law also induces the creation and expansion of domestic regulatory agencies. The TRIPS agreement empowered new intellectual property agencies around the world, often housed in new state-of-the-art buildings financed in part by new and enhanced filing fees, creating new bureaucratic interests.[74] WTO law indirectly raised the prominence of standard-setting agencies, exemplified particularly by China's internal initiatives. WTO rules, in addition, explicitly permit governments to provide economic protection through antidumping, countervailing duties, and safeguard regulations, which catalyzed the creation of entirely new national bureaucracies after developing countries lowered their tariffs. Complementarily, multiple WTO agreements require mechanisms of judicial review, which can empower courts and tribunals, such as for customs, import relief, and intellectual property law. Countries such as China created new specialized intellectual property courts. Trade liberalization institutionalized through the WTO facilitates these transnational legal ordering effects by engaging domestic interests that harness trade law to oppose or support changes in regulatory institutions and policy.

Catalyzing New Professions and Forms of Expertise

The transnational legal ordering of trade catalyzed *new professional specializations* and shifts in professional authority, creating new incentives for individuals and institutions. These developments trigger shifts toward more technocratic forms of governance, enhancing expert authority. The legalization and judicialization of the trade regime unleashed competition for new expertise to take advantage of the opportunities offered. Law firms, consultancies, business associations, nongovernmental organizations, think tanks, universities, institutes, and government ministries invested in it. New professions developed, professional markets changed, and existing career paths adapted to new opportunities.

The fields of intellectual property and import relief law exemplify these shifts, which had even broader indirect implications in the fields of business and corporate law. The WTO agreement on international property rights helped create and bolster the profession of the patent examiner, the patent attorney, the patent bar, specialized administrative officials, and new judges. In parallel, as protectionism became legalized through import relief law regulated under WTO agreements, lawyers and accountants developed legal expertise, representing both petitioners and respondents before new administrative bodies and courts. In this transnational field, some lawyers specialize in assisting respondents, some in representing claimants, and

---

[74] Peter Drahos, *The Global Governance of Knowledge Patent Offices and their Clients* (Cambridge: Cambridge University Press, 2010).

some act for both. They work with accountants to analyze price differentials and sometimes economists to develop causal arguments regarding injury. Their activation places pressure on investigating authorities to develop legal and factual justifications of agency findings. Government officials and private practitioners write brochures and books to educate industry and attract clients. Expertise pits against expertise in developing the law that becomes ever more demanding, requiring further investment in expertise.

Shaping Associational Patterns and Normative Frames

Transnational legal ordering generates shifts in *patterns of association* that are *institutionalized through accountability mechanisms*, which operate *within particular normative frames*. Individuals and groups inside and outside of government study and work abroad, interact transnationally, and develop new relations of authority. These processes can shape the legal culture and legal consciousness of elites and (potentially) broader publics.

A central transnational accountability mechanism is monitoring, surveillance, and reporting that triggers peer pressure, giving rise to processes of justification, learning, and persuasion.[75] In the WTO context, WTO members report to a series of WTO committees and councils on their compliance with WTO commitments. Those reports are prepared, discussed, and evaluated within the normative frame of WTO rules. In the area of import relief, for example, the WTO secretariat (in the Rules Division) helps arrange meetings in which technical antidumping officials discuss their laws and practices, in addition to the regular meetings of the Committee on Anti-Dumping practices held in Geneva twice per year.[76]

Although the WTO normative frame focuses on liberalizing markets, frames are not simply given. They are shaped through recursive rounds of engagement among actors with differing epistemologies and interests at different levels of governance.[77] In practice, the positions taken by state representatives in the WTO often assume more of a mercantilist nature, as they defend their export and their import-competing business interests. These processes provide an opening for contestation and argumentation in which officials must simultaneously look at their own practices when challenging others' measures. For example, the WTO's central norm is nondiscrimination and a central aim of its promoters is to instill this norm within national regulatory cultures. The nondiscrimination norm, however, can be defined in different ways. It is complemented by others, such as the norm of science-based

---

[75]   Andrew Lang and Joanne Scott, "The Hidden World of WTO Governance," *European Journal of International Law* 20 (2009): 575–614.

[76]   Interview, WTO Secretariat official, June 29, 2017.

[77]   Alastair Iain Johnston, "Treating International Institutions as Social Environments," *International Studies Quarterly* 45 (2001): 487–515; Stone Sweet, Sandholtz, and Fligstein, *The Institutionalization of Europe*.

risk assessment for sanitary and phytosanitary regulations. These norms induce state regulators to engage in justification of their measures, including to affected foreign traders.

National officials who participate in WTO meetings go home, whether in their government capacity, or, if they leave the government, then in a private capacity. They lobby for regulatory change and provide input regarding regulatory proposals and the interpretation and application of existing national regulations. International trade law norms, in this way, can become transnationalized. They enter national regulatory systems conveyed through the intermediary of national officials and private sector experts who interact with them. The norms circulate, build on each other, and their meaning settles and unsettles in light of ongoing contestation. The impact of the WTO normative frame is not seamless. The norms are resisted, debated, translated, hybridized, and transformed within national contexts. But the regulatory debates are informed, sometimes directly, but often diffusely, by WTO legal norms.

B. *State Change in Historical Context: Emerging Powers as "Developmental" or "Neoliberal" States*

External legal and epistemic developments affect the state's internal organization and trajectory along these dimensions to different degrees, depending on the state and historical period. Yet, these processes intensified for trade-related matters following the WTO's creation and its legalization and judicialization of trade policy. Starting in the 1940s and 1950s, developmental theorists argued for import protection and state intervention to jumpstart growth and industrialization.[78] Unconstrained by the GATT,[79] Brazil, India, and China were all inward-looking and focused on import substitution industrialization and state-directed policies. In India, while Gandhi and Nehru differed in their views on modernization, with Gandhi calling for indigenous development through textile crafts, and Nehru pushing for industrialization, they were similar in their inward-looking, self-sufficient prescriptions. That was not surprising given India's emergence from its oppressive colonial fetters. Brazil likewise adopted import substitution policies, as did Mao's China. Their choices reflected the developmental-economics expertise of the day, although Mao's autarkic China paid no heed of it either.[80]

---

[78]   Albert O. Hirschman, *The Strategy of Economic Development* (New Haven: Yale University Press, 1958); P. N. Rosenstein-Rodan, "Problems of Industrialisation of Eastern and South-Eastern Europe," *The Economic Journal* 53, no. 210/211 (1943): 202–211.

[79]   To recall, China was not a member of the GATT, and Brazil and India benefitted from special and differential treatment under the GATT so that their tariff lines tended to be unbound or set at higher levels.

[80]   David Kennedy, "The 'Rule of Law', Political Choices and Development Common Sense," in *The New Law and Economic Development*, eds. David M. Trubek and Alvaro Santos (Cambridge: Cambridge University Press, 2006), 95–173. Compare the era of Mao's successors in Julian Gewirtz, *Unlikely Partners: Chinese Reformers, Western Economists, and the Making of Global China* (Cambridge: Harvard University Press, 2017).

By the late 1980s, however, state corruption and inefficiencies began to fuel a backlash against such policies. An onslaught of public-choice critiques contended that state bureaucrats pursue their own self-interest rather than the public good, which in turn affected development theory. International financial institutions and leading development theorists increasingly advocated privatization, state downsizing, and the unleashing of market forces – known as the "Washington Consensus."[81] International Monetary Fund (IMF) structural adjustment programs, IMF surveillance (under Chapter IV of its charter), and IMF and World Bank technical assistance to developing countries, reflected this neoliberal approach.

The success of export-oriented development models behind the East Asian economic miracles also challenged import-substitution strategies.[82] In Brazil, Fernando Henrique Cardoso, a leading formulator of "dependency theory," which had provided an intellectual basis for import substitution industrialization to build national manufacturing capacity, became minister of finance in 1994 and then, in 1995, president of the republic for two four-year terms. Cardoso's shift from being a leading theorist of "dependency theory" to being a strong advocate of Brazilian integration in the global economy exemplifies the significant ideological changes among Brazilian governing elites.[83] Although the political left won the election of 2002, the government of President Luiz Inácio Lula da Silva maintained Brazil's economic policies of greater budgetary discipline and relatively liberalized trade, combined with compensatory, redistributive policies for the poor.

Some commentators view these shifts in emerging economies, institutionalized through their joining the WTO, as taking a "neoliberal" turn in which the state defers to markets, transnational capital is empowered in relation to labor, and the state gradually hollows out.[84] They see the state "in retreat."[85] There is something to

---

[81] John Williamson, "Latin American Adjustment: How Much Has Happened?," *Washington: Institute for International Economics* (1990) (on Washington consensus); Mukherji, *Globalization and Deregulation*, 6–9, 66–69 (regarding India).

[82] In practice, there were major differences between export-led models in East Asia, such as Japan, for which Chalmers Johnson coined the term "developmental state," and countries like India and Brazil that focused on import-substitution. Compare Chalmers Johnson, "The Developmental State: The Odyssey of a Concept," in *The Developmental State*, ed. Meredith Woo-Cumings (Ithaca: Cornell University Press, 1999); Peter Evans, *Embedded Autonomy: States & Industrial Transformation* (Princeton: Princeton University Press, 1995); Alice Amsden, *The Rise of "The Rest"* (Oxford: Oxford University Press, 2003); Robert Hunter Wade, *Governing the Market: Economic Theory and the Role of Government in East Asian Industrialization* (Princeton: Princeton University Press, 2003).

[83] Winston Fritsch and Gustavo Franco, "Brazil and the World Economy in the 1990s," in *Latin America's Integration into the World Economy*, ed. Winston Fritsch (Washington, DC: The Brookings Institution, 1991), 9; Pedro da Motta Veiga, "Trade Policy-Making in Brazil: Changing Patterns in State-Civil Society Relationship," in *Process Matters: Sustainable Development and Domestic Trade Transparency*, eds. Mark Halle and Robert Wolfe (Winnipeg: International Institute for Sustainable Development, 2007), 143, 144.

[84] Hopewell, *Breaking the WTO*.

[85] Kenichi Ohmae, *The Borderless World: Power and Strategy in the Interlinked Economy*, rev. ed. (New York: HarperCollins, 1999), 188–189; Susan Strange, *The Retreat of the State: The Diffusion of Power in the World Economy* (Cambridge: Cambridge University Press, 1996), 3; Thomas Friedman,

this story given the rise of neoliberal norms regarding the role of free trade, foreign investment, capital flows, and intellectual property protection in the 1990s and early 2000s.[86] Along the five dimensions of state change just discussed, Brazil, India, and China not only opened their markets and changed their laws but also created new institutions and engaged in new accountability mechanisms within a trade liberal frame, catalyzing new professions and professional specializations. By incorporating global rules and institutions in their domestic systems, these countries did much of what the United States and European Union wanted, giving rise to a trade order governed by rules. Indeed, in all three countries, the market, private sector, and trade, investment, intellectual property, and business law grew in importance. For some, it seemed like the end of history – a rules-based order supporting and governing global capitalism.[87]

Yet, the Asian financial crisis of 1997 and the global financial crisis of 2008 first impugned and then upended the Washington consensus. A revived developmental-state model emerged that called for an active state engaged with economic globalization, while still providing a significant role for private actors and markets. In practice, the approach varied by country in terms of the degree of state coordination. Some labeled a variant of this trend the *"new developmental state,"* noting its antecedents in previous, export-oriented models in East Asia, but then differentiating it in that the state is less dominant and is pressed to become more open and transparent to the private sector and civil society.[88] This version of the developmental state relies more on the private sector and global markets for investment and trade as part of development policy. Other variants provide a greater role for state capitalism, as reflected in China's model for economic ordering, sometimes called the "Beijing consensus," discussed in Chapter 7. In each case, the government retains a steering role that requires a highly competent and activist state bureaucracy, but the state also engages in substantial collaboration and communication with the private sector, invests and stimulates investment in professional and technical expertise, and provides a greater role for economic and business law. The

The World is Flat: A Brief History of the Twenty-first Century (New York: Farrar, Straus and Giroux, 2006).

[86] Rawi Abdelal, *Capital Rules: The Construction of Global Finance* (Cambridge: Harvard University Press, 2007); Dani Rodrik, *Straight Talk on Trade: Ideas for a Sane World Economy* (Princeton: Princeton University Press, 2017); Quinn Slobodian, *Globalists: The End of Empire and the Birth of Neoliberalism* (Cambridge: Harvard University Press, 2018).

[87] Francis Fukuyama, "The End of History?," *National Interest*, Summer 1989, 3 ("What we may be witnessing is not just the end of the Cold War, or the passing of a particular period of postwar history, but the end of history as such: that is, the end point of mankind's ideological evolution and the universalization of Western liberal democracy as the final form of human government ... [t]he victory of liberalism has occurred primarily in the realm of ideas or consciousness.").

[88] David M. Trubek, *Law and the New Developmental State: The Brazilian Experience in Latin American Context* (Oxford: Hart Publishing, 2013). This version of a new developmental state is an ideal type, and it is in part a normative, and not just a descriptive, label. Compare Richard Stubbs, "The East Asian Developmental State and The Great Recession," *Contemporary Politics* 17 (2011): 151–166.

government encourages the private sector to develop innovation and entrepreneurship to be competitive on domestic and global markets, including through subsidies. It creates mechanisms to monitor, evaluate, and adapt industrial policy initiatives.[89] It combines these economic policies with greater state intervention in social policy that redistributes income to the poor, with the aim of enhancing individual capabilities and social development, such as *Bolsa Familia* in Brazil, *Aadhar* – the brand name for the National Identity Program – to distribute public goods in India,[90] and China's plans for universal health insurance for its 1.3 billion people.[91]

Developmental state policy favors public–private partnerships because neither the state nor the private sector alone has the knowledge to pick the right path for a form of growth that offers broad-based benefits. The country can then better tap into global production networks and value chains.[92] These states engaged new coordination mechanisms among government officials, professionals, business actors, and civil society organizations.[93] Political contests within them determine the relative role of the state and the private sector, which varies over time. Because of the greater role of markets combined with an ongoing role for state coordination, some commentators dub this model state neoliberalism,[94] and others state capitalism.[95] Regardless of the label used, these countries engaged in different forms of public–private coordination to engage with the global trade and broader economic legal order.

Major shifts in the global economy helped drive changes in development models that contributed to such economic opening. Technological change, such as the transport revolution of container ships and air cargo, and the transformation of information processing and communication, reducing time as a trade barrier, spurred a new focus on trade-led development. New parts of the production process could be outsourced, leading to the "unbundling" of production and trading in "tasks" for producing goods (as opposed to simply trading final products).[96] This great unbundling contributed to a "manufacturing miracle" in China,[97] a services

---

[89] Ricardo Hausmann, Dani Rodrik, and Charles Sabel, "Reconfiguring Industrial Policy: A Framework with an Application to South Africa," *HKS Working Paper*, no. RWP08-031 (2008).

[90] The Indian government also created the *Jan Dhan Yojana* program, which seeks to ensure universal access to banking facilities with at least one basic banking account for every household, to enhance access to credit, insurance, and pensions. To eliminate intermediaries and ensure the speedy transfer of government benefits, the government introduced a direct benefit transfer scheme.

[91] Alvin Y. So and Yin-Wah Chu, *The Global Rise of China* (Hoboken: John Wiley & Sons, 2015), 89.

[92] Gary Gereffi, "Global Value Chains in a Post-Washington Consensus World," *Review of International Political Economy* 21, no. 1 (2014): 9–37.

[93] Seán Ó Riain, *The Politics of High-Tech Growth: Developmental Network States in the Global Economy* (Cambridge: Cambridge University Press, 2004); Trubek, *The Brazilian Experience*.

[94] So and Chu, *The Global Rise of China*, 14.

[95] Branko Milanovic, *Capitalism, Alone: The Future of the System that Rules the World* (Cambridge: Harvard University Press, 2019).

[96] Baldwin, *The Great Convergence*.

[97] By 2015, China produced "about 80% of the world's air conditioners, 70% of its mobile phones, and 60% of its shoes." "Made in China?," *Economist*, March 12, 2015.

revolution in India,[98] and a commodity boom in Brazil.[99] In each case, the state formed alliances with these key sectors, including for trade negotiations and litigation regarding the rules of the game.

These changes are a product of the global economic and legal context in interaction with contests among domestic factions. In line with a developmental state model advocating public–private partnerships for innovation and growth, governments fashioned trade law strategies to leverage, mediate, cope with, resist, and compensate for global economic forces. They did so by enhancing transparency to better work with the private sector, private professionals, and nongovernmental organizations.

This book's account of the development and role of trade law capacity in state change complements earlier accounts of economic transformation in developmental states. What is new in this book is the focus on law. Peter Evans, in his book *Embedded Autonomy: States & Industrial Transformation*, earlier assessed the "*economic transformation*" of developmental states during the 1980s and early 1990s through industrial policy. He found that their success was contingent on the state's ability to seed and incentivize key industrial sectors through creating close, "embedded" relations with them, which, in turn, was "defined in global terms."[100] This book similarly examines states' building of broad-based capacity embedded in the public and private sectors in the context of the global trading system. The book does so, however, through *the lens of law and institutions* in shaping the rules of the game, both domestically and internationally. The international trade regime "seeded" incentives for institutional changes within states to develop trade law capacity.[101] The embedding of public and private legal expertise regarding trade within these states enabled them to build state capacity to adapt, respond to, and potentially and recursively shape the transnational legal order for trade.

These countries still wish to "construct" comparative advantage (as assessed by Evans) to become dominant in particular sectors (from manufacturing to services to agribusiness). But since the rules of the game structure how they might do so, they built complementary legal capacity and adapted institutions in light of the rules. In other words, just as "comparative advantage" for a country's economic production and trading profile is subject to human agency and innovation where the state may

---

[98]   India became the top exporter of information and communication technology services. "WIPO Global Innovation Index 2019" (World Trade Organization, Trade in Commercial Services database, based on the International Monetary Fund Balance of Payments database), www.globalinnovationindex.org/user files/file/reportpdf/gii-full-report-2019-appendix2.pdf. Ireland's listing should be adjusted because of tax planning that inflates its figures.

[99]   Brazilian agribusiness became the world leader in exports of soybeans, coffee, sugar, orange juice, and chicken, and the world's second biggest exporter of beef, while Brazil was also the second leading exporter of iron ore and third largest of bauxite. "The Observatory of Economic Complexity (OEC)," *Macro Connections Group* (data for soybeans, coffee, sugar, orange juice, poultry meat, frozen bovine meat, iron ore, and bauxite); "The Miracle of the Cerrado," *Economist*, August 28, 2010, 50–52.

[100] Evans, *Embedded Autonomy*. Chapter 3 further explains parallels with Evans's work.

[101] I thank Joseph Conti for his comments on the relation to Evans's work.

play a catalyzing role, so too law is not simply "given" and static. Law is subject to human agency and innovation, which spurs the development of legal capacity, and, in the case of this book, trade law capacity to shape the rules of the game.

The state can play a coordinative and directive role by catalyzing the diffusion of expertise on international trade issues outside of the trade ministry to include broader public–private networks. The participants in these networks can form communities of trade policy specialists, ones that are transnationally linked to the broader trade policy field. Such transnational links can empower them in domestic contests. Although this field can be conceptualized in terms of an "epistemic community," contestation arises within it as actors respond to political and social developments and the implications of trade law and its interpretation.[102] To understand these processes, one must open the black box of the state and engage in domestic institutional analysis as part of transnational legal ordering.

International trade law creates legal obligations to liberalize markets and curtail subsidies and performance requirements, which can constrain the state. To mediate between international trade rules and state development strategies, state officials harness private sector input. Transnationally connected private actors offer expertise that enhances the state's competencies to address the demands of international trade law. Public and private actors use trade law's opportunities and constraints to advance their interests and normative perspectives. Because there is a risk of capture if the state relies alone on the private sector and private lawyers to advance state priorities, the state also builds corresponding expertise within state bureaucracies. These bureaucracies, in turn, deploy it to advance their own (at times conflicting) policy goals and priorities. The result is that state officials, lawyers, and economists come together (and clash) because of economic globalization and its institutionalization in the WTO and other trade and investment fora.[103] The state did not withdraw from global and transnational influences per the import substitution model of the 1950s. The international trade legal order, rather, helped catalyze the building of new state capacity through public–private coordination mechanisms, including legal and regulatory capacity, even though its raison d'être was oriented toward freeing markets and liberalizing trade.[104]

---

[102]   Peter M. Haas, "Introduction: Epistemic Communities and International Policy Coordination," *International Organization* 46 (1992): 3. Compare field theory that highlights the role of power and contested positioning. Pierre Bourdieu and Loïc J. D. Wacquant, *An Invitation to Reflexive Sociology* (Chicago: University of Chicago Press, 1992), 16 ("a field consists of a set of objective, historical relations between positions anchored in certain forms of power (or capital)").

[103]   Aseema Sinha, "Global Linkages and Domestic Politics: Trade Reform and Institution Building in India in Comparative Perspective," *Comparative Political Studies* 40 (2007): 1183–1210.

[104]   Compare Steven Vogel, *Free Markets More Rules: Regulatory Reform in Advanced Industrial Countries* (Ithica: Cornell University Press, 1996); David Levi-Faur and Jacint Jordana, *The Rise of Regulatory Capitalism: The Global Diffusion of a New Order* (2005); Aseema Sinha, *Globalizing India: How Global Rules and Markets are Shaping India's Rise to Power* (Cambridge: Cambridge University Press, 2016).

The overall result of these transnational processes was not the weakening of the state, but rather, the strengthening of the state's capacity to play an active role internationally in the legal ordering of trade. Brazil, India, and China used mechanisms of public–private coordination to gather information and define and advance government and constituency interests in trade negotiations and dispute settlement. They adapted mechanisms analogous to those first developed in the United States and Europe, but these mechanisms now reflected their own institutional heritages and constraints. They reinvented and repurposed US and E models of public–private coordination, while transforming themselves in the process. The relative power of the private sector and the state, and political contests within the state, determine the extent to which policies reflect more of a neoliberal or state-led capitalist model – or, put differently, the hybrid contours of public–private, state-market combinations. These processes gave rise to a certain amount of institutional isomorphism,[105] reflecting transnational legal ordering, but with distinct national variants resulting from distinct domestic contests and institutional legacies. The changes within these countries were far more complex than captured in simple invocations of "neoliberalism."[106]

In sum, unlike those who contend that the world has moved toward a post-national order where the state has weakened, this book shows how these countries' enmeshment in the transnational legal ordering of trade spurred the strengthening of state capacities to engage with international trade law and institutions. These states' greater engagement with private stakeholders and professionals enabled them to better mediate between global markets, the pursuit of state development strategies, and international trade rules. Many trade rules are highly contestable from a development perspective, such as those governing intellectual property rights and the role of industrial policy in development.[107] Indeed, actors contested these processes within all three countries. Yet, in all three, the state – in different ways – continued to play a central role in economic development, to the consternation particularly of the United States. To define, defend, and pursue its policies, the state expanded and tapped into both public and private expertise. These changes were not autonomous of globalization and the trade rules that organize and facilitate it, but were a product of them. At the same time, these states were not simply casualties of

---

[105]   Paul DiMaggio and Walter Powell, "The Iron Cage Revisited: Institutional Isomorphism and Collective Rationality in Organizational Fields," *American Sociological Review* 48 (1983): 47–160; John Meyer, John Boli, George Thomas, and Frank Ramirez, "World Society and the Nation-State," *American Journal of Sociology* 103 (1997): 144–181.

[106]   Rodgers provides an acute overview of the history, risks, and limits of the term "neoliberalism," which variously refers to "finance capitalism" to describe the late capitalist economy, "market fundamentalism" to name an intellectual project in economics, "disaster capitalism" to critique a policy of austerity, and "commodification" of culture to describe an overarching "governing rationality." Daniel Rodgers, "The Uses and Abuses of Neoliberalism," Dissent (Winter 2018).

[107]   Keith Maskus, *Intellectual Property Rights in the Global Economy* (Washington, DC: Peterson Institute, 2000); Dani Rodrik, *Straight Talk on Trade*.

globalization. They responded to globalization in new ways that had profound implications within the United States and for the international trade legal order.

IV. IMPLICATIONS FOR THE INTERNATIONAL TRADE LAW SYSTEM

Domestic legal and institutional change is just one component of transnational legal ordering. The other is the direct and indirect recursive impacts of domestic developments on the international legal order itself. It is this dynamic, recursive, transnational component that John Ikenberry's theory of a liberal hegemonic international order – of the United States ruling through rules – elides.[108] It is this component that the theoretical framework of transnational legal orders illuminates because it places national and international lawmaking and practice within a single analytic frame.

The legal ordering of trade involves specialized knowledge. Much of that knowledge involves US and European expertise.[109] From the perspective of transnational legal ordering, it can be viewed as globalized localisms – that is, the export, transfer, and hybridization of US and European legal and economic know-how and practice.[110] This book assesses how emerging powers and constituencies within them enrolled and adapted this US and European specialized legal and economic expertise to advance their interests through trade negotiations, litigation, import relief law, intellectual property, investment law, and domestic trade-related policy. This analysis leads to the book's third question: What are the implications for the transnational trade legal order and broader economic governance?

To recapitulate, emerging powers' deployment of trade law capacity could shape the trade legal order in multiple ways. As regards WTO *negotiations*, it enabled them to thwart US and European proposals, shape new negotiating initiatives, and

[108] John Ikenberry, *After Victory: Institutions, Strategic Restraint, and the Rebuilding of Order after Major Wars* (Princeton: Princeton University Press, 2000); John Ikenberry, *Liberal Leviathan: The Origins, Crisis, and Transformation of the American System* (Princeton: Princeton University Press, 2011). The Gramscian concept of hegemony concerns the ability to dominate not solely through coercion but also through consent. Robert Cox, "Gramsci, Hegemony and International Relations: An Essay in Method," *Millennium: Journal of International Studies* 12 (1983): 162. There is obvious tension, if not contradiction, in Ikenberry's account of an order that is both "liberal" and "hegemonic." As Oliver Stuenkel writes from the vantage of Brazil and the periphery, countries' "consent" was not given without a considerable amount of coercion, and the United States, in the name of American exceptionalism, always was better able to flout the rules and strategically use ambiguities and exceptions within them without the consequences suffered by others. Oliver Stuenkel, *Post-Western World: How Emerging Powers are Remaking Global Order* (Cambridge: Polity Press, 2016), 3, 182.

[109] Yves Dezalay and Bryant Garth, "Marketing and Selling Transnational 'Judges' and Global 'Experts': Building the Credibility of (Quasi)judicial Regulation," *Socio-Economic Review* 8, no. 1 (2010): 113–130; Yves Dezalay and Bryant Garth, *Asian Legal Revivals: Lawyers in the Shadow of Empire* (Chicago: University of Chicago Press, 2010).

[110] Boaventura de Sousa Santos, *Toward a New Common Sense: Law, Science and Politics in the Paradigmatic Transition (After the Law)*, 2nd ed. (Abingdon: Routledge, 2002).

become critical for any agreement's conclusion. As regards *monitoring and litigation*, it empowered them to launch or threaten to launch legal cases, including against major trading powers. Where successful, they could spur change in foreign regulatory practices that were the subject of dispute and could shape the interpretation of WTO legal texts in systemic ways that affect regulatory practices more broadly across countries. As regards *implementation*, it facilitated their design and application of regulatory practices in ways that could serve as models for others, whether for investment facilitation, standard setting, industrial policy, import relief measures, or patent protection.

The book shows how emerging economies' investment in trade law capacity enhanced their position in the international trade legal order.[111] The three countries studied are widely touted as among the most successful users of the international trade law system in negotiation and litigation. Their relative success received national and international attention, which paid off politically. It first helped them to become critical players in WTO negotiations and litigation. Then, as the WTO declined as a negotiating forum, it provided resources for them to develop their own models and initiatives for transnational legal ordering, shaping the changing ecology of the trade and broader economic law system.

The book shows how these countries' investments in legal capacity helped to shape the trade legal order in three interconnected ways, which paradoxically triggered the WTO's decline. Their investments contributed to stalemate at the WTO as a negotiating forum, fragmentation of the trade law system into webs of regional and bilateral agreements, and the potential demise of binding multilateral dispute settlement, at least through a WTO Appellate Body operating as a world trade court. As a result, competitive and overlapping bilateral and regional initiatives have partially displaced the WTO's centralized system of negotiation and dispute settlement.

First, through their investments in trade law capacity, these countries collectively *countered US and European dominance* of the trading system through WTO negotiations and dispute settlement. Brazil, India, and China became major players in WTO negotiations as first witnessed at the Cancun ministerial meeting. By 2008, the Doha round of negotiations collapsed but limped on until the United States announced in late 2015 that it was unwilling to pursue the round further.[112] No longer could the United States and Europe drive rulemaking in the WTO. No longer could they revise rules multilaterally to address new challenges, such as those posed by China's successful model of state capitalism and industrial policy. As

[111] Position is a critical concept in field and ecology theory, as actors' positions place them in more (or less) central or peripheral relations within a field. Liu and Emirbayer, "Field and Ecology," 63.

[112] Paul Blustein, *Misadventures of the Most Favored Nations: Clashing Egos, Inflated Ambitions, and the Great Shambles of the World Trade System* (New York: Public Affairs, 2009); "U.S., Other WTO Members Dispute Meaning of Doha Language in Declaration," 33 *Inside U.S. Trade* 50, December 25, 2015.

China became increasingly important in the global economy, its higher tariffs and other barriers to market access frustrated the United States, which had little negotiating leverage in the WTO given the already low level of US tariff bindings. The political process in the WTO largely deadlocked when these countries refused to make the market access concessions that the United States desired, leading to US disillusionment regarding the WTO as a negotiating forum. In parallel, through WTO litigation, these countries successfully challenged US and European trade measures against them, and in particular import relief measures through which the United States could raise tariffs against their products. In the process, they shaped the understanding of existing international trade law requirements.

Second, stalemate at the multilateral level led the United States and European Union to turn to regional and bilateral negotiations and thus *fragmentation* of the trading system. After the collapse of the Cancun ministerial in 2003 in the wake of Brazil's and India's forging of a G-20 negotiating group with China, United States Trade Representative (USTR) Robert Zoellick announced that the United States would pursue free trade agreements "with can-do countries," ones that would constitute a new coalition of the willing.[113] The aim was to create new templates, since the agreements expanded rights for US investors, service providers, and intellectual property holders.[114] The Obama administration subsequently negotiated much more ambitious regional agreements in the Trans-Pacific Partnership (TPP) and Transatlantic Trade and Investment Partnership that together were to cover 60 percent of the global economy. The TPP created a further template of new rules, including ones designed to constrain and rein in Chinese practices. Although the Trump administration abandoned the TPP, it used the TPP as a template for many chapters in its renegotiation of NAFTA – under the 2020 United States–Mexico–Canada Agreement – and these provisions will continue to serve as a guide for other US agreements.

In parallel, emerging economies developed their own models and initiatives through regional and bilateral trade and investment agreements. Most notably, China is using its trade law capacity to develop its Belt and Road Initiative and potentially create a new Sino-centric economic order. To support this initiative, China is expanding a web of trade and investment agreements that includes a massive Regional Cooperation Economic Partnership and that excludes the United States. India, in parallel, developed first a "Look East" and then an "Act East" policy to enhance trade and investment agreements with ASEAN and other

---

[113]   Robert Zoellick, "America Will Not Wait for the Won't-Do Countries," *Financial Times*, September 22, 2003 ("As WTO members ponder the future, the US will not wait: we will move towards free trade with can-do countries").

[114]   These US agreements were typically with smaller countries (such as with Bahrain, Chile, the Dominican Republic and Central America, Morocco, Peru, and Singapore), and not major ones (such as the European Union, Brazil, India, or China). Australia and South Korea were the largest economies with which the United States ratified a comprehensive bilateral trade agreement, respectively entering into force in 2005 and 2012.

Asian nations. Brazil ramped up negotiation of trade and investment agreements in Latin America through Mercosur and independently of it, while also negotiating new agreements with the European Union, Canada, Japan, South Korea, and others. In sum, these countries are deploying the legal capacity that they previously developed for the WTO in new ways.

Third, these countries' ability to counter the United States and Europe, coupled with US perceptions of China as a geopolitical threat, was a major contributing factor to US *disenchantment* with the WTO, manifested in US attacks on its dispute settlement system.[115] The inability of the United States to change WTO rules through the WTO political process coupled with WTO Appellate Body decisions not to its liking, catalyzed the potential collapse of the judicial system. Already under the Bush and Obama administrations, the United States became circumspect as it lost cases at the WTO regarding antidumping, countervailing duty, and safeguard measures.[116] With China's rise, especially following the 2008 financial crisis, important factions within the United States felt that WTO rules, as interpreted and enforced by the Appellate Body, constrained its ability to protect US industries from "unfair competition" from Chinese imports. The Office of the USTR increasingly challenged Appellate Body decisions against the United States and expressed its discontent by taking more aggressive positions in the selection of Appellate Body members.[117]

The Appellate Body consisted of seven members who decided cases in panels of three. These members held four-year terms, which were renewable once. Appointing them required consensus of all WTO members so that any member could veto a candidate's selection. Under the Bush and Obama administrations, the USTR twice refused to renominate the current US member for a second term as a signal of US dissatisfaction (replacing each with a new US member). The Obama administration then blocked consensus over the appointment of a Kenyan law professor based in the United States for an African regional slot, as well as the reappointment for a second term of a South Korean law professor.[118] The Obama administration, nonetheless, eventually agreed to the filling of Appellate Body vacancies with individuals who had less of an academic and more of a diplomatic background. The administration appeared to hope that an appointee with a diplomatic background would be more politically astute, more deferential to state import relief law, and less likely to take an expansive view of the Appellate Body as an independent, quasi-constitutional judicial body.

[115] Gregory Shaffer, "A Tragedy in the Making? The Decline of Law and the Return of Power in International Trade Relations," *Yale Journal of International Law Online* (2018): 37–53.

[116] Andrew Stoler, "The WTO Dispute Settlement Process: Did the Negotiators Get What They Wanted?," *World Trade Review* 3 (2004): 99–118.

[117] Gregory Shaffer, Manfred Elsig, and Sergio Puig, "The Law and Politics of WTO Dispute Settlement," in *Handbook on The Politics of International Law*, eds. Wayne Sandholtz and Christopher Whytock (Cheltenham: Edward Elgar Publishing, 2016), 269–306.

[118] Formally there are no regional slots, but they have existed in practice to ensure representativeness of the WTO membership.

In contrast, the Trump administration, generally hostile to international legal constraints, strategically and frontally blocked the launching of the formal process for selecting any new Appellate Body members. In December 2019, the Appellate Body died, as other WTO members sought to jerry rig and negotiate a revised system for appeals. It beckoned the end of binding third-party dispute settlement and the return of power-laden diplomacy where the United States is free to wield its economic weight through unilateral threats, deployment of trade sanctions, and the launching of a trade war that primarily targets China but directly and indirectly encompasses all major economies.

Viewed more broadly, emerging powers' deployment of legal capacity in the WTO, linked with structural changes in the global economy, *indirectly* affected the international trade legal order by facilitating the election of an economic nationalist in the United States. As Chapter 8 explains, economic globalization, supported by international trade law, generated a *double-edged shift in inequality*. On one side, the income of the working and middle classes in the United States and Europe stagnated and job security became precarious, such that there is *increasing inequality within countries*, with the United States being the leading example.[119] This shift triggered social conflict and revolt against the "elites" who benefitted from globalization, preparing the way for a populist nativist. On the other side, there is *decreasing inequality between the United States and emerging economies, and particularly China*. This shift facilitated a new framing of China as a strategic rival economically and militarily, especially given the dual uses of cutting-edge technologies for artificial intelligence and "smart" manufacturing. Moreover, now it is people of a different ethnicity – Chinese (in manufacturing), Indians (in services), and Brazilians (in agriculture) – who outcompeted Americans and Europeans and who thus must be "cheating."[120] Forged as a single, doubled-edged sword, the two edges do not bode well for multilateral trade law. The blade cuts multiple ways. The fallout from the 2020 coronavirus pandemic could deepen the blade's cuts.

In this context, these emerging powers continue to negotiate and sign trade and investment agreements. The trade legal know-how that they first developed in the WTO context is, in part, transportable, as they now have well-trained lawyers who can work on new trade and investment initiatives. The goal of creating and shaping transnational legal orders continues to serve as a tool among others in the new geopolitical context given the impact of law in shaping the rules of the game. Today,

[119] Emmanuel Saez and Gabriel Zucman, *The Triumph of Injustice* (New York: W.W. Norton & Company, 2019), 6 ("The United States is unique, among advanced economies, to have witnessed such a radical change in fortune"); Thomas Piketty, *Capital in the Twenty-First Century* (Cambridge: Harvard University Press, 2014), 1000–1004.

[120] Jeff Cox, "Trump Says China Cheated America on Trade, But He Blames US Leaders for Letting it Happen," CNBC, November 12, 2019. In the 1980s, this also contributed to anti-Japanese sentiment in the United States, but China has become a more formidable rival, both economically and geopolitically.

these countries engage in the construction of complementary and rival transnational legal orders for trade in a more pluralist system.

This book empirically examines these three emerging powers' development and use of trade law capacity, and not that of developing countries generally.[121] All three of these countries are powers in their regions and among the world's ten largest economies. Of the three, China is best positioned to shape the international trade legal order regionally and globally through webs of agreements, which is why the book dedicates an additional chapter to its initiatives. The future ecology of the transnational legal ordering of trade continues to unfold. These countries, working with stakeholders within them, will be key players in it.

In sum, this book does not contend that these countries' development of trade law capacity is the sole or main cause of US disenchantment with the WTO and the decline of WTO judicial authority, unrelated to other causes. Rather, the book provides a complementary (and necessary) "legal" explanation of such US disenchantment. This book *braids* the legal story's strands with the economic and geopolitical ones.[122] The stories are interwoven and thus reinforce each other. Take away the legal braid and the whole would be weaker. This book shows how building legal capacity to take on the United States and Europe at the WTO was a *critical reason* – if not a *necessary condition* – for the United States becoming disenchanted with the system.[123] Legal capacity was critical because it was *the medium through which change became expressed in institutional terms*. Counterfactually, if law and legal capacity do not matter, why would these states have invested in the ways the case studies document? Similarly, why else would the United States neutralize the WTO legal order if it had no material or normative consequence? These emerging powers' investment in legal capacity directly and indirectly reshaped the rules of the game for trade.

This book documents both the settling of a centralized transnational legal order for trade, with the WTO at its pinnacle, and its (at least partial) unsettlement. What does this augur for the future? The decline of the trade transnational legal order? A world in which lawfare plays a greater role than the public goods dimension of law? A reformed and moderated legal order for trade? Fragmentation into multiple, overlapping, and competing transnational legal orders for trade? This book provides a critical guide for such assessment.

---

[121] Compare *Dispute Settlement at the WTO: The Developing Country Experience*, eds. Gregory Shaffer and Ricardo Mélendez-Ortiz (Cambridge: Cambridge University Press, 2010).

[122] I thank Anthea Roberts for the metaphor.

[123] I reference but do not use the term "necessary condition" because, although historical institutional change tends to be gradual and layered, revolutionary change is possible where law is of little relevance.

3

The Challenges of International Trade Law

The WTO created incentives for Brazil, India, and China to develop trade law capacity. But before turning to how they invested in developing it, we should recognize the major challenges posed to effective participation in international trade negotiations, monitoring, and dispute settlement in the WTO and the broader ecology of the trading system. Only then will we have a better sense of how differences in legal capacity matter in practice. Building trade law capacity is not a simple matter. The demands are significant and are beyond many countries' hopes, although much progress has been made since the WTO's creation, including through collective efforts.[1] As the scope of trade agreements expanded and as countries negotiated in other fora, creating parallel dispute settlement mechanisms, the challenges grew.

Whatever one's perspective on trade agreements and their enforcement, emerging economies and their constituents started at a significant disadvantage before the WTO, its dispute settlement regime, and the broader ecology of the trading system, as compared to the United States and European Union. The United States and European Union led WTO negotiations and successfully exported many areas of their laws into the WTO system, from intellectual property to import relief law. Similarly, the United States and European Union have expanded the scope of regulatory commitments through bilateral and plurilateral trade agreements, which create templates for the future.

Unlike other countries, the United States and European Union generally do not need to adapt their national laws since trade agreements reflect them. They generally upload their domestic law into international treaties, which other countries are then expected to download. As the editors of a comprehensive volume on the Trans-Pacific Partnership wrote, "The US national regulatory system is already aligned with TPP11, as the United States had been able to influence the TPP12 terms toward

---

[1] *Dispute Settlement at the WTO: The Developing Country Experience*, eds. Gregory Shaffer and Ricardo Mélendez-Ortiz (Cambridge: Cambridge University Press, 2010); *Building Legal Capacity for a More Inclusive Globalization: Barriers to and Best Practices for Integrating Developing Countries into Global Economic Regulation*, eds. Joost Pauwelyn and Mengyi Wang (Geneva: The Graduate Institute, 2019).

a US model to such an extent that almost no regulatory changes within the United States would have been needed."[2] The US negotiating mandate set by Congress generally provides that the executive is to obtain commitments that reflect current US law. For example, its mandate for negotiating over intellectual property rights is to ensure "that the provisions of any trade agreement governing intellectual property rights that is entered into by the United States reflect a standard of protection similar to that found in United States law."[3] Even the procedural timelines of the WTO's dispute settlement system grew out of those used in the United States' unilateralist Section 301 mechanism pursuant to which the US government may investigate and take retaliatory action against countries for their "unjustified" and "unreasonable" trade-related measures.[4] And even the seemingly technocratic "trade facilitation agreement" regarding customs matters largely reflected "the current practices of developed countries" such as the United States.[5]

In contrast, WTO commitments and US bilateral and plurilateral trade agreements often require major changes in domestic laws and institutions in other countries. Thus, for implementation, the United States often includes provisions that the other country must receive US approval of their implementing statutes in order for the agreement to come into effect. Practitioners call this process "certification," which "commits the other Party to adopt in the case of IP, the necessary implementation legislation that meets the expectations of the US."[6] Think counterfactually if the United States were pressed to revise its domestic laws and institutions through international trade agreements, and if implementing Congressional legislation had to be approved by a foreign government. That would be unthinkable. Even if the United States were no longer a global hegemon, it would never have such a subordinate status. Much more was thus at stake at the implementation stage for these countries and stakeholders within them, further incentivizing investments in trade-related legal capacity.

The United States and European Union also have dominated trade litigation, shaping the interpretation and application of trade law. In the WTO, the United States has been a party in 67 percent of the cases decided by the Appellate Body, the European Union in 42 percent, and one or the other of them in 86 percent.[7] Where

---

[2] *Megaregulation Contested: Global Economic Ordering After TPP*, eds. Benedict Kingsbury, David Malone, Paul Martenskotter, Richard Stewart, Thomas Streinz, and Atushi Sunami (Oxford: Oxford University Press, 2019), 2.

[3] 19 U.S.C. 4201 (b)(5)(A)(i)(II).

[4] Louise Johannesson and Petros C. Mavroidis, "The WTO Dispute Settlement System 1995–2016: A Data Set and its Descriptive Statistics," *Journal of World Trade* 51, no. 3 (2017): 357, 367.

[5] Nicolas Lamp, "Legislative Innovation in the Trade and Climate Regimes: Towards a Framework for the Comparative Analysis of Multilateral Lawmaking," in *Global Environmental Change and Innovation in International Law*, eds. Neil Craik, Cameron Jefferies, Sara Seck, and Tim Stephens (Cambridge: Cambridge University Press, 2018), 290.

[6] Pedro Roffe, *Intellectual Property Provisions in Bilateral and Regional Trade Agreements*: CIEL. October 6, 2006.

[7] Author's calculation from worldtradelaw.net, based on 145 Appellate Body reports circulated as of December 31, 2019. One was formally adopted on January 7, 2020.

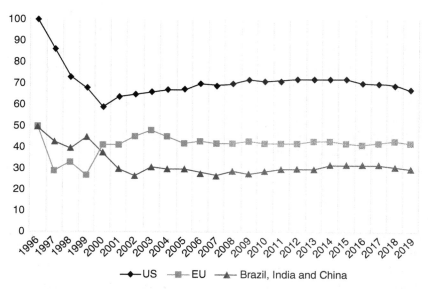

FIGURE 3.1 Percentage of total Appellate Body cases over time (complainants and respondents)[8]

they are not a party, they have been an active third party in almost every case. They thus exercised significant influence in introducing arguments and shaping WTO jurisprudence. Nonetheless, through their investments in legal capacity, Brazil, India, and China have participated individually and in aggregate, so as to exercise considerable influence as well, as reflected in Figure 3.1 regarding WTO litigation.

The United States and European Union employ dozens of well-trained governmental lawyers for trade-related matters and they benefit from significant assistance from private consultants and law firms hired by the world's largest corporations and trade associations who do research, prepare negotiating modalities, and write legal briefs for dispute settlement. They thus have more legal resources at their disposal than other WTO members. They have been the most successful in developing new concepts and texts for negotiations and then litigating them, both as complainants and as respondents. They surpassed the average success rate of the BRICS countries by twenty-two percentage points as a complainant and by thirteen percentage points as a respondent.[9] They have, in short, used legal resources to construct international trade law. Brazil, India, and China needed to develop significant legal capacity to offset, in part, the disadvantages they faced against the United States and European Union.

---

[8] Appellate figures generated from worldtradelaw.net.
[9] Johannesson and Mavroidis, "The WTO Dispute Settlement System 1995–2016," 383–384 (BRICS countries lowest in each category of the breakdown).

Countries generally face four primary challenges if they are to participate effect-ively in international trade negotiations, monitoring, and dispute settlement. These challenges are:

(i)   the development of *technical capacity*, including legal capacity, to organize information to understand the implications of trade law choices in order to defend and advance one's interests, including through developing one's own negotiating initiatives and model agreements, on the one hand, and to identify, bring, and bargain over claims in dispute settlement, on the other. This challenge directly involves the development of specialized legal expert-ise and complementary technical know-how related to it, the first of the three questions assessed in this book;

(ii) the allocation of sufficient *financial resources*, in light of other government priorities, to hire and work with specialized experts, including internal and external economic consultants and legal counsel to effectively negotiate, monitor, and litigate in the trade law system. This challenge involves mater-ial resources that implicate a country's ability to build trade law capacity;

(iii) concern with *political and economic repercussions* from countries with large markets, and in particular the United States and European Union, which could neutralize legal capacity once developed. This challenge implicates a country's incentives to build legal capacity. It particularly affects small developing countries, but emerging powers have to address it as well, includ-ing in relation to each other; and

(iv) *internal governance* obstacles, including interministerial coordination and government relations with the private sector and civil society. This challenge directly affects a country's development of legal capacity because it impli-cates its ability to seed, incentivize, and harness legal capacity built in the private sector. It involves domestic institutions, professions, and their adap-tation, the second of the three questions that this book addresses.

These four challenges involve constraints of technical legal knowledge, financial endowment, political/market power, and internal state–society relations – or, more simply put, constraints of *knowledge, money, power,* and *governance*. These con-straints are more formidable for smaller developing countries.[10] Brazil, India, and China do not face them to nearly the same degree because of their economic size. Nonetheless, it took considerable effort for them to develop requisite legal capacity to take on the United States and European Union in trade negotiations and dispute settlement before the WTO and in other fora, including for monitoring obligations

[10]   Gregory Shaffer, "The Challenges of WTO Law: Strategies for Developing Country Adaptation," *World Trade Review* 5 (2006): 177–198; Gregory Shaffer, "Developing Country Use of the WTO Dispute Settlement System: Why It Matters, the Barriers Posed," in *Trade Disputes and the Dispute Settlement Understanding of the WTO: An Interdisciplinary Assessment*, ed. James C. Hartigan (Bingley: Emerald Publishing, 2009): 167–190.

and for bargaining in the shadow of the law. This chapter examines these four challenges and, in doing so, it provides preliminary examples of how they apply to Brazil, India, and China and how these countries addressed them.

I. THE CHALLENGE OF TECHNICAL LEGAL CAPACITY (LAW)

Countries need to develop legal capacity to overcome an array of challenges they face if they are to participate effectively in order to defend and advance their interests in the international trade legal order. As the journalist Paul Blustein wrote in his study of WTO trade negotiations, "One of the biggest disadvantages [developing] countries face as WTO members – mustering the technical expertise needed to participate effectively in an organization where the giants, especially the United States and the European Union, have much larger staffs, better equipment, deeper knowledge, and more experience playing the game."[11] Yet, he does not break down the different ways that such expertise is critical in light of the multiple challenges posed, as done here.

First, there is the challenge of *the substantive scope of WTO and other trade law.* The WTO expanded the scope of the 1948 General Agreement on Tariffs and Trade to include nineteen agreements under a single framework and a vastly expanded membership, consisting of 164 members today. Countries significantly reduced tariff rates and the WTO legally constrained the use of other barriers to trade.[12] The agreements contained ongoing negotiation mandates and members launched a new round of negotiations in 2001. These states' new legal commitments and ongoing negotiations made investment in trade law capacity essential.

Second, *the expanding number of trade and trade-related agreements* required increased technical expertise. The demands on a country's legal capacity intensified when the WTO became just a big meatball in a spaghetti bowl of agreements. As of October 2020, countries had ratified 688 bilateral and plurilateral trade agreements and signed many others. These agreements comprised approximately 7,549 dyadic pairings of countries.[13] Collectively these agreements constitute a broader ecosystem of trade and trade-related economic law and institutions. The demand on these countries' legal and negotiating resources escalated.

Third, the *judicialization* of trade relations posed significant new challenges. The WTO's judicialized dispute settlement system required enhanced technical legal

---

[11] Paul Blustein, *Misadventures of the Most Favored Nations: Clashing Egos, Inflated Ambitions, and the Great Shambles of the World Trade System* (New York: Public Affairs, 2009), 20.

[12] Brazil reduced its average applied tariffs from about 50 percent in 1989 to 13.4 percent in 2017. India reduced them from 37.95 percent in 1996 to 8.9 percent in 2017. And China did so from 19.3 percent in 1996 to 8.5 percent in 2017. These rates, however, were not bound rates. World Bank, Index Mundi, www.indexmundi.com/facts/indicators/TM.TAX.MRCH.SM.AR.ZS/rankings (based on WTO and UNCTAD data).

[13] Andreas Dür, Leonardo Baccini, and Manfred Elsig, *The Design of Trade Agreements*, March 1, 2017, www.designoftradeagreements.org/project-description/ (updated through October 2020).

expertise involving increasingly complex legal procedures. The WTO created a judicialized dispute settlement system with compulsory jurisdiction and an appellate process that helped to enforce these countries' undertakings, and they were quickly put on the defensive. This system developed in a highly legalistic manner, driven by lawyers representing government and business clients, creating opportunities but also challenges for countries with fewer legal, financial, and political resources.[14] The legal procedures and substantive case law became exceedingly complex and technically demanding. By January 31, 2020, WTO members had filed 594 complaints, giving rise to the adoption of over 50,000 pages of case reports (approaching 100,000 when including annexes). WTO dispute settlement panels and the Appellate Body developed this jurisprudence in more than 300 decisions (and more than 400 when including compliance- and retaliation-related reports).[15] At an extreme, the 2006 WTO panel decision in the *European Communities-Biotech* case was 1,087 pages in text, contained 2,187 footnotes, and was over 2,400 pages when including annexes.[16] Generalist diplomats are not trained for such matters, nor are most countries' attorneys. It is a system in which specialized lawyers play central roles. The new bilateral trade and investment agreements that these countries negotiated came with distinct dispute settlement provisions, adding to the complexity. Even though the WTO system remained the main recourse for trade disputes because of its multilateral nature, these countries also required legal capacity for the design of new mechanisms that potentially could be deployed.

Fourth, *the depth of the implications of these rules for regulation* and policy space within developmental states created an array of new challenges.[17] The TRIPS agreement required massive changes in intellectual property law and institutions within developing countries. The WTO Agreement on the Application of Sanitary and Phytosanitary Measures demanded costly changes in states' regulatory systems for food and agriculture. The Agreement on Technical Barriers to Trade obliged countries to rationalize standard setting and enhanced the salience of global standard-setting organizations. The Agreement on Subsidies and Countervailing Measures and

[14] Gregory Shaffer, Manfred Elsig, and Sergio Puig, "The Extensive (but Fragile) Authority of the WTO Appellate Body," *Law and Contemporary Problems* 79 (2016): 237–274.

[15] The number of adopted reports can be broken down to 196 adopted Panel Reports; 120 adopted Appellate Body Reports; 36 adopted Article 21.5 Panel Reports (on compliance); 25 adopted Article 21.5 Appellate Body Reports (on compliance); 33 adopted Article 21.3(c) Arbitration Decisions (on reasonable period of time to comply); 24 adopted Article 22.6 Arbitration Decisions (on amount of authorized retaliation); and 1 Article 25 Arbitration Award (as an alternative dispute settlement mechanism).

[16] Panel Report, *European Communities – Measures Affecting the Approval and Marketing of Biotech Products*, WT/DS291/R, WT/DS292/R, WT/DS293/R. September 29, 2006.

[17] J. Michael Finger and Philip Schuler, "Implementation of Uruguay Round Commitments: The Development Challenge," *The World Economy* 23 (2000): 511 ("For most of the developing and transition economies – some 100 countries – money spent to implement the WTO rules in these areas would be money unproductively invested"); J. Michael Finger, "Implementing the Uruguay Round Agreements: Problems for Developing Countries," *The World Economy* 24 (2001): 1097.

the Agreement on Trade-Related Investment Measures created limits on states' industrial policy programs. And the trio of WTO import relief agreements governing antidumping law, countervailing duty law, and safeguards law pressed countries to create new institutions and professions to oversee the legalization of protectionism.

To address these challenges, a country must develop different, interrelated forms of trade policy capacity. For *trade negotiations*, a country must determine its sectoral priorities regarding goods and services sectors, gather information regarding the consequences of different negotiating outcomes, and form a clear bargaining strategy (including in terms of issue linkages).[18] Technical expertise is required to craft the scope of coverage of agreements, and then to draft precise legal language to protect and advance the state's and its constituents' interests and priorities. These negotiations involve market access commitments, affecting both export interests and internal industrial policy. They increasingly involve behind-the-border regulatory issues, affecting internal institutions and policy space more broadly.[19] In each case, countries need trade law capacity to assess the effects of tariff reductions and other commitments on their economy, and thus the relation of legal change to their economic prospects and the distributional implications. Determining the proper balance between rules (to protect exports) and exceptions (to protect regulatory policy space) is critical. In WTO negotiations, countries develop modalities for tariff cuts and limits on domestic agricultural support. In doing so, they must understand the implications of these modalities for their economic sectors and broader economic development, including industrial, agricultural, and services policies. The United States and European Union long took the lead in developing modalities for negotiations and getting text they preferred into the "Chair's text."[20] Other countries were placed in the position of having to respond. The WTO ministerial meeting in Cancun changed that, as Brazil took the lead with India in developing negotiating modalities for agriculture with the assistance of Brazilian and Indian think tanks to counter a US–EU joint proposal.[21] They continued playing key roles through the collapse of the Doha round in 2008 and thereafter.

For trade *dispute settlement*, countries must develop cost-effective mechanisms to perceive injuries to its trading prospects, identify who is responsible, and mobilize resources to bring a legal claim or negotiate a favorable settlement. In the socio-legal literature, these stages of dispute resolution are referred to as naming, blaming, and claiming.[22] In the WTO context, a member's participation in the system is, in part, · a function of its ability to process knowledge of trade injuries, their causes, and their

---

[18]   John S. Odell, "Negotiating from Weakness in International Trade Relations," *World Trade Review* 45 (2010): 545–566 (differentiating distributive and integrative bargaining strategies).

[19]   Kingsbury et al., eds., *Megaregulation Contested.*

[20]   John Braithwaite and Peter Drahos, *Global Business Regulation* (Cambridge: Cambridge University Press, 2000), at 196.

[21]   Blustein, *Misadventures of the Most Favored Nations,* 142–144.

[22]   William L. F. Felstiner, Richard L. Abel, and Austin Sarat, "The Emergence and Transformation of Disputes: Naming, Blaming and Claiming," *Law & Society Review* 15 (1980–1981): 631.

relation to WTO rights. This first involves *monitoring* other countries' policies and practices. Hiring lawyers to defend WTO and other claims is of little help if countries lack cost-effective mechanisms to identify and prioritize claims in the first place. Even where countries become aware of actionable injuries, this awareness will not be transformed into legal claims if, based on experience, officials lack confidence that a claim is worth pursuing in light of litigation costs, weak remedies, and political risks. Even where a country decides to bring a case, it will need to adhere to the dispute settlement system's demanding procedural requirements, including its tight deadlines for legal submissions and responses to panel questions.

Given the broad scope of coverage of WTO and other trade negotiations, trade law affects multiple ministries that have distinct regulatory goals and agendas. As negotiating mandates spread to cover trade in services and behind-the-border regulatory issues, countries are needed to develop trade-related expertise across ministries to ensure appropriate commitments and constraints affecting their regulatory domains. Countries likewise had to develop *mechanisms to coordinate officials* across ministries to reconcile ministerial goals. A broad range of ministries had to take international trade law much more seriously given its implications for domestic regulation and policy space. They needed to develop and tap into technical, trade-related legal expertise.

The United States and European Union were the first to develop formal and informal mechanisms to identify foreign trade barriers, prioritize them according to their impact, and mobilize resources for WTO complaints.[23] They did so through interagency coordination and networking with the private sector, which, in turn, engaged private law firms. It was a great challenge for them, involving a "huge learning curve,"[24] but nothing like the challenges faced by other countries. Although Brazil, India, and China are large and have significant trading stakes, they faced significant internal bureaucratic hurdles.

Even where countries coordinate bureaucracies and ensure some continuity of representation, most countries' ministries lacked *legal* expertise.[25] Limits to legal capacity in relation to bureaucratic coordination, both in the home capital and between it and the Geneva mission, undermine a country's ability to follow and participate in WTO matters. For example, it constrains a country's ability to participate effectively in dispute settlement as a third party to protect the country's *systemic interests in the rules' interpretation*. As a third party, a WTO member may make written submissions and oral presentations to panels and the Appellate Body so as to shape WTO jurisprudence. This jurisprudence has had systemic implications for future disputes because it created a form of de facto precedent given the system's

[23]   Gregory Shaffer, *Defending Interests: Public-Private Partnerships in WTO Litigation* (Washington, DC: Brookings Institution Press, 2003).

[24]   Comments from Jennifer Hillman, former General Counsel at USTR (and subsequently member of the US International Trade Commission and the WTO Appellate Body), Irvine, February 29, 2020.

[25]   Shaffer, "The Challenges of WTO Law." Brazil's lead ministry at the WTO, for example, is the Ministry of Foreign Affairs, and its career officials generally did not have legal training.

desire to handle like cases alike. Without direction and close coordination with the capital, countries are unable to participate in shaping jurisprudence in this way.

To address legal issues, Brazil and China thus created specialized WTO dispute settlement units in their respective lead ministries, and India created a group of think tanks annexed to its Ministry of Commerce to help coordinate for trade and investment negotiations and disputes. Each of these countries also worked to catalyze the development of specialized trade law knowledge in its private bar so that private lawyers could assist the government in international trade law cases, as well as in developing new dispute settlement frameworks and chapters covering trade and investment. As regards third-party participation, Brazil was particularly creative. It created internship programs for young attorneys in private law firms in its Geneva mission, in the capital, and in its embassy in Washington. The Geneva-based attorneys helped develop submissions where Brazil was a third party. In the process, they built experience and contacts so that they could be useful for the government and national stakeholders in the future.

Even in developing such expertise, the WTO legal order posed a particular challenge for many delegations because of *language* and its mix of *common and civil law* reasoning for handling disputes. Even though English, French, and Spanish are the three official languages of the WTO, English predominates. This has been a particular challenge for China compared to India and Brazil. Moreover, the legal culture of the WTO dispute settlement system poses greater challenges for lawyers and diplomats raised in legal cultures where dispute settlement is less factually contextualized and legal submissions require less parsing of prior court jurisprudence. Lawyers from Brazil and China have relatively little experience with this type of factually contextualized legal reasoning. As one Brazilian lawyer stated, "Lawyers in Brazil are not used to the fact-finding part of WTO cases. The way attorneys write in Brazil is fashioned by Brazilian civil law traditions. It's not a natural way for them, the way they are trained to write. Brazilians can write in English, but they will think as Brazilian lawyers."[26] Adapting to the WTO legal culture was more challenging for them.

Finally, the need for legal capacity is particularly significant where a country wishes to develop *its own initiatives* to shape the trade legal order. As Nicolas Lamp writes regarding negotiations, "Identifying a potential issue for a lawmaking initiative, developing a textual proposal in coordination with domestic stakeholders, defending the proposal in meetings of the relevant WTO bodies, and incorporating feedback from other WTO members, with uncertain chances of success, requires both human and financial resources that most developing countries do not possess."[27] More recently, these emerging economies began to

---

[26] Interview, Brazilian Attorney in a major law firm in São Paulo, Brazil, April 23, 2004.

[27] Nicolas Lamp, "Strategies for Developing Countries in Multilateral Trade Negotiations at the World Trade Organization," in *Building Legal Capacity for a More Inclusive Globalization: Barriers to and Best Practices for Integrating Developing Countries into Global Economic Regulation*, eds. Joost Pauwelyn and Mengyi Wang (Geneva: The Graduate Institute, 2019): 9–30.

develop their own models for economic integration not only through developing new proposals in the WTO, but also in negotiating new trade and investment agreements outside of it as part of the changing ecology of the trade legal order. China, most ambitiously, is developing its Belt and Road Initiative, which includes a plethora of agreements and new dispute resolution mechanisms, supported by new trade and investment agreements (Chapter 7). It has developed a policy of pragmatically expanding trade agreements to first cover trade in goods before expanding them to cover trade in services. Brazil has developed a new alternative model for investment facilitation, and it has tested out new regulatory agreements with smaller countries such as Peru in preparation for negotiations with major powers such as the European Union. India has formulated "Look East" and "Act East" policies to forge closer economic relations in Asia, and it has developed government-sponsored think tanks with lawyers, including one on regional integration, to support its efforts. In each case, developing legal capacity became critical.

There are increasing returns to such investments in trade law capacity because of the high start-up costs relative to maintenance costs, and the fact that legal expertise deepens through experience. Once an investment is made, the marginal cost of maintaining trade law capacity is much lower. Professionals who have developed expertise, both in the public and private sectors, are now on tap. The initial decision to invest in building trade law capacity involves a critical juncture. On the one hand, it generates increasing returns as the country and its stakeholders defend their interests and work to shape the rules of the game. On the other hand, it creates path dependencies through the development of new institutional processes and professional know-how, identities, and networks.

II. THE FINANCIAL CHALLENGE (MONEY)

Developing legal capacity is not free and it is thus not autonomous from other factors, including money. Participating in international organizations so as to shape the conception, drafting, and negotiation of international trade-related obligations is costly. Countries not only need to staff specialized agencies at home but also ensure adequate representation at the WTO and the World Intellectual Property Organization in Geneva, the Food and Agricultural Organization in Rome, the World Customs Organization in Brussels, the major standard-setting organizations in Geneva, Rome, and Paris, the OECD in Paris, ICSID in Washington, DC, and UNCITRAL in Vienna. To ensure technical expertise, they ideally wish to send specialized officials from ministries in the capital to these organizations. Given the distance of these organizations from Brazil, India, and China, the costs can be considerable, much more so, for example, than for the European Union. As the ecology of trade law expanded through bilateral and regional agreements and institutions, these countries had to hire specialized staff to engage in these parallel and competing processes as well.

In order to be responsive to others' initiatives and proactively launch their own, high-level specialists were needed.

To complement their bureaucratic staff, emerging powers invested in think tanks and consultancies. China's think tanks are staffed largely by former government officials. India created new think tanks under the auspices of the Ministry of Commerce. The private sector funded new think tanks and consultancies in Brazil. In each case, these entities hire economists and lawyers. These think tanks work to help coordinate public–private joint initiatives and partnerships to ensure the flow of information and the sharing of expertise (linked to the fourth challenge of internal governance involving state–private sector relations).

When it comes to trade dispute settlement, countries face four primary types of costs in determining whether to bring a WTO case. First, they need to develop mechanisms to monitor whether countries are meeting their obligations. To do so, they need to establish overseas networks to collect and analyze information and need to coordinate with the private sector. In this way, more eyes can identify violations where claims might be brought. Second, where a government decides that it does not have the necessary expertise internally to litigate a WTO case, it faces the direct out-of-pocket cost of hiring specialized, outside legal counsel.[28] Third, even if assisted by outside legal counsel, the government must dedicate personnel with expertise to oversee and provide necessary support in bringing a complaint. This is necessary to ensure that the government's long-term systemic interests are addressed because the government may be a respondent and complainant in future cases that the jurisprudence implicates. Fourth, a government faces the opportunity cost of expending scarce resources and personnel time for dispute settlement as opposed to other social priorities, which affects a government's perception of the cost.

Many countries dedicate fewer resources to spend on trade law matters in light of other government priorities. Of these three countries, India's Ministry of Commerce faced the greatest financial challenge in light of the country's other needs. India has the lowest per capita income of the three (at just over $2,000 in 2018 on a nominal basis, which is highly unevenly distributed),[29] and it has correspondingly allocated the fewest resources to WTO, other trade missions, and to trade dispute settlement. It has not hired the leading US and European law firms for its cases. Rather, it turned to using the Advisory Centre on WTO Law (ACWL), an international organization in Geneva created to provide developing countries with lower cost legal assistance.[30] It used the ACWL more than any other developing country until it developed a pool of Indian law firms that it could hire, which further enabled it to save costs. It did so, even

---

[28] This has been necessary for Brazil, India, and China given the complexities of trade jurisprudence.

[29] The World Bank, GDP per capita (current US$) (visited January 4, 2020).

[30] Chad Bown, *Self-Enforcing Trade: Developing Countries and WTO Dispute Settlement* (Washington, DC: Brookings Institution, 2009) (chapter 6); Gregory Shaffer, "Assessing the Advisory Centre on WTO Law from a Broader Governance Perspective," *Minnesota Legal Studies Research Paper* (2011), 11–46.

though these lawyers do not have nearly as much experience as their US and European counterparts. India also has a much smaller staff handling WTO matters, both in its mission in Geneva and in its capital compared to the other two. In contrast, China has always hired both a Chinese law firm and a top-tier foreign law firm for its cases pursuant to separate bidding processes. Brazil has at times conferred only with Brazilian law firms, but it has used a foreign firm for its most complex cases.

Private companies and trade associations can pay for a private law firm to work with the government in preparing a WTO case to ease the pressure on government budgets. Since private business ultimately is affected by trade barriers, it has the incentive to do so where stakes are high, particularly if it is a large company or a well-funded trade association. Brazil has worked with the private sector to hire private law firms to assist it in bringing WTO complaints. In contrast, the private sector has not funded cases brought by India or China so that the government has assumed the costs. Moreover, not all companies and trade associations are willing to front these costs, especially where the remedy is weak. Countries thus particularly face challenges if they wish to address foreign trade barriers adversely affecting their less-organized economic sectors.

Finally, countries face implementation challenges to comply with their international trade-related obligations in ways that facilitate their development goals.[31] Since compliance involves interpretive choices, countries need to hire sophisticated staff to evaluate, tailor, and defend their development options. China, moreover, has to translate all of its laws and regulations into English pursuant to its WTO Accession Protocol, unlike any other WTO member.

Developing technical expertise, in sum, requires material resources. Governments that face multiple priorities may not invest in the requisite legal capacity for trade negotiations, monitoring, dispute settlement, and implementation. This affects their ability to shape rules and their interpretation, as well as bargaining in the shadow of the law. One reason they may attempt to develop public–private partnerships is to enhance the financial resources available to participate effectively in the trading system.

III. THE POLITICAL CHALLENGE (MATERIAL AND STRUCTURAL POWER)

Political asymmetries because of differences in material and structural power present a third challenge. These asymmetries implicate a country's decision to invest in trade law capacity. Given the importance of US and European markets, Brazil, India, and China have been subject to US and EU leverage in negotiations. In the buildup to the WTO's creation, Brazil and India faced considerable threats and sanctions that the United States would withdraw preferential tariff access under their general system of preferences (GSP) programs.[32] The United States continued to

---

[31] Finger, "Implementing the Uruguay Round Agreements."
[32] Thomas Bayard and Kimberly Ann Elliott, *Reciprocity and Retaliation in U.S. Trade Policy* (Washington, DC: Peterson Institute, 1994).

wield these threats to pressure them regarding intellectual property protection and services trade after the WTO's creation.[33] In its trade war with China, the United States again uses its market power to induce China to change its laws and practices. It is doing the same in skirmishes over trade with Brazil and India. For the receiving countries, as a Brazilian official complained, it is like negotiating with "a gun to your head."[34]

To enhance their leverage against the United States and European Union, particularly in negotiations, countries can form *alliances with each other* or *with civil society organizations*.[35] Brazil, India, and China formed an alliance when they organized the G-20 negotiating group on agriculture at the WTO Ministerial Meeting in Cancun in 2003.[36] Similarly, Brazil and India joined forces in bringing joint WTO complaints against the European Union to stop the Netherlands from seizing Indian generic drugs on flights destined for Brazil and other developing countries.

The BRICS countries for a time fostered greater solidarity in their negotiating positions through organizing annual summits of the BRICS presidents and high-level ministers, starting in 2009, with South Africa joining the group in 2010. Although at times fruitful, these countries have distinct trading interests and BRICS solidarity is unraveling as geopolitical tensions rise. India criticizes China's Belt and Road Initiative because of its adverse implications for India's sphere of influence in South Asia, its relations with Pakistan, and its border conflicts with China.[37] Brazil's President Bolsonaro and other Brazilian commentators periodically have lashed out at China's neo-colonialist trade relationship with the country.[38] India has been highly critical of Brazil's and China's new initiative to address investment facilitation in the WTO.[39]

China thus has looked beyond the BRICS to create broader alliances that now are useful in the context of the US-launched trade war. The Belt and Road Initiative

---

[33]   Ed Taylor, *"Brazilian Official Vows to Strengthen IPR In Effort to Avoid Losing U.S. GSP Benefits,"* *International Trade Reporter* 21 (2004): 1602; Rossella Brevetti, *"Administration Cuts GSP Benefits for Brazil, India, Venezuela, Others,"* *International Trade Reporter* 24 (2007): 939. China and Brazil graduated out of the European Union's program on January 1, 2015. The United States revoked India's GSP status in 2019.

[34]   Interview, Brasília, March 9, 2018 ("The U.S. says we can take everything, but since we like you just give us 70 percent."). He was referring to the US offer to negotiate quotas with Brazil after the United States announced a 25 percent tariff on steel imports and a 10 percent tariff on aluminum imports on national security grounds in 2018. Brazil agreed to the quotas.

[35]   Odell, "Negotiating from Weakness."

[36]   Amrita Narlikar and Diana Tussie, "The G20 at the Cancun Ministerial: Developing Countries and their Evolving Coalitions in the WTO," *World Economy* 27 (2004): 947–966.

[37]   Darshana M. Baruah, "India's Answer to the Belt & Road: A Road Map for South Asia," *Carnegie India* (2018).

[38]   As a candidate, Bolsonaro claimed, "China isn't buying in Brazil. It's buying Brazil." As a President, he is pressed to be more circumspect. Guy Burton, "What President Bolsonaro Means for China-Brazil Relations," *The Diplomat*, November 9, 2018.

[39]   Bryce Baschuk, *India Sparks WTO Discord, Blocks General Council Meeting*, 34 *Int'l Trade Rep.* (BNA) 752, 34 ITR 752 (BL) (May 18, 2017); Brett Fortnam, "India Blocks WTO General Council Meeting Over Investment Agenda Item," *Inside U.S. Trade*, May 12, 2017.

helps it create closer connections with political and economic elites in countries around the world. In turn, India is working to create alliances with other developing countries, particularly in Asia and Africa. Brazil long worked with the other members of Mercosur and is known for its successful diplomacy in obtaining support for Brazilians to lead international organizations, such as the WTO. These alliances are particularly important for advancing their policy initiatives. China, for example, has gotten most developing countries to recognize it as a "market economy" for purposes of import relief investigations, and Brazil is signing a new investment facilitation model with a growing number of countries.

By enhancing trade relations with third countries, these emerging economies could reduce US and EU economic and political leverage over them because they are less dependent on US and EU markets.[40] China's Belt and Road Initiative makes it less dependent on the US market. Brazil, in parallel, is less subject to US leverage today than during the negotiations that led to the WTO's creation because of its increased trade with China. More generally, each of these countries is developing its own regional and bilateral trade and broader economic law initiatives so that it is less dependent on the WTO as the WTO's authority erodes.

Countries also benefit from forming *alliances with nongovernmental organizations* in the United States and Europe, possibly combined with other international organizations, to reframe legal issues and counter trade-related pressure from the United States and European Union. When successful, they can harness favorable media coverage that adopts frames that they prefer to enhance their position's normative authority.[41] Because of law's partial autonomy where norms matter, weaker countries can increase their leverage in bargaining and litigating by creating such alliances.

Brazil and India most notably used these strategies to combat pressure regarding their levels of pharmaceutical patent protection. In June 2001, the Bush administration withdrew the United States' claim against Brazil's patent law in the context of widespread protest against the US action from advocacy groups who maintained that the US government placed corporate interests above public health involving life and death.[42] International organizations complemented this

---

[40] Odell, "Negotiating from Weakness."

[41] John S. Odell and Susan Sell, "Reframing the issue: the WTO coalition on TRIPS and Public Health," in *Negotiating Trade: Developing Countries in the WTO and NAFTA*, ed. John S. Odell (Cambridge: Cambridge University Press, 2006), 85–114; Bown, *Self-Enforcing Trade* (chapter 7).

[42] Doctors Without Borders declared that Brazil's patent policy was key to the success of the Brazil's strategy to offer universal access to HIV/AIDS medication in Brazil. Oxfam, the British NGO, backed Brazil's efforts, maintaining that the US complaint was an assault on public health. "Drug Companies vs. Brazil: The Threat to Public Health," *Oxfam*, May 2001. The United States soon backpedaled. "U.S., Brazil End WTO Case on Patents, Split on Bilateral Process," *Inside U.S. Trade* 19 (2001): 2 ("Informed sources said the U.S. backpedaling from the WTO panel, which it had requested in February, reflected an unwillingness on the part of U.S. Trade Representative Robert Zoellick to give opponents of trade liberalization a red-hot issue that appeared to give credence to the idea of the WTO interfering with poor countries' health policies").

NGO pressure.[43] USTR Robert Zoellick eventually abandoned the US pharmaceutical industry with little consultation in agreeing to the "Declaration on the TRIPS Agreement and Public Health" at Doha.[44]

There are many other examples. Oxfam was a major supporter of Brazil's challenges to US and European agricultural subsidy programs in WTO cases that were highly covered in the international media, placing normative pressure on WTO decision makers.[45] Brazil also received support from a coalition of Brazilian, Latin American, US, and European NGOs in defending its ban on retreaded tire imports from an EU challenge in the *Brazil-Tyres* case.[46] It did so by raising a defense grounded on environmental and human health concerns. India rallied NGOs to support its position on public stockholding of grains "to protect food security."[47] China, however, has been less able to tap into international civil society support, which disadvantages it when it raises environmental defenses, such as the environmental cost of mining rare earths to justify high taxes on their export.

Structural and material power remain important determinants of global governance. However, the partial autonomy of law incentivizes weaker countries to develop alliances with other states, civil society actors, and international organizations to enhance their normative positions in negotiations and litigation, as well as in bargaining in the law's shadow. The Trump administration's trade war and attack on WTO institutions can be understood as an attempt to shrink the law's shadow and thus enhance US political leverage through withholding or threatening to withhold market access. Doing so, nonetheless, imposes costs on the United States, including in terms of its reputational effects as a norm breaker, as public surveys reflect.[48]

---

[43]   For example, fifty-two countries of a fifty-three-member United Nations Human Rights Commission endorsed Brazil's AIDS policy and backed a resolution sponsored by Brazil that called on all states to promote access to AIDS drugs. "UN Rights Body Backs Brazil on AIDS Drugs," *News24.com*, April 24, 2001.

[44]   Washington-based trade specialist, email message to author, June 27, 2002 (concerning the lack of consultation); Gary Yerkey and Daniel Pruzin, "Agreement on TRIPS/Public Health Reached at WTO Ministerial in Doha," *International Trade Reporter* 18 (2001): 1817.

[45]   "Busted: World Trade Watchdog Declares EU & US Farm Subsidies Illegal," *Oxfam*, September 10, 2004, www.oxfam.org.nz/news/busted-world-trade-watchdog-declares-eu-us-farm-subsidies-illegal.

[46]   The following NGOs filed an amicus curiae brief in support of Brazil: Associação de Combate aos Poluentes (ACPO), Brazil; Associação de Proteção ao Meio Ambiente de Cianorte (APROMAC), Brazil; Center for International Environmental Law (CIEL), USA and Switzerland; Centro de Derechos Humanos y Ambiente (CEDHA), Argentina; Conectas Direitos Humanos, Brazil; Friends of the Earth Europe; The German NGO Forum on Environment and Development; Justiça Global, Brazil; Instituto O Direito por Um Planeta Verde Planeta Verde, Brazil. CIEL Press Release, "CIEL and a Coalition of European and Latin American NGOs Submit an Amicus Curiae Brief to the WTO's Appellate Body in the Brazil-Retreaded Tyres Case," October 11, 2007.

[47]   Jitendra, "Global Civil Society Organizations Support India's Stand at WTO," *Down to Earth*, July 16, 2015.

[48]   Richard Wike, Bruce Stokes, Jacob Poushter, Laura Silver, Janell Fetterolf, and Kat Devlin, "America's International Image Continues to Suffer," *Pew Research Center* (October 1, 2018).

IV. THE CHALLENGE OF GOVERNANCE (STATE–BUSINESS, STATE–SOCIETY RELATIONS)

A fourth challenge is a country's internal governance, which affects the role of law and expertise within it, its ability to avoid capture by corrupt political and economic elites, its capacity to coordinate among ministries to harness sector-specific expertise, its facility to manage relations with lower level units of government, and its capability to harness business and civil society support. Critically, a country's internal governance implicates its capacity to receive information from, incentivize the formation of expertise in, and steer collaboration with the private sector.[49] As Schneider and Maxfield write regarding business and the state in developing countries, "The lack of trust between economic agents can inhibit all types of beneficial exchanges and retard overall development . . . . Trust increases the voluntary exchange of information, makes reciprocity more likely even without active monitoring and disciplining, and generally reduces uncertainty and increases credibility on all sides."[50]

State capacity relies both on the building of internal bureaucratic expertise and on the development of complementary private expertise. This is why, in his influential book *Embedded Autonomy: States & Industrial Transformation*, Peter Evans contends that "'embedded autonomy' combines Weberian bureaucratic insulation with intense connection to the surrounding social structure."[51] According to Evans, for a developmental state to meet its "global challenges," it must incentivize entrepreneurial groups through what he calls "husbandry" and "midwifery," where state institutions assist, cajole, and induce private groups to venture into new areas for the state to meet its development goals.[52] An effective state, Evans theorizes, must have autonomy to ensure independence, cohesiveness, and coherence, but it also must be embedded in society to receive necessary input and incentivize key investments. "Embeddedness," he contends, "provides sources of intelligence and channels of implementation that enhance the competence of the state."[53] To turn back to this

---

[49] For quantitative analysis that suggests that this latter factor is important, see Christina Davis and Sarah Blodgett Bermeo, "Who Files? Developing Country Participation in GATT/WTO Adjudication," *The Journal of Politics* 71 (2009): 1033–1049; Marc Busch, "Democracy, Consultation and the Paneling of Disputes Under the GATT," *Journal of Conflict Resolution* 44 (2000): 425–446.

[50] Ben Ross Schneider and Sylvia Maxfield, "Business, the State, and Economic Performance in Developing Countries," in *Business and the State in Developing Countries*, eds. Sylvia Maxfield and Ben Ross Schneider (Ithaca: Cornell University Press, 1997), 14. Compare Vivek Chibber, *Locked in Place: State-Building and Late Industrialization in India* (Princeton: Princeton University Press, 2006); Charles F. Sabel, "Learning by Monitoring: The Institutions of Economic Development," in *The Handbook of Economic Sociology*, eds. Neil J. Smelser and Richard Swedberg (Princeton: Princeton University Press, 1994), 137–165.

[51] Peter Evans, *Embedded Autonomy: States and Industrial Transformation* (Princeton: Princeton University Press, 1995) (distinguishing predatory, rent-seeking bureaucracies from "developmental" types), 50.

[52] Evans, *Embedded Autonomy*, 13–14. I thank Joseph Conti for this point.

[53] Evans, *Embedded Autonomy*, 12, 248.

book's argument, the state similarly needs strong state–business and state–society relations to help it participate in developing and enforcing the rules of the game for the global economy. The state benefits when it develops public–private coordination mechanisms for negotiations, monitoring, litigation, and bargaining in the shadow of the law to defend and advance state and stakeholder interests, and, in turn, potentially shape the international legal order.

First, countries need to institutionalize *autonomous public sector expertise* to develop, coordinate, and advance state positions and to avoid regulatory capture. The trade bureaucracies of Brazil, India, and China are known for their meritocracy, which grants them a degree of autonomy. In Brazil, the Foreign Affairs ministry has a strong elite esprit de corps. To enter the high-level civil service in India, such as the Indian Administrative Service, and advance within it, is highly competitive. China has committed the largest amount of resources of the three to its trade bureaucracy, which presents China's public face as being globally and multilaterally committed.[54]

Given the implications of trade rules across ministries, the country's lead ministry also needs to develop and tap into internal systems of *bureaucratic coordination* on trade matters because different bureaucracies receive input from different constituencies. These internal processes can give rise to considerable internal bureaucratic wrangling. But they also can enhance the coherence and effectiveness of the state's external strategies in developing and supporting state positions. Although Brazil, India, and China are large and have significant trading stakes, they faced significant internal bureaucratic hurdles. These hurdles included, to varying degrees, a bureaucratic tradition of ministries assuming the lead on trade matters in which they were subject to traditional diplomatic rotations (inhibiting their ability to retain technocratic expertise and thus posing a major challenge for continuity), a lack of support from home capitals to the Geneva mission, and a lack of financial and informational support from the private sector.

To ensure that investments in legal capacity are effective, a country must overcome challenges of *continuity* in light of its diplomatic and bureaucratic traditions and professional career incentives. Studies of representation in international organizations find that, "besides the representatives from the key member states [such as the United States], the attribute most widely shared among the more influential actors in ... international organizations ... was long association with the organization."[55] Yet, the career advancement of many representatives in Geneva does not depend on their competence in technical WTO matters. As a result of the diplomatic rotation and career advancement system, a country's WTO unit in

[54]   Its ambassador to the WTO, Zhang Xianchen, for example, presents an image of a cosmopolitan China. In his opening remarks to the General Council in 2017, he cited Voltaire, David Ricardo, and Ecuadorian Quechuan muralist Oswaldo Guayasamín, as he stressed the importance of liberalized trade. "China Elevates 'Good Cop' on Trade to Counter Trump Barbs," *Bloomberg News*, April 11, 2017.

[55]   Robert Cox and Harold Jacobson, *The Anatomy of Influence: Decision-Making in International Organizations* (New Haven: Yale University Press, 1973), 395.

Geneva can suffer from a severe lack of continuity. By the time a replacement becomes versed in WTO matters, the delegate will move to an unrelated post. As a result, once diplomats are trained in WTO negotiations, monitoring, and dispute settlement, they can be replaced by personnel with little to no knowledge of the substantive and procedural complexities. These career trajectories and incentives undermine a country's defense of its trading and regulatory interests. These bureaucratic traditions can be difficult to change.

As we will see, this was a particular challenge for Brazil and India. For India, its bureaucratic organization provides that officials go to Geneva for a three-year term and those in the elite Indian Administrative Service then must return to India and work for a state government within the federal system on completely unrelated tasks, such as managing municipal waste. This worthy attempt to address the internal challenges of federalism in such a diverse country creates severe challenges for India's representation internationally, in particular where involving a highly technical organization such as the WTO. Continuity is also a challenge for Brazil where officials rotate to new positions every two to three years in the foreign affairs ministry. Brazil and India thus aimed to develop new ways to ensure continuity of trade expertise. China, in contrast, created a more specialized WTO track within its Ministry of Commerce. Even when officials move within the ministry, it is usually from one trade-related division to another. China still faces challenges of officials leaving the government (such as for higher salaries), but even then, many of them choose to work in trade, such as in a law firm, commercial firm, or in academia.

Many WTO missions also suffered from a lack of *support from national capitals*. In light of the considerable complexity of WTO rules and the WTO institutional structure, a delegate cannot possibly follow all WTO developments. There are over seventy different WTO councils, committees, working parties, and other groupings, involving thousands of meetings each year.[56] Through these processes, officials can advance national agendas, help ensure other countries respect their legal commitments, and defend regulatory policy space. These committee processes help countries monitor what their trade partners are doing, place pressure on them in a multilateral arena, and use them as part of bargaining in the shadow of the law. They also enable countries to advance and defend their positions in the development of new trade agendas.[57] Yet, unlike the United States and European Union, most countries cannot and do not fly officials from the capital for specific meetings, and overburdened Geneva-based delegates may receive little other support.

In addition, internal governance systems are critical for enabling bureaucratic autonomy to be embedded so that a country may build *public–private coordinative mechanisms* for trade negotiations, monitoring, litigation, and bargaining in the

---

[56] Bernard Hoekman, "Proposals for WTO Reform: A Synthesis and Assessment," *Minnesota Journal of International Law* 20 (2011): 324–364 (estimating over 5,000).

[57] Andrew Lang and Joanne Scott, "The Hidden World of WTO Governance," *European Journal of International Law* 20 (2009): 575.

shadow of the law. These mechanisms enhance a country's ability to access knowledge and expertise not only from different ministries but also from the private sector, local lawyers, academics, and civil society. Developing expertise within academia is key for generating new students and professionals on whose knowledge the state can subsequently draw, together with that of the professors. Transparency is important for obtaining input and avoiding regulatory capture.

Countries benefit when they develop routinized relations with the private sector to identify trade barriers and investigate, prioritize, and potentially challenge them. The private sector in many countries, such as India and China, however, has typically viewed international trade dispute settlement as the government's job. This perspective can pose a problem for trade officials who, in addition, have fewer public resources than their US and EU counterparts, who had already developed mechanisms to work with their own private sectors.[58] Even when governments compile lists of trade barriers, as China and Brazil have done, if they do not coordinate with the private sector, nothing may come of their efforts. As Denning writes, "Organizations that focus completely on collecting information with little or no effort to foster people connections end up with repositories of dead documents."[59]

Countries like Brazil, India, and China thus engage in programs to educate their firms and industry associations. In Brazil, the private sector has worked closely with the government. In India, the private sector has kept more distance from the government on trade dispute settlement, but it has become much more engaged with trade negotiations. Although China has worked to build relations with all of these groups, the private sector can be wary of too close scrutiny of the government. China's internal governance, in other words, could impede its access to information and thus effective interaction with the private sector and civil society. It is an open question whether its authoritarian turn under President Xi could curtail information flows and negatively affect economic growth.[60] The government nonetheless has found ways to incentivize other actors to work with it.

Given the judicialization of the WTO legal order, the role of domestic *courts and legal culture* is another important component of internal governance that helps explain variation in countries' challenges.[61] Courts and litigation long played a more

---

[58]   Shaffer, *Defending Interests*; Chad P. Bown and Bernard M. Hoekman, "WTO Dispute Settlement and the Missing Developing Country Cases: Engaging the Private Sector," *Journal of International Economic Law* 8 (2005): 861–890.

[59]   Stephen Denning, "Technical Cooperation and Knowledge Networks," in *Capacity for Development: New Solutions to Old Problems*, eds. Sakiko Fukuda-Parr, Carlos Lopes, and Khalid Malik (Sterling: Stylus, 2002), 242.

[60]   Statistically, there is evidence that democracies perform better economically, likely because of the effects of participation. Daron Acemoglu, Suresh Naidu, Pascual Restrepo, and James A. Robinson, "Democracy Does Cause Growth," *National Bureau of Economic Research, Working Paper No.* 20004 (2014).

[61]   David Nelken, "Legal Culture," in *Encyclopedia of Law and Society: American and Global Perspectives* 1 (2007): 370.

important role in Brazil and India, for example, than in China.[62] Litigation at the international level thus diverged less from their internal legal culture, which could give them advantages. This barrier, however, can be overcome, as a country adapts internally as part of its transnational engagement with the international trade legal order. China was quite reticent about WTO dispute settlement when it first joined, but since became active, normalizing the use of law and courts to resolve its international trade disputes. In parallel, despite China's authoritarian turn, courts and lawyers play an increasing role domestically so long as disputes are not politically sensitive or implicate powerful parties.[63] The growing role of courts in China potentially enhances its ability to use courts and arbitration for its own transnational legal ordering initiatives, which Chapter 7 examines.

This book assesses the development of trade law capacity as a key part of internal governance that affects broader state capacity. These processes can spur changes in domestic institutions that, recursively, can affect a country's ability to shape international ones.[64] The development of such internal legal capacity implicates the construction and flow of norms and practices both domestically and internationally.

V. CONCLUSION

To participate effectively in the international trade system, countries needed to build and maintain trade law capacity. They needed to develop coordinative mechanisms within government, complemented by mechanisms to obtain information and support from the private sector and civil society. Capacity-building endeavors generally are most sustainable if they permeate broadly throughout institutions and societies. If the focus of legal capacity building is on individual capacity instead of larger institutional and societal capacity, then countries will lose that capacity once individuals' career paths shift.[65] Legal capacity is not unrelated to material and structural power. Brazil, India, and China were much better positioned than small developing countries for this reason. Nonetheless, legal capacity was

---

[62] Megan J. Ballard, "The Clash Between Local Courts and Global Economics: The Politics of Judicial Reform in Brazil," *Berkeley Journal of International Law* 17 (1999): 239; Hiram E. Chodosh, Stephen A. Mayo, A. M. Ahmadi, and Abhishek M. Singhvi, "Indian Civil Justice System Reform: Limitation and Preservation of the Adversarial Process," *N.Y.U. Journal of International Law & Politics* 30 (1998): 1.

[63] Ji Li, "The Power Logic of Justice in China," *American Journal of Comparative Law* 65 (2017): 95, 139–140; *The Chinese Legal Profession in the Age of Globalization: The Rise of the Corporate Legal Sector and its Impact on Lawyers and Society*, eds. David Wilkins and Sida Liu (New York: Cambridge University Press, forthcoming).

[64] Compare Henry Farrell and Abraham Newman, "Domestic Institutions Beyond the Nation-State: Charting the New Interdependence Approach," 66 *World Politics* (2014): 331–363.

[65] Gregory Shaffer, "Can WTO Technical Assistance and Capacity Building Serve Developing Countries?," in *Reforming the World Trading System: Legitimacy, Efficiency, and Democratic Governance*, eds. Ernst-Ulrich Petersmann and James Harrison (Oxford: Oxford University Press, 2005), 245–270.

a necessary condition for them to become important players within the international trade legal order. As any country, they had different institutional heritages and faced discrete challenges, so that there was no single strategy that fit all of them. They each faced much greater challenges in developing trade law capacity than the United States and European Union. We turn now to examine how they respectively built it and adapted themselves in light of their own contexts to defend their interests and take on the major Western powers, thereby affecting the evolving ecology of the international legal order for trade.

PART II

The Cases of Brazil, India, and China

4

Building Legal Capacity and Adapting State Institutions in Brazil

With *Michelle Ratton Sanchez Badin*

Brazil has long shown promise of becoming an emerging power but never quite gotten there. After strong economic growth in the 2000s amid a commodity boom – culminating in a 7.5 percent growth rate in 2010 – its ambitions once more crumbled. A devastating recession struck; GDP plunged 3.5 percent in each of 2015 and 2016, and political scandal and crisis triggered the impeachment of President Dilma Rousseff. Despite these setbacks, Brazil remains among the world's ten largest economies, the dominant economy in Latin America – with around half of South America's landmass, population, and GDP – and a global leader in agribusiness that rivals the United States, being the world's top exporter of soybeans, poultry, sugar, and coffee. Although right-wing President Jair Bolsonaro personally aligns with the cultural populism of Donald Trump, China has become Brazil's most important trading partner so that Brazil's economy, including its powerful agribusiness sector, increasingly depends on China and the East.

Importantly for this book, Brazil was the first emerging economy to build the *legal capacity* to seriously challenge the United States and European Union in the WTO system. In doing so, it created models that India and China later borrowed, while adapting them to their own contexts. The Brazilian model involved significant shifts in its internal government organization and the government's relations with the private sector, civil society, and the legal profession, which officials referred to as the Brazilian three-pillar model.

The transnational legal order for trade, with the WTO at its head, had deep *implications within Brazil* along multiple dimensions, beyond changes in Brazilian law. It shaped the role of markets, the relative powers of Brazilian institutions, professional development, and accountability norms and processes. Through engaging with the WTO and the transnational legal ordering of trade and economic policy, Brazil significantly enhanced government transparency and developed new public–private partnerships. It reorganized its government institutions, while the private sector created new think tanks and hired foreign and domestic private law firms and consultants to engage with the government. Within the domestic Brazilian context, constituencies pushed for rival developmentalist and neoliberal policies. These contested internal processes responded to opportunities and constraints created by the WTO system, and they, in turn, attempted to shape that system for their own ends.

In adapting to the WTO, Brazil contributed to the *trade system's transformation*. Along with India and China, it blocked US and EU initiatives for new rules, symbolizing a major shift in power within the organization. It helped shape the development of WTO jurisprudence as a litigant, particularly regarding agricultural subsidies. In the process, it helped catalyze agricultural reform in Europe and the United States, as it pressed for new WTO rules on agricultural support, which eventually abolished agricultural export subsidies. Its early ability to use WTO law against the United States in politically sensitive areas portended what was to come with China (Chapter 6), which triggered US disenchantment, lambasting, and then neutering of the WTO Appellate Body. Brazil, in parallel, developed a complementary investment law model that provides an alternative to dominant US and European approaches. It also was active on intellectual property issues, involving struggles between competing domestic constituencies, and implicating the interface between patent law and the right to health. As the WTO lost relative authority and new trade and investment agreements proliferated, Brazil remains an important player in international economic governance as a large, emerging economy. Its trajectory is important for understanding the interaction of domestic and international processes as part of transnational legal ordering, the rise of emerging powers and decline of US and European dominance, US backlash, and the future of the international legal order for trade, investment, and economic relations.

I. THE BRAZILIAN STATE AND THE CATALYSTS OF CHANGE

A. *Brazil at the Time of Joining the WTO*

Institutional change occurs transnationally in light of a mix of internal and external factors. Brazil, like many Latin American countries, has veered left and right in its trade and development policies over time, but with the state always playing a key role in the economy, and with trade representing a relatively small percentage of GDP in comparison with other emerging economies, such as China and India.[1] In the 1960s and 1970s, in line with the development economics of the time, Brazil implemented highly protectionist "import substitution" policies to support industrialization and diversification of its economy. It did so both under the left-wing Presidency of Joao

---

[1] Trade as a percentage of GDP, for Brazil only reached a height of 29.58 percent in 2004, which compares to the US maximum of 30.89 percent in 2011, and which is much less than the height for China of 64.48 percent in 2006, and for India of 55.79 percent in 2012. In 2017, the figures were 24.2 percent for Brazil, compared to 26.58 percent for the United States, 37.8 percent for China and 40.64 percent for India. For figures on trade openness, www.theglobaleconomy.com/Brazil/trade_o penness/.

Goulart and the military dictatorship that overthrew him and maintained power until 1985.[2] Following the collapse of the Soviet Union and the success of export-oriented Asian economies, Brazil moved haltingly toward more export-oriented, trade-liberalizing policies, but it never followed a linear, consensual path, and the state always played a key role in regulating the market. Its development policy shifted in line with its politics, from enhanced social and industrial policies supporting a developmentalist state under the administrations of Lula and Dilma, to a return to a more liberal orientation under the administration of Temer (following Dilma's impeachment) and an uncertain mix of neoliberal and nationalist policies under the right-wing Bolsonaro administration.[3]

The country's political orientations always have been polymorphous.[4] On the one hand, Brazil wishes to be the regional leader of South America and a supporter of South–South collaboration. With this aspiration, it drove the development of the Mercosur customs union, which for some Brazilian officials represents the hope of a Latin American counterpart to US hegemony; collectively, Mercosur members constitute the world's fifth largest economy. Yet, many of its business and professional elites have close ties with the United States and some have long favored liberalizing trade and capital flows along a US model. The Bolsonaro administration has reoriented Brazil's policies toward greater alignment with the United States.

Joining the WTO in 1995 was a critical event for Brazil. The demands were severe, not only in terms of the reform of laws and institutions because of the WTO's vastly expanded scope compared to the GATT but also for the development of legal capacity if Brazil was to defend its interests in this highly legalized and soon to be judicialized international organization. Brazil benefitted from three attributes that helped it build trade law capacity to defend its interests: its renowned foreign diplomats, its well-funded trade associations, and its elite, cosmopolitan law firms.

First, Brazil has a professionalized Ministry of Foreign Affairs with a strong esprit de corps, where selection and advancement of officials are merit-based. The ministry is known for its unified institutional structure, relative autonomy, professionalism, and ability to adjust to outside developments. Other relevant ministries handling international trade matters, such as the Ministry of Trade, Industry and Services, partially replicated this structure. This professionalism facilitated Brazilian officials'

---

[2] Kathryn Sikkink, *Ideas and Institutions: Developmentalism in Brazil and Argentina* (Ithaca: Cornell University Press, 1991).

[3] For historical background: Matthew M. Taylor, *Decadent Developmentalism: The Political Economy of Stagnation in Brazil, 1985–2018* (Cambridge: Cambridge University Press, 2020); David Trubek, Diogo Coutinho, and Mario Schapiro, "New State Activism in Brazil and the Challenge for Law," in *Law and the New Developmental State: The Brazilian Experience in Latin American Context*, eds. David M. Trubek, Helena Alviar Garcia, Diogo R. Coutinho, and Alvaro Santos (Cambridge: Cambridge University Press, 2013), 28–62. Peter Evans labeled Brazil an "intermediate state" since the public sector did not meet the ideal type of the developmental states of East Asia because of greater corruption among elite factions. Peter Evans, *Embedded Autonomy: States & Industrial Transformation* (Princeton: Princeton University Press, 1995), 60–66.

[4] As the bossa nova singer-songwriter Tom Jobim quipped, "Brazil is not for beginners."

success in being appointed to serve as Director-General of key international organizations for trade, including of the United Nations Conference on Trade and Development (Rubens Ricupero, from 1995 to 2004), the Food and Agriculture Organization (José Graziano da Silva, from 2012 to 2019), and the WTO (Roberto Carvalho de Azevêdo, from 2013 to 2020).

Second, Brazil has well-funded and well-staffed trade associations, together with large individual companies, which facilitate businesses' ability to overcome collective action problems and work with the government. Brazilian legislation long included a compulsory tax, the proceeds of which went to all business associations, which often use the funds to hire economic expertise.[5] As elites circulate between government, business, and business associations, relatively close relations develop between the government, trade associations, and companies. The Brazilian government taps these human and financial resources to defend its and their interests under the trade legal order.

Third, in the past decades the largest, elite law firms in Brazil include lawyers who have trained abroad, combining international degrees with experience in large US law firms and international organizations. A number of them developed international trade practices handling trade remedies domestically and WTO and other trade-related work internationally. The law firms then could assist both the private sector and the government on trade issues. The WTO work was limited, but significant trade law capacity developed.

The international trade-related initiatives of these three groups – government, trade associations, and law firms – spilled into and linked with those of academia, thinks tanks, and civil society organizations. These links gave rise to further public–private coordination on trade matters. They fed into not only WTO work but also Brazil's negotiation and development of other trade, investment, and broader economic integration agreements involving relations with Mercosur, other Latin American countries, the European Union, United States, China, India, the OECD, and others. As a Brazilian official stressed to us, "don't forget that the trade focus of Brazil is not just on the WTO," but also includes the Food and Agricultural Organization for agriculture, different international standard-setting organizations, commodity organizations, the World Customs Organization, the OECD, and so on. "It's a big field and the challenge is how to be present in all of them," which requires intergovernmental coordination.[6] That

---

[5] Ben Ross Schneider, *Business Politics and the State in Twentieth-Century Latin America* (Cambridge: Cambridge University Press, 2004), 93–94, 101 ("[T]he statutory provisions for financing compulsory associations bankrolled some of the wealthiest business associations in Latin America," which included "compulsory membership dues," a "union tax," and "an additional 1 percent tax on payrolls to fund worker training").

[6] Interview, Brazilian official, Brasília, March 9, 2019. Moraes provides an example of the importance of intergovernmental coordination to address the interface between customs law, trade, and intellectual property protection before the WTO. Henrique Choer Moraes, "International Lawmaking by Transgovernmental Networks: Using Domestic Coordination to Address Asymmetries in Participation," *Journal of International Economic Law* 19 (2016): 821–843.

coordination is not easy because Brazil's positions before these institutions can be highly contested internally. These institutions provide opportunities for Brazilian interest groups in domestic policy contests. The outcomes of these internal contests determine Brazil's positions, which, in turn, help to shape the transnational legal order for trade.

B. *How Being on the Defensive Catalyzed Brazil's Investment in Trade Law*

Being on the defensive in two early, high-profile cases spurred Brazil to build trade law capacity. At the end of 1996, Canada challenged Brazil's subsidization of the aircraft company Embraer – the crown jewel for Brazil's industrial policy and a poster child of its privatization program in the 1990s. The case triggered widespread coverage in Brazilian media and politics and awakened the private sector regarding WTO law's implications. An even more controversial case followed when the United States challenged Brazilian patent law provisions in 2000 during the height of the AIDS crisis. The case rallied civil society organizations in Brazil and around the world behind the Brazilian government, once more generating significant media coverage.

These two cases helped spur the Brazilian government, private sector, and civil society to devote greater resources to WTO and other trade negotiations and dispute settlement.[7] After being placed on the defensive, Brazil developed systemic strategies involving a reorganization of the government bureaucracy and enhanced engagement with the private business sector, private lawyers, academics, and civil society organizations. This bolstering of Brazilian domestic WTO-related capacity led to Brazil's most highly touted successes in challenging the United States and European Union before the WTO, changing perceptions of the system within Brazil and internationally.

II. DIFFUSING EXPERTISE BY BUILDING A TRADE POLICY COMMUNITY

Brazilian public officials realized their need for outside legal and technical economic assistance, and Brazilian business, lawyers, and consultants developed expertise to work with the Brazilian government in international trade negotiations and dispute settlement, giving rise to a more pluralist trade law community.[8] To respond to the challenges and opportunities of WTO dispute settlement, Brazil developed

---

[7] Michelle Ratton Sanchez Badin, "Developmental Responses to the International Trade Legal Game: Cases of Intellectual Property and Export Credit Law Reforms in Brazil," in *Law and the New Developmental State: The Brazilian Experience in Latin American Context*, eds. David M. Trubek, Helena Alviar Garcia, Diogo R. Coutinho, and Alvaro Santos (Cambridge: Cambridge University Press, 2013), 246.

[8] Brazilian trade policy became more pluralistic in terms of the diffusion of trade-related expertise and the incorporation of views of different stakeholders in trade policymaking, involving business, consultants, and civil society.

what officials in the Ministry of Foreign Affairs call a "three-pillar" structure for WTO dispute settlement,[9] composed of:

(1) A specialized WTO dispute settlement division located in the capital, Brasília (the "first pillar");

(2) Brazil's WTO mission in Geneva (the "second pillar"); and

(3) Brazil's private sector, supported by foreign and domestic law firms and economic consultants, creating a critical mass of transnationally connected domestic expertise (the "third pillar"). The creation of this critical mass had spillover effects, spurring investments in trade-related expertise in the Brazilian private sector, academia, think tanks, and NGOs to contest and shape Brazil's positions on international trade and economic governance.

Although the "three-pillar" model focused on trade litigation, the diffusion of expertise had broader implications affecting the development of legal capacity for trade negotiations and implementation, as this chapter shows.

A. *Pillar 1: Reorganizing Government in the Capital*

The Ministry of Foreign Affairs, which has longstanding responsibility for representing Brazil before international organizations and with foreign governments, adapted its organizational structure by overhauling its departments for trade in the early 2000s. Until 2001, only one department in the Ministry handled all trade-related matters. When Celso Lafer, a former ambassador at the Brazilian mission in Geneva, became foreign minister in 2001, the Ministry created six specialized departments for trade to which it allocated increased human and budgetary resources for trade negotiations, monitoring, and litigation.

The Ministry prioritized international economic and trade matters. Brazil's three foreign ministers from 1995 to 2011 served previously as the country's ambassadors to either the GATT or the WTO, and its foreign minister from 2011 to 2013 also worked in the country's WTO mission.[10] As a result, Brazil's foreign ministers had in-depth experience with the WTO's organizational culture and the substantive economic issues at stake. Brazil's capital thus gave its Geneva mission strong political and logistical support.

In response to the demands of the WTO and broader trading system, multiple Brazilian ministries developed their own trade-related expertise, which the government

---

[9] Celso de Tarso Pereira, "Mission of Brazil to the WTO, Reactions: The Experience of Brazil and a Comment on Some Reform Proposals," *Presentation at International Trade and Sustainable Development Conference: Making the Dispute Settlement System Work for Developing and Least Developed Countries* (February 7, 2003).

[10] Luiz Felipe Lampreia served as Foreign Minister from 1995 to 2001, Celso Lafer from 2001 to 2002, and Celso Amorim from 2002 through 2011, in each case after previously serving as Brazil's ambassador to the GATT or WTO. Antonio Patriota served as Foreign Minister from 2011 to 2013 and had worked with Amorim at the mission from 1999 to 2001.

coordinated through different interministerial groupings. In 1995, following the WTO's creation, the government created an interministerial body, the Chamber of Foreign Trade (CAMEX), to formulate, adopt, coordinate, and implement trade policy.[11] CAMEX became a center of constant debate between the Ministry of Finance and the Ministry of Development, as well as other ministries, embodying the struggles between Brazilian liberals and developmentalists over trade policy. The government, in parallel, opened and restructured a series of other agencies, including an export promotion agency (*Agência de Promoção às Exportações*, APEX), an export insurance agency (*Seguradora Brasileira de Crédito*, SBCE), and export credit programs (PROEX at Banco do Brasil/BNDES and FINAMEX at BNDES) to help exporters cope with tight monetary policy and an appreciated currency.

Before 1995, no institutionalized forum existed within the Brazilian government where ministries could reach consensus regarding Brazil's positions on international trade matters. To participate effectively in CAMEX, ministries invested in developing trade-related expertise. As a Brazilian official stressed, "CAMEX has had a crucial role" in bringing trade issues to the attention of other ministries and clarifying issues for them, which has generated increased "expertise on trade matters within these ministries."[12] CAMEX includes a formalized body that provides a focal point for the private sector, the Private Sector Consultative Council (CONEX).[13] The government created CONEX to catalyze private sector engagement with trade negotiations and dispute settlement.

CAMEX brought together six ministers plus the presidential staff.[14] Three ministries bore primary responsibility for implementing Brazil's trade policy under CAMEX guidelines. Externally, the Ministry of Foreign Affairs played the central role, both in trade negotiations and in trade dispute settlement. Internally, the Ministry of Industry, Commerce and Service and the Ministry of Finance divided primary responsibility for implementing Brazil's trade policy for import protection and export promotion. The Ministry of Industry took responsibility for antidumping and countervailing duty investigations and general export promotion, while the

---

[11] CAMEX was created by Decree No. 1.386 (September 6, 1995).

[12] Welber Barral communication, when head of the Department of Foreign Trade (SECEX) within the Ministry of Industry, March 31, 2008.

[13] CONEX was created in 2003, but it started to operate in 2006 with up to twenty representatives from the private sector entities and civil society organizations. Resolução CAMEX No. 11, April 25, 2005. According to Decree N. 10.044 (October 4, 2019), CONEX was incorporated within the interministerial Council CAMEX.

[14] CAMEX's composition historically included representatives of the Presidential Chief of Staff; the Ministry of Industry, Commerce and Services; the Ministry of Foreign Relations; the Ministry of Economy; the Ministry of Agriculture; the Ministry for Planning and Public Management; the Ministry of Transports; and the President's General Secretariat (Ordinance n. 9,029, of April 10, 2017). The organization is in flux under the Bolsonaro government, but according to Decree 10,004 (October 4, 2019), CAMEX has been divided into a committee-like structure, comprised of the Strategic Trade Council, CAMEX Executive Committee, CAMEX Secretariat, CONEX, and a series of specialized committees.

Ministry of Finance handled customs and export credits.[15] The Ministry of Agriculture, in parallel, supported agribusiness, which became key for Brazil's exports and its current account balance.[16]

To engage more effectively on trade policy, Brazilian ministries invested in creating trade policy expertise. In 1998, the government created career tracks for foreign trade analysts ("*analistas de comércio exterior*").[17] Such candidates must have a background in international law, international economics, or international relations, and must pass an extremely competitive exam. After a training program, they work in the ministries associated with CAMEX, particularly the Department of Foreign Trade (*Secretaria de Comércio Exterior*, SECEX), which (until a reorganization under the Bolsonaro administration) was located within the Ministry of Industry. This highly competitive track attracted around 250 applicants per position.[18] In 2017, there were 730 foreign trade analysts, which were mainly allocated to the Ministry of Industry.[19]

During the *Embraer* case, Brazil's Ambassador to the WTO, Celso Lafer, needed increased support from Brasília to respond to the legal and technical demands of the WTO judicialized system. In 2001, the Ministry of Foreign Affairs responded by creating a specialized Dispute Settlement Unit (*Coordenação Geral de Contenciosos*), consisting of up to eight professionals in Brasília, complemented by two or three based in Geneva.[20] The Dispute Settlement Unit analyzes the legal and factual grounds for a WTO complaint, defines strategies, prepares and oversees outside lawyers' legal submissions, and represents Brazil in hearings before WTO panels and the Appellate Body and in settlement negotiations conducted after legal procedures begin. The unit also handles disputes arising under Mercosur, and it oversees the negotiation of new dispute settlement chapters in trade agreements, such as that between Mercosur and the European Union.[21]

The Dispute Settlement Unit provides a central contact point for affected businesses, trade associations, and their lawyers regarding foreign trade problems. Private

---

[15]   Under Decree 9679 of January 2, 2019, the Ministry of Industry, the Ministry of Finance and the Ministry of Planning merged into the Ministry of Economy.

[16]   Raw materials constitute about 50 percent of Brazil's exports, led by soybeans and soy products at around 17 percent, as of November 2019. Brazil Exports, Trading Economics, at https://tradingeconomics.com/brazil/exports.

[17]   Law n. 9,620, of April 2, 1998. The foreign trade analyst career track was created during the Cardoso administration to extend the professionalization of the Foreign Affairs Ministry's selection process to other ministries.

[18]   Barral Communication, April 2, 2008.

[19]   Associação dos Analistas de Comércio Exterior, www.aace.org.br/. In 2019 (under the Bolsonaro administration), they became part of the Ministry of Economy.

[20]   The Dispute Settlement Unit ranged from eight to three fully dedicated diplomats in a period of just a year (2016–2017). Interview by the authors with Brazilian officials, Ministry of Foreign Relation, March 8, 2018, and March 22, 2018. One Brazilian diplomat noted that they should have from twelve to thirteen people working in Brasília to be at the same level as the United States and the European Union. Interview with Member of the Brazilian WTO Mission in Geneva, June 28, 2017.

[21]   Interviews by the authors with Brazilian officials, March 8, 2018.

parties tend to first contact sectoral ministries and departments, which then work with the specialized unit. Once the Dispute Settlement Unit identifies a potential case, it works with other units within the Ministry of Foreign Affairs and other ministries regarding the substantive issues raised. Together they gather and evaluate factual support. The Dispute Settlement Unit then coordinates between the private sector, government agencies, and outside counsel assisting on the case.

The growing importance of trade law for Brazil triggered multiple ministries' interest. Within the Ministry of Finance, officials trained in trade policy pushed for a more liberal orientation within CAMEX during the Temer administration (2016–2018). They benefitted from the merging of the Ministry of Industry into the Ministry of the Economy in 2019 under the direction of Paulo Guedes, a University of Chicago-trained economist who earlier ran a major Brazilian investment bank and created the Brazilian neoliberal "advocacy think tank" Instituto Millenium in 2005 in Rio de Janeiro. Guedes represents the first time that a neoliberal economist reached a high position of power in Brazil.

WTO trade litigation also piqued the interest of the Federal Solicitor General's Office (known as AGU), which created a division on international affairs in 2010 and sought a lead role in the preparation of WTO cases. AGU is a decentralized federal agency that posts officials in Brazilian ministries who defend the federal government in domestic legal proceedings.[22] In 2014, AGU signed a memorandum of understanding with the Ministry of Foreign Affairs for the training of public attorneys in international cases with the possibility of integrating them into Brazilian dispute settlement delegations. In 2014 and 2015, the Federal Solicitor General's Office signed agreements with the World Trade Institute (WTI) in Berne and a trade policy institute (IELPO) in Barcelona to train its lawyers in WTO law, once more expanding the understanding of trade law and policy in Brazil, including in terms of domestic implementation in administrative law.[23]

B. *Pillar 2: Brazil's Mission in Geneva*

The Brazilian mission in Geneva forms the second pillar in Brazil's organization for WTO affairs. Since 2008, it has had a staff of around twenty diplomats dedicated to WTO and other international economic issues, which is among the largest delegations to the WTO alongside those of China and the United States. It represents

[22]   According to Article 131 of the 1988 Federal Constitution, the Federal Solicitor General's Office (Advogado-Geral da União) represents the Federal State in judicial and extra-judicial processes, and it is responsible for providing legal assistance and counsel to the Executive branch. On March 2, 2017, Decree N. 8,995 established that the Federal Attorney's General Office has the mandate to prepare the submissions to, and represent the Brazilian state before, the Inter-American Court of Human Rights and/or any other legal body established by an international treaty (Article 27.IV).

[23]   Interview with Boni de Moraes Soares, head of the international division at the Federal Solicitor General's Office (AGU), March 9, 2018 ("we want to have a team to support the Ministry of Foreign Affairs" so that Brazil has "more autonomy to bring cases").

Brazil in WTO Council and committee meetings in close coordination with Brasília. More broadly, it works to provide information and build capacity on trade matters in the government, the private sector, civil society organizations, and academia. The Geneva mission organizes a four-month internship program for private lawyers, academics, private sector representatives, and civil servants.[24]

The Ministry of Foreign Affairs created the internship in 2003 in response to pressure from Brazilian law firms to hire them for WTO matters rather than foreign firms, illustrating the more bottom-up process of capacity building in Brazil compared to India and China.[25] Through the internship, the Ministry believed that Brazilian lawyers could gain experience and be better positioned to compete in rendering legal services to the government and private sector. The Ministry hired an outside trade specialist to oversee the four-month program, which each year issued three calls for applications. In 2007, the mission expanded the program to include government officials from other ministries and agencies (such as for agriculture, import relief, finance, and intellectual property), as well as business professionals (such as from Brazil's largest industry associations, the Federation of Industries of São Paulo and the National Confederation of Industry). The internship had a significant impact in diffusing expertise. For example, the first intern from another ministry to complete the internship subsequently became head of Brazil's anti-dumping investigative unit. One of her successors likewise came from the internship program. The interns remain in contact, fostering subsequent interministerial coordination and public–private partnerships. By the end of 2018, after sixteen years, 205 interns had completed the internship, helping to expand, deepen, and refresh the Brazilian trade policy network.[26] The Geneva program's success spurred the Dispute Settlement Unit within the Foreign Affairs Ministry to create its own internship program in Brasília in 2004, and the government also created internship programs in its domestic import relief authority (applying Brazil's antidumping law) and in Brazil's embassy in Washington, DC, further diffusing expertise.

As a government official noted to us, "We are trying to spread knowledge of the system in order to create a critical mass."[27] As another official emphasized, the internship program helps "train Brazilian lawyers to facilitate their contact with WTO rules and procedures so that in the future they can help Brazil's private sector."[28] The program was widely admired by missions in Geneva. Although India and China did not directly copy it, its success helped catalyze their creation

---

[24] It also has a twitter account – @OMCBrasil – which regularly provides an update on WTO developments and work opportunities in the mission, which replaces its former bulletin *Radar Genebra*. The publication was previously known as *Carta de Genebra*, until it changed its name to *Radar Genebra*.

[25] For more detail, Gregory Shaffer, Michelle Ratton Sanchez, and Barbara Rosenberg, "The Trials of Winning at the WTO: What Lies Behin Brazil's Success," *Cornell International Law Journal* 41, no. 2 (2008): 383–502.

[26] Email from Beatriz Stevens, Coordinator of Internship Program from 2016 to 2018, June 24, 2019.

[27] Interview with Brazilian Representative, Geneva, February 1, 2005.

[28] Interview with Member of Dispute Settlement Unit, Brazil Foreign Ministry, April 19, 2004.

of their own variants for building trade law capacity in the private sector and private law firms, as Chapters 5 and 6 document, in turn helping to circulate WTO norms through professional training and career competition.

C. *Pillar 3: Private Business, Law Firm, Academic, and Civil Society Networks*

Until the 2000s, most knowledge of international trade law matters in Brazil, from negotiations to dispute settlement, was limited to government representatives predominantly located within the Ministry of Foreign Affairs. Few law firms or economic consultants dealt with international trade-related issues. The legalization and judicialization of international trade relations changed this situation. The WTO catalyzed the development of trade law expertise in the private sector, including business, law firms, think tanks, academia, media, and civil society networks. The resulting Brazilian private sector initiatives deepened knowledge about international trade issues among an array of individuals and groups, many of whom are linked to transnational networks. It is this community that Brazilian officials called the "third pillar" for trade policy and dispute settlement.

Brazilian Trade Associations and Consultancies

Brazil's major business associations reorganized to respond to the significant challenges posed by the liberalization of Brazil's internal market and the new trade opportunities abroad. They wished to engage more effectively with government officials over Brazil's negotiating positions in the WTO and other trade negotiations, such as the proposed Free Trade Agreement of the Americas (negotiated from 1994 through 2005), the EU-Mercosur Free Trade Agreement (signed but not ratified in 2019), and other bilateral and regional agreements. Industry and agricultural trade associations held different views, with industry being much more protectionist and even hostile, but they worked to strengthen their alliances to coordinate their demands.

To prepare for the negotiation of a Free Trade Agreement of the Americas in the late 1990s, Brazil's industrial and agricultural sectors created a novel trade association – the Brazilian Business Coalition (*Coalizão Empresarial Brasileira*) – which broke with Brazil's traditions of sectoral interest groups.[29] It focused on one issue – trade negotiations. The National Confederation of Industries (CNI) assumed leadership to consult with members, formulate the private sector's position on negotiations, and advocate before government agencies. In parallel, Brazil's large industry

---

[29]   The Coalition brought together more than 170 Brazilian business associations and enterprises under a single umbrella. Pedro da Motta Veiga, "Trade Policy-Making in Brazil: Transition Paths," in *The trade policy-making process, level one of the two level game : country studies in the Western Hemisphere,* eds. Sylvia Ostry, Peter Hakim, and Juan José Taccone (Washington, DC: Inter-American Development Bank, 2002): 13–21.

and agricultural associations and companies created new international trade departments and personnel positions. The Industry Federation of São Paulo (FIESP),
which represents eighty percent of the country's industrial production, and CNI,
both had departments on foreign trade policy since the 1950s, but they dealt
primarily with customs matters.[30] By the end of the 1990s, business associations
developed specialized trade policy departments that proactively analyzed and lobbied on trade.

In parallel, entrepreneurs created think tanks and consultancies to inform, advise,
and assist the government and private sector on trade negotiations and litigation.
Examples include:

(1) Agroicone, a consultancy founded in 2003 by large agribusiness associations
    to conduct research and support Brazil and its agribusiness in international
    trade negotiations. It was central to Brazil's WTO negotiating agenda for
    agriculture in the Doha Round;

(2) DATAGRO, a consultancy of economists and statisticians who provide global
    market analysis and statistical studies for companies and government minis-
    tries in Brazil and abroad. It provided critical statistical analysis for the *EC-
    Sugar* and *US-Cotton* cases;

(3) Barral M. Jorge Associates (BMJ), created in 2011 by former Minister of Trade
    Miguel Jorge and former Secretary of Commerce Welber Barral, which
    combines international trade work with government relations. It played
    a key role in preparing Brazil's challenge in the *Indonesia-Chicken* case
    while working for the main poultry association, the Brazilian Producers and
    Exporters of Poultry (ABEF);[31] and

(4) Uno International Trade Advisors, a consultancy formed by ex-interns from
    the Ministry of Foreign Affairs program in Geneva that is linked to an
    international network of consultancies working on trade remedies, technical
    barriers to trade, and trade strategies.

This expertise circulated in and out of government, like in the United States but
unlike in India and China. Trade associations and companies hired former government officials for their knowledge and access to trade policymaking. A former deputy
minister in the Ministry of Agriculture, Pedro de Camargo Neto, engineered the
gathering of funds through Brazil's cotton trade association to hire the US law firm
Sidley Austin and successfully challenge US cotton subsidies. The Brazilian
Sugarcane Industry Association hired Elisabeth Serodio, who alternated between
it and appointments in agriculture-related government agencies. She then became

---

[30] Interview, Christian Lohbauer, Director, International Relations Department, FIESP, São Paulo,
     April 23, 2004.
[31] In 2018, the consultancy had around twelve consultants working in the international trade department,
     including lawyers, economists, and accountants. Interviews with trade lawyers and consultants in
     Brasilia in November 2017, and March 2018.

a private consultant who provided technical support to the association and the government in Brazil's acclaimed challenge to EU sugar subsidies.

Individuals moved among enterprises to develop their professional careers. For example, Christian Lohbauer, after working as director of the International Relations unit at FIESP, transferred to the Brazilian Producers and Exporters of Poultry (ABEF) (2006–2009), then to the Association of Exporters of Citrus (CitrusBR) (2009–2013), and then to the pharmaceutical company Bayer Brazil where he became Vice President of Government Relations (2013–2017).[32] Another former member of the FIESP trade department, Beatriz Stevens, coordinated the government's internship program in its WTO mission in Geneva from 2016 to 2018 before returning to the private sector. Similarly, lawyers who started their careers in law firms moved to private trade associations to work on trade issues.

Brazilian Law Firms

The government and private sector benefitted from private Brazilian law firms' and lawyers' investments in trade law expertise, as was the case in India and China. Although the market is limited, knowledge of trade law within Brazilian law firms grew significantly.[33] Brazil's elite law firms are the largest in Latin America and they long worked on cross-border matters, specializing in inbound investment and commercial transactions, antitrust law, and (more recently) "compliance work" relating to anti-bribery law. These firms have an association named the *Centro de Estudos das Sociedades de Advogados* (CESA, or the Law Firm Study Center) that created a technical group on international trade, bringing together twenty-five private lawyers in 2002, the year that Brazil launched the *US-Cotton* and *EC-Sugar* cases. This group coordinated meetings among lawyers and government representatives to discuss trade issues, including the role of the private bar in representing Brazil's commercial interests.

Private lawyers, through CESA, complained that the government only hired foreign law firms to assist it in WTO disputes.[34] The Ministry of Foreign Affairs responded that the government did not select the law firms since the affected private parties paid the attorneys' fees, but emphasized that it would welcome the development of expertise on WTO law within the Brazilian bar.[35] On the law firms' urging, the Ministry of Foreign Affairs created its internship programs. Although the amount

---

[32] Other examples include Antonio Josino Meirelles Neto who worked at CNI, moved to large private entities, and then the Brazil Industries Coalition (BCI) in Washington, DC. Diego Bonomo, currently at CNI, earlier worked at BCI.

[33] Rubens Glezer et al., "Transforming Legal Capacity in Brazil: International Trade Law and the Myth of a Booming Practice," in *The Brazilian Legal Profession in the Age of Globalization*, eds. Luciana Gross Cunha et al. (Cambridge: Cambridge University Press, 2018), 264–293.

[34] "Cesa Realiza Estudos Sobre Comércio," *Valor Econômico*, July 28, 2003; Shaffer, Sanchez, Rosenberg, "The Trials of Winning."

[35] Interviews with Brazilian Officials and Law Firm Representatives, in Brasilia and São Paulo, 2005 and 2017.

of law firm work is small compared to other areas, the Brazilian business sector hired ex-interns to provide counsel on some trade disputes and other trade law matters, starting with the *EC-Bananas* arbitration procedure in 2005, followed by the *Brazil-Tyres* and *Brazil-Taxation* cases.[36]

The government formalized its hiring of Brazilian law firms for certain categories of WTO cases through a legally regulated bidding process. Responding to pressure from law firms, the government launched for the first time a bid to hire lawyers to assist it in the *Brazil-Tyres* case in 2005. The European Union had challenged a Brazilian regulation banning the import of retreaded tires on health and environmental grounds. The government viewed it as a matter of public interest and so it did not accept private sector funding from the tire industry to hire an outside law firm. It rather hired its own law firm, although the tire industry also hired the Demarest firm to follow the case. Following this bid, and after a lawsuit that Brazilian law firms brought against the government (which would be unthinkable in China), all public bids for the following types of WTO cases must include a foreign and Brazilian law firm hired by the government: (1) where there is a broader public interest at stake (such as environmental and health protection) or where government public policy does not coincide with that of the affected economic sector (such as when multiple economic sectors have different interests); (2) when Brazil is a respondent; and (3) when a complex case before the Appellate Body level raises systemic concerns.[37] Otherwise, the government typically will work with a private law firm that the affected private sector selects and hires, as in the *US-Cotton* and *EC-Sugar* cases where sectoral trade associations hired the US law firm Sidley Austin. The sequence of public tenders served to enhance networking between domestic law firms and foreign law firms to work on trade disputes, gradually enlarging the number of Brazilian firms involved.[38]

Media, Academic, and Civil Society Networks

Brazilian media covered the country's engagement with the WTO on the front pages, diffusing interest in and knowledge about international trade in the country.[39]

---

[36] For example, Demarest Advogados worked for the tire industry in the *EC-Tyres* case and the government in *Brazil-Taxation*. Demarest partner Jose Diaz was among the first interns in Brazil's Geneva mission. As of 2018, his group included nine trade lawyers and two interns working exclusively on international trade issues. Interview at firm's office, São Paulo, March 7, 2018. The law firm of Machado, Meyer, Sendacz e Opice worked for the Brazilian banana sector in the *EC-Bananas* arbitration case (brought by its associate André Brickmann Areno who had been an intern).

[37] The firms brought judicial action n. 2007.34.00.030189–7 because under the Notice of Bidding Brazilian law firms could only participate as a subcontractor. Interviews with ministry officials working in the dispute settlement unit, in Brasilia, October 2018.

[38] Interviews with lawyers and government officials from 2017 until 2018.

[39] During the late 1990s, two leading newspapers (*Gazeta* and *O Estado de São Paulo*) posted full-time journalists in Geneva to follow WTO issues. In 2017, one full-time specialized journalist working for *Valor Econômico* and a part-time journalist working for *O Estado de São Paulo/ Folha de São Paulo-UOL* remained. Interview with Brazilian Mission official and Geneva-Based journalist, 2017.

To ensure sophisticated coverage, the business community, under the leadership of agribusiness, created a program to train Brazilian media on trade issues – a bottom-up process that again differs from China.[40] In 2004, "the most commented news item in Brasília – and certainly by President Lula's Administration – was the Brazilian victory in two international disputes before the World Trade Organization," the cotton and sugar cases respectively against the United States and European Union. The media's coverage increased Brazilian public awareness of WTO rules and their importance for the Brazilian economy. In the 2006 Presidential election, "the two main candidates argued tirelessly about which party (the Workers' Party or Social Democratic Party) won more claims at the WTO."[41] When President Dilma Rousseff advocated her developmentalist industrial policy (named *"Plano Brasil Maior"* or Greater Brazil Plan), she too spoke of WTO law, in this case about fair trade to protect Brazilian competitiveness.[42]

Academics taught and wrote on international economic law, disseminating Brazilian perspectives in global debates, starting with trade law and then turning to investment law – a process that mirrors developments in India and China.[43] New trade law study networks and trade policy institutes developed. Think tanks on international economic relations formed, sponsoring research and organizing symposia on a broad range of international economic law issues.[44] In 2010, the Fundação Getulio Vargas (FGV), which is ranked among the world's top ten think tanks, founded the Center for the Study of International Trade and Investment (*Centro de Estudo do Comercio Global e Investimento*) in São Paulo, led by Vera Thorstensen after she led the government's internship program in Geneva. In 2014, the WTO recognized and funded FGV as a regional WTO Chair program to organize research, conferences, workshops, and online training on trade.

[40] From 2004 until 2007, the agribusiness-funded think tank ICONE and the American Chamber of Commerce in São Paulo organized courses of "trade for journalists" which trained around fifty journalists in São Paulo and Rio de Janeiro. These and other journalists took further courses on trade organized by Brazil's largest private foundation and think tank, such as the regular specialization course at the Getulio Vargas Foundation (GVlaw). Shaffer, Sanchez, and Rosenberg, "The Trials of Winning."

[41] Welber Barral, "The Brazilian Experience in Dispute Settlement," *U.N. Economic Commission for Latin America & The Caribbean*, 21 U.N. Doc. LC/W. (August 2007), 147 (citing Carolina Glycerio, "Política Externa Gera Embate Acalorado Entre Lula e Alckmin," *BBCBrasil.com*, October 9, 2006).

[42] Portal do Planalto, Press Release, *Presidenta Dilma lança Plano Brasil Maior, Nova Política Industrial do País*, August 10, 2011.

[43] Shaffer, Ratton Sanchez, and Rosenberg, "The Trials of Winning" (referencing different academic networks).

[44] In 1998, a group of intellectuals, businessmen, government authorities, and academics founded the Brazilian Center of International Relations (*Centro Brasileiro de Relações Internacionais*) in Rio de Janeiro, which models itself in some ways on the U.S. Council of Foreign Relations. In 2006, a group of trade experts that had worked for the National Confederation of Industry founded CINDES (*Centro de Estudos de Integração e Desenvolvimento*), which in turn works within the Latin America Trade Network coordinated in Buenos Aires. Ibid. (also referencing ICONE).

Trade concerns spurred civil society demands for transparency and access. In 2001, leading Brazilian NGOs formed the Brazilian Network for the Integration of Peoples (*Rede Brasileira pela Integração dos Povos, REBRIP*), a coalition of around fifty-three NGOs that include major Brazilian trade unions and social movement organizations, as well as branches of foreign NGOs and alliances with other social movements. REBRIP gained access to government officials and to international fora during the administrations of Lula and Dilma, focusing particularly on negotiations. REBRIP also has supported the government as respondent in WTO cases that raise social policy concerns.[45] REBRIP organizations became active in the creation of the Reflection Group on International Relations (Grupo de Reflexão sobre Relações Internacionais, GR-RI) in 2012 to cover other issues in Brazilian foreign policy and to enhance access for social movement groups.[46] After President Rousseff's impeachment, REBRIP organized resistance to the neoliberal policy agenda of the interim government, which it continues today. Greater institutionalization of trade liberalization incited civil society reaction in Brazil, India, and other countries, which, in turn, played into the ongoing development of the international trade law regime.

III. TRANSNATIONAL LEGAL ORDERING OF TRADE POLICY

The Brazilian government harnessed this trade-related legal capacity to enhance its ability to participate in trade negotiations, monitoring, and litigation, and to implement international rules in line with its priorities. Brazilian public officials and private lawyers have overlapping interests. The government benefitted from the diffusion of WTO legal expertise in Brazil so that qualified Brazilian specialists were available for consulting with government and industry. Through working with the government, Brazilian practitioners learned about trade law and dispute settlement to market themselves to companies, trade associations, and the government as consultants. Brazil's engagement with the WTO and other international trade-related institutions not only shaped the international legal order for trade. It also shaped Brazilian law, institutions, and practice. Actors contested these developments given their conflicting perspectives and interests, as they aimed to shape domestic and international law and policy.

A. Negotiations: Becoming a Critical Player at the WTO

Brazil was never a driver of trade negotiations during the GATT years, including those that led to the WTO in 1995 when the United States and European Union

---

[45] Juana Kweitel and Michelle Sanchez Badin, "Participação da Sociedade Civil: Comércio, Saúde e Meio Ambiente na OMC," *Cadernos Direito GV* N. 17, 2007.

[46] GR-RI was more active in consulting with and submitting comments to the Ministry of Foreign Affairs when the ministry was more open to public participation under the Workers' Party, as was Brazilian foreign policy generally. The group publishes and maintains a website regarding its activities: http://brasilnomundo.org.br/.

largely controlled the agenda. Although Brazil, like India, was invited to restricted "green room" meetings during the GATT, it lacked a significant voice in shaping negotiations.[47] After the WTO was created and a new "development" round of trade negotiations launched in Doha in late 2001, Brazil established itself as an essential party in WTO negotiations. It aimed to build bridges among WTO members to advance its primary goal of eliminating export subsidies for agriculture, significantly reducing domestic agricultural support around the world, and enhancing market access through tariff reductions.[48] Celso Amorim, the foreign minister at the time, described his feeling of being part of a group viewed as the "new brats in the neighborhood," which included India.[49]

In preparation to the WTO Ministerial Meeting in Cancun in 2003, Brazil worked with others to create a more level-playing field in agricultural trade through reducing US and European subsidies. The government harnessed expertise from the private sector through public–private networks to advance its positions, working closely with the agribusiness sector. The agribusiness-funded think tank ICONE provided the econometrics and simulations that enabled the government to devise negotiating modalities to counter a US and EU joint proposal. The government worked closely with India to ensure that the proposal accommodated India's need to safeguard its rural population, and together they built a new negotiating group, the G-20 trade group of developing nations that included China.

The United States and European Union realized that they would have to work with the G-20 if a deal were to be made. For a time, a new "quad" for trade negotiations arose, consisting of the United States, European Union, Brazil, and India, producing what one ambassador in Geneva called a "tectonic shift" in the WTO.[50] For the first time, emerging economies were critical to the WTO's functioning. Suddenly the United States and European Union were no longer the sole

---

[47] According to Blustein, the fact that Brazil and India looked for exceptions to the rules on their behalf catalyzed a GATT working rule that if you do not commit, you should not block a decision, Paul Blustein, *Misadventures of the Most Favored Nations: Clashing Egos, Inflated Ambitions, and the Great Shambles of the World Trade System* (New York: PublicAffairs, 2009), 66. Compare Nicolas Lamp, "How Some Countries Became 'Special': Developing Countries and the Construction of Difference in Multilateral Trading," *Journal of International Economic Law* 18 (2015): 743–771, 770 ("Just as the term 'special' is inextricably linked to a conception of what is normal', the concept of 'special and differential treatment' is premised upon an acceptance that what the developed countries do in the trading system is 'normal', and that the developing countries should aspire to eventually do the same"). Nonetheless, Brazil was a member of the Cairns Group of agricultural exporting countries that, broadly speaking, allied with the United States in creating greater liberalization and legal disciplines for agricultural trade.

[48] The World Bank projected that Brazil, along with China, would be the largest beneficiaries among developing countries from the round's conclusion. Blustein, *Misadventures of the Most Favored Nations*, 217.

[49] Celso Amorim, *Breves Narrativas Diplomáticas* (São Paulo: Benvirá, 2013), 79.

[50] Kristen Hopewell, *Breaking the WTO: How Emerging Powers Disrupted the Neoliberal Project* (Stanford: Stanford University Press, 2016), 81; Amrita Narlikar, *New Powers: How to Become One and How to Manage Them* (New York: Columbia University Press, 2010). The identity of the inner circle would change, becoming the "Five Interested Parties" in 2004 (with the inclusion of Australia)

"demandeurs" for trade liberalization, and they were placed on the defensive to reduce their massive agricultural subsidies.

Brazil used its success in WTO dispute settlement to advance its negotiating proposals. The *US-Cotton* and *EC-Sugar* cases helped it catalyze support for the elimination of agricultural export subsidies and significant changes in domestic support. These cases generated considerable international political and media attention regarding the impacts of US and European agricultural subsidy programs on agricultural production in developing countries, and they provided tools for opponents of the subsidies in US and European internal political debates.[51] Although the Doha round of negotiations collapsed, and members turned to bilateral and plurilateral trade agreements, Brazil catalyzed normative settlement over the issue of agricultural export subsidies, which WTO members agreed to eliminate at the 2015 WTO Ministerial meeting in Nairobi. In the process, the European Union completely revamped its agricultural support programs, starting in 2003, to reduce their trade-distorting effects by decoupling them from production and retooling them toward sustainability and rural development. The United States also revised its farm programs toward less trade-distorting forms of support.[52]

Specialized bodies working inside government and the private sector supported these efforts. In the public sector, the Ministry of Foreign Affairs and a new Department of International Affairs of the Ministry of Agriculture (created in 2005) worked increasingly together. This specialized department facilitated the appointment of agriculture attachés in Brazilian embassies and missions in major capitals.[53] Private sectoral associations individually and collectively (through the National Agriculture Confederation) prepared studies and worked with them on negotiations. The agribusiness-funded think tank ICONE was central. As one Brazilian negotiator stated, its "technical capacity was the miracle making it possible for us to make proposals and convince people."[54] In parallel, Brazilian officials "met frequently with NGOs in Geneva, giving them 'a free pass' to the Brazilian mission and sharing strategy, analysis, talking points, and messaging."[55]

---

and a G-7 in 2007 (with the addition of China and Japan). Blustein, *Misadventures of the Most Favored Nations*, 183, 262–263.

[51] As one Brazilian official stated, "The cotton case showed not only internationally but I think mostly domestically in the U.S. how distorting and unfair [US] agricultural policies are. And that may be in [the] long run, a very positive development." Interview with Brazilian official, May 20, 2005, in Joseph A. Conti, "The Good Case: Decisions to Litigate at the World Trade Organization," *Law & Society Review* 42, no. 1 (2008): 145.

[52] Hopewell, *Breaking the WTO*, 84.

[53] In 2010, a first group of eight agricultural attachés were appointed to important missions in Buenos Aires, Washington, Brussels, Geneva, Moscow, Pretoria, Beijing, and Tokyo. In 2016, the Brazilian government created thirteen additional positions for agriculture attachés. The Ministry of Foreign Affairs trained them on international trade policy before they started.

[54] Hopewell, *Breaking the WTO*, 116 (citing an interview).

[55] Ibid., 119 (citing an interview with Brazilian diplomat).

After 2015, when it became clear that the Doha Round negotiations had collapsed, Brazil significantly shifted its position on negotiating "new" issues at the WTO on a "plurilateral" basis.[56] In 2017, after a change in government following the impeachment of President Rousseff, Brazil made new proposals for negotiations on electronic commerce, electronic signatures, small and medium enterprises (SMEs), and investment facilitation. Similar to US and EU strategies, Brazil proposed what it already accomplished or was developing in Mercosur regarding these issues, just as the United States brought what it accomplished through NAFTA to the WTO in the 1990s.[57] In these new negotiations, Brazil recognized that "the only way to make progress at the WTO" would be through ad hoc plurilateral agreements.[58] The European Union's ambassador to the WTO told us that "the biggest conversion" in attitudes toward WTO negotiations is Brazil, which formed "an offensive trade agenda, and not only in agriculture."[59] Brazil understood that it did not fare well in the 1980s when it was beset by US unilateral pressure. It thus did what it could to support the multilateral system.[60]

B. *Negotiating New Webs of Trade and Economic Law Agreements*

Brazil long favored *multilateral* negotiations and coordination over bilateral ones. Its success in coordinating the G-20, however, spurred a shift in US and European tactics, which moved to bilateral negotiations outside the WTO, affecting the ecology of transnational legal ordering.[61] Brazil was wary of this shift. As the United States challenged the WTO and multilateralism, and as the United States, European Union, and others turned to bilateral trade agreements, Brazil continued to defend the importance of trade multilateralism, both for purposes of opening access for Brazilian agricultural goods and for protecting national autonomy from great power coercion. It nonetheless recognized the need to engage with these developments pragmatically. More recently, policymakers of a neoliberal orientation in the Temer and Bolsonaro administrations went further and began to prioritize bilateral trade negotiations. They are using international economic law and institutions, in part, to advance their domestic policy goals. In doing so, they tap into

[56]   Interview, Brazilian official, Geneva, June 28, 2017 (Brazil became "more realistic and open to new issues in the WTO"); Interview, Brazilian official, Geneva, July 11, 2019.

[57]   Interview, WTO Secretariat official, July 5, 2017.

[58]   Interview, Brazilian official, June 28, 2017. WTO members effectively adopted a plurilateral approach with the Trade Facilitation Agreement (on customs processing) at the Bali Ministerial Meeting in 2013. Groups of WTO members have since been discussing and negotiating plurilaterally over trade in services, investment facilitation, and other initiatives, in the General Council and at the 2017 WTO Ministerial in Buenos Aires. Interview, Brazilian official, Brasília, March 9, 2018.

[59]   Interview, EU Ambassador, Marc Van Heukelven, Geneva, June 30, 2017.

[60]   Interview, Brazilian official, June 28, 2017.

[61]   After the Cancun ministerial meeting collapsed, USTR Robert Zoellick announced a new program of bilateral agreements with "can-do countries." Robert Zoellick, "America Will Not Wait for the Won't-Do Countries," *Financial Times*, September 22, 2003.

existing trade-related expertise, illustrating the links between international and national legal change.

The 2014–2016 economic crisis and the ensuing political instability in Brazil triggered a reorientation of its trade policy. After the Rousseff administration responded to the crisis with protectionist policies, businesses pushed for more active Brazilian engagement in bilateral, regional, and plurilateral trade negotiations, organized around the Brazilian Business Coalition.[62] Celebrating its twentieth anniversary, the Coalition launched a new *International Agenda for Industry* in 2016. This annual publication sets forth industry's priorities for Brazilian foreign trade and investment policy. The industry works closely with government officials, and it launches its proposals with government representatives present. In 2019, the CNI launched 110 trade policy proposals, stressing that "a country more integrated to the world, produces, innovates and generates more jobs, [which requires . . .] greater and better participation of Brazil in the international market."[63] Despite high tariffs, Brazil's industries were losing market share in Brazil to Chinese imports and sought a new strategy to enhance their competitiveness. This development represents a significant change from their earlier protectionist positions.

Brazil faces particular challenges concluding bilateral trade agreements since all tariffs must be negotiated under the auspices of Mercosur, requiring consensus within the Mercosur bloc. Most of Brazil's bilateral agreements traditionally have been with other Latin American countries, conducted within the framework of the Latin American Integration Association (known as ALADI), based in Montevideo, Uruguay. Under the ALADI framework, Mercosur concluded free trade agreements with Bolivia (1997), Chile (1996), and Peru (2005), and preferential trade agreements (covering fewer tariff lines) with Colombia (2005), Ecuador (2005), Mexico (2002), and Venezuela (2005).[64] These agreements' coverage is expanded through periodic negotiations.

More recently, Brazil initiated a series of more ambitious negotiations on trade-related regulatory issues with countries in the Pacific Alliance – the trade liberal bloc of Chile, Colombia, Mexico, and Peru that represents about 35 percent of regional

---

[62] According to Diego Bonomo of the International Affairs Department at CNI, which serves as the Secretariat for the Brazilian Business Coalition, the main axes of its work are market access and trade facilitation. Interview, Diego Bonomo, March 8, 2018.

[63] CNI, "CNI Launches the 2019 International Agenda for Industry," *Global Business Coalition*, March 20, 2019, http://globalbusinesscoalition.org/gbc-news/cni-launches-the-2019-international-agenda-of-industry/ (quotation from the CNI's Director of Industrial Development, Carlos Abijaodi).

[64] The Association was created in 1980 under the Montevideo Treaty and it promotes the gradual development of a common market for Latin America. The dates within parentheses are those for the treaty's entry into force, unless otherwise indicated. Around 70 percent of trade among ALADI countries is exempt from tariffs. Ministry of Foreign Affairs, "The Latin American Integration Association," *Governo do Brasil*, www.itamaraty.gov.br/en/politica-externa/integracao-regional/5975-aladi-en- The Montevideo Treaty is covered under the 1979 Enabling Clause to the GATT, which allows for preferential trade agreements among developing countries that do not cover "substantially all trade," which is otherwise required by GATT Article XXIV.

GDP. In 2016, it made its first commitments on government procurement and regulatory coherence in its agreement with Peru, following which it announced in 2020 that it would join the WTO plurilateral Government Procurement Agreement. In 2018, it signed its first trade agreement with Chile apart from Mercosur, which included nontariff subjects such as trade facilitation, regulatory coherence, trade in services (covering all services except those expressly excluded in a "negative list"), electronic commerce, and anticorruption rules. These agreements served as testing grounds for the government to coordinate among ministries and with the private sector before negotiating with larger developed countries, where the economic consequences are higher.[65] Through these agreements, Brazil also aimed to better position itself as a potential node for global value chains.[66]

Under the Temer and Bolsonaro administrations, Brazil prioritized bilateral trade negotiations with major economies. Brazil had not signed any ambitious agreement with a country outside of Latin America until a landmark one between Mercosur and the European Union in June 2019, after twenty years of on-and-off negotiations. Before then, Brazil had signed free trade agreements outside of Latin America only with three Middle Eastern governments, done mainly for political reasons.[67] In contrast, the European Union agreement is massive, as it is Brazil's second largest trading partner after China. If ratified, the reduction of Brazilian tariffs for EU producers will give them a significant advantage over foreign rivals and put competitive pressure on Brazilian manufacturers. The agreement contains chapters on sanitary and phytosanitary standards, services, intellectual property, government procurement, and an environmental and labor chapter, among others. It notably excludes an investment chapter providing for investor–state arbitration and many intellectual property provisions often found in US free trade agreements and included in the EU's Comprehensive Economic and Trade Agreement with Canada.

Through Mercosur, Brazil not only concluded negotiations with the European Union but launched trade talks with Canada (in 2018), Japan (in 2017, since suspended), the EFTA countries (in 2016), South Korea (in 2017), Lebanon and Tunisia (in 2016), Singapore (in 2018), and Mexico (in 2019).[68] Brazilian officials also signaled interest in negotiating an agreement with the United States.[69] They

---

[65]   Interview, Official of Ministry of Industry, March 8, 2017.

[66]   Comisión Económica para América Latina y el Caribe (CEPAL) and Instituto de Pesquisa Econômica Aplicada (IPEA), "La Matriz de Insumo-Producto de América del Sur: Principales Supuestos y Consideraciones Metodológicas," CEPAL/IPEA, June 2016, www.ipea.gov.br/portal/images/stories/PDFs/mip-sudamericana-junio2016.pdf.

[67]   Brazil signed agreements with Israel (2010) and Egypt (2017) that are in force, but the Brazilian Congress has yet to approve that with the Palestinian Authority (2011).

[68]   EFTA is the European Free Trade Area, composed of Iceland, Liechtenstein, Norway, and Switzerland.

[69]   "Brazilian Official Says Country is Ready of 'USMCA-like' Trade Deal With U.S.," *World Trade Online*, November 6, 2019.

even threatened to leave Mercosur if a populist government in Argentina thwarts its trade agenda.[70]

Although Brazil's trade is increasingly oriented toward Asia, with China being Brazil's largest trading partner since 2009, Brazil likely will not sign a trade agreement with China or formally join China's Belt and Road Initiative, at least under the Bolsonaro administration. Nonetheless, the two countries have engaged in regular trade and investment facilitation talks, and Brazil remains in need of Chinese funding for infrastructure, whether through Chinese state banks or the New Development Bank (the BRICS Bank).[71] Brazil's agribusiness and extractive industries have opened key offices in Asia,[72] and, in 2018, the government reassigned two important officials from its WTO mission in Geneva to Beijing, exemplifying China's rise in importance for trade and investment and the WTO's decline.[73] Meanwhile, Brazil also is exploring the possibility of expanding the scope of its preferential agreement with India.[74]

C. *Monitoring and Dispute Settlement*

The government and private sector monitor compliance with WTO commitments and, in particular, the application of nontariff barriers that concern Brazil's agribusiness sector. Agricultural and semi-processed food products are subject to sanitary, phytosanitary, and other technical barriers to trade. Brazil developed specialized agencies in the late 1990s, such as INMETRO and the Brazilian Export and Investment Promotion Agency (APEX), which help monitor foreign nontariff trade barriers.[75] Brazil's foreign embassies do as well.[76] Private consultancies and law firms work with the government and industry to monitor and challenge them

[70] Simone Preissler Iglesias and Rachel Gamarski, "A Latin American Brexit? Analyzing Brazil's Threat on Mercosur," *Bloomberg*, September 14, 2019.

[71] Chapter 7 of this book. Gustavo de L. T. Oliveira and Margaret Myers, "The Tenuous Co-Production of China's Belt and Road Initiative in Brazil in Latin America," *Journal of Contemporary China* (2020).

[72] For example, Marcos Jank, who earlier founded ICONE to assist agribusiness on trade issues and then became President of Brazil's trade association for sugar, moved to Singapore where he was CEO of the Asia–Brazil Agro Alliance, which unites the Brazilian agribusiness associations for beef, poultry, and sugar with the Brazilian Export and Investment Promotion Agency and the Brazilian Ministries of Agriculture and Foreign Affairs. He then led the Center on Global Agribusiness at Insper, an educational institution in Brazil.

[73] Key diplomats Celso de Tarso Pereira (former head of Brazil's Dispute Settlement Unit) and Felipe Hees (former head of Brazil's antidumping authority) moved from the Geneva mission to Beijing in 2018.

[74] Brazil concluded preferential trade agreements having minimal coverage with India (2009) and the Southern African Customs Union (2016). President Bolsonaro visited China in October 2019 and India in January 2020, during which the countries signed agreements to improve bilateral trade and investment.

[75] Interview, Augusto Castro, General Manager of APEX, March 9, 2018. INMETRO is the national agency in charge of technical regulation.

[76] Email exchange with Brazilian diplomat in Brussels, July 23, 2019.

bilaterally, within WTO committees, and eventually in WTO dispute settlement. For example, UNO Trade prepared studies on nontariff trade barriers for INMETRO, in close dialogue with industry associations.[77] Similarly, BMJ's work for agribusiness on nontariff barriers eventually led to a WTO case against Indonesia for blocking imports of chicken from Brazil.[78]

Figure 4.1 summarizes Brazil's annual and cumulative participation as a complainant and respondent in WTO dispute settlement. Although Brazil primarily was a respondent in the WTO's first years, it filed a flurry of complaints from 2000 to 2002; it was the most active WTO complainant in 2001, from which it gained experience as a repeat player. Many of these cases were strategically important, factually and legally demanding, and broke new ground in WTO dispute settlement, such as the *US-Cotton* and the *EC-Sugar* cases challenging agricultural subsidies. After 2002, Brazil continued to be a party on average around once per year, and was frequently a third party, as captured in Figure 4.2.

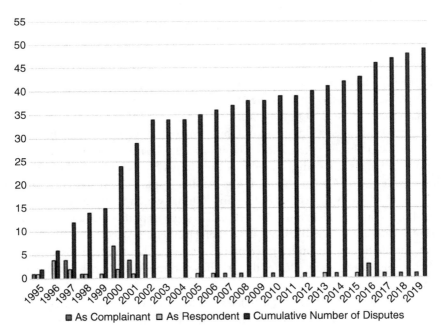

FIGURE 4.1 Brazil as complainant and respondent in WTO dispute settlement (1995–2019)[79]

---

77 Interview, Roberto Kanitz, Head of UNO Office in São Paulo, March 6, 2018. Some of UNO's studies can be found at http://unotrade.com/br-office/publicacoes/.

78 *Indonesia – Measures Concerning the Importation of Chicken Meat and Chicken Products*, WT/DS484. Interviews with Barral, October 2017 and March 2018, Brasília. Barral reported that non-tariff barriers had become central to his consultancy, which he had not expected.

79 Compilation from the WTO database (January 2020).

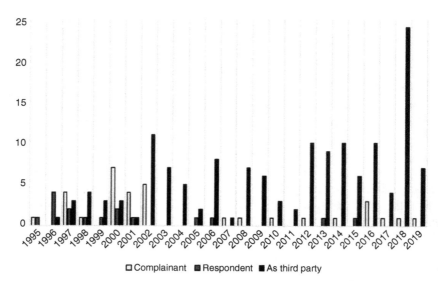

□ Complainant   ■ Respondent   ■ As third party

FIGURE 4.2 Brazil as party or third party (1995–2019)[80]

The years 2001 and 2002 were the high points of Brazil's activity, where it commenced thirteen cases. Overall, it was a party in forty-nine cases as a complainant or respondent in the WTO's first twenty-five years, which makes it the sixth most active WTO member in WTO dispute settlement, after the United States (279), European Union (190), China (sixty-five), Canada (sixty-three), and India (fifty-six), through 2019. Moreover, it was a third party in 147 additional cases. Its primary targets as a complainant were the United States (eleven), the European Union (seven), and Canada (four). It also was the first emerging economy (besides Mexico) to file a WTO complaint against China, which it did in October 2018 regarding a Chinese safeguard against Brazilian sugar imports – breaking an implicit rule of *détente* among the BRICS.[81] Brazil's engagement in WTO dispute settlement as a party and third party built a reservoir of knowledge about WTO substantive law, judicial procedures, and strategies that it diffused through its domestic trade policy network.

Brazil's tit-for-tat cases against Canada on subsidies for their aircraft manufacturers represented the dawn of a new era for Brazilian (and subsequent Indian and Chinese) public–private partnerships in trade dispute settlement.[82] The cases lasted

[80] Ibid. This chart is based on the dates on which cases were filed, and not the dates on which the WTO Dispute Settlement Body adopted the rulings.
[81] Brazil hired a Brazilian along with a US law firm for the case. Interview, Brazilian lawyer, São Paulo, March 2018. Brazil also has brought a case against Indian domestic support for the sugar producers in 2019.
[82] The Brazil-Canada (Embraer-Bombardier) case numbers at the WTO are WT/DS46; WT/DS70; and WT/DS222.

seven years from 1996 to 2003, and they involved intensive interaction between Brazilian officials and law firms hired by Embraer to defend its interests. In the words of one Washington counsel, the legal complexities involved in the cases were "light years away" from the GATT.[83] No longer was there any pretense that this was a quasi-legal, quasi-diplomatic process of state-to-state dispute settlement. Embraer funded Brazil's case, engaging a US team of lawyers to respond to Canada's initial complaint against Brazil's subsidies and commence Brazil's own complaint against Canada's subsidization of Embraer's rival Bombardier. Brazil included the lawyers hired by Embraer in its delegation to the WTO hearings.

At the time, the Brazilian government lacked a legal unit in Brasília to handle the cases. A young diplomat at Brazil's Geneva mission, Roberto Carvalho de Azevêdo, successfully oversaw the outside lawyers' work and handled the oral argument, together with Brazil's Ambassador to the WTO. Azevêdo's success in the cases helped catapult his rise within the Ministry of Foreign Affairs to become Brazil's Ambassador to the WTO and then the Director General of the WTO itself. This highly technical, time-demanding case motivated government and private sector efforts to systematize public–private coordination for WTO dispute settlement, catalyzing the government's creation of its Dispute Settlement Unit in Brasília, the internship program for private Brazilian attorneys at the Geneva mission, and WTO research groups and networks in major Brazilian cities. The cases spurred Brazil's creation of its three-pillar model.

Brazil's subsequent complaints against US and EU agricultural subsidies in 2002 – *US-Cotton* and *EC-Sugar* – were even more demanding, with WTO implementation proceedings lasting until 2005 in the sugar case and 2009 in the cotton case.[84] These two cases had huge implications for agricultural trade. The government would not have brought them without private sector support. The Brazilian cotton sector consisted of many producers, of varying size, with limited capacity to address trade law issues. Entrepreneurs, therefore, had to organize and convince the producers to pool their resources through a trade association to help pay the outside legal counsel and consultant fees, particularly those of the US law firm Sidley Austin.[85] In parallel, Oxfam and other NGOs rallied support against the US subsidies, and Brazil attached a statement from Oxfam to its legal submissions regarding the subsidies' adverse impact on West African producers, which the panel referenced.[86] In the *EC-Sugar* case, the sugar trade association again hired Sidley Austin, but it also worked with a Brazilian consulting firm, DATAGRO, to provide economic analysis of the subsidies' impact on world prices. It was the first time that a Brazilian consulting firm worked on a WTO dispute.

---

[83]   Interview, Counsel, Washington, DC, February 19, 2008.
[84]   The United States and Brazil finally settled the cotton case by an agreement in 2014 based on a final US payment to Brazil in the amount of US $300 million, following earlier payments of US $497 million, in addition to US changes to its subsidies to the cotton sector. Congressional Research Service, *The WTO Brazil-U.S. Cotton Case* (2014).
[85]   The actual amount of the costs may have exceeded $2 million. Interview, Private lawyer, July 20, 2005.
[86]   *United States – Subsidies on Upland Cotton*, WT/DS267/46 (2004), para. 7.54.

DATAGRO later provided technical support in the *EC-Bananas* arbitration regarding the EU's revised bananas import regime, and in the *Brazil-Tyres* case.[87]

This process became systematized. In 2018, the private sector again funded Brazil's WTO complaints in *Canada-Aircraft* (DS522) and *China-Sugar* (DS568). In the aircraft case, Embraer hired the US law firm King & Spalding, which also counseled Embraer when Brazil was a third party in US and EU challenges to each other's aircraft subsidies in the so-called Boeing-Airbus disputes.[88] In the sugar case, the Brazilian sugar association hired a Brazilian law firm, a US-based law firm, and a consortium of Brazilian experts in Asia.[89]

Brazil also provided a potential model to other emerging economies by working successfully with domestic law firms without the participation of a US or European counterpart. In the early 2000s, the Brazilian Poultry Association (ABEF) and Brazil's soluble coffee industry association (ABICS) funded the São Paulo-based law firm Veirano Advogados to work with the government in two successful WTO cases against Argentina and the European Union.[90] Then, André Brickmann Areno of the Brazilian law firm of Machado, Meyer, Sendacz e Opice, who earlier gained experience as an intern at the Brazilian mission in Geneva, worked with the government in the *EC-Bananas Arbitration*. Del Monte, the largest exporter of bananas from Brazil, funded the case.[91] In 2014, Brazil again used only Brazilian lawyers in a case challenging Indonesian technical and phytosanitary barriers against Brazil's poultry industry.[92] The Brazilian Poultry Association and the Brazilian Association of Animal Protein (ABPA) hired the Barral M. Jorge consultancy, to work with the government. Barral and Renata Amaral, then director of BMJ's international trade group, had worked in Brazil's department for antidumping investigations and with Brazil's private sector on nontariff barriers to trade, once more illustrating public–private career linkages.[93] The WTO panel ruled in Brazil's favor in 2017, and the two countries agreed to an implementation schedule in 2018.

---

[87]   Interviews with Brazilian officials, Ministry of Foreign Affairs, April 20, 2004.

[88]   King & Spalding had assisted Embraer in Brazil's participation as third party in the Boeing-Airbus cases (WT/DS353, WT/DS347). Interview, Government official, March 8, 2018. In 2017, Boeing acquired 80 percent of Embraer, following Airbus's acquisition of 50.1 percent of Bombardier in 2017.

[89]   Interview, Brazilian lawyers, March 6, 2018.

[90]   WT/DS241 (2003); WT/DS269 (2005). The 2000 complaint in *EC – Measures Affecting Soluble Coffee* followed an earlier one brought by Brazil against the European Union's system of preferences program. The lead lawyer Ana Caetano had worked at O'Melveny & Myers in Washington, DC, in an earlier complaint brought by Brazil against the European Union (*EC – Measures Affecting Differential and Favourable Treatment of Coffee*, 1998). After receiving an LLM degree at Georgetown University Law Center, Caetano continued working with the sector and leads a team of four trade lawyers. Interviews, Ana Teresa de S. L. Caetano, April 23, 2004, and March 6, 2018.

[91]   The Bananas Arbitration was linked to EU compliance with the decision in the original *EC-Bananas* case (WT/DS27).

[92]   WT/DS484 (2014).

[93]   While at SECEX, Barral worked on WTO negotiations and was a panelist in WTO cases. At the consultancy, they increasingly worked on issues involving technical barriers to trade. Interview, Barral, March 2018.

These cases show how Brazil adapted its institutions and broadened its internal expertise so that the Brazilian government and private parties could obtain domestic WTO-related legal assistance at a lower cost. Although Brazilian law firms are relatively less experienced than leading US and European firms in WTO disputes, the firms' fees are much lower. In the words of a Sidley Austin lawyer, the American firm lost business to these Brazilian law firms because "Brazil has done what it promised to do" – create domestic legal capacity on WTO matters.[94]

Brazil's success with WTO litigation – using a public–private partnership model coordinated by a specialized dispute settlement unit – enhanced Brazil's credibility. Its reputation, in turn, strengthened its hand in settlement negotiations conducted in the shadow of potential litigation.[95] Brazil settled nineteen of its first thirty-three WTO complaints without litigation. Through diffused expertise, the state was strengthened in its international trade relations.

D. Implementation, Policy Space, and Regulatory Coherence

It is a mistake to view the development of the international trade law system only at the international level, with its multilateral, regional, and bilateral dimensions. The trade legal order is a transnational one, shaped by and deeply implicating domestic institutions, professions, and practices. Contests among domestic actors over domestic law, policy, and institutions form part of its ecology. We have assessed how Brazil developed domestic institutions to shape the international trade legal order through negotiation, monitoring, and litigation. Yet the trade legal order also affects Brazilian domestic institutions, law, and policy. Viewed transnationally, the trade legal order not only requires legal expertise to implement international commitments in ways that are supportive of domestic policy goals but also provides leverage for those pushing for certain types of domestic policy change.

Harnessing Legal Capacity as a Respondent; the Implications for Domestic Policy

Many WTO complaints raise developmental and social concerns that implicate domestic policy. Brazil needed legal capacity to defend its policy space in these

---

94   Interview, Brazilian lawyer, São Paulo, March 7, 2018 (recalling a conversation when the lawyer worked at Sidley Austin).

95   For example, Brazilian officials cite disputes with Thailand regarding barriers to Brazilian sugar exports and South Africa regarding an antidumping preliminary determination on Brazilian poultry exports where the threat of WTO litigation was helpful in formulating a settlement. The sugar association hired Brazilian lawyer Adriana Dantas, who had earlier worked at King & Spalding in Washington, DC, to assist it in the case against Thailand. Interviews, Brazilian official, Geneva, June 28, 2017; Brazilian Official, Brasilia, March 22, 2018.

cases, which involve the implementation of WTO law.[96] In some cases, such as the aircraft subsidy cases, the affected private sector will fund private lawyers to defend the case.[97] In others, the Brazilian government will directly hire a law firm to protect the country's systemic interests.[98] In cases implicating social policy, civil society activists may pressure and directly or indirectly assist the government in its response.

The *Brazil-Tyres* dispute exemplifies a case of systemic importance because, although the government's ban on the import of retreaded tires clearly violated WTO law, the government had a defense in light of environmental and health concerns with waste tires. The case rallied civil society organizations. The Ministry of Foreign Affairs coordinated with the Environment Ministry, which provided key support on the environmental issues, in contact with the NGOs.[99] For the first time, Brazilian NGOs filed an *amicus curiae* brief before a WTO panel backing the government, together with a US-based NGO.[100] The NGOs spurred media coverage from an environmental and health perspective in support of the government's position. The WTO panel and Appellate Body found largely in favor of Brazil and its right to ban the importation of retreaded tires on health and environmental grounds.[101]

Brazil's response to the US challenge to its patent law in 2000 further exemplifies civil society's potential role, in this case to help offset US leverage. In the *Brazil-Patent* case, the United States dropped its complaint regarding Brazil's requirement of "local working" of patents after the government orchestrated an international campaign that framed the case in public health terms, supported by

---

[96]   As of December 31, 2019, WTO members had filed requests for consultations sixteen times against Brazil, but only five of these complaints were fully litigated, and Brazil largely prevailed in two of them. The Brazilian government worked with private law firms in all five cases in which a panel was formed, whether funded by it or the private sector.

[97]   The private sector also funded Brazil's defense in the early case *Brazil – Measures Affecting Desiccated Coconut* (1996).

[98]   The Brazilian government engaged Sidley Austin through a public bid. Private trade associations nonetheless hired Brazilian lawyers to follow and provide input. As Dias Varella writes, "The national actors in favor of restricting imports came both politically and legally stronger than those against it." Marcelo Dias Varella, "Implementing DSB Reports: An Analysis Based on Brazil's Retreaded Tires Case," *Wisconsin International Law Journal* 32, no. 4 (2013): 699, 722.

[99]   "Brazil Tyres Update," *BRIDGES Monthly* v. 10, n. 6, September to October 2006; *Bridges Weekly Trade News Digest*, July 11, 2006, p. 6 (noting that "Brazilian Environment Minister Marina Silva met with civil society representatives in Geneva … following the first panel hearing." The government also took "the unusual step of making all of its written submissions and oral statements in the tyre dispute publicly available," both in English and Portuguese).

[100]   The *amicus curiae* brief was filed by Associação de Combate aos Poluentes (ACPO), Associação de Proteção ao Meio Ambiente de Cianorte (APROMAC), Center for International Environmental Law (CIEL), Centro de Derechos Humanos y Ambiente (CEDHA), Conectas Direitos Humanos, Justiça Global, Instituto O Direito por Um Planeta Verde Planeta Verde.

[101]   The Appellate Body found that Brazil violated the most-favored-nation clause because it permitted the import of tires from Mercosur. Brazil complied by extending the ban to such imports. WT/DS332/AB/R (December 3, 2007).

national and international civil society groups. Advocacy groups maintained that the US government had placed corporate interests above life-and-death medical concerns.[102] Under political pressure, catalyzed by human rights and AIDS activists, as well as international organizations, the Bush administration withdrew the US complaint.

Space for Industrial Policy Experimentation

As Alvaro Santos writes, it is important to view trade law both as "a sword to open markets and a shield for heterodox policies."[103] Santos rightly contends that "developmental legal capacity" is thus required, one that is grounded in a state's development context and is open to experimentation to enhance its developmental prospects. Given that Brazil has implemented WTO law through statutes and is bound by WTO law, the head of the international division of the Federal Solicitor General's Office told us that, in relation to the WTO, the office's "first role" is to "ensure compliance with WTO law by Brazilian public authorities."[104] What compliance means, however, is subject to legal interpretation, affecting implementation. A country thus needs legal capacity to assess WTO legal constraints and flexibilities. Constituencies advance their different interpretations of WTO commitments to advance their policy preferences.

Brazil has attempted to support industrial innovation through state support, such as through the tax incentives of the Lula administration's Program for Productive Development and the Dilma administration's Greater Brazil Plan, whose motto was "innovate to compete, compete to grow."[105] The government created new institutions, such as the Brazilian Agency for Industrial Development and renamed the Ministry of Industry, which became the Ministry of Development, Industry and Foreign Trade, reflecting a developmentalist orientation. Most funding came through the Brazilian National Development Bank (BNDES), which has an annual

---

[102] The United States brought the complaint under the TRIPS agreement against Article 68 (paragraph 1) of the Brazilian Intellectual Property Law, which requires the "local working" of a patent – that is, the local production of a patented invention as a condition for the recognition of an exclusive patent right. Sanchez Badin, "Developmental Responses to the International Trade Legal Game," 246–300.

[103] Alvaro Santos, "Carving Out Policy Autonomy for Developing Countries in the World Trade Organization," in *Law and the New Developmental State: The Brazilian Experience in Latin American Context*, eds. David Trubek, Helena Alviar Garcia, Diogo R. Coutinho, and Alvaro Santos (Cambridge: Cambridge University Press, 2013), 167–245.

[104] Interview, Boni de Moraes Soares, Head of the International Division of AGU, March 9, 2018. Some officials nonetheless question the extent to which lawyers within ministries from the Office of the Attorney General are prepared to play an important role in consulting on WTO-related matters. Email, Brazilian Official (July 23, 2019).

[105] After the Greater Brazil Plan (2011–2014), the Dilma administration adopted the *Plano Nacional de Exportações* (2015–2018). While the former focused on tax relief, financing, and protection of the domestic market through trade remedies, the latter included trade promotion, market access through trade agreements, and trade facilitation.

loan portfolio that at times has tripled that of the World Bank.[106] Before Brazil's economic crisis of 2014–2016, BNDES created new innovation financing instruments and strategies through which it took equity positions as an angel investor and worked with capital market investment groups to form venture capital funds.[107] It sought to parallel government finance of innovation in East Asia, aiming for Brazilian companies not simply to be buyers but also makers of innovation.[108]

In 2013, Brazil faced a major WTO legal challenge to its industrial policy, which formed a key part of the Rousseff administration's Greater Brazil Plan. The European Union and Japan challenged seven programs benefiting different Brazilian industrial sectors, including autos electronics, information technology, and semiconductors, mostly involving fiscal relief.[109] According to the European Union, this case – *Brazil-Taxation* – was "one of the most comprehensive disputes ever launched by the EU."[110] As one of the Brazilian lawyers working on the disputes remarked, this case raises "big issues" involving "philosophical" questions about the role of the state in the economy and economic development.[111]

The case went not only to the heart of the Rousseff administration's Greater Brazil Plan but also to the longstanding role of Brazil's developmentalist state. Brazil's response demanded expertise not only to defend its developmental policy space in the litigation. It also required legal capacity for implementation choices following the ruling. For sophisticated attorneys, the issues addressed in WTO litigation and

---

[106] Shunko Rojas, "Understanding Neo-Developmentalism in Latin America: New Industrial Policies in Brazil and Colombia," in *Law and the New Developmental State: The Brazilian Experience in Latin American Context*, eds. David M. Trubek, Helena Alviar Garcia, Diogo R. Coutinho, and Alvaro Santos (Cambridge: Cambridge University Press, 2013), 107.

[107] Mario Schapiro, "Rediscovering the Developmental Path? Development Bank, Law, and Innovation Financing in the Brazilian Economy," in *Law and the New Developmental State: The Brazilian Experience in Latin American Context*, eds. David M. Trubek, Helena Alviar Garcia, Diogo R. Coutinho, and Alvaro Santos (Cambridge: Cambridge University Press, 2013).

[108] Compare Evans, *Embedded Autonomy*; and Alice Amsden, *The Rise of the "Rest": Challenges to the West from Late-Industrializing Countries* (Oxford: Oxford University Press, 2001), 277–281.

[109] The challenged policies were: (i) Incentive Scheme for Technological Innovation and Consolidation of the Automotive Supply Chain – *Programa de Incentivo à Inovação Tecnológica e Adensamento da Cadeia de Fornecimento Automotivo* (Inovar-Auto); (ii) Informatics program – *Lei de Informática*; (iii) Special Regime for the Purchase of Capital Goods for Exporting Enterprises – *Regime Especial de Aquisição de Bens de Capital por Empresas de Exportação* (RECAP); (iv) Digital Inclusion programme – *Programa de Inclusão Digital*; (v) Programme of Incentives for the Semiconductors Sector – *Programa de Apoio ao Desenvolvimento Tecnológico da Indústria de Semicondutores e Displays* (PADIS); (vi) Programme of Support to the Technological Development of the Industry of Digital TV Equipment – *Programa de Apoio ao Desenvolvimento Tecnológico da Indústria de Equipamentos para TV Digital* (PATVD); and (vii) an additional program applied for exporter companies, Regime for Predominantly Exporting Companies, known as PEC. For more details, WT/DS472/R-WT/DS497/R and WT/DS472/AB/R-WT/DS497/AB/R.

[110] "The EU Wins WTO Dispute Challenging Brazil's Tax Subsidies in the ICT, Electronics and automotive Sectors," *European Commission*, August 30, 2017, http://trade.ec.europa.eu/doclib/press/index.cfm?id=1708.

[111] Interview, Brazilian lawyer, São Paulo, March 6, 2018.

implementation intersect. Brazil sought clarity in the case regarding which industrial policy options were available to it. The litigation, in turn, shaped interpretive possibilities in Brazil, so that actors probe flexibilities that the rulings leave open, whether by design, inadvertence, or context.

A group of Brazilian private sector associations organized to fund the defense and hired three law firms based in São Paulo to support different aspects of the case. Veirano Advogados represented the Association of the Electrical and Electronics Industry (ABINEE), Pinheiro Neto represented the Brazilian National Association of Vehicle Manufacturers (ANFAVEA), and Demarest Advogados represented a group of exporters coordinated through the Brazilian National Confederation of Industries.[112] The Ministry of Foreign Affairs' Dispute Settlement Unit worked directly with these law firms and the federal ministries and agencies whose programs were challenged. In parallel, the Ministry of Foreign Affairs launched a public solicitation for a law firm to help oversee the case before the WTO Appellate Body, and selected Pablo Bentes of the US firm Steptoe & Johnson, together with a local Brazilian partner.[113] Although Brazil lost most aspects of the case, the Appellate Body reversed the panel's findings against two of the seven programs and it granted Brazil more time for implementation of the rulings regarding the other five.[114]

A key issue was how Brazil would implement the Appellate Body report, which would have significant domestic policy implications regarding Brazil's industrial policy, triggering internal policy contestation. The implementation choices are both political and legal, and they attract competing constituencies. Trade associations hire law firms and consultants to prepare analyses on compliance, such as Pinheiro Neto regarding reform of the Inovar-Auto program in light of the WTO decision.[115] Officials in the more neoliberal-oriented Finance Ministry hoped to leverage the

---

[112]   Interviews, São Paulo and Brasília, March 2018. Pinheiro Neto partner Rene Guilherme da Silva Medrado, after studying at Columbia Law School, worked at Sidley Austin and was an intern in the WTO Rules Division. He has since been a panelist in a WTO antidumping case. Pinheiro Neto has a team of eight lawyers working on trade issues. Interview, da Silva Medrado, March 6, 2016.

[113]   Interview, Government officials, October 2018. Bentes is a Brazilian who earlier was an intern in the Brazilian embassy in Washington, DC, and, in 2006, joined as Legal Officer at the WTO Appellate Body Secretariat. As part of the bid, Steptoe worked with the Brazilian law firm Barbosa Mussnich Aragao (BMA). Adriana Dantas was the lead partner at BMA before she left to create her own law firm in São Paulo in 2019.

[114]   AB Report, *Brazil-Certain Measures Concerning Taxation and Charges*, WT/DS472/AB/R-WT/DS497/AB/R (2018), paras 6.20–6.21 (concerning the PEC and RECAP programs for exporting companies), 6.43–6.45 (concerning the panel's ruling on implementation within ninety days). Although the Appellate Body upheld most of the panel's rulings against the other programs, it reversed the panel's findings against Brazil regarding Brazilian production requirements that do not require local production of inputs (called nested basic production processes). Paras 6.26–6.31.

[115]   Interview, da Silva Medrado, March 6, 2016. Similarly, in the earlier aircraft subsidy cases against Canada, although Brazil had to change its export financing programs, it implemented the changes "gradually," while "carefully testing the limits of the restriction and moving its measure to a threshold point where it could be considered permissible." Santos, "Carving Out Policy Autonomy," 241.

decision to rein in industrial policies they found inefficient and a waste of public resources.[116] Developmentalists and nationalists, in contrast, looked for means to continue to provide state support to critical sectors. Government lawyers help coordinate implementation among the implicated federal agencies in the context of these debates.

Internal political developments have called into question Brazil's developmentalist orientation, implicating its industrial policy. The Temer administration dropped the word "development" from the title of the Ministry of Industry. The more neoliberal-oriented Ministry of Finance rose in prominence and advocated for more open markets to attract foreign direct investment and link with global value chains. It represented yet another change in Brazil's policies, recalling the neoliberal orientation of former Minister of Finance Pedro Malan under the Cardoso administration, who remarked, "the best industrial policy is not having an industrial policy."[117]

The Transnational Legal Ordering of "Regulatory Coherence"

The United States, international organizations such as the OECD, and business groups have promoted "regulatory coherence" as a means to reduce nontariff barriers to trade while "rationalizing" domestic regulation.[118] It encompasses the concept of "good regulatory practices" that include "regulatory impact assessments" and thus implicitly some form of cost–benefit analysis. Regulatory coherence that entails some form of transnational cooperation to solve regulatory problems is important and does not necessarily infringe on policy space. Nonetheless, some commentators view the initiative as a neoliberal one because of its focus on the removal of nontariff barriers to trade rather than regulatory problem solving.

In 2007, Brazil (along with China, India, and other large emerging economies) entered into an enhanced relationship as a "key partner" with the OECD – the group of developed nations that Brazilian developmentalists long critiqued as a hegemonic Northern club. The OECD has an established program on good regulatory practices involving peer review. It integrated Brazil into its statistical reporting and sector-specific peer reviews, and it invited the country to participate in some OECD committees. In 2015, it launched the OECD-Brazil Programme of

---

[116]   Interview, Brazilian official, July 11, 2019 (referring to the new Ministry of Economy which has absorbed the Ministry of Finance and Ministry of Industry). As one anonymous government source noted before the ruling went public, "we are already considering how to realign these tax incentives to a new reality that is also consistent with our fiscal situation." Silvio Cascione, "WTO Defeat Likely to Bolster Brazil's Free-Market Shift," *Reuters*, August 29, 2017.

[117]   Cited in Schapiro, "Rediscovering the Developmental Path?," 125. Malan worked there through 2003.

[118]   The United States incorporated this issue in its free trade agreements, including as a chapter of the Trans-Pacific Partnership, which became part of the 2018 Comprehensive and Progressive Agreement for Trans-Pacific Partnership, as well as the 2020 United States-Mexico-Canada Agreement that replaced NAFTA.

Work to inform Brazilian public policy and regulatory reform. As part of this relationship, Brazil receives periodic analyses based on "indicators of regulatory policy and governance." In May 2017, Brazil sent a formal request to accede to the OECD, while it heightened its engagement with OECD regulatory coherence programs, such as regulatory impact assessments and ex post evaluations.[119] At a 2019 joint press conference at the White House, President Trump expressed support for Brazil's bid to join the OECD, while Brazil would give up its claims for special and differential treatment as a developing country in future WTO negotiations.[120] In the words of Vera Thorstensen of FGV, "It would be a huge deal if Brazil joins as [the OECD] is part of the larger ecosystem of trade; . . . it is the master of indicators [and] works by peer pressure."[121] Thorstensen references how OECD indicators are used to measure a government's regulatory performance that can create pressure for reform through peer review mechanisms.[122]

Brazil is now negotiating bilateral agreements that contain provisions and chapters on regulatory coherence aiming to shape domestic administrative law. In 2015, it signed a Memorandum of Understanding Regarding Joint Cooperation on Good Regulatory Practices with the United States that recognizes the importance of evidence-based decision making, cost minimization in light of regulatory benefits, and market-based incentives.[123] In 2018, it signed its first trade agreement with a chapter on "Good Regulatory Practices" with Chile, which covers public consultation and comment, regulatory impact assessment, and procedures for ex post regulatory evaluation.[124] Brazil is negotiating regulatory coherence chapters in trade agreements with Canada and Mexico, in addition to the one it concluded with the European Union.

After the fall of the Rousseff administration, CAMEX created an internal technical group to oversee the revision of the country's foreign trade policy and

[119] The letter is available at www.fazenda.gov.br/noticias/2017/junho/governo-brasileiro-solicita-ingresso-a-ocde-como-pais-membro.

[120] Lise Alves, "Brazil Agrees to Surrender Special WTO Status for OECD Entry," *The Rio Times*, March 20, 2019.

[121] Interview, Vera Thorstensen, CCGI, São Paulo, March 5, 2018.

[122] Compare *The Quiet Power of Indicators: Measuring Governance, Corruption, and Rule of Law*, eds. Sally Engle Merry, Kevin E. Davis, and Benedict Kingsbury (New York: Cambridge University Press, 2015).

[123] These MOUs provide a framework under which standard-setting agencies meet and coordinate regarding the harmonization of product certification and industry standards. Memorandum of Understanding between the Executive Secretariat of the Foreign Trade Council of the Federative Republic of Brazil and Casa Civil of the Federative Republic of Brazil, of the one part, and the International Trade Administration of the United States Department of Commerce and the Office of Information and Regulatory Affairs of the United States Office of Management and Budget, of the other part, Regarding Joint Cooperation on Good Regulatory Practices, signed at meeting of the Plenary Session of the 16th edition of the U.S.-Brazil Commercial Dialogue, at www.whitehouse.gov/wp-content/uploads/2018/10/US_Brazil_MOU_Regarding_Joint_Cooperation_Good_Regulatory_Practices.pdf.

[124] Foreign Trade Information System, "Implementación de Buenas Prácticas Regulatorias," *Trade Agreement Between Chile and Brazil* (1980), ch. 3, art. 3.6, www.sice.oas.org/TPD/BRA_CHL/FTA_CHL_BRA_s.pdf.

regulations to ensure greater coherence.[125] Since then, CAMEX has developed an agenda of "regulatory coherence" to reduce nontariff barriers in Brazil and for Brazilian products in foreign markets. As one official states, this is "a milestone for Brazil since it is the first time that the country is incorporating a 'regulatory agenda' for trade."[126] It implicates Brazil's "regulatory culture" because it will require agencies to conduct impact studies and engage in notice and comment and consultation processes with the affected private sector, which will include foreign companies and their domestic affiliates. CAMEX works with the Executive Office of the President (Casa Civil) to give political salience to this initiative. It is "one of the largest projects at CAMEX," involving internal consultations with twenty-eight different Brazilian ministries and agencies, together with lawyers from the Solicitor General's Office,[127] exhibiting the extent of transnational legal ordering at stake. CAMEX invited US and UK officials to come and "share their practices and experience" with Brazilian agencies, once more illustrating transnational legal ordering at work.[128]

CAMEX coordinates the regulatory coherence agenda in consultation with the private sector. It invites law firms, consultancies, think tanks, and academics to contribute to the public debate and provide studies. Such transnational legal ordering processes implicate the regulatory state. While Brazil works to open export markets, it applies these initiatives to reform its internal regulations and regulatory procedures. In doing so, the government again harnesses the trade law capacity built in the public and private sectors, an ongoing legacy of joining the WTO now used to engage with the evolving transnational legal order for trade.

Domestic law and international trade negotiations are, in short, intertwined. As one Brazilian official noted regarding the liberalization policies of the Bolsonaro and Temer administrations, "trade agreements are part of the domestic reform process. They are instruments of reform."[129] They are a way for Brazilian policymakers to bind current and future Brazilian regulatory officials through leveraging international rules.

E. *Transnational Legal Ordering of Protectionism: Import Relief*

The WTO creates legal restraints on protectionism that implicate national laws, institutions, and professional practices. In particular, the WTO affects domestic import relief law under three agreements respectively addressing antidumping law,

---

[125] This was formalized in Resolution n. 52, August 9, 2018. It represents a significant development from the Rousseff administration's earlier initiative known as Institutional Capacity for Regulatory Management, or Pro-Reg, which was aimed at enhancing regulators' technical skills.

[126] Interview, CAMEX official, March 8, 2018.

[127] Ibid.

[128] It also launched a public consultation and received 886 comments from seventy-one entities – mainly from companies and trade associations, but also from foreign governments. Ibid.

[129] Interview, Brazilian official, July 11, 2019.

countervailing duty/subsidy law, and safeguards law. Brazil was largely a taker and not a shaper of these WTO rules so that the rules can be viewed as US, EU, and Canadian legal exports that largely reflect North American and European regulations and regulatory practices. Indeed, between July 1980 and June 1988, in the run-up to the launch of the negotiations creating the WTO, the United States, European Union, Canada, and Australia applied 97.5 percent of the world's antidumping measures.[130] Because Brazil's economy was already sheltered by high tariffs, it did not develop an import relief practice until 1988 and its use of import relief laws was insignificant prior to the WTO's creation in 1995. However, once Brazil reduced tariffs and other nontariffs barriers, it turned to antidumping law to offer protection to key industrial sectors,[131] as did India and China, requiring the development of new professional expertise in government and the private sector

As petitions for antidumping relief rose, the Brazilian government needed to build new institutions.[132] In December 1994, it implemented the WTO antidumping agreement by decree. In 1995, it created a new Department of Trade Defense (DECOM) to handle all import relief investigations, which it lodged within the Secretariat of Foreign Trade (SECEX) in the Ministry of Industry.[133] It also created CAMEX (the interministerial body) to oversee and make final decisions on import relief measures. The government divided institutional responsibility between these institutions. SECEX determined whether to initiate an antidumping investigation; DECOM conducted the investigation and recommended relief; and CAMEX decided on the adoption of any relief measure, taking into consideration the technical analysis.[134] The decision by CAMEX is, in addition, subject to administrative legal challenge through administrative and then judicial review before the federal courts.

Because this is a decentralized system where private parties trigger domestic administrative proceedings and drive the legal process, the private sector has been

---

[130] In addition, the United States has been the most frequent user of countervailing duty law and safeguard law, which is less used in Brazil and elsewhere. Michael Trebilcock and Robert Howse, *The Regulation of International Trade*, 3rd ed. (Abingdon: Routledge, 2005), 232–233, 275.

[131] Cynthia Kramer, "Brazilian Trade Remedies Practice against China," in *Settlements of Trade Disputes between China and Latin American Countries*, ed. Dan Wei (London: Springer-Verlag Berlin Heidelberg, 2015), 39–40. Around two-thirds of Brazil's antidumping measures apply to just three sectors – plastics and rubber products, chemical and allied industries, and base metals and products made from them. In addition, the textiles and electronics sectors are frequent beneficiaries. World Trade Organization, "Anti-Dumping," *World Trade Organization*, 2019 (noting sectors most frequently covered by Brazilian antidumping measures).

[132] There is much more antidumping work than on safeguards or countervailing duties in Brazil. Interviews, Brazilian Trade Lawyers, March 2018.

[133] SECEX was created in 1992, three years before DECOM. Since 2019, the bureaucracy of DECOM became part of the Ministry of Economy as the Undersecretariat of Trade Remedies and Public Interest. See Decree n. 9,279 of January 2, 2019 and its amendments.

[134] Rabih Nasser and Luciana Costa, "Brazil: The Need for Enhanced Effectiveness," in *Domestic Judicial Review of Trade Remedies: Experiences of the Most Active WTO Members*, ed. Müslüm Yilmaz (Cambridge: Cambridge University Press, 2013), 107.

particularly active, illustrating how transnational legal ordering often works. Individuals, including lawyers, economists, consultants, and accountants, invested in developing this specialized practice to build their careers, working both sides of antidumping cases. Many of the lawyers were former interns in Brazil's Geneva and Washington, DC missions.[135] Some earlier worked with US law firms on antidumping investigations involving Brazilian products.[136] Some circulated between the public and private sectors. Most built connections with foreign antidumping law firms to collaborate on investigations in Brazil and abroad, particularly involving major trading partners such as China and the United States.[137] In this way, expertise diffused transnationally, giving rise to a transnational community of import relief practice.

Brazil's administration of trade remedy law intensified as a fallout from the 2008 financial crises when its currency appreciated. Chinese imports particularly threatened Brazilian industry, raising high-level political concern. In 2011, Brazil received the highest number of petitions for antidumping measures in its history. From July 2011 to June 2012, it led the world in the initiation of antidumping investigations and was second in the application of antidumping measures.[138] Overall, from January 1, 1995, to December 31, 2016, Brazil ranked fourth in terms of number of antidumping investigations, behind India, the United States, and European Union.[139] Its largest targets were imports from China (ninety-eight investigations), followed by the United States (forty-three), Korea (twenty-three), India (twenty), and Taiwan (nineteen).[140]

The Rousseff administration responded to the crisis by announcing its "Greater Brazil Plan" for industrial and trade policy in 2011, which included the goal of "strengthening trade remedies . . . and restructuring investigations."[141] The president went public regarding the importance of combatting product dumping as part of the Plan, particularly regarding imports from China.[142] It was the first time that antidumping formed part of a high-level Brazilian Presidential speech. She declared,

---

[135]   Interview, Beatriz Stevens, Geneva, June 28, 2017.
[136]   For example, after working with O'Melveny & Myers in Washington, DC, Ana Caetano returned to Brazil to work on antidumping investigations. Her first case with the poultry trade association involved an Argentine antidumping measure.
[137]   Interviews, Lawyers, Brasília, October 2017; Interviews, Lawyers, São Paulo, March 2018.
[138]   Fernando Pimentel, "As Investigações Antidumping e o Sistema Brasileiro de Defesa Comercial," *RBCE*, July to September 2013, 64–71. DECOM published an Annual Report, available in Portuguese.
[139]   World Trade Organization, "Anti-Dumping," *World Trade Organization*, 2019 ("Anti-dumping initiations: by reporting Member").
[140]   World Trade Organization, "Anti-Dumping," *World Trade Organization*, 2019 ("Anti-dumping initiations: reporting Member vs exporter").
[141]   Luiz Eduardo Salles, "Navigating Brazil's New Antidumping Regulations: Acceleration, Codification, Proceduralization," in *Settlements of Trade Disputes between China and Latin American Countries*, ed. Dan Wei (London: Springer-Verlag Berlin Heidelberg, 2015), 131–147.
[142]   Although China succeeded in having the Lula administration formally recognize it as a "market economy," which is a key goal of Chinese trade policy, Brazil continues to use surrogate prices from

"We are going to act with strength in international organizations and, at the same time, we will adopt all of the safeguards possible to defend our companies, our jobs, and the income of our workers."[143] Under the Greater Brazil Plan, Brazil used antidumping law to support its industrial policies.

The government needed to rapidly develop new administrative expertise to respond to the petitions. Brazil's Ministry of Industry launched the "biggest public opening in its history," recruiting over one hundred new personnel, of which around eighty percent were for trade remedy investigations.[144] These professionals follow WTO jurisprudence. The more senior ones participate in technical discussions coordinated by the WTO Secretariat with a network of import relief specialists. SECEX also brought officials from the U.S. Department of Commerce to Brazil to learn from their experience.[145]

As a central part of the Greater Brazil Plan, Brazil adopted Decree 8,058/13 in 2013, which aimed to revamp Brazilian antidumping law to provide greater predictability and to streamline investigations. The reforms rationalized the bureaucratic process by increasing the technical quality, efficiency, and transparency of Brazil's regulations.[146] The government used expertise gained in Geneva to revamp its laws, illustrating transnational legal processes at work.[147] One feature of Brazilian antidumping procedures became notably cosmopolitan. Pursuant to the reforms, any company subject to a Brazilian investigation may submit its filings in any of the three WTO official languages – English, Spanish, or French – in place of Portuguese.[148]

Brazil's antidumping law, however, is not a mere "legal transplant," and different Brazilian factions contest its application. Within the framework of WTO antidumping law, Brazil adopted its own procedures. For example, Brazil applies a "lesser duty rule" that the WTO antidumping agreement does not require, but that the European Union and some other WTO members use. Under this rule, Brazil can apply an antidumping duty that is lower than the dumping margin where the lower

third countries for purposes of calculating the "normal value" of Chinese products in practice, which enables it to increase antidumping duties to protect Brazilian industry from Chinese imports.

[143] *Portal do Planalto* quoting President Rousseff 2012, "Discourse of President Rousseff, During the Ceremony of Announcement of New Measures of the Greater Brazil Plan and the Installment of the Sectorial Counsels of Competitiveness," *Portal do Planalto*, April 2012 (authors' translation).

[144] Abrão Neto, for example, who subsequently became Secretary of SECEX, joined the ministry in 2001 from the industry association FIESP as part of this hiring wave. Interview, Prazeres, Geneva, June 28, 2017.

[145] Interview, Prazeres, June 28, 2017.

[146] Dan Wei, "The Use of Trade Defense: Some Considerations for Brazil-China Bilateral Trade Relationship," in *Settlements of Trade Disputes between China and Latin American Countries*, ed. Dan Wei (London: Springer-Verlag Berlin Heidelberg, 2015), 19–20, 33 (noting "Brazil's confidence and leadership as an emerging power in applying the AD rules"). Prazeres, the former Secretary of SECEX, stresses that Brazil has transparently published its antidumping determinations, including its reasoning for opening investigations and behind its conclusions. Interview, Prazeres, June 28, 2017.

[147] Felipe Hees, who had been posted to the Geneva mission where he participated in WTO meetings and cases, played a key role.

[148] Law, No. 12,995, of 2014. Interview, Prazeres, June 28, 2017.

amount is sufficient to eliminate the domestic industry's injury. Brazil also applies anti-circumvention rules, which it uses to counter businesses that shift production to a third country to evade antidumping duties. Commentators find that the rules are "novel" and "much more detailed than procedures adopted in the E.U and in the U.S."[149] Brazil's 2013 Decree also excludes the use of "zeroing" in the calculation of antidumping margins in response to WTO Appellate Body rulings regarding what constitutes a "fair comparison" of export and home market prices.

Domestic actors contest these laws' application. For example, Brazil instituted a procedure pursuant to which CAMEX may suspend or not impose antidumping measures because of the "public interest." Brazilian importers, downstream produ-cers, and trade liberal policymakers attempt to trigger this process, which is not required under WTO law and is not used in the United States, although the European Union, Canada, and New Zealand have analogous procedures. Brazil created a Technical Group for Evaluation of Public Interest in 2012 that reviews data, whose secretariat became based in the Ministry of Finance.[150] Following the increased use of antidumping, the Ministry of Finance became active in debates in CAMEX over import relief's implications for the "public interest." Desiring to exercise more influence, the ministry hired officials trained in trade policy and sent others to gain experience in Brazil's Geneva mission.[151] During the Temer administration (from 2016 to 2018), it actively invoked the public interest to suspend antidumping measures. The growing influence of its Secretariat provoked a strong reaction in the Brazilian antidumping law community. Private lawyers successfully pressed for the specification of technical criteria and opportunities for interested parties to provide information and express their views.[152] The Bolsonaro administra-tion created a new secretariat in 2019 named SDCOM to consolidate review of both antidumping investigations and public interest analysis.

---

[149]   Wei, "The Use of Trade Defense: Some Considerations for Brazil-China Bilateral Trade Relationship," 27. WTO Secretariat officials found that Brazil's trade remedy system had become quite "sophisticated." Interview, member of WTO Rules Division, June 29, 2017.

[150]   The technical group known as GTIP was created by CAMEX Directive N. 13/2012. The Secretariat of International Affairs in the Ministry of Finance took charge of the procedure in 2016 under CAMEX Directive N.30/2016.

[151]   For example, Fernando Alcaraz, executive secretary for foreign trade and regional integration at the Secretariat on International Affairs of the Ministry of Finance, was trained at the World Trade Institute in Bern, Switzerland. In 2018, the Secretariat of International Affairs sent two members of its team for training at the Geneva Mission. Interview with Fernando Alcaraz, March 8, 2018. Alcaraz told us that the aim of the Secretariat is "to make the economy more open." In this endeavor, he stated that the Finance Ministry received the support of the Presidency and Brazil's main trade associations CNI and FIESP.

[152]   CAMEX Directive n. 20/2017 on the creation of the Technical Group; and CAMEX Directive n. 29/2017 on transparent and detailed procedures for GTIP, favoring the due process and the participation of interested parties. The "public interest" is largely viewed in terms of the impact on inputs for downstream Brazilian industries. In April 2019, SDCOM published a Guideline for the Public Interest Analysis, www.economia.gov.br/central-de-conteudos/publicacoes/guias/guia-processual_ip.pdf.

Brazilian exports are subject to increased tariffs under foreign antidumping laws, such that government officials, private attorneys, and consultants who specialize in this area also monitor developments abroad. Their experience at the domestic level enables them to assist Brazilian companies subject to foreign investigations,[153] as is the case with practitioners in China and India. The Brazilian antidumping authority maintains a database in Portuguese regarding measures imposed by the country's main trading partners and informs exporters about investigations that could affect them. When the foreign government requires local inspections regarding prices in Brazil, the antidumping authority follows the process. When the foreign authority attempts to settle the matter through price undertakings, the Brazilian authority works with the exporter's legal counsel together with the Ministry of Industry and the Ministry of Foreign Affairs.[154]

The government, in other words, is Janus-faced since it participates on both sides of the transnational legal ordering of antidumping and other import relief law. It thus has a greater interest in ensuring compliance with WTO rules. For example, in response to China's opening of an antidumping investigation against Brazilian chicken exporters in August 2017, the Brazilian government announced that it would support the companies to ensure that "WTO rules are followed strictly."[155]

Different factions and constituencies in Brazil contest import relief law's implementation and practice at the domestic and international levels. They work with professionals who form part of a semi-autonomous field of law. Both international law and domestic law jurisprudence form part of the transnational ordering of import relief law. These processes implicate domestic laws, institutions, and practices for protectionism, and the place of law and lawyers within the regulatory state. What Brazil has done, in turn, recursively can shape the practice of import relief law transnationally, such as through litigation and through technical discussions of practices at WTO committee meetings.

IV. TRANSNATIONAL LEGAL ORDERING OF INTELLECTUAL PROPERTY: DOMESTIC CONTESTS AND INSTITUTIONAL CHANGE

Much has been written on the intersection of the trade regime, Brazilian patent law, and the right to health, particularly in relation to the AIDS crisis.[156] The policies at

---

[153] In total, Brazilian entities were subject to 156 foreign antidumping investigations between 1995 and 2018, which gave rise to 105 antidumping measures. Argentina, its Mercosur partner to which it exports a relatively greater percentage of manufactured products, conducted the largest number of investigations (sixty-three), followed by the United States (seventeen) and India (ten). World Trade Organization, "Anti-dumping," WTO, 2019.

[154] Tatiana Prazeres interview, Geneva, June 28, 2017. The Ministry of Industry explains such assistance on its website, at www.mdic.gov.br/index.php/comercio-exterior/defesa-comercial/852-apoio-expo. The authority was DECOM. Pursuant to Law n. 13.844 (June 18, 2019), it was renamed the Subsecretariat for Trade Remedies and Public Interest (acronym in Portuguese, SDCOM).

[155] "Brazil Vows to Support Chicken Exporters in Chinese Anti-Dumping Case," *Reuters*, August 18, 2017.

[156] Kenneth Shadlen, *Coalitions and Compliance: The Political Economy of Pharmaceutical Patents in Latin America* (Oxford: Oxford University Press, 2017); Amaka Vanni, *Patent Games in the Global*

stake engaged different factions in Brazil. These competing forces are complex and so patent issues are not just a North–South struggle. On the one hand, the AIDS crisis in Brazil and the US challenge to Brazil's patent law helped catalyze civil society knowledge of trade law, giving rise to new civil society organizations, such as REPRIP with its Working Group on Intellectual Property, and new civil society pressure on the reform and application of patent law. On the other hand, the Brazilian government wishes to develop innovative industries and attract foreign direct investment to be a manufacturing leader in South America, including of pharmaceuticals where it has the seventh (and projected to have the fifth) largest market in the world.[157]

Brazil, along with India, unsuccessfully fought the inclusion of intellectual property rights in the WTO. Because of the TRIPS agreement, Brazil revised its law in 1996 to provide for patenting of pharmaceutical products and chemical processes. Yet, Brazil went even further than required, as it did not take advantage of all flexibilities under the TRIPS agreement and it implemented the agreement in 1997, eight years earlier than required. Most significantly, Brazil, unlike India, granted protection to "pipeline patents," thus covering pre-1995 applications outside of Brazil. As a result, drugs that came on the market in late 1990s and early 2000s, nearly all based on pre-1995 applications, were patented in Brazil, which the TRIPS agreement did not require. Brazil purportedly did this in the hope of attracting foreign direct investment and reducing the risk of US unilateral sanctions, such as the removal of benefits under the US General System of Preferences program.[158]

By strengthening patent protection, expanding it to cover the chemical/pharmaceutical sector, and including "pipeline patents," Brazil unleashed a flurry of patent applications, creating new professional opportunities. Today, about half of all patent applications in Brazil come from the chemical/pharmaceutical sector, with about 60 percent of all applications for second-use patent protection, raising civil society concerns over the "evergreening" of patents to maintain monopoly rents.[159] Professional markets responded, illustrating the multiple dimensions of state change catalyzed by transnational legal ordering. Universities created new courses, a specialized profession grew, and large law firms developed their intellectual property practices, working largely on behalf of multinational companies. Brazil's patent office, the *Instituto Nacional da Propriedade Industrial* (INPI), was both empowered and overwhelmed, facing a huge backlog of over 243,000 pending files

South: *Pharmaceutical Patent Law Making in Brazil, India and Nigeria* (London: Hart Publishing, 2020).

[157] IQVIA Institute, *The Global Use of Medicine in 2019 and Outlook to 2023: Forecasts and Areas to Watch* (January 2019): 50, www.iqvia.com/institute/reports/the-global-use-of-medicine-in-2019-and-outlook-to-2023.

[158] Shadlen, *Coalitions and Compliance*, 113–118, 134.

[159] Jae Sundaram, *Pharmaceutical Patent Protection and World Trade Law: The Unresolved Problem of Access to Medicines* (Abingdon: Routledge, 2018), 104.

in 2016, such that it takes an average of over ten years to process a patent.[160] Brazil created four new specialized intellectual property trial courts, complemented by two specialized appellate chambers, to hear intellectual property disputes. Companies challenge administrative decisions on patents before these tribunals, engaging lawyers, incentivizing the development of new expertise, which shapes and provides a conduit for transnational legal ordering.

Brazil and other developing countries obtained some provisions in the TRIPS agreement that provide policy space to address social policy concerns, such as the granting of compulsory licenses for essential medicines, which other factions in Brazil used. Having incorporated the right to health in the Brazilian constitution, and as the first developing country to provide universal free access to antiretroviral drugs, Brazil soon faced significantly increased drug costs. It thus revised its patent law in 2001 to enhance its ability to meet its public health obligations. The Brazilian government is one of the largest purchasers of medicines in the world because of its commitments under the country's public health system. The government created an institutional innovation for the assessment of pharmaceutical patents by giving a prominent role to the National Health Surveillance Agency (known as ANVISA) within the Ministry of Health, which was to provide its "prior consent" before a patent would be granted. ANVISA asserted itself to delay or block the issuance of many pharmaceutical patents on patentability grounds.

Brazil provided an alternative framing of pharmaceutical patents as a health issue that other developing countries could adopt and promote internationally to facilitate their access to medicines. It was a leader in pushing for the 2001 Declaration on TRIPS and Public Health and the 2003 WTO General Council decision implementing paragraph 6 of the Declaration regarding the conditions for granting compulsory licenses. In his autobiographical account of his life as a Brazilian diplomat, Amorim calls the TRIPS declaration the most important achievement of his diplomatic career.[161] Brazil was also central to establishing the Development Agenda of the World Intellectual Property Organization (WIPO) in 2007, which works to constrain the adoption of ever-stronger intellectual property protection and led to the suspension of negotiations of a new Substantive Patent Law Treaty that industrial powers promoted. The government issued a compulsory license for an antiretroviral medication in 2007 and used the threat of a compulsory license to negotiate significant price discounts from pharmaceutical producers.[162] In addition,

[160] Peter Drahos, *The Global Governance of Knowledge: Patent Offices and Their Clients* (Cambridge: Cambridge University Press, 2010). Brazil has the worst record of major patent offices. World Intellectual Property Organization, *Patents* (2017), www.wipo.int/edocs/pubdocs/en/wipo_pub_941_2017-chapter2.pdf, 75.

[161] Celso Amorim, *Breves Narrativas Diplomáticas*, 79.

[162] Interestingly, Brazil issued the compulsory license under a "public interest" provision, and not the "local working" provision that the United States had earlier challenged before the WTO, possibly because of the larger industrial policy issues raised by the "local working" provision. We thank Ken Shadlen for this point.

it worked with India to challenge European seizures of generics destined from India to Brazil before the WTO dispute settlement system, leading to a favorable settlement. Brazil's actions and its framing of the issues contributed to broader processes of diffusion and emulation that facilitate other countries' use of flexibilities under the TRIPS agreement to reduce drug prices.

However, like India and China, Brazil also desires to move up the value-added chain of production, which requires innovation policies. Through its industrial policy, it aimed to develop the domestic pharmaceutical sector to create production capacity, which makes the threat of a compulsory license more effective. The domestic sector, in turn, became interested in filing patents, including for secondary uses, complicating the political economy within Brazil, which saw the rise of a new innovation-intellectual property complex.[163] International producers challenged ANVISA's actions before the courts and found allies in Brazil's patent agency (INPI) that wished to protect its own institutional authority. National firms, now interested in patenting, no longer came to ANVISA's defense.[164] In 2017, following an opinion from the Federal Solicitor General's Office, INPI reached an agreement with ANVISA in a Joint Ordinance. Under it, ANVISA operates only as an advisory body on patentability issues implicating health, so that the INPI makes the final decision.[165] Brazilian civil society groups nonetheless remain vigilant and they challenge INPI's granting of patents in the courts, lobby agencies and the legislature, and network with other civil society groups, academics, and think tanks to coordinate positions in international forums, including before the United Nations, WIPO, and the World Health Organization.

One could summarize Brazil's competing tendencies by stating that it includes patent protection as part of its innovation policies while incorporating measures to meliorate impacts on the provision of public goods. In practice, however, the equilibrium is always contested and involves struggles between competing constituencies. Outside of agribusiness where the public and private sectors invest significant amounts in research and development of plant varieties to be highly competitive in global markets, Brazil still depends largely on its vast internal market, and it remains much less competitive in innovative sectors globally.[166] It continues to rely on foreign direct investment, and those investors demand intellectual property protection, leading to net royalty outflows. The vast majority of patents that Brazil grants

---

[163] Shadlen, *Coalitions and Compliance*, 218–219.

[164] Ibid., 218–221.

[165] INPI will only shelve an application if ANVISA finds that the product or pharmaceutical process "presents a risk to public health," which is understood to occur when it results in a "substance whose use has been prohibited," such as a narcotic substance. INPI-ANVISA Joint Ordinance no. 01/2017 (authors' translation).

[166] The share of Brazilian exports incorporating "high technology" declined from over 10 percent in 2000 to 5 percent in 2010. This is explained not only by the "commodity boom," but also because of slow growth of Brazilian manufactured exports that incorporate such technology. Arturo C. Porzecanski, "Brazil's Place in the Global Economy," in *Brazil on the Global Stage*, eds. Oliver Stuenkel and Mathew M. Taylor (London: Palgrave Macmillan, 2015), 145.

are to nonresidents – 4,736 compared to 714 granted to residents in 2017.[167] Moreover, in the years 2014–2016, the filing of patents declined in Brazil, dropping it out of the top ten most active patent offices.[168] Brazil, in short, continues to lag behind other emerging economies such as India and particularly China in developing innovative, high-tech sectors.

V. TRANSNATIONAL LEGAL ORDERING OF INVESTMENT: A NEW BRAZILIAN MODEL

Brazil remained largely outside of the transnational legal ordering of investment law until recently. Most of Brazil's exports are commodities, and Brazil's imports are generally not used as inputs for export production as part of global value chains. Indeed, "Brazil is one of the most self-sufficient of nations, with no more than one-tenth of the value-added of its exports incorporating foreign made inputs" – which compares to over one-fifth for India and around one-third for China.[169] Brazil has not taken part in the Western model of ratifying bilateral investment treaties (BITs) subject to investor–state dispute settlement (ISDS) in which investors may bring cases against states before international arbitral tribunals. Brazil signed fourteen conventional BITs between 1994 and 1999 that were mostly with developed countries, but its National Congress never ratified them because the BITs limited the state's right to regulate and granted greater rights to foreign investors than domestic ones.[170] Brazil's ability to attract foreign investment did not suffer, for Brazil remained one of the world's top destinations for foreign investment, largely because of its huge domestic market.[171]

Since 2015, the Brazilian government has created its own approach to international investment treaties called Cooperation and Facilitation Investment Agreements (CFIAs), which are more respectful of state sovereignty and yet aim

[167] WIPO, *Statistical Country Profiles: Brazil* (Geneva: WIPO, 2019), www.wipo.int/ipstats/en/statistics/country_profile/profile.jsp?code=BR.

[168] WIPO, *World Intellectual Property Indicators 2017* (Geneva: WIPO, 2017), 30, www.wipo.int/edocs/pubdocs/en/wipo_pub_941_2017-chapter2.pdf (foreign applicants constitute 87 percent of the total).

[169] Porzecanski, "Brazil's Place in the Global Economy," 145.

[170] Daniela Campello and Leany Lemos, "The Non-Ratification of Bilateral Investment Treaties in Brazil: A Story of Conflict in a Land of Cooperation," *Review of International Political Economy* 22, no. 5 (2015): 1055–1086 (noting a cohesive opposition referencing these grounds and an unresolved executive for which the BITs were not a priority).

[171] Martino Maggetti and Henrique Choer Moraes, "The Policy-Making of Investment Treaties in Brazil: Policy Learning in the Context of Late Adoption," in *Learning in Public Policy: Analysis, Modes and Outcomes*, eds. Claire Dunlop, Claudio Radaelli, and Josef Philipp Trein (London: Palgrave Macmillan, 2018), 295–316 (table showing Brazil varying from 5 to 8 from 2010 to 2015). Investors found other means to protect their investments, such as through contractual clauses providing for arbitration. Brazil passed an arbitration law in 1996 that reconciled Brazilian law with the 1958 New York Convention on the Recognition and Enforcement of Foreign Arbitral Awards, which Brazil ratified in 2002, constituting a parallel transnational legal order. Campello and Lemos, "Non-Ratification," 1065.

to support Brazilian multinationals in their foreign expansion.[172] The Brazilian model provides an alternative to those long promoted by the United States and Europe. It focuses on investment facilitation and dispute avoidance rather than extensive investor protection backed by ISDS. To facilitate investment, the parties aim to create ongoing "agendas" to improve the process, including expediting visas for business persons.[173] Substantively, although they vary in light of negotiation dynamics, the CFIAs limit the scope of investor protections to claims such as direct expropriation, discrimination, and unreasonable treatment in violation of due process of law, while generally obliging investors to comply with state laws, as well as a range of corporate social responsibility endeavors.[174]

At the CFIA model's core are national focal points – or ombudsmen – that provide a new institutional interface between local officials, foreign investors, and their governments. These ombudsmen can propose amendments to national legislation and regulation to facilitate and provide assurance to foreign investment. In addition, they can help manage and resolve conflicts.[175] Brazil designated a new Ombudsman of Direct Investments within CAMEX as its focal point, which, pursuant to a 2019 decree, is available for all investors and not just those covered under CFIAs.[176] If the dispute remains unresolved, then a contracting state may bring the matter to a "Joint Committee" of state representatives before which investors and other stakeholders can voice their concerns. Only if these processes fail to resolve the matter may a state pursue traditional state-to-state arbitration, and the investor is granted no recourse to ISDS.

Brazil has been the most active country in the world in signing new investment agreements since 2015, although it has so far negotiated and signed CFIAs only with developing countries. By January 2020, it had signed fifteen agreements, eight in Latin America (with Chile, Colombia, Ecuador, Mexico, Peru, its Mercosur partners, Suriname, and Guyana), five in Africa (Angola, Mozambique, Malawi, Ethiopia, and Morocco), one in the Middle East (United Arab Emirates), and one

---

[172] Michelle Sanchez-Badin and Fabio Morosini, "Navigating between Resistance and Conformity with the International Investment Regime," in *Reconceptualizing International Investment Law from the Global South*, eds. Fabio Morosini and Michelle Ratton Sanchez-Badin (Cambridge: Cambridge University Press, 2018), 218–250.

[173] Brazil and Angola, for example, signed a Visa Protocol together with the CFIA. Sanchez-Badin and Morosini, "Navigating," 225.

[174] The CFIAs expressly do not include indirect expropriation or "fair and equitable treatment" commitments, which have been the most frequently invoked and expansively interpreted clauses in ISDS jurisprudence. Moreover, the national treatment and most-favored nations clauses limit non-discrimination claims to the treatment of investors "in similar circumstances." The CFIAs also exclude protection for investments obtained through corruption.

[175] The ombudsmen are to assess complaints submitted by the treaty party or its investors and "recommend, as appropriate, actions to improve the investment environment." Article 18.4(c) of Model CFIA. Brazil borrowed this aspect of its model from South Korea.

[176] Decree 9770, April 22, 2019, and CAMEX Resolution N. 1, December 11, 2019 approving the rules of procedure for the National Committee on Investments.

with India.[177] Through the CFIAs, Brazil is engaged in a form of transnational ordering of investment law that aims to update national laws and practices to facilitate investment, and to create new national institutions to facilitate foreign investment and resolve disputes – the ombudsmen.

Brazil is diffusing its model largely through example, although it also has brought key aspects of its model to regional and multilateral institutions as a "rulemaker." Regionally, it incorporated the model within Mercosur in 2017 with Argentina, Paraguay, and Uruguay.[178] It has since taken the model to the WTO. In April 2017, it helped launch an Informal Dialogue on Investment Facilitation for Development within the WTO General Council.[179] It worked to coordinate a new group of WTO members named the "Friends of Investment Facilitation for Development," which created groundwork for a Joint Ministerial Statement on Investment Facilitation for Development by seventy WTO members at the 2017 WTO Ministerial Meeting in Buenos Aires.[180] The United States and India opposed the initiative, while China and the European Union supported it, upsetting old alliances. Brazil immediately followed the Ministerial Meeting with a January 30, 2018, Communication to the General Council that attached a draft agreement incorporating core elements from the Brazilian model. The draft included the concept of national focal points, provisions to enhance transparency and predictability for investors, and principles of corporate social responsibility.[181] By bringing the model to the WTO, the model can be further diffused and potentially multilateralized as an alternative transnational legal order for investment.

The process that lay behind the creation of the Brazilian investment model involved intensive interministerial coordination and stakeholder coordination that

---

[177] Authors calculations from UNCTAD Investment Policy Hub database, at https://investmentpolicy .unctad.org/international-investment-agreements and the Brazilian Ministry of Foreign Affairs database https://concordia.itamaraty.gov.br/. However, only the agreement with Angola has been ratified by both state parties as of June 2019. Brazil has concluded CFIAs with all South American countries other than Bolivia and Venezuela.

[178] Facundo Pérez Aznar and Henrique Choer Moraes, "The MERCOSUR Protocol on Investment Cooperation and Facilitation: Regionalizing an Innovative Approach to Investment Agreements," *EJIL: TALK!*, September 12, 2017.

[179] Argentina and Brazil: Possible Elements of a WTO Instrument on Investment Facilitation (JOB/GC/ 124), April 26, 2017.

[180] The declaration called for the WTO to develop "a framework for facilitating foreign direct investments that would: improve the transparency and predictability of investment measures; streamline and speed up administrative procedures and requirements; and enhance . . . relations with relevant stakeholders, including dispute prevention." WTO, *Joint Ministerial Statement on Investment Facilitation for Development*, WT/MIN(17)/59, December 13, 2017. This in turn built from technical work on trade facilitation within UNCTAD and the G20 in which Brazil was an active participant. Henrique Choer Moraes and Felipe Hees, "Breaking the BIT Mold: Brazil's Pioneering Approach to Investment Agreements," 112 *AJIL Unbound* (2018): 197–201.

[181] Brazil's WTO proposal also called for the national establishment of a "single electronic window" for submitting all documents for regulatory approvals of investments, a mechanism that Brazil has yet to establish domestically. Brazil: Proposal for an Investment Facilitation Agreement (JOB/GC/169), February 1, 2018.

the government earlier institutionalized for trade negotiations. After an initial study, CAMEX formed technical groups that worked in coordination with the private sector, academics, and consultants to develop the model.[182] Foreign trade analysts within the Ministry of Industry – who had been hired as part of the wave of professionalization in response to the international trade regime – played a key role. Many in the Brazilian trade law community offered their expertise in constructing the model and they now help to diffuse it.[183] Trade-related legal capacity, which was initially catalyzed by the WTO, in other words, was transportable for Brazil's ongoing engagement in transnational legal ordering of economic law. The CFIA model initially reflected the Lula and Dilma administrations' turn to the development of South–South relations. It is now embedded as a new model for transnational legal ordering of investment.

VI. CONCLUSION

To recount and respond to this book's three questions, Brazil was the first emerging power to invest significantly in building trade law capacity after being placed on the defensive in WTO litigation. To do so, its institutions and professions adapted, transforming Brazilian state, private sector, and civil society relations in relation to international economic law. In the process, Brazil became a forerunner to India and China in shaping the transnational legal order for trade.

"Power," in the words of former Minister of Foreign Affairs Ramiro Saraiva Guerreiro is not just material. It is also about a country's "level of economic, scientific, cultural, and technological development."[184] One way to characterize this form of power is in terms of expertise, including legal capacity to shape the law and its application through negotiation, litigation, bargaining in the shadow of the law, and implementation. Different Brazilian constituencies acquired new expertise to shape Brazilian law, institutions, and practices in more neoliberal or developmentalist directions, as well as to help Brazil engage with and recursively shape the international trade and broader economic law system. After joining the WTO, Brazil transformed institutionally along multiple dimensions. In parallel, its early success before the WTO foreshadowed the challenges that the United States and European Union would later face more dramatically with China.

Brazilian trade policy is changing as neoliberal, nationalist, and developmentalist forces clash, working in the shadow of the international system. The Bolsonaro administration includes both neoliberal and nationalist forces. The minister of the

---

[182] CAMEX, *Internacionalização de Empresas Brasileiras* (Brasília: CAMEX, 2009).

[183] Michelle Ratton Sanchez Badin, coauthor of this chapter, for example, wrote a series of articles and edited a book in this vein with Fabio Morosini, *Reconceptualizing International Investment Law from the Global South*.

[184] FUNAG, *Brazilian Diplomatic Thought Vol. 1* (Brasília: Fundação Alexandre de Gusmão, 2013), 370. He was Minister of Foreign Affairs from 1979 to 1985.

transformed super-Ministry of the Economy, Paulo Guedes, is a neoliberal econo-mist, while the Minister of Foreign Affairs, Ernesto Araújo, is a nationalist like President Bolsonaro. Historically, Brazil has a long developmentalist tradition that will not be easily discarded. The Bolsonaro administration sought to deepen its relationship with the United States in the context of the US trade war against China. Yet, it is highly unlikely that Brazil will cut back on economic ties with China, which is its most important trading partner, particularly for its powerful agribusiness sector, and an increasingly important investor in critical infrastructure. Which path Brazil takes is uncertain, but what is clear is that the international and national dimensions of trade law and policy will continue to interact through transnational legal ordering processes.

The ecology of the international trade legal order is changing rapidly. Brazil is caught in a difficult place, torn between its long-term, strategic commitment to multilateralism and pressure to engage in bilateral and regional negotiations so as not to be left behind in the emerging trade legal order. A key challenge for Brazil is how to manage its relations between its most important trade and investment partners – China, the United States, and the European Union – while retaining its traditional commitment to enhancing regional ties in Latin America, on which much of its industry was built. In this shifting landscape, Brazil is redeploying in new ways the trade law capacity it developed in the public and private sectors since joining the WTO. Its choices will implicate the future ecology of the transnational legal order for trade.

5

India: An Emerging Giant's Transformation and Its Implications

With *James Nedumpara and Aseema Sinha*

To take from the title of a book by Amartya Sen, India is the argumentative nation.[1] Many countries have viewed it as arrogant, reputed for its lecturing and moralizing.[2] Within the WTO, it is tagged for being obstructionist.[3] It has fiercely defended its sovereignty, and in the case of trade, its imposition of high tariffs and other trade barriers to protect domestic producers. After the WTO's creation, India quickly found itself on the defensive. To respond, it needed to develop trade law capacity as part of state capacity. It gradually did so, and it used both offensive and defensive means to defend its exports and support its vulnerable sectors such as agriculture and textiles.

Through engaging with the WTO and the transnational legal ordering of trade, India transformed itself along multiple dimensions, implicating its institutions, professions, and policy frames. It placed greater emphasis on foreign trade and intellectual property protection, increased government transparency, and developed public–private coordination mechanisms for trade policy. The government reorganized its institutions, created new think tanks, and coordinated with the private sector and private professionals. Indian private law firms began to routinely work for the government in trade litigation and other trade and investment-related matters. These government changes were not an autonomous policy choice, but rather the result of internal clashes in light of the global context in which the WTO and WTO law forms a part. Without the WTO, India would not have changed its internal institutions as it did.[4] Reciprocally, by building legal capacity, India aimed to shape the construction, interpretation, and practice of the international trade and broader economic law order.

---

[1] Amartya Sen, *The Argumentative Indian: Writings on Indian History, Culture and Identity* (London: Macmillan, 2005). India is of course one of the world's most diverse nations and generalizations are problematic. We cite this text in light of India's reputation in the WTO.

[2] Amitav Acharya, *East of India South of China: Sino-Indian Encounters in Southeast Asia* (Oxford: Oxford University Press, 2017), 150.

[3] Kristen Hopewell, *Breaking the WTO: How Emerging Powers Disrupted the Neoliberal Project* (Stanford: Stanford University Press, 2016).

[4] Aseema Sinha, *Globalizing India: How Global Rules and Markets are Shaping India's Rise to Power* (Cambridge: Cambridge University Press, 2016).

I. THE INDIAN STATE AND THE CATALYSTS OF CHANGE

A. *India and the GATT Years – Little Role for Law or Lawyers*

When India gained its independence and emerged from colonization in 1947, its leaders sought to build a developmental state autonomous and unconstrained by Western-dominated institutions, law, and policy. Indian businesses' primary market was domestic. They were unable to compete internationally. As the Oxford development economist I.M.D. Little – the professor of Manmohan Singh who later became the architect of India's 1991 reforms and future prime minister – wrote in a widely read text in the early 1980s, "developing countries never expected to be able to export manufactures [manufactured products] to the developed countries."[5]

Until 1991, India maintained a closed economy, built on a socialist model of five-year plans. The country introduced high tariffs and quantitative restrictions as part of a policy of import substitution to build domestic manufacturing and safeguard India's balance of payments.[6] It was wary of international commitments given its colonial heritage. Yet, also following that heritage, the government employed a centralized bureaucracy to administer what was called the "License Raj." The Indian bureaucratic system was both powerful and sclerotic, insular and nontransparent, creating delays, uncertainty, and opportunities for corruption. Decision making was time- and resource-consuming. It slowed entrepreneurial endeavor, while demanding nimbleness for businesses to navigate. Firms were preoccupied with obtaining licenses to import, and subsidies to export, as part of complicated government policies to manage India's balance of payments. In-house public relations personnel – not lawyers – were critical for obtaining licenses.[7]

The Indian government did not need to pay as much attention to the GATT, the WTO's predecessor, as it made few legal commitments. At the time that Uruguay Round negotiations accelerated in 1990–1991, India's maximum tariff rate was 355 percent and its simple average applied tariff rate was a whopping 128 percent.[8] Moreover, India bound only 6 percent of its tariff lines, meaning that it could raise rates on most items at any time. India complemented the tariff regime with different types of

[5] Ian Malcom David Little, *Economic Development: Theory, Policy and International Relations* (New York: Basic Books, 1982), 61.
[6] Jagdish N. Bhagwati and T. N. Srinivasan, *Foreign Trade Regimes and Economic Development: India* (Cambridge: National Bureau of Economic Research, 1975); Aseema Sinha, *The Regional Roots of Developmental Politics in India: A Divided Leviathan* (Bloomington: Indiana University Press, 2005). India partially liberalized the License Raj in in the 1980s, but it still largely isolated the country's economy.
[7] Successful Indian businesses engaged in *"juggad"* – a term that captures the ability of a business to find quick fix solutions when the law and regulatory environment disfavor it. India's "Grand Advocates" engaged in occasional ex poste litigation to defend large businesses under the licensing system, but they had no expertise in trade law. Marc Galanter and Nick Robinson, "Grand Advocates: The Traditional Elite Lawyers," in *The Indian Legal Profession in the Age of Globalization: The Rise of the Corporate Legal Sector and Its Impact on Lawyers and Society*, eds. David Wilkins, Vikramaditya Khanna, and David Trubek (Cambridge: Cambridge University Press, 2017), 455.
[8] Sinha, *Globalizing India*, 8.

quantitative restrictions to help monitor its unfavorable balance-of-payments situation. It was a small inward-oriented economy incapable of affecting international trade and thus less interested in shaping international trade rules and their application except to ensure that they would not constrain its tariff and other policy choices.

In such a closed, nontransparent system, trade law and trade lawyers played no role. During the forty-seven years of the GATT dispute settlement system, India was a party in just three minor cases, none of which resulted in a GATT panel decision. Because of India's lack of significant tariff commitments and legal engagement under the GATT, one could not speak of a transnational trade legal order permeating the Indian state, or the need to develop professional, trade-related legal capacity to respond to it.

B. *Catalytic Contestation: India on the Defensive in the 1990s*

Like Brazil, the Indian development model changed in the 1990s. With the fall of the Berlin Wall in 1989 and the Soviet and socialist models discredited, Indian officials eyed with envy East Asian economies' export-oriented growth models. A growing faction of policymakers and technocrats became more receptive to greater liberalization and engagement with the global economy. While East Asia grew, a severe economic crisis struck India in 1991 with the Gulf War oil shock and the country's dependence on petroleum imports. The government went to the IMF for emergency credits of US$2.3 billion dollars, and, to its humiliation, exported gold to the vaults of Great Britain as the value of the rupee plunged and the country could not otherwise pay its debts.[9]

As a condition for financing, the IMF called for Indian reforms, including to open the country to foreign trade. Under duress, the Indian government responded. Prime Minister Narasimha Rao and Finance Minister Manmohan Singh spun these reforms as homegrown, known as the "1991 reforms," which is how Indians conventionally reference them today. Yet the reforms were part of a transnational context. As a former high-level member of the Indian Administrative Service told us, "the IMF and international institutions helped to provide an excuse to do what otherwise was more difficult to do politically, as change was otherwise very difficult to obtain."[10]

Internally, the Ministry of Finance supported the reforms in inter-ministerial struggles against the Ministry of Commerce.[11] A key group of economists and technocrats within it drove the reform effort. Transnationally embedded, they included Finance Minister Singh (BA from Cambridge, PhD from Oxford, who had worked at UNCTAD and led the South Commission in Geneva), Finance Secretary Montek Singh Ahluwalia (a former Rhodes Scholar at Oxford on deputation from the IMF and who would later lead

[9] Vijay Joshi and Ian Malcom David Little, *India's Economic Reforms 1991–2001* (Oxford: Oxford University Press, 1996).
[10] Interview, January 16, 2012.
[11] Sinha, *Globalizing India*, 88–90 (noting the IMF and WTO India-Quantitative Restrictions case in particular).

India's powerful Planning Commission), and Deepak Nayyar (who became Chief Economic Advisor of India after receiving his PhD at Oxford and teaching in India and England). Shankar Acharya, an equally prominent economist who worked at the World Bank after receiving degrees from Oxford and Harvard, then became India's Chief Economic Adviser between 1993 and 2001, the most important phase of India's economic liberalization. Within India, the 1991 economic crisis, and the need to go to the IMF for financing, provided an opportunity for those advocating reforms.

These officials had close intellectual ties with leading Indian economists abroad, as Indian economic expertise looked increasingly toward the United States.[12] A number of Indian economists held positions in elite US universities, such as Jagdish Bhagwati at Columbia and T.N. Srinivasan at Yale. Others held major research posts at the World Bank, Asian Development Bank, GATT, and WTO, such as Aditya Matoo, Arvind Subramanian (who became India's Chief Economic Advisor from 2014 to 2018), and Arvind Panagariya (who headed India's new think tank "NITI Aayog" – the National Institution for Transforming India – from 2014 to 2017).[13] International and national policy making, with their implications for transnational legal ordering, were enmeshed.

The reforms of the early 1990s and India's subsequent WTO commitments sparked protests in India. India's vibrant civil society includes many NGOs that vociferously contested economic globalization and the WTO, including such global figures as Sunita Narain, Vandana Shiva, and Arundhati Roy.[14] Many business elites likewise strongly opposed trade liberalization. This opposition, however, lost steam after 2000–2002 as domestic liberalization reforms became politically accepted, even though it is still present.[15] The reforms altered business incentives and empowered traders and exporters that formed new linkages with state officials concerning trade policy.

The Uruguay Round negotiations and the resulting WTO agreements vastly expanded trade law's scope, affecting manufacturing, agriculture, textiles, intellectual property, services, and investment measures. India bound almost 74.4 percent of its tariff lines,[16] and, in practice, lowered its applied tariff rates vastly beyond its actual commitments to an average of around 9.5 percent on nonagricultural goods by 2015, rising slightly to 10.2 percent in 2016.[17] India also made market access

---

[12] Rahul Mukherji, *Globalization and Deregulation: Ideas, Interests and Institutional Change in India* (Oxford: Oxford University Press, 2014), 76–82.

[13] The NITI Aayog replaced the Planning Commission, which had a more socialist heritage, but itself gradually changed over time.

[14] Balakrishnan Rajagopal, *International Law from Below: Development, Social Movements and Third World Resistance* (Cambridge: Cambridge University Press, 2003).

[15] Sinha, *Globalizing India*, 16, 275; Mukherji, *Globalization and Deregulation*. Compare B. S. Chimni, "A Just World Under Law: A View from the South," *American University of International Law Review* 22, no. 2 (2007): 199–220, 211 (noting "two Indias" of the rich and mobile, and the "poor and marginal"); Rana Dasgupta, *Capital: The Eruption of Delhi* (New York: Penguin Press, 2014).

[16] WTO, Trade Policy Review Body, *Trade Policy Review: India, Report by the Secretariat* (2015).

[17] WTO, *World Tariff Profile* (2016). The trade weighted applied rate on non-agricultural products was 7.5 percent as of 2016.

TABLE 5.1 *India's relative openness to trade under the GATT and WTO*[18]

	Percentage of bound tariffs	Average applied tariff (percent)	Trade (imports + exports as percentage of GDP)
1970	6	125	8
2018	74.4	13.8	40.8

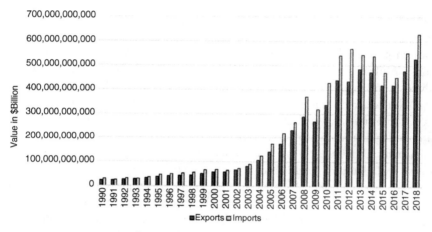

FIGURE 5.1 *India's trade in goods and services (1990–2018)*[19]

commitments regarding services for the first time, involving thirty-three service sectors. Table 5.1 summarizes the shift in relative openness of the Indian economy to trade.

The ensuing reforms significantly reoriented the Indian economy toward trade. The proportion of trade of goods and services (imports and exports) to India's GDP was a mere 8 percent in 1970, rising to 15.5 percent in 1990, and soaring to 56 percent by 2012, before declining to 41 percent in 2018, a proportion higher than China's.[20] With growing trade, inbound and outbound investment and capital also flowed (Section V), creating new prospects and challenges for business, while offering new opportunities for lawyers.

The actual meaning and impact of WTO rules depend on their interpretation and application. The Indian government and Indian business did not immediately engage in legal capacity building in response to the WTO's creation. Rather, they

[18] Sources: The World Bank, *Trade (% of GDP) – India*, https://data.worldbank.org/indicator/NE .TRD.GNFS.ZS?locations=IN; WTO, *World Tariff Profile (2018)*, 10.

[19] UN Comtrade, https://comtrade.un.org/data/.

[20] World Bank, *Trade (% of GDP) – India*, https://data.worldbank.org/indicator/NE.TRD.GNFS.ZS? locations=IN.

responded to the WTO law-in-action after they faced politically sensitive complaints brought by the United States and European Union in the WTO's first years. These cases pressed the Indian bureaucracy to develop new partnerships with the private sector and engage technical experts such as economists and lawyers. Being on the defensive drove India's development of trade law capacity, as was the case with Brazil and (as we will see) with China.

Two key WTO cases spurred this process, respectively covering India's implementation of the Agreement on Trade-Related Aspects of Intellectual Property Rights (Section IV), and its use of quantitative restrictions on balance-of-payments grounds and thus India's License Raj. The most broad-reaching case affecting Indian industry and agriculture was the WTO's quantitative restrictions decision that implicated the reform of India's import licensing regime. When India went to the IMF in 1991 to receive its US$2.3 billion dollars credit, it agreed to remove quantitative restrictions and import licensing on most goods.[21] In practice, India maintained them on consumer goods involving 2,714 tariff lines, which was nearly 30 percent of its total number. Before the WTO, the United States challenged India's invocation of quantitative restrictions on balance-of-payments grounds for these remaining lines. The case was a "wake up" call for India given its importance for India's import controls. The government wished to keep the measures in effect until at least 2006, and, in its defense, it invoked GATT provisions granting special and differential treatment to developing countries facing balance-of-payment difficulties. But it did not prevail. Rather, WTO and IMF rules were closely aligned on the issue.[22] An IMF representative reported that India no longer faced a balance-of-payments crisis, and the panel and Appellate Body cited the IMF report in support of their decisions. Critically, India's Ministry of Finance helped undercut the Department of Commerce's position before the WTO by writing a letter to the IMF confirming that India faced no balance-of-payments crisis.[23]

The case exhibited the role of judicialization under the WTO. Formerly, GATT disputes over balance of payments had only been addressed politically within the GATT committee system.[24] India contended that this preexisting practice precluded the dispute settlement panel from hearing the case. Yet the WTO panel found that it had the authority to consult the IMF under Article 13 of the WTO Dispute Settlement Understanding, and India failed with its defense.[25]

---

[21] Arvind Panagariya, *India: The Emerging Giant* (Oxford: Oxford University Press, 2008), 106.
[22] Gregory Shaffer and Michael Waibel, "The (Mis)Alignment of the Trade and Monetary Legal Orders," in *Transnational Legal Orders*, eds. Terence Halliday and Gregory Shaffer (Cambridge: Cambridge University Press, 2015), 187–231.
[23] Sinha, *Globalizing India*, 89 (confirming in interviews that "this action was deliberate and not accidental").
[24] Richard Eglin, "Surveillance of Balance-of-Payments Measures in the GATT," *The World Economy* 10 (1987): 1–26.
[25] Panel Report, *India- Quantitative Restrictions on Imports of Agricultural, Textile and Industrial Products*, WT/ DS 90/R (April 6, 1999).

The WTO decision spurred fears in India that foreign products would flood the Indian market, and, in particular, marine and dairy products, confectionary items, and fruits and vegetables.[26] The Commerce Ministry promised to establish a "war room" to keep a vigil on around three hundred sensitive products, and it constantly assured stakeholders that it had put adequate monitoring mechanisms in place.[27] The government established a committee headed by the Commerce Secretary and the Secretaries of Agriculture and of Small-Scale Industries to identify any safe-guards required and to forewarn industries and trade bodies.

In each of these disputes, India had to defend its system in a losing case, but, in the process, learned the importance of developing capacity to engage with WTO law, including adapting domestic measures to protect its development strategies. These politically sensitive cases raised government, private sector, and civil society aware-ness about the implications of the WTO dispute settlement system. As Atul Kaushik, the lawyer in the government who handled WTO dispute settlement in Geneva from 2003 to 2006, states, "these disputes were of high visibility for India. The government felt it needed to build capacity regarding WTO law."[28]

The United States itself used public–private partnerships in these cases as govern-ment lawyers worked with private law firms hired by US companies. Brazil was the first to adapt this model among developing countries (Chapter 4). India learned to follow suit, adapting the model to its own institutional context. The diffusion and localization of these models of public–private coordination in trade litigation illus-trate how the trade legal order catalyzed domestic institutional and professional adaptations.

When WTO members launched the Doha Round in 2001 to cover a broad array of policy areas, the Indian government and business quickly realized that they needed to invest more resources. As a high-level representative of the Federation of Indian Chamber of Commerce and Industry told us, the federation realized that it was "imperative" that business become more involved "because of our sense of failure to do so in the Uruguay Round."[29] Although the Doha Round collapsed, trade negoti-ations remain active in bilateral and regional forums and continue within the WTO, representing new forms of competitive trade liberalization shaping the transnational legal ordering of trade.

By late 2009, advocates of a "new India" touted the global shift of economic power away from the United States and European Union toward India and other emerging

---

[26]   Sukumar Muralidharan, "Opening the Floodgates," *Frontline* 18 (2001), https://frontline
       .thehindu.com/other/article30250264.ece.
[27]   Interview with government official, New Delhi, January 11, 2012. The government set up an inter-
       ministerial monitoring body consisting of the Secretaries for Commerce, Revenue, Agriculture, Small
       Scale Industries, Animal Husbandry, and the Director-General of Foreign Trade to monitor surges on
       imports of products where quantitative restrictions were eliminated, and potentially intercede under
       India's new import relief laws.
[28]   Interview, July 9, 2010.
[29]   Interview, January 19, 2010.

economies. India's share of global trade in goods and services (exports plus imports) quadrupled in the two decades since the WTO was created, from around 0.61 percent in 1994 to 2.5 percent in 2018; its share of global foreign direct investment (outbound and inbound) increased tenfold from 0.41 percent in 1994 to 4.34 percent in 2018; and its share of global GDP (PPP) more than doubled from 3.6 percent to 7.74 percent between 1994 and 2018, largely at the expense of Europe and the United States (whose combined proportion declined from 50 percent to 35 percent during this period).[30] Yet, to be a global leader in shaping and resisting transnational legal ordering, India needed to continue to enhance its institutional infrastructure and professional capacity in the public and private sectors. While economists tradition-ally have been most important for Indian policymaking analysis within and outside of the government, and they continue to be so today, the bureaucratic establishment and economists were pressed to recognize the importance of law and lawyering for national and international institutional adaptation, resistance, and reform.[31] Since legal capacity was not built into the traditional Indian government service, new methods were needed that could work with India's bureaucratic heritage.

II. DIFFUSING EXPERTISE: BUILDING PUBLIC–PRIVATE COORDINATION ON TRADE

The Indian government responded to the challenges of the WTO by investing in greater trade expertise in the Indian bureaucracy and government think tanks, and by working with the private sector and private legal counsel. The government reformed state institutions where it could, investing in state capacity within the Ministry of Commerce and Industry as a node for trade policy. It opened the state bureaucracy to build and tap into new legal capacity in the private sector. It created, in particular, a series of government think tanks, starting with the Centre for WTO Studies, to engage in policy-relevant research and act as a liaison between the Ministry of Commerce, the private sector, and private lawyers and consultants. By advancing more outward-oriented state development strategies through developing closer coordination with the private sector and professional expertise, the Indian state significantly transformed itself, illustrating the multiple dimensions of institu-tional change spurred by transnational legal ordering. It did so, in large part, to strengthen its capacity to engage with the transnational legal ordering of trade. These processes were largely elite-driven and technocratic, since the major political parties accepted India's economic reforms and public contestation over trade policy diminished.

---

[30] The trade statistics are our calculations from the UNCTADstat: World Statistical Database and the IMF Data Mapper. PPP signifies purchasing power parity, which equalizes the purchasing power of countries' currencies by accounting for cost of living and inflation differences.

[31] Interview with officials at Indian think tank, New Delhi, January 18, 2010.

A. *Building Expertise in the State*

In 1996, the government reconstituted the small, low-profile Trade Policy Division in the Commerce Ministry to enhance its competence on trade matters and support India's mission to the WTO in Geneva. The ministry increased staff strength from nine to almost forty officials within a few years.[32] By 2019 the government employed over one hundred officials with the rank of undersecretary or above,[33] complemented by those in other ministries working on international trade issues. The status of trade positions increased so that officials increasingly sought them and the best officials were posted. Within the Ministry of Commerce and Industry, the government created three new specialized agencies to handle matters implicated by WTO law: a new Tariff Commission, a reorganized Directorate General of Antidumping and Allied Duties, and an intellectual property rights administration within the Department of Industrial Policy and Promotion (since renamed the Department of Promotion for Industry and Internal Trade). In 1999, the government formed for the first time an inter-ministerial group to coordinate India's positions before the WTO and help resolve conflicts among ministries, such as between the Agriculture and Commerce ministries regarding agricultural tariffs and import restrictions.[34]

The government concurrently more than doubled the size of its mission in Geneva for WTO matters and enhanced coordination between the Geneva mission and the Commerce Ministry in New Delhi. In 1995 when the WTO started, the Indian mission in Geneva had one ambassador and three officers. By 2019, the mission had eight to nine officers, including two dispute settlement specialists with legal training.[35] In the early years, officials from the Legal and Treaty Division filled this division. Subsequently, the government chose officials from the more elite Indian Administrative Service and Indian Foreign Service with formal training from India's top law schools. For example, M.S. Srikar, the First Secretary (Legal) from 2014 to 2017, and his successor, Gitanjali Brandon, both graduated from India's top law school, the National Law School of India University, Bangalore. The government's expansion of its trade units and its selection of highly qualified personnel in New Delhi and the Geneva mission enhanced deliberation and coordination between Geneva and New Delhi-based officials. As a former Ambassador of India to the WTO noted, "in the old days, the Geneva mission received no meaningful inputs from the capital," but now officials in New Delhi are closely and continuously engaged.[36] Indian delegations in WTO meetings now

---

[32] Sinha, *Globalizing India*, 81

[33] Department of Commerce, Ministry of Commerce and Industry, *Officer Contact*, New Delhi, http:// commerce.gov.in/OfficerContact.aspx.

[34] Sinha, *Globalizing India*, 88–92.

[35] WTO Directory, June 2013. Increase confirmed in personal interview, Permanent Mission of India official, April 30, 2020.

[36] Interview, January 16, 2012.

comprise not only capital-based officials from the Department of Commerce, but also officials from other departments and sometimes private lawyers.[37]

B. *The UNCTAD Capacity-Building Project and the Creation of New Government Think Tanks*

Despite the relative growth in capacity of trade officials in the Commerce Ministry, the government still faced challenges, and thus needed to tap into expertise from outside government. It obtained critical external support for this endeavor through a transnational capacity-building project. UNCTAD, an organ of the United Nations, led the project, which India's Commerce Ministry and Britain's Department for International Development supported. The project, named "Strategies and Preparedness for Trade and Globalisation in India," lasted eight years, from January 2003 to December 2010.

Aiming to strengthen institutional trade capacity, the UNCTAD project organized a series of broad-based and sector-specific stakeholder consultations in India. It aimed to mobilize, for the first time, organizations representing farmers, fishermen, and small producers to articulate their interests and concerns and inform the government's approach to WTO and other trade agreement negotiations.[38] The UNCTAD project helped to spur the Ministry of Commerce and Industry to work with various state governments to establish WTO departments – known as "WTO cells" – with the responsibility of enhancing awareness of WTO law in the state government and providing a liaison to the ministry for WTO matters.

Transnational intermediaries were crucial for developing Indian trade-related capacity, exhibiting the links between transnational processes and state institutional change. The UNCTAD project was led by Veena Jha, an Indian trade economist whose husband, Harsha Singh, became one of the WTO's four Deputy Director Generals.[39] High-ranking Indian civil servants similarly held important posts in the WTO and GATT. The former Chief Economic Advisor of India (Subramaniam) and a former member of India's Policy Commission (Anwarul Hoda) worked in the GATT, and Hoda also was a Deputy Director-General (part of the inaugural slate at the WTO). Indian lawyers worked in each of the WTO secretariat's three legal divisions, serving respectively the Rules, Legal Affairs, and Appellate Body divisions.

To maintain the new networks after the UNCTAD project ended, and because of the difficulty of changing the bureaucracy from within, the Ministry of Commerce

---

[37] Interview with Sachin Kumar Sharma, CWS, November 20, 2017. The Department of Commerce is one of two Departments within the Ministry of Commerce and Industry.

[38] Compare Rajeev Kher, "India's Trade Disputes: Implications for Public Policy," in *WTO Dispute Settlement at Twenty: Insiders' Reflections on India's Participation*, eds. Abhijit Das and James Nedumpera (Singapore: Springer, 2016), 23 ("[M]ost of the time the State has pursued the interest of small producers," such as in "textiles and clothing, marine products . . .. The reason is not difficult to find, as much of India's export is represented by the small sector").

[39] Interview with acting director, January 21, 2010.

and Industry outsourced research and the building of public–private collaboration to government-sponsored think tanks. It created the Centre for WTO Studies in 1999, housed in the Indian Institute of Foreign Trade, a public management school in New Delhi. The last head of the UNCTAD project, Abhijit Das, became the government think tank's director, once more reflecting its transnational dimension.

Indian policymakers had long considered the need to strengthen the country's capacity in negotiating trade agreements. In 2016, after several years of internal debates, the Ministry of Commerce and Industry, with the approval of the Union Cabinet (India's highest decision-making body), established a new think tank named the "Centre for Research in International Trade" (CRIT) with a view to significantly augment India's ability to participate in WTO, regional, and bilateral trade and investment negotiations and dispute settlement. The Centre for WTO Studies was to be subsumed within CRIT and four additional centers were proposed. It was a state-led model quite different than in Brazil where the private sector funded the key think tanks.

The ministry created CRIT to develop research capabilities in India, as well as to develop ties with researchers in other countries in the region. CRIT undertakes substantive research on emerging trade-related issues, such as regarding digital trade, exchange rate policy, and climate change, in each case with a development orientation. As one senior official within the ministry responded to us, "fear of the unknown" is still a major factor that impedes developing countries' participation in trade negotiations.[40] Trade agreements have long-term implications and it is difficult to foresee their consequences. A recent example is India's participation in the Information Technology Agreement. As a rising power in the software sector, the government assumed that the Indian sector would capitalize on the WTO agreement's zero percent tariff commitments on computer and technology products. Its expectations were belied when more competitive Chinese and ASEAN exporters used the agreement to expand their share in India's internal market. Because many developing countries are wary of new negotiations, they are often ill prepared and on the defensive, pressed to react to developed country proposals, instead of being proactive.

In line with the Cabinet's decision, the Ministry of Commerce and Industry established two new centers in 2017: the Centre on Trade and Investment Law (CTIL) and the Centre for Regional Trade (CRT). These new centers, together with the Centre for WTO Studies, hire lawyers and economists. They recruit law graduates from India's National Law Schools and other leading institutions as professional and research staff. As of the start of 2019, over eighty professionals worked in these three centers. These centers illustrate how legal capacity originally catalyzed by the WTO is transportable and deployed elsewhere in the changing ecology of the trade system. James Nedumpara, coauthor of this chapter, developed

---

[40] Interview with a Joint Secretary, Ministry of Commerce and Industry, July 24, 2017.

expertise first regarding WTO law and then became the founding head of the Centre on Trade and Investment Law.

These centers aim to generate development-oriented negotiating positions and provide a platform to influence international discourse and discussions on international trade and investment law. The Centre on Trade and Investment Law, for example, hosts a pool of lawyers who respond to requests from the ministry and other government departments for legal research support and advice. The government wanted a think tank that it controlled to act and advise it without conflicts of interest because of other clients or donors. The center serves as a sort of in-house counsel that oversees the work of outside law firms, think tanks, and consultants as needed.

CRIT also aims to foster closer regional connections on trade policy, with India serving as a node. In this way, the centers can help India forge coalitions and like-minded groups to offset power imbalances and defend its interests in international trade and investment negotiations. CRIT aims to serve as a regional trade-related capacity-building agency for other countries. Working with the Centre for WTO Studies, the ministry had already conducted trade-related capacity building for countries such as Afghanistan, Kyrgyzstan, Kazakhstan, Mongolia, Myanmar, and other ASEAN countries. The creation of CRIT furthered these endeavors to facilitate policy dialogue and develop common negotiating positions.

For years, India had not explored economic cooperation with Central Asian countries. China's launch of the Belt and Road Initiative (Chapter 7) triggered Indian security and sovereignty concerns, especially in light of China's growing economic links with Pakistan and its building of major roads and other infrastructure close to China's contested border with India. China's trade initiatives compelled India to actively explore economic cooperation agreements with Eurasian economies. Through the Centre for Regional Trade within CRIT, it hopes to further regional economic cooperation among countries along the old Central Asian silk route that once traversed India.

The government typically works through the following process. The Commerce Ministry refers trade and investment law and policy questions to the research centers, whether relating to international negotiations, litigation, or domestic policy. The centers conduct the majority of the work in-house, but they outsource work to private contractors as well, such as to private lawyers, thereby strengthening state capacity through tapping private expertise.

C. *The Emergence of New Trade Law Expertise: Tapping into Indian Lawyers*

To participate in the negotiation of international trade rules, to shape the interpretation of rules, and to implement them in line with government priorities, the government needed to develop and tap into private legal expertise. The government did so in part because of the path dependence of the bureaucracy (which has a traditional diplomatic rotation system that does not involve lawyers and thus could not internally develop and retain the requisite expertise), in part because of the legal and technical demands of the WTO system, and in particular because harnessing private expertise would enhance government competence to form, defend, and justify its policy decisions domestically and internationally. The government began to foster the development of a small group of private professionals, and, in particular, transnationally-connected Indian lawyers, who developed expertise in trade law and policy, reflecting both the opening of the state bureaucracy and the strengthening of state capacity. In developing their own professional careers, these individuals provided critical assistance to the government in order for it to adapt and (potentially) contribute to the evolving trade legal order. As Abhijit Das, the head of the Centre for WTO Studies, states, as a consequence, trade policy making became more "participatory" and "based on stronger empirical foundations."[41]

This process gave rise to "a small industry of [legal] consultants growing around the Department of Commerce that helps to fill the government's needs."[42] For major WTO dispute settlement rulings, the ministry tried to organize a session where a private lawyer/consultant made a presentation to the department and other ministries, recounting their experience.[43] Participants included officials from the Department of Commerce and law firms and consultants that work with the government. The discussions raised awareness and enhanced the capacity of Indian domestic lawyers by keeping them abreast of WTO developments.[44] The meetings also helped the Department of Commerce to identify the core strengths of law firms that it could hire subsequently.[45]

The Indian private lawyers who work with the government on trade law are highly educated and are part of the rising professional classes that develop transnational social and educational connections, facilitating transnational legal ordering. Some are part of older elites that retool themselves, while others reflect an expansion of the Indian professional classes in light of new economic opportunities. These lawyers often received graduate legal education in the United States or Europe. The first Indian lawyer to take a lead in WTO cases was Krishnan Venugopal, the son of one of India's most renowned Supreme Court litigators who became Attorney General in 2017 (K.K. Venugopal). He went to Harvard Law School where he received an LLM and started an SJD, and then practiced with the US law firm Paul Weiss. Suhail Nathani, who started the boutique firm Economic Laws Practice based in Mumbai and Delhi, received a BA from Cambridge and an LLM from Duke Law School. Samir Gandhi, who worked earlier with Nathani, went to the London

---

[41] Interview, New Delhi, January 21, 2010.

[42] Interview with government official handling trade disputes, New Delhi, July 9, 2010.

[43] The Department of Commerce organized presentations by lawyers on important cases (such as the *China – Raw Materials*, *US – Carbon Steel*, *India – Agricultural Products*, *India – Solar Cells*, and *EC – Seals* cases) which have significant implications for government policymaking. Interviews, including with Joint Secretary, January 13, 2013.

[44] Interview with Indian trade official, New Delhi, January 13, 2013.

[45] Interview with Tapan Mazumder, Counsellor at India's Mission in Geneva, August 22, 2017.

School of Economics for his LLM. R.V. Anuradha, who founded Clarus Law Associates, received a master's at SOAS at the University of London and was a global law scholar at NYU Law School. Atul Sharma, a Partner at Seetharaman Associates, received his masters from NYU Law School. Moushami Joshi, a former partner at Luthra & Luthra who became a foreign attorney with Pillsbury Winthrop Shaw Pittman in Washington DC, received her LLM from George Washington University Law School. As Joshi says regarding her experience in the United States, "I had an interest in international trade and it just got strengthened when I was in DC. And DC being an international place, you get to attend so many conferences; you are constantly going to all these meetings that think tanks have, which was great because I think it just opened up my mind to this whole new world of law and legal practice."[46]

This new generation of highly skilled lawyers largely works within boutique firms, although such firms can have over one hundred attorneys overall. The largest elite Indian law firms generally have not developed a major international trade law practice, although a partner (at the time) in Luthra & Luthra (Moushami Joshi) worked on trade matters as part of her portfolio, and the founder of Clarus Law Associates (R.V. Anuradha), a small boutique firm, was formerly a partner at one of India's largest law firms, Amarchand & Mangaldas & Suresh A Shroff & Co. The total number of these trade lawyers is relatively small in light of the primarily intergovernmental nature of the WTO and broader trade law system, and they typically develop complementary practices, as in Brazil and China.[47]

The government facilitated the rise of these professionals through its creation of highly selective national law schools, which helped catalyze the development of this expertise. In 1996, just after the WTO's creation, the government funded a WTO Chair at the leading Indian law school, the National Law School of India University, Bangalore. The government's funding of a chair in trade law signaled the subject's importance, as well as the hope that the government would benefit from top students specializing in it.[48] K.M. Chandrasekhar, who was instrumental in the chair's creation when he was Joint Secretary in the Ministry of Commerce, told us that "the idea was to get young lawyers who can follow and provide expertise on WTO matters. The idea was to create new structures within the Indian context."[49]

---

[46] Interview, New Delhi, January 20, 2010.
[47] Some firms aim to build a complementary competition law practice, which somewhat overlaps with antidumping law-type analysis, such as regarding the definition of an industry, injury from unfair competition, and causation. Larger firms such as L & L Partners Law Offices, Economic Laws Practice, and Lakshmikumaran & Sridharan complement their WTO work with tax, customs, competition, and antidumping law practices.
[48] Interview with government official, July 9, 2010.
[49] Interview, January 16, 2012.

In practice, the vast majority of these students went to serve business clients in the "rising" India. However, many Indian international trade lawyers came from these national law schools.[50] Moreover, the students started a number of initiatives that helped build knowledge of international trade law in India. The National Law School in Bangalore, for example, created one of the first student-edited journals on international trade law, *The Indian Journal of International Economic Law*. The National Law University in Jodhpur followed by creating a specialization in International Trade and Investment Law and a journal entitled *Trade, Law and Development*. The student who started the journal in 2009, then got his LLM at Yale, worked at the Centre for WTO Studies, and became the first Indian member of the WTO Appellate Body secretariat. In parallel, a new generation of academics at Jindal Global Law School organized a concentration on international trade law and trade remedy law for LLM students, and it began a research center on international trade and economic law where students from law schools in India and abroad can receive a paid internship. Jindal Global Law School also works on TradeLab with the Graduate Institute in Geneva and Georgetown University Law Center to provide a clinical opportunity for students to advise clients on international trade and investment law issues, representing a significant change in the traditional Indian law school model.[51]

The government and the private sector created internships in trade law to attract these students. Building from Brazil's internship model (Chapter 4), which was prominently covered in Geneva, the Department of Commerce created trade policy internship programs for law students overseen by the Centre for WTO Studies and the Centre for Trade and Investment Law within CRIT. The NGO CUTS International did so as well, as have Indian law and consulting firms. Placement in these internships is highly competitive. Top law graduates pursued them despite opportunities to work in the more lucrative corporate law sector. These internships facilitate subsequent public–private collaboration and reflect a significant shift in the previously closed Indian state bureaucracy.

---

[50]   R. V. Anuradha, Samir Gandhi, and Moushami Joshi, respectively, graduated from National Law School Bangalore in 1995, 1998, and 2001. Shashank Kumar (in the WTO Secretariat for the Appellate Body and then Rules divisions), Atul Sharma, and Adarsh Ramanujam (who represented India in the *US – Carbon Steel* case) graduated from National Law University, Jodhpur. Parthasrathi Jha and Rishab Raturi, who worked on India's claim against the United States in the case *US – Renewable energy*, are graduates of the National Law Schools and respectively received graduate degrees from Harvard and the World Trade Institute (in Switzerland). Within the Centre for WTO Studies, Shailaja Singh joined as a legal consultant after receiving a degree from the West Bengal National University of Juridical Sciences, Kolkata, followed by an LLM at Cambridge University. Satwik Shekar, a legal consultant in the Centre for Trade and Investment Law in CRIT, graduated from the National Law School in Patiala and received an LLM from the Graduate Institute in Geneva.

[51]   Yves Dezalay and Bryant Garth, "Battles Around Legal Education Reform: From Entrenched Local Legal Oligarchies to Oligopolistic Universals. India as a Case Study," *UC Irvine Journal of International, Transnational, and Comparative Law* 3 (2018): 143.

D. *Tapping into Economic Expertise and External Consultancies*

International trade negotiations demand, in particular, economic expertise since they have large economic implications. Such expertise and legal know-how complement each other. Indian officials began to feel the need for enhanced economic expertise as international trade negotiations intensified in the 2000s and the negotiations became technically complex. As Sinha writes, "while India has many world-class economists, the civil service was traditionally quite insular and relied on 'in-house research' through the Indian Economic Service," whose officials were considered of much lower rank to the generalist officials of the Indian Administrative Service.[52] Most of the research conducted within the Indian civil service was poor, and it was not used in a significant manner. This began to change after India lost the *India – Quantitative Restrictions* and *India – Patents* cases in the late 1990s, and the government sought external economic expertise in a more systematic, rigorous, and sustained way.

The government began to consult many external research agencies and institutions while also enhancing the funding of state research institutions, such as the Research and Information System for Developing Countries (RIS) and the new Centre for WTO Studies, which were asked to focus attention on international economic issues. The Indian Ministry of Commerce and Industry also extensively consulted with and hired independent research institutes, such as ICRIER (the Indian Council for Research and International Economic Relations), NCAER (the National Council of Applied Economic Research), the Madras Institute of Development Studies, the Centre for Management in Agriculture, and the Indian Institutes of Management, among others.[53] In 2002–2003 alone, it commissioned eleven new studies at a cost of 8 million rupees.[54] This funding, in turn, catalyzed new investment in expertise within universities and think tanks, which hired economists to work on commissioned studies, creating a recursive feedback loop for capacity building across the policy community. Universities and research institutions began to generate a large quantity of research reports, databases, analysis, and commissioned studies, funded by the Indian state. The state's cognitive capacity for international trade negotiations significantly increased.

E. *The Transformation of State–Business Relations on Trade*

Indian business associations and companies were also insular during the GATT years, concerned with domestic policy and domestic licenses more than the international trade regime.[55] During the Uruguay round (1986–1994), industry prepared

---

52   Sinha, *Globalizing India*, 83.
53   Anwarul Hoda, Deputy Director General at the WTO from 1995 to 1999, headed ICRIER's WTO initiatives.
54   Sinha, *Globalizing India*, 84.
55   Interview with a business association officer, January 2012.

little for international trade negotiations or their implications. A 1999 report of the Confederation of Indian Industry (CII) acknowledged that the Indian Industry was "not so much concerned with what was happening in the Uruguay round. It was not even fully aware of the items of agenda that were being negotiated."[56]

Once industry became aware of the importance of WTO law in the early cases against India, it changed. In parallel, the government increasingly needed to become more transparent and consultative to enhance state capacity.[57] As one senior Indian official observed, the new Trade Policy Division decided to "open its doors" to the private sector and civil society during the Doha Round of negotiations.[58] The government increasingly invited industry and civil society representatives for consultations. It agreed to share the cost of internal industry consultations and it provided technical support, recognizing its ultimate dependence on private sector support.[59]

Industry associations responded. The Federation of Indian Chamber of Commerce and Industry (FICCI) established a new WTO, FTA, and Foreign Trade Division. The Confederation of Indian Industry created a new Trade Policy Section. They, in turn, conducted their own stakeholder consultations with their members.[60] Other industry organizations such as ASSOCHAM and PHD Chamber did as well, conducting industry-wide consultations on trade negotiation matters before and after key events such as WTO Ministerial conferences and other trade agreement negotiations. Organizations led by CII started an "India Everywhere" campaign with a view to showcasing India to the outside world.[61] Indian business and political leaders became a regular feature at the annual meeting of the World Economic Forum in Davos. In November 2012, the World Economic Forum organized a session entirely on India in New Delhi. The Confederation of Indian Industry opened an office in Geneva in 2003 to monitor the developments in the WTO negotiations and update industry about developments.

Indian businesses increasingly recognized the implications of trade negotiations. As Kaushik states, as India opened its economy to international trade, "industries recognized the need for internal capacities to deal with international trade matters."[62] The process started with the creation of WTO cells within Indian trade associations and large companies in the late 1990s and early 2000s. Trade associations representing different sectors created specialized WTO cells, such as for auto components, financial services, and textiles. The cells handled market access issues in trade negotiations, export control matters, trade remedy matters such as

---

[56] Sinha, *Globalizing India*, 103 (quoting CII report).
[57] Sinha, *Globalizing India*, 99–106.
[58] Interview with high-level Indian official, January 2012.
[59] Interview, academic consultant, New Delhi, January 9, 2012.
[60] Interview with FICCI representatives, New Delhi. January 19, 2010 and January 12, 2012.
[61] Knowledge@Wharton, *Delhi in Davos: How India Built its Brand at the World Economic Forum* (2006).
[62] Interview with Atul Kaushik, New Delhi, July 9, 2010.

antidumping, countervailing duty and safeguard investigations, technical regulations and standards, and other trade-related regulatory matters. Tata Iron and Steel
Company, the largest Indian steel maker, for example, engaged a senior consultant
to advise the company and the consortium of Indian steel companies in the OECD
steel subsidies negotiations. Tata also played a key role in mobilizing domestic
support for participation in the Global Forum on Steel Excess Capacity, an initiative
of the G-20 and the OECD to address trade distortions and excess capacity in the
steel sector.[63]

In 1998–1999, the government took initial steps to involve business groups in trade
policymaking. These business groups responded by supporting the government's
economic reforms, including "liberalization across India's states."[64] The government delegation to the 1999 WTO ministerial in Seattle for the first time included
members from the three main trade associations, FICCI, CII, and ASSOCHAM.[65]
Although the Seattle ministerial spectacularly collapsed, the experience highlighted
the need for broader government consultations with industry as a "stakeholder."
After the Seattle ministerial debacle, the government created a group of experts and
business representatives under the "Prime Minister's Council on Trade and
Industry" to produce a strategy paper on the WTO. For three months, the group
met at FICCI's office one-to-two days each week to discuss issues and produce
a report and set of recommendations.[66]

By the early 2000s, there had been a sea change in the nature and extent of
consultations conducted with private business. The government launched public
seminars to disseminate information about the WTO and India's obligations to other
ministries, state governments, and the broader public, including through trade
associations, trade unions, farmer representatives, NGOs, intellectuals, political
parties, and other interest groups. Government officials prominently issued public
statements on WTO-related issues, organized press conferences, and met various
actors. From just April to September 2003, "the government held at least thirty
seminars, conferences, and meetings to educate the public and interested parties" in
preparation for the WTO ministerial meeting in Cancun.[67] While contestation
remained, and the opening primarily engaged business, the result was a more
transparent process than in traditional bureaucratic policy making, whether for
international relations or purely domestic policy.

***

The Indian system remains government-driven and the government aims to steer the
process so that the consultants and lawyers are on tap, and not on top. The private

---

[63] Interview with Koustav Kakati in New Delhi, October 18, 2017.
[64] Aseema Sinha, "Understanding the Rise and Transformation of Business Collective Action in India,"
      Business and Politics 7, no. 1 (2005): 16.
[65] Interview with CII official, January 1, 2012.
[66] Sinha, *Globalizing India*, 106.
[67] Sinha, *Globalizing India*, 100.

sector still plays a more limited role than in comparison with the United States, as well as Brazil. These institutional and professional changes, nonetheless, were significant for India. As Professor Bipin Kumar of the National Law University Jodhpur, who formerly worked in the Centre for WTO Studies, told us, "the new mantra in India is public-private partnerships. The old mentality regarding government is changing."[68] These changes involving greater government transparency, public–private coordination, and outward engagement with the global economy reflect key aspects of what has been called a new developmental state model involving enhanced state capacity through greater coordination with the private sector.[69] They are explained, in significant part, by India's enmeshment in the WTO and the broader transnational legal order for trade. Trade law capacity is thus critical.

III. TRANSNATIONAL LEGAL ORDERING OF TRADE POLICY

The transnational legal order for trade develops through negotiation, litigation, and practice. It entails both top-down and bottom-up processes; it is shaped by states and private actors; in turn, it shapes their practices through recursive processes. Public and private lawyers engage with the trade transnational legal order in different ways. Lawyers and economists advise the government in the development of its negotiating positions, and they assist the government in evaluating, litigating, and settling WTO cases for and against it. They provide input on the drafting of legislation and regulation and the consideration of domestic policy alternatives in light of international trade law. In doing so, they embed and shape the transnational legal order for trade, implicating law and policy within India.

A. WTO Negotiations: Primarily a Veto Player But with a New Agenda for Services

With the launch of the Doha negotiating round in 2001, India adapted its institutions in order to play a more engaged role in the WTO system. To do so, the government created new linkages with stakeholders and it consulted with them more regularly and transparently. While the trade policy division was previously known for being remote and nontransparent, the government began more proactively and regularly to share analysis and documents with the private sector and seek economic studies from consultants and legal opinions from law firms. The government did so because of a sense that it would embarrass itself if the administration did not become more proactive and effective in tapping into and making use of the information and

---

[68] Interview, Jodhpur, January 9, 2012.
[69] David M. Trubek, *Law and the New Developmental State: The Brazilian Experience in Latin American Context* (Oxford: Hart Publishing, 2013); Sinha, *Globalizing India*.

expertise of the private sector and a new generation of professionals engaged with global issues.[70]

India is known for being wary and on the defensive in GATT and WTO trade negotiations. It was a leader of the Group of 77 of developing countries that called for a radical overhaul and establishment of a New International Economic Order in the 1970s and a key member of the "Like-Minded Group" and G-33 of developing countries that blocked the inclusion of three of the so-called Singapore issues (investment, competition law, and government procurement) as part of the WTO's negotiating mandate in 2004, and demanded special and differential treatment for developing countries in WTO negotiations over market access in agriculture and industry.[71] Although such special and differential treatment was part of the Doha Round negotiating mandate,[72] India's position contributed to US disenchantment with the WTO as a negotiating forum because emerging powers' had become more successful in blocking US demands in trade negotiations. For the United States, their economies (and particularly China's) had become more competitive while their market access commitments remained much less than those of the United States.

Crucially, at the 2003 WTO Ministerial meeting in Cancun, India worked with Brazil to respond to a Joint EU-US proposal on agriculture that failed to reflect the interests of Brazil and India. In practice, Brazil had strong export interests and India protectionist ones. Indian politicians are particularly concerned about the impact of opening India's market to increased agricultural imports because of the huge percentage of its population still employed in agriculture – about one-half – and the Maoist/Naxalite insurgencies threatening many Indian rural areas. The US-EU proposal managed to account for the divergent interests of the United States and Europe while alienating both Brazil and India. Brazil and India creatively responded by developing a counter proposal that accommodated their differing interests while challenging US and EU agricultural subsidies. They organized a new group of developing countries known as the G-20, which included China, to co-sponsor it.[73] This proactive developing country stance on negotiating

---

[70] Interview with official, New Delhi, July 9, 2010.

[71] Nicolas Lamp, "Strategies for Developing Countries in Multilateral Trade Negotiations at the World Trade Organization," in *Building Legal Capacity for a More Inclusive Globalization: Barriers to and Best Practices for Integrating Developing countries into Global Economic Regulation*, eds. Joost Pauwelyn and Mengyi Wang (Geneva: The Graduate Institute, 2019): 9–30.

[72] Doha Declaration, para. 13 on agriculture ("special and differential treatment for developing countries shall be an integral part of all elements of the negotiations"); para. 16 on non-agricultural products ("the negotiations shall take fully into account the special needs and interests of developing and least-developed country participants, including through less than full reciprocity in reduction commitments").

[73] Committee on Agriculture, *Agriculture – Framework Proposal – Joint Proposal by Argentina, Brazil, Bolivia, China, Chile, Colombia, Costa Rica, Cuba, Ecuador, El Salvador, Guatemala, India, Mexico, Pakistan, Paraguay, Peru, Philippines, South Africa, Thailand and Venezuela*, JOB (03)/162 (August 29, 2003).

modalities was a "defining moment of change for the WTO" and its negotiating system.[74] It was the first time that developing countries had come together to submit an integrated, detailed proposal on modalities that reflected their development concerns.[75] Following this initiative, commentators referred to a new Quad, consisting of the United States, European Union, India, and Brazil, constituting the key players for WTO negotiations (with India and Brazil having replaced Japan and Canada).[76]

This shift would not have happened without the development of trade law capacity involving new public–private partnerships. The Brazilian and Indian governments worked with think tanks in their respective countries to develop new modalities for WTO agricultural negotiations. The think tanks' analyses provided the analytic heft for the G-20 in the Doha Round agricultural negotiations. While Brazil's focus was to expand access for its highly competitive agribusiness sector, India pushed defensively for a "special safeguards mechanism" and "special product exemptions" for its agriculture, as well as a permanent exemption for public stock-holding of grains for food security.[77]

In the key meetings in 2008 in Geneva, the inner group was expanded to a G-7 that included China, Australia, and Japan.[78] There, India insisted on the adoption of a Special Safeguard Mechanism for agricultural products, leading to blockage. India also joined forces with Brazil and China to refuse US demands to make "further market access" commitments through sectoral negotiations (including for chemicals, industrial machinery, and electronics and electrical products) beyond those set forth in a "Swiss formula."[79] This eventually led to US withdrawal from the negotiations on the grounds that emerging economic powers needed to "catch up" with making greater tariff commitments to balance existing US tariff bindings.[80] The Doha Round then collapsed.

[74]   Shaffer discussed with K. M. Chandrasekhar, India's ambassador to the WTO from 2001–2004 who was central to the Cancun ministerial meeting, in Trivandrum, India (Interview, January 16, 2012). India's Ambassador Ujjal Singh Bhatia (to the WTO from 2004–2010) calls this a "watershed moment" in the history of the WTO. Ujjal Singh Bhatia, "G-20 – Combining Substance with Solidarity and Leadership," in *Reflections From the Frontline: Developing Country Negotiators in the WTO*, ed. Pradeep S. Mehta (New Delhi: Academic Foundation, 2012), 239, 245 (arguing that the formation of G-20 challenged the hegemony of the US and EU in agenda setting at the WTO); David Deese, *World Trade Politics: Power, Principles and Leadership* (Abingdon: Routledge, 2007), 155 (noting that in 2004, "the Brazilian and Indian ministers established themselves as co-leaders in the most contentious issue area, agriculture, because they were able to gradually press the US and EC for substantial agricultural reforms they would not offer on their own").

[75]   Bhatia, "G-20 – Combining Substance with Solidarity and Leadership," 239, 245.

[76]   Deese, *World Trade Politics*. The Old Quad consisted of the United States, European Union, Japan, and Canada.

[77]   India feared Brazil would later compromise as it did. Paul Blustein, *Misadventures of the Most Favored Nations: Clashing Egos, Inflated Ambitions, and the Great Shambles of the World Trade System* (New York: Public Affairs, 2009), 187–188, 267; Hopewell, *Breaking the WTO*, 87.

[78]   Hopewell, *Breaking the WTO*, 215. This inner group periodically changed during the Doha round.

[79]   Blustein, *Misadventures of the Most Favored Nations*, 270–276.

[80]   Report by the Director-General on His Consultations on NAMA Sectoral Negotiations, TN/C/14, April 21, 2011, para. 8, 12.

Although the WTO Doha Round of negotiations effectively ended, trade negotiations continued in a less ambitious manner within the WTO. Once more, India continued to oppose new initiatives, frustrating other members. It delayed adoption of the WTO Trade Facilitation Agreement in 2014 to extract a commitment for a permanent exemption of its stockholding programs under the WTO Agreement on Agriculture on food security grounds. Although it did not receive an exemption, it did obtain a "peace clause" that its policies would not be challenged.[81] It also opposed the launch of initiatives on investment facilitation and e-commerce supported by Brazil and China on the grounds that they focus on concerns of developed countries (bringing back one of the "Singapore issues") and do not incorporate developing countries' concerns, which had been the rationale for the Doha "development round."[82]

Nonetheless, India became more proactive in negotiations to liberalize a key area for trade in services. It took an offensive position involving the movement of personnel for services trade (known as "mode 4"), which would liberalize visas, and which is important for many Indian service providers, such as the information technology industry. India's liberalization initiative in a trade negotiation, in the words of one of its former negotiators, represented "a paradigm shift."[83] The government worked closely with its service sectors, and in particular the National Association of Software and Services Companies, as well as CII and FICCI. As one industry representative stated, "Whatever inputs we have given to the government, they have taken them."[84] The government found support from NGOs, such as Oxfam, and international organizations, such as the World Bank.[85] After the round's collapse, India proposed an analogue to the Trade Facilitation Agreement for services trade in 2016, and then followed up with a "draft legal text" the following year. Even though the proposal became dormant, India had deployed its legal capacity to be proactive.[86]

India used its new technical capacity to become part of the inner circle of trade negotiations. It made detailed proposals to protect its policy space (as in agriculture) and to expand its exports (as in mode 4 services). It created new alliances with Brazil and the G-20, and it maintained old ones with developing country negotiating groups. It worked with the private sector and civil society groups. It consulted with lawyers to provide support for its proposals. Without the development of such broad-based technical capacity, it would have been much less effective. In WTO negotiations, it often acted as a veto player more than a shaper of new norms. Nonetheless, WTO members eventually did agree to ban agricultural export subsidies and India did obtain a peace clause for its public stockholding of grains.

[81] Lamp, *Strategies for Developing Countries*, 21–23.
[82] Interviews with two high-level Indian officials, July 10, 2019.
[83] Hopewell, *Breaking the WTO*, 157 (citing an interview).
[84] Hopewell, *Breaking the WTO*, 155 (citing an interview).
[85] Hopewell, *Breaking the WTO*, 164.
[86] Lamp, *Strategies for Developing Countries*, 24–25.

B. *Adapting to the Changing Ecology of the Trade Legal Order: The Turn to Bilateral and Regional Trade Agreements*

As the Doha Round collapsed and WTO negotiations stalemated, bilateral and regional trade negotiations triggered competition among countries to gain market access. India formerly had focused largely on maintaining close ties in South Asia where it was the regional power. It signed its first bilateral trade agreements with Nepal (1991) and Sri Lanka (1998). It then drove a new Agreement for a South Asia Free Trade Area (SAFTA) in 2004 that includes Bangladesh, Bhutan, India, Maldives, Nepal, Pakistan, and Sri Lanka.[87] As WTO negotiations stalemated and countries turned to other negotiating fora, these competitive processes spurred India to enter a much broader array of trade negotiations and agreements.

Most importantly, India worked to build economic ties in East Asia, in part to counterbalance China. The Rao government formally launched a *Look East* policy in 1991 as part of its trade liberalization initiatives. With China's rise and development of the Belt and Road Initiative (Chapter 7), the Modi government ramped up this policy, relabeling it *Act East* in 2014.[88] India worked to build closer relations with ASEAN and other East Asian nations. The policy, however, has remained largely aspirational, and for some commentators, hype,[89] since China's Belt and Road Initiative dwarfs it. Implementing the Act East policy has not been easy, and India has persistent trade deficits with most ASEAN countries.[90] Within Asia, Indian companies' integration with global and regional supply chains is less impressive. Yet, India's trade is increasing significantly with East Asia, and ASEAN countries generally welcome India's engagement.[91] Integration with the ASEAN countries is key to India being part of global value chains, including through obtaining access to raw material and industrial inputs. This regional policy signals Indian government awareness of China's growing economic clout and the need to respond through forging closer economic ties in Asia, including through trade and investment agreements.

India signed a slew of agreements with countries in the region, including with Afghanistan (2003), Thailand (2004), Singapore (2005), South Korea (2009), Japan

---

[87]   SAFTA is linked to the South Asian Association for Regional Cooperation (SAARC) created in 1984. The development of SAARC has been limited by India's tense relations with Pakistan. Regional trade increased following SAFTA but it is still rather minimal, constituting only around 1 percent of the region's GDP.

[88]   Frederic Grare, *India Turns East: International Engagement and US-China Rivalry* (Oxford: Oxford University Press, 2017).

[89]   Chietgj Bajpaee, "Dephasing India's Look East/Act East Policy," *Contemporary Southeast Asia* 39, no. 2 (2017): 348–372.

[90]   Veena Jha, Pankhuri Bansal, and Vipin Kumar, "India's Position in the International Economic Order," *Global Trade & Customs Journal* 14, no. 7–8 (2019): 325, 331 (noting that India's trade deficit with ASEAN, Japan and South Korea in FY 2017 increased to US$24 bn as compared to US$15 bn in FY 2011).

[91]   Acharya, *East of India*.

(2011), and Malaysia (2011), as well as with regional groups such as APTA (2004) and ASEAN (2009, 2010, 2014). It then began to expand these agreements into "comprehensive economic partnerships" that include investment as well as trade in goods, services, e-commerce, government procurement, standards, and regulations regarding the movement of people. It already has signed comprehensive economic partnership agreements with Singapore (2005), South Korea (2009), Malaysia (2011), Japan (2011), and ASEAN (2010, 2014). It is negotiating others with Australia, Indonesia, and New Zealand. It is also expanding its free trade agreements concluded with Sri Lanka (1998), BIMSTEC (1997), and APTA (1987) to include additional chapters, such as for services.[92]

India also has launched negotiations for free trade agreements outside of Asia, including with the European Union, the European Free Trade Association, Canada, Egypt, Israel, and the United States. It concluded agreements with Chile (2005) and Mercosur (2008). It is working, in particular, to develop close economic relations with the United States, including as part of its broader geopolitical concerns regarding China.[93]

India nonetheless remains highly cautious in its trade agreements, which have been much narrower in scope than those negotiated by the United States and Europe. They sometimes start with mere framework agreements. They have tended to constitute "preferential agreements" – rather than free trade agreements – in that they exempt large numbers of "sensitive" product lines and, for those lines covered, often only reduce tariffs over an extended period as opposed to cutting them to zero. India, for example, participated in the negotiation of a Regional Comprehensive Economic Partnership (RCEP) – with the ASEAN group, Australia, China, India, Japan, New Zealand, and South Korea – but suspended its participation in November 2019. It first constrained the ambitions of the RCEP by demanding the right to retain tariffs on at least 20 percent of goods that it deems sensitive.[94] It then dropped out of the negotiations because of its fear of Chinese trade dominance.[95]

---

[92] BIMSTEC is the Bay of Bengal Initiative for Multi-Sectoral Technical and Economic Cooperation, comprised of seven countries. APTA is the Asia-Pacific Trade Agreement, previously named the Bangkok Agreement, and is the oldest preferential trade agreement in the region. V. S. Sheshadri, "Evolution in India's Regional Trading Arrangements," *Journal of World Trade* 43, no. 5 (2009): 903–966.

[93] India's desire to develop closer ties with the United States also is reflected in the 2105 US–India Joint Strategic Vision for the Asia-Pacific and Indian Ocean Region and its follow-up. It joined the United States in announcing in 2020 their aim to conclude a free trade agreement, though commentators imagine it will be of limited ambition, if reached. Anubhav Gupta, "Despite the Trump-Modi 'Love', Trade is Still the Weak Link in U.S.-India Relations," *World Politics Review*, March 9, 2020.

[94] Amiti Sen, "RCEP Hanoi Talks: India Not Willing to Go Beyond 80% Tariff Elimination in Goods," *The Hindu Business Line* (May 23, 2017): www.thehindubusinessline.com/economy/rcep-hanoi-talks-india-not-willing-to-go-beyond-80-tariff-elimination-in-goods/article9710892.ece.

[95] Benjamin Parkin and John Reed, "India Decides Not to Sign China-Backed Pan-Asian Trade Deal," *Financial Times*, November 4, 2019.

For these negotiations, the government consults outside lawyers to bolster state capacity. The lawyers at times work with economists who address the economic implications of different negotiating positions and modalities, whether for trade in goods, trade in services, or investment.[96] The government has hired private law firms for specialized assistance on intellectual property, services, standards, import relief, government procurement, and investment issues.[97] These firms provide the government with advice, including at the stage of "legal scrubbing" and finalization of the schedules of concessions.[98]

India realizes that the ecology of the trade legal order is changing. It is thus negotiating and has concluded a growing number of bilateral and regional trade agreements to advance its trading interests. These agreements can expand over time as India cautiously opens its economy. Developments in these different bilateral and regional fora both complement multilateral negotiations and agreements and compete with each other to shape transnational legal norms and practices for trade. In the process, India has enhanced state capacity by tapping into the broader legal expertise that WTO cases first catalyzed.

C. Trade Litigation

The WTO system became unique in providing a global judicialized system for dispute settlement with compulsory jurisdiction. The WTO Appellate Body created a complex system of de facto legal precedent, for which legal expertise became particularly important. India became one of the leading users of this system, in contrast to India's earlier (half century) disengagement from litigation under the GATT. Through January 1, 2020, India was a complainant in twenty-four WTO disputes, a respondent in thirty-two, and a third party in 162 additional ones, totaling 218 cases in twenty-five years. Third-party submissions became important because decisions in WTO cases involving other countries could have systemic implications for the understanding and future application of WTO law (Chapter 3). India increasingly asserted third-party rights, becoming the fourth most active third-party participant (after Japan, the European Union, and China), as well as the fifth most active party in WTO dispute settlement (after the United States, European Union, China, and Canada). Figure 5.2 shows India's annual and

---

[96] Shaffer interviews with Indian attorneys, economists in think tanks, and government officials, January 2010 and January 2012. In 2018, for example, the Department of Commerce hired the services of Ajit Ranade, Chief Economist with Aditya Birla Group, to evaluate the trade impact of United States' non-compliance with the WTO ruling in *US – Carbon Steel*, a dispute that India had won.

[97] The firms include Economic Laws Practice, Clarus Law, PLR Chambers, TPM Consultants, APJ-SLG, and Lakshmikumaran and Sridharan. For example, the government worked with CRIT and external lawyers to examine the implications of "Brexit" and its effects on trade concessions in goods and services.

[98] Shaffer interviews with officials in Ministry of Commerce, New Delhi, January 12, 2012.

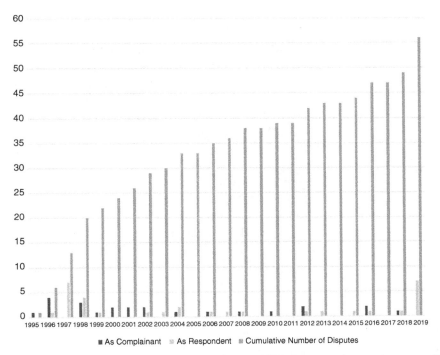

FIGURE 5.2 India as complainant and respondent in WTO dispute settlement (2001–2019)[99]

cumulative number of cases as a respondent and complainant through 2019, illustrating how India became a repeat player.

This engagement with transnational legal ordering required new legal expertise and public–private coordination. The government first turned to the former head of the GATT legal secretariat, Frieder Roessler, initially in his private capacity, and then as the first Executive Director of the Advisory Centre on WTO Law (ACWL) in 2002, an international organization in Geneva providing developing countries with subsidized legal assistance. India quickly became the ACWL's most active user. Roessler worked for India in the *India – Quantitative Restrictions*[100] and *India – Auto* disputes in his individual capacity, and in the *EC – Tariff Preferences*[101] and the *US – Rules of Origin*[102] disputes as part of ACWL. The government also turned to foreign lawyers in cases involving foreign application of import relief laws against Indian imports, such as with a Brussels-based law firm in

[99] Compilation from the WTO database (January 2020).
[100] WT/ DS 90/R (April 6, 1999).
[101] WT/DS 246/R (December 1, 2003).
[102] WT/DS 243/R (June 20, 2003).

the *EC – Bed Linen* dispute,[103] and a US law firm in the *US – Steel Plate* dispute challenging US antidumping practices.[104]

The government, however, wished to develop indigenous Indian expertise given the legal costs as well as the broader implications of the interpretation of WTO rules, its need to respond to cases brought against India, and its desire to use WTO rules to support its exports. It started to use, and then began to groom, specialized, transnationally connected, private Indian lawyers instead of government attorneys. The government began to work on WTO cases with Krishnan Venugopal, first in parallel with Roessler and the ACWL, and later alone. Venugopal worked on a series of cases, either alone or jointly with other lawyers.[105]

Over time, a small group of Indian lawyers in the private sector became increasingly important for providing counsel to the government on potential and actual WTO trade disputes, including Economics Law Practice, Clarus Law Associates, Luthra & Luthra Law Offices, and Lakshmikumaran & Sridharan.[106] These Indian law firms increasingly provided legal analysis and drafting support for India's third-party submissions in WTO cases as well.[107] As a result, India participated more regularly in WTO disputes that implicated WTO law's interpretation and future application. In September 2014, Lakshmikumaran & Sridharan, which at the time was assisting the government in the *US – Carbon Steel (India)* case,[108] became the first non-US or European law firm to establish an office in Geneva, although it closed the office in 2017 because of its inability to attract work beyond the Indian government.

[103] WT/DS 141/R (October 30, 2000). The firm was Vermulst Waer & Verhaeghe (VWV), which also represented Indian textile exporters in the underlying antidumping case in Brussels. The Indian government worked with the Indian textiles industry through Texprocil, the textiles export promotion council in the case.

[104] WT/DS 206/R (June 28, 2002). The law firm was Sidley Austin. Scott Anderson and Deepak Raju, "India's Initial Disputes – An Analysis in Retrospect," in *WTO Dispute Settlement at Twenty: Insiders' Reflections on India's Participation*, eds. Abhijit Das and James Nedumpara (Singapore: Springer Nature, 2016): 45–67.

[105] He worked on the *India – Patents, India – Quantitative Restrictions, India – Autos, EC – Tariff Preferences* (AB 2005), and *US – Customs Bond Directive* cases, among others.

[106] The government hired Economics Laws Practice in the cases *India – Additional Duties*, WT/DS 360/R (June 9, 2008); and *US – Renewable Energy*, WT/DS510/R (June 27, 2019). It hired Luthra & Luthra Law Offices in the case *India – Agricultural Products*, WT/DS 430/R (September 14, 2014). In the subsequent arbitration and compliance proceedings in *India – Agricultural Products*, the government also engaged ACWL because of the complexity of the matter, but it ensured that the Indian law firm played a part. It engaged Clarus Law Associates in *India – Solar Cells* and in the preparatory stages for a complaint against restrictive US visa requirements in *US – Visa Fees*. Interview with Indian official at ambassadorial level, New Delhi, May 21, 2012 (regarding DS 503 concerning the U.S. Southwest Border Protection Act and the James Zadroga Act). A full list of cases and counsel is provided in Gregory Shaffer, James Nedumpara, and Aseema Sinha, "Indian Lawyers and the Building of State-Trade Related Authority," *Minnesota Legal Studies Research Paper* No. 14–08 (2014).

[107] Interview with private Indian lawyer, New Delhi, January 12, 2012.

[108] WT/DS 436/R (July 14, 2014). The firm had represented the steel industry in the underlying U.S. import relief case.

The government created more systematized procedures for the selection of trade lawyers. In 2010, the Department of Commerce, in consultation with the Department of Legal Affairs, enlisted seventeen law firms to help defend the country in WTO disputes, which it periodically updated based on past performance and new panel requests. For individual cases, the Department of Commerce issued calls to law firms with expertise in the subject. Responding law firms submit information about their legal team's relevant experience, together with a legal opinion regarding the case.

India brought systemically important claims before the WTO system that shaped WTO jurisprudence and thus affected the trade legal order. The *US – Shrimp-Turtle* dispute is arguably the most referenced WTO case regarding the interpretation of the GATT exception clause, Article XX, addressing the interaction of trade rules with environmental protection measures.[109] The *EC – Tariff Preferences* case clarified the legal requirements under the General Systems of Preferences affecting imports from developing countries. The *Turkey – Textiles* case for the first time recognized the jurisdiction of the WTO dispute settlement body over the legality of measures taken to form regional trade agreements. In India's early complaint, *US – Shirt and Blouses*, the Appellate Body clarified the burden of proof in WTO cases.[110] India also brought important cases affecting the interpretation of antidumping and countervailing duty law to the consternation of the United States, as discussed below (section E). Given the systemic implications of these decisions, India's aim was to win the case while also shaping the understanding of WTO law in line with its broader policy objectives to protect its policy space, on the one hand, and support its export interests, on the other.[111] India has not been as successful in shaping WTO jurisprudence as has Brazil, for example, in Brazil's strategic cases against US and EU agricultural subsidies. However, India's use of WTO dispute settlement has provided it with greater policy space domestically, has shaped import relief law (Section E), and has protected its exports (such as of generic drugs, Section IV).

D. *Implementation and Policy Space*

The implementation of WTO law has significant implications for law and policy within emerging economies. Choices over implementation involve interpretation of the flexibilities permitted under WTO law where lawyers can be helpful. WTO rules and dispute settlement implicated India's dismantling of its License Raj, its adoption and implementation of intellectual property law, its revision and application of

---

[109]   WT/DS 58/R (May 15, 1998).
[110]   WT/DS 33/AB/R (April 25, 1997), 16.
[111]   India also aimed to shape WTO jurisprudence as a respondent. In *India – Agricultural Products*, the Appellate Body clarified the regionalization requirements under the Agreement on Sanitary and Phyotsanitary Measures, which was the first decision under this agreement against a developing country.

Indian import relief laws, and its development of industrial policy. Changing domestic laws and institutions to comply with WTO requirements was highly contested in India, most publicly in the area of intellectual property rights and agriculture, but also in other areas. The demands catalyzed the development of new institutional capacity, complemented by new public–private coordination for implementing trade law requirements.

Different Indian government departments worked directly with private consultants or indirectly through first contacting the Commerce Department as the government node for WTO and trade-related questions. Other departments frequently sent questions to the Commerce Department regarding the WTO compatibility of draft legislation and regulation. The Department at times outsourced these questions to private consultants, including through CRIT and the centers within it. Departments have done so, for example, for policy documents such as the National Standards Policy and the Manual of Operating Practices for trade remedy investigations. In 2013, the Joint Secretary in the Ministry of Commerce informed us that it "gets references about every single day" regarding the WTO implications of legislation, regulation, and policies.[112]

As government departments became aware of trade law's implications, they sometimes engaged private lawyers directly. WTO law affects industrial policy choices, such as the use of subsidies and domestic content requirements, affecting many Indian ministries. The powerful Indian Planning Commission (since replaced by the NITI Aayog), for example, contacted private attorneys regarding power infrastructure initiatives, including policy options for applying tariffs and local content requirements to build domestic manufacturing capacity.[113] In the past, the Planning Commission would never have consulted outside lawyers, much less regarding international trade law. The government likewise consulted private law firms regarding WTO law's implications for India's renewable energy policies affecting utilities, as well as regarding climate change policies (from the Ministry of Environment and Forests) and e-commerce policies (from the Department of Industry Policy and Promotion). NITI Aayog likewise has worked with trade lawyers to explore policy options. These developments illustrate the broader implications of the WTO for Indian law and policy, including as it tries to link its industrial policies with global supply chains.[114]

WTO law grants countries some flexibility in interpreting its provisions so that India had some leeway in determining how to revise its laws and adapt its institutions. Although international lawyers and international relations scholars tend to focus on the issue of "compliance" as a binary issue, and commentators like Thomas Friedman refer to the "golden straitjacket" of global markets,[115] countries retain

---

[112] Interview, January 13, 2013.
[113] Interview, Moushami Joshi, January 12, 2012.
[114] ENS Economic Bureau, "New Industrial Policy Linking Global Supply Chain on the Anvil: Suresh Prabhu," *The Indian Express*, March 11, 2020.
[115] Thomas Friedman, *The Lexus and the Olive Tree* (New York City: Anchor Books, 1999).

flexibility to engage in hybrid policymaking within constraints. In implementing, they may invent; in adopting, they may indigenously adapt.

India has lost a number of WTO cases affecting its industrial policies to develop particular industries, but has, in the process bought time and redesigned industrial policies to enhance their effectiveness. At times, the country's policies clearly violated WTO rules, but it raised defenses under such rules in new ways, leading to clarification of WTO constraints and flexibilities. At other times, it largely played for time to maintain or adapt its policies while pursuing its objectives. And at times, the cases helped to catalyze consultations to improve the effectiveness of its policies.

For example, the United States challenged India's policy to support the development of a national auto sector, which included Indian local content, foreign exchange, and trade balancing requirements as conditions for imports and investment.[116] India lost the case, but, in practice, was able to use the dispute settlement system (which does not provide retrospective remedies) so as to delay compliance and continue its program for a number of years to develop local manufacturing know-how and enhance competitiveness.[117] Government officials contend that the policy was successful, as India now exports autos to the Middle East, Latin America, Africa, South Asia and Central Asia, and created a new hub in competition with Thailand and Indonesia in the region.[118]

Similarly, India launched a National Solar Mission in 2010 to increase its solar power generation and establish India as a global leader in the solar energy sector. Following vigorous domestic debate that pitted solar equipment manufacturers against power project developers who wanted low-cost access to foreign products, the plan included domestic content requirements for the use of Indian equipment. The United States challenged these requirements in the *India – Solar Cells* case in 2013. India invoked a defense under GATT Article XX(j) concerning "products in general or local short supply." The panel and Appellate Body ruling clarified the scope and contours of this exception which had never been invoked in the history of the GATT and WTO.[119] Although India lost the case and revised its regulations, the United States challenged India's compliance, which remained pending. India, in turn, challenged US state policies to enhance its leverage in settlement negotiations. It won its case against the United States at the panel stage in June 2019, but the appeal was suspended

---

[116] WT/DS 146/R (December 21, 2001); Kyle Bagwell and Alan Sykes, "India – Measures Affecting Automotive Sector," *World Trade Review* 4, no. 1 (2005): 158–178. The United States did so after its victory in the broad-based challenge to India's system of quantitative restrictions and licenses.

[117] Interview with officials at Indian think tank, New Delhi, January 18, 2010. Compare Rachel Brewster, "The Remedy Gap: Institutional Design, Retaliation, and Trade Law Enforcement," *George Washington Law Review* 80 (2011): 102–158 (noting how nations can take advantage of protracted WTO dispute settlement to buy time).

[118] Interview with officials at Indian think tank, New Delhi, January 18, 2010.

[119] WT/DS/456/AB/R (September 16, 2016).

given the hamstringing of the Appellate Body.[120] Meanwhile, industrial policy and public–private partnerships remain central to India's National Solar Mission, and some local content requirements were expanded, complemented by new subsidies and import safeguards, which the government tried to tailor in light of WTO rulings. The country's robust defense of its programs before the WTO helped buy it time to advance its objectives to become a low-cost producer of solar power. This relatively nascent sector is growing faster than the government had targeted, although it also has encountered setbacks in light of Chinese competition and WTO legal constraints.[121]

The United States continues to press India to curtail its industrial policies. In 2018, it challenged India's export incentive schemes, including its Special Economic Zones policies, in the case *India – Export Related Measures*.[122] The case affected a broad range of industrial sectors, the leading ones being information technology, electronics, semiconductors, pharmaceuticals, engineering, and textiles. As Manoj Mate shows, even though India lost at the panel stage, with the appeal process once more suspended, the government was much more proactive at an early stage in initiating internal consultations for the adaptation of its policies.[123] India used this time to proactively introduce an otherwise WTO permissible border tax adjustment scheme for various non-reimbursable duties and taxes on exported products.[124] Importantly, the government did so not only in relation to the WTO dispute, but also to improve policy effectiveness as part of its New Industrial Policy. In this case, the policy interests of economic operators coincided regarding the special economic zone policies, unlike in the solar energy case, illustrating how internal contexts affect outcomes. Moreover, WTO rules on subsidies are more flexible than those on local content, which enabled greater experimentation.

In sum, international trade law and dispute settlement interact with internal domestic policy debates and economic contexts. They serve both as important tools in domestic policy clashes over the contours and details of regulatory policy, as well as catalysts for the development of new forms of industrial policy. Legal capacity plays a key role in providing opportunity to shape the understanding of the rules internationally and their implementation domestically, as well as the interaction between the two, affecting the settlement of legal norms.

---

[120]   WT/DS/510/R (June 27, 2019).

[121]   Manoj Mate, "The WTO and Development Policy Space in India," *Yale Journal of International Law* 45 (2020): 285 (noting India's move to "domestic manufacturing requirements" while continuing some domestic content requirements that may still be not compliant).

[122]   WT/DS541/R, October 31, 2019. India launched its Special Economic Zones policy in 2000 and enacted a Special Economic Zones Act in 2005.

[123]   Mate, "The WTO and Development Policy Space in India."

[124]   Press Information Bureau, "Cabinet Approves Schemes for Remission of Duties and Taxes on Exported Products," March 13, 2020, https://dgft.gov.in/sites/default/files/RoDTEP.pdf (under the acronym "RoDTEP").

E. *Transnational Legal Ordering of Protectionism: Import Relief*

Import relief law, in many ways, is a North American and European legal export incorporated into the WTO. But since the WTO's creation, India has brought a number of cases before the WTO affecting the interpretation of these rules, proposed new rules, and adapted WTO law domestically in ways that provide new models for antidumping law that can be diffused to other developing countries. In these ways, it contributes to the transnational legal order of trade – in this case regarding import protection. Overall, India has become the world's greatest user of antidumping law since the WTO's creation in 1995.

This specialized import relief practice is the most active area of trade law in India, as in other major trading nations. The participating law firms range from India's largest, Amarchand Mangaldas, which has around 600 lawyers, to specialized boutique firms.[125] TPM Consulting, a firm started by a former cost accountant in the antidumping directorate (who was not part of the legal elite) initiates the largest number of antidumping petitions in India, and it has handled hundreds of antidumping investigations. This vibrant legal practice constitutes part of a transnational legal order where expertise that was originally developed in the United States and Europe became localized after being catalyzed by India's commitments under the WTO agreements.

This practice area involves intense public–private interaction, including through officials leaving government to develop their own private practice and bring and defend cases before government bodies. In India, many of the leading lawyers came from government service, moving to private practice because of the fees. The three largest practitioners in the antidumping field, V. Lakshmikumaran, Sharad Bhansali, and A.K. Gupta, all came from government services. In 2012, Neeraj Varshney likewise left his position as director within the Ministry of Commerce's antidumping directorate to join the accounting firm Ernst & Young and establish its trade remedy practice.[126] He did so with Tashi Kaul who later joined the WTO Rules Division, illustrating how transnational processes operate in multiple directions as individuals move from public to private sector work, and between the national and international levels.[127]

---

[125] Pallavi Shroff, the wife of Shardul Amarchand Mangaldas's lead senior partner, developed its practice that was among the first in India. She is the daughter of P. N. Bhagwati, the former Chief Justice of India's Supreme Court, and niece of renowned trade economist Jagdish Bhagwati, reflecting the adaptation of old, highly educated elites to the new transnational context. Mark Wu, "Indian Corporations, the Administrative State, and the Rise of Indian Trade Remedies," in *The Indian Legal Profession in the Age of Globalization: The Rise of the Corporate Legal Sector and Its Impact on Lawyers and Society*, eds. David Wilkins, Vikramaditya Khanna, and David Trubek (Cambridge: Cambridge University Press, 2017), 672.

[126] In 2018, Agneshwar Sen, former Additional Director General in India's Directorate General of Trade Remedies, similarly joined Ernst & Young in 2018 to further their trade division.

[127] Varshney wrote a book on WTO import relief law while engaged in domestic practice, further illustrating the transnational links. Neeraj Varshney, *Anti-Dumping Measures Under the WTO Regime: Law, Practice, and Procedure* (Delhi: Universal Law Publishing Company, 2007).

Import relief laws implicate domestic policies. Firms, industries, and the government often deploy them for purely protectionist purposes. Yet the laws also offer safety valves that can "provide Indian corporations with the 'breathing space' to become competitive."[128] They thus can be used to advance industrial policy objectives. Mark Wu shows, for example, how these practices worked for the Indian telecommunications equipment company M/s Sterlite Industries.[129] After an antidumping award, it became one of the ten fastest growing Indian technology companies and a leading exporter of optical fibers. Similar practices affected the India solar cells and modules sector, which is critical for clean energy needs.[130]

India helped shape the meaning and practice of antidumping and countervailing duty law through international litigation. Most notably, India was the first to challenge the controversial practice of "zeroing" used by the European Union and the United States, which created biased calculations of dumping margins against imports. India won the litigation in the *EC – Bed Linen* case, which established new precedent that led to a series of subsequent cases against US antidumping regulations and regulatory practices, which the United States lost before the Appellate Body. The United States argued vehemently that the Appellate Body holdings were contrary to the parties' intentions under the WTO antidumping agreement, but to no avail. It became an explosive issue, catalyzing US challenges to the authority and very existence of the WTO Appellate Body.[131] Similarly, regarding countervailing duty law, following India's complaint in *US – Carbon Steel*, the Appellate Body refined its jurisprudence that sets the conditions under which a state-owned enterprise may be deemed to constitute a "public body" granting subsidies, thereby constraining a country's ability to impose countervailing duties, once more infuriating the United States.[132]

These cases were part of a series of Indian challenges to US import relief measures that engaged Indian public–private partnerships. Indian shrimp exporters pressed the government to join other countries in successfully challenging the US Byrd Amendment (known in the WTO as the *US – Offset Act*). Under the Act, the United States distributed revenue obtained from US antidumping and countervailing duty proceedings to the petitioning US domestic industry, thereby subsidizing it. Once more, the United States contended that WTO rules did not extend to this practice. Once more, the United States lost the case and complained that the Appellate Body was engaged in inappropriate gap filling to impose new requirements on the United States. India similarly successfully challenged US practices using "facts available" for dumping

[128] Wu, "Indian Corporations."
[129] Ibid.
[130] Kher, "India's Trade Disputes," 28.
[131] "Zeroing" refers to the US practice of setting at zero the negative differences between the foreign domestic prices of a product when compared to its US import prices. Because negative amounts are excluded, this practice often results in the finding of dumping when otherwise there would be none, as well as the calculation of a higher dumping margin and thus the imposition of a higher antidumping duty.
[132] WT/DS 436/R (July 14, 2014).

determinations in *US – Steel Plates*, once again constraining US practices and creating important precedent.[133] And it likewise won its challenge of US enhanced bond requirements in antidumping proceedings in the *US – Custom Bond Directive* case, again involving close industry-government coordination.[134] Through this litigation, India helped to define the transnational legal order for import relief, even though the initial rules came out of US and other developed countries' laws and practices.

India also affected transnational legal ordering through its practices in antidumping law tailored to India's developmental context. Before the WTO's creation, India had import relief laws on the books, but it did not use them because its industries were already protected by high tariffs and other import restrictions. After India bound its tariffs and removed its quantitative restrictions, it updated its trade remedy legislation and practice. The government reorganized the Indian bureaucracy for import controls, and it reformed the Directorate-General of Foreign Trade within the Department of Commerce, to enhance expertise. In 1998, it established a Directorate General of Antidumping and Allied Duties with greater autonomy to handle antidumping cases. In early 2018, it reorganized this department and created a new body – the Directorate General of Trade Remedies.[135] In addition to conducting antidumping, countervailing duty, and safeguards investigations, the Directorate General supports the interests of micro, small- and medium-sized enterprises and other exporters in trade remedy cases filed against them in foreign jurisdictions,[136] as do Brazil and China.

India did not simply copy the practices of the United States and Europe. It rather indigenized its antidumping law in the context of WTO rules by simplifying them compared to US practices, such as by adopting a lesser duty rule (a variant also used in Europe and Brazil) that it found to be easier to calculate.[137] India actively participated in negotiations involving antidumping law. To participate effectively, it again hired a private law firm, in this case the Strategic Law Group, to propose its "lesser duty rule" as a global rule.[138] Even if not formally required in the WTO system, these practices potentially diffuse to other developing countries.

To educate Indian industry, government officials within the Commerce Department organized workshops and seminars for Indian corporations and trade

---

[133]   Anderson and Raju, "India's Initial WTO Disputes."
[134]   WT/DS343/AB/R (July 16, 2008); Gregory Shaffer, James Nedumpara, and Aseema Sinha, "State Transformation and The Role of Lawyers: The WTO, India, and Transnational Legal Ordering," *Law & Society Review* 49 (2015): 595–629 (using the case to illustrate public-private coordination of Indian expertise).
[135]   Ministry of Commerce and Industry, Press Information Bureau, *Creation of Directorate General of Trade Remedies (DGTR) in Department of Commerce* (May 9. 2018), http://pib.nic.in/newsite/PrintRelease.aspx?relid=179195.
[136]   Ministry of Commerce and Industry, Mid-Term Review, *Foreign Trade Policy 2015–2020* (December 4, 2017).
[137]   Wu, "Indian Corporations."
[138]   Interview, January 12, 2012. James Nedumpara during his employment at the UNCTAD program in New Delhi organized the review process where the proposal was revised and submitted to the WTO negotiating committee.

associations, and they wrote books and brochures. The petitions followed. From 1995 to 2016, India initiated 839 antidumping investigations (out of a total of 5,286 investigations for all WTO members), which was more than any other WTO member.[139] These investigations required increasing legal and accounting expertise, and they exemplify the reach of the transnational legal order within legal and law-related institutions and professions.

Under WTO antidumping and countervailing duty law, national courts or administrative tribunals are to review executive agency decisions. Judicial authority is enhanced as a result, which further empowers the technocrats within national administrations. Indian courts reference WTO law even though India is a dualist system in which international law formally has no direct effect. By the end of October 2017, we estimate that lawyers had filed over 397 appeals before the Customs Excise and Service Tax Appellate Tribunal and its predecessor Central Excise and Gold Appellate Tribunal, a specialized court that hears antidumping matters. In addition, various parties filed numerous writ petitions before the state High Courts.[140] The Indian Supreme Court alone heard 39 petitions on antidumping cases between 2000 and 2017, "more than any other Supreme Court in the world," and invalidated a number of the antidumping directorate's practices.[141] Law gradually and increasingly encroached on administrative discretion.

These developments in Indian import relief laws and practices reflect transnational legal ordering's institutional and professional impact. The state continues to be the central decision maker in providing protection and it can potentially do so to advance industrial policy goals, but it now engages in a legalistic process in which legal capacity is central, especially compared to lawyers' minimal roles during the License Raj. India's tailoring of antidumping laws in light of its development situation and its engagement to shape the negotiation, interpretation, and practice of the rules show how this transnational legal order is a dynamic one. A purely international lens fails to capture these processes that permeate nation states and recursively shape the international legal order.

IV. TRANSNATIONAL LEGAL ORDERING OF INTELLECTUAL PROPERTY: DOMESTIC CONTESTS AND INSTITUTIONAL CHANGE

With the WTO's creation, intellectual property law became a core part of the trade regime, which has since been further developed through bilateral and regional trade agreements. The transformation of Indian intellectual property law further exhibits how transnational legal ordering of trade works, and its implications for India's developmental state. India, as many other developing countries, did not provide

---

[139] Own calculations and Chad Bown, "Global Antidumping Database," *The World Bank* (2015). http://people.brandeis.edu/~cbown/global_ad/cvd/.

[140] Own calculations and Jha, "India's Position in the International Economic Order," 29.

[141] Wu, "Indian Corporations," from which we updated the figures.

patent protection for pharmaceutical medicines or chemical products used in agriculture, such as fertilizers and pesticides, on public interest grounds. The TRIPS agreement, however, eliminated this option, which the United States, European Union, and Japan successfully imposed on developing countries as a condition for joining the WTO. Article 27 of the TRIPS agreement provides: "patents shall be available for any inventions, whether products or processes, in all fields of technology."

In 1996, the year after the WTO's formation, the United States and European Union targeted India to press for compliance. In the *India – Patents* case, they successfully challenged India's implementation of its commitment to create a transitional "mail-box system" where companies could file patent applications to establish priority and obtain exclusive marketing rights during India's ten-year transition period India.[142] The WTO decision spurred significant contention in India over the government's development priorities. Social movements organized mass protests and the Parliament acrimoniously debated alternatives. At the last moment, the Indian President issued a decree on January 1, 2005 to comply with the TRIPS agreement deadline (when India's 10-year transition period terminated), which remained in effect until the Parliament passed an amendment to the Patents Act months later to implement the changes.

The TRIPS agreement's implementation created new incentives for Indian companies, as Indian government and business norms shifted toward a greater focus on innovation. In 2010, the government created a National Innovation Council aimed at fostering a change of mindset toward innovation strategies, declaring 2010–2020 the "Decade of Innovation." Swaminathan Aiyar, a prominent editor, wrote: "The sad truth is that they [the pharmaceutical companies in India] were dragged kicking and screaming into new territory, and only then discovered that it was the promised land."[143] As a former Indian Ambassador to the WTO quipped to us, "now one speaks of patent or perish; whereas before the mantra was no patents or perish."[144] From 1990 to 2014, Indian pharmaceutical companies collectively increased their R&D from less than 50 crore (under US$ 7.2 million) in 1990 to over 7,000 crore (over US$ 1 billion) by 2013, constituting a 13,900 percent increase.[145] They substantially increased R&D as a percentage of sales to 8.5 percent in 2018, even though India is the world's largest exporter of generic medicines.[146] Patent filings ensued. Indian applicants' filings are rising faster than foreign ones, and they constituted almost a quarter of all filings in India by 2013.[147] In 2018, India registered the world's highest rate of growth in terms of international patent applications (at 27 percent),

[142] TRIPS agreement, Art. 65 (on transitional period); Art. 70.8 (on mailbox).
[143] Sinha, *Globalizing India*, 109.
[144] Interview, December 14, 2013.
[145] Sinha, *Globalizing India*, 148.
[146] India Brand Equity Foundation, "Pharmaceuticals" (March 2019), 11–12.
[147] Government of India, Office of CGPDTM, *Annual Report 2012–2013* (2014).

although it still fell far below the United States, China, and Japan in terms of volume.[148]

The TRIPS agreement created not only new incentives for industry but also new stakes for Indian professionals, especially given the interpretive issues arising from India's implementation of the agreement. Around 2004, India began to modernize its patent infrastructure and the process then accelerated, illustrating the multiple dimensions of institutional change that transnational legal ordering implicates.[149] The government created four new Patent Offices in the four largest metropolitan areas, hired new patent examiners, and established an Intellectual Property Training Institute in Nagpur (Maharashtra). The government increased the size, capacity, and skills of its administration, but more capacity is needed given the volume of patents filed. In the private sector, India developed an important industry that provides transnational services for drafting patents, wherever they might be filed. Taking advantage of English language and technical skills, an Indian patent law army arose. In 2018, applicants filed over 50,000 patent applications in India.[150]

The TRIPS agreement grants countries flexibility in interpreting its provisions so that India had some leeway in determining how to revise its laws and adapt its institutions.[151] Although India radically revised its patent law, expanding protection to pharmaceutical and agricultural chemical products, it did so in an innovative manner after a long internal study and consultations with industrial and civil society stakeholders. First, unlike Brazil, India did not retrospectively recognize "pipeline patents" for pre-1995 inventions before the WTO's creation.[152] India refused to cover them, as was its right, which involved the majority of marketed drugs for many years. Second, it created new definitions of what a patent must show in terms of novelty and an inventive step, thus narrowing the scope of patent claims and facilitating the development of generics. Famously in patent law circles, under section 3(d) of its Patents Act, India denied the grant of a pharmaceutical patent based on "a new form of a known substance" that does

---

[148] World Intellectual Property Organization, *WIPO 2018 IP Services: Innovators File Record Number of International Patent Applications, With Asia Now Leading* (Geneva, March 19, 2019).

[149] Peter Drahos, *The Global Governance of Knowledge Patent Offices and their Clients* (Cambridge: Cambridge University Press, 2010), 199–220.

[150] WIPO, Statistical Country Profiles: India, visited January 9, 2020; Government of India, Office of CGPDTM, *Annual Report 2017–2018* (2018). WIPO reports show that patent filings increased 605 percent from 1997 to 2011 in India, and by a further 175 percent between 2013 and 2016.

[151] Gregory Shaffer and Susan Shell, "Transnational Legal Ordering and Access to Medicines," in *Patent Law in Global Perspective*, eds. Ruth L Okedji and Margo A. Bagley (Oxford: Oxford University Press, 2014), 8 (noting that developing countries may benefit particularly from "the right of parallel importation; the right to grant compulsory licenses; and 'Bolar' exceptions for generic drug companies to prepare a drug under patent for marketing authorization once the patent expires").

[152] Kenneth Shadlen, *Coalitions and Compliance: The Political Economy of Pharmaceutical Patents in Latin America* (Oxford: Oxford University Press, 2017), 38–40 (on pipeline patents compared to mailbox patents).

not enhance a drug's therapeutic "efficacy," or based on a "new use for a known substance" that does not result in a "new product." This provision helps India combat the "evergreening" of drugs, while ensuring that pre-1995 drugs remain unpatented in India. It also raises outcry from US and European pharmaceutical companies and keeps India on the United States Trade Representative's Priority Watch List,[153] even though the policy is TRIPS-compliant. India simultaneously eased the ability to challenge patent claims by including pre- and post-grant challenges before an administrative body whose processes are more efficient and less costly than a court.[154] Neither the United States nor Europe provide these opportunities to challenge patents, and they oppose their use in India. The Indian generic industry uses them to delay and oppose patents. In parallel, the government actively imposes price controls for pharmaceutical products on public interest grounds, including patented medicines.[155] In 2017, it introduced price controls for some medical devices, including cardiac stents and knee implants – a policy measure which helped trigger US revocation of preferential tariff rates for Indian products under the General System of Preferences.[156]

The Indian Supreme Court and state High Courts adjudicate cases that implicate the interpretation of India's commitments under the TRIPS agreement, further shaping transnational legal ordering within India but also (potentially) transnationally. In 2013, the government successfully defended itself in a case reported in the global media before the Indian Supreme Court against the Swiss pharmaceutical firm Novartis, who challenged its refusal under section 3(d) to recognize a patent based on a slight modification of an existing drug.[157] The United States fears that other countries will emulate different parts of India's patent law as a model, which is why such litigation is important. Indeed, India's section 3(d) has had a modelling effect as a number of countries are adopting different variants of the Indian approach to combat the extension of patents and thus the "evergreening" of drugs. The Philippines incorporated the section 3(d) exception in its law, Thailand introduced a similar standard, China has used variants to invalidate the anti-cancer drug at issue

---

[153]   USTR, 2019 *Special 301 Report* (April 2019).

[154]   Amy Kapczynski, "Harmonization and Its Discontents: A Case Study of TRIPS Implementation in India's Pharmaceutical Sector," *California Law Review* 97 (2009): 1571–1650.

[155]   The National Pharmaceutical Pricing Authority (NPPA) maintains a list of essential medicines which are subject to price control. The Supreme Court of India dismissed a challenge instituted by the Indian Pharmaceutical Alliance against the NPPA and the Government of India for fixing a maximum retail price on Sitagliptin, a patented medicine and prescribed for the treatment of diabetes. *Indian Pharmaceutical Alliance v. Union of India* (Special Leave Petition No. 30089/2016).

[156]   President of the United States, "Proclamation 9902 of May 31, 2019," *Federal Regulations* 84 (2019): 182, https://ustr.gov/sites/default/files/Proclamation_9902.pdf.

[157]   In this case, the original Novartis drug was invented pre-1995 and so it received no patent protection in India. Bhaven Sampat and Kenneth Shadlen, "Drug Patenting in India: Looking Back and Looking Forward," 14 *Nature, Biobusiness Briefs* (July 17, 2015): 1–2 (noting the critical relation of India's non-recognition of pipeline patents and section 3(d)).

in the landmark Novartis case, and the Brazilian, Kenyan, and South African governments have considered adopting similar legislation.[158]

To protect against multinational firms patenting traditional knowledge (called bio-piracy), India developed a digital library of traditional knowledge. In parallel, it created a Traditional Knowledge Resource Classification system designed for easy use by patent examiners around the world to verify whether a patent claim involves a "prior art."[159] If it does, then the claim is ineligible for a patent. India relatedly has played a leading role in international negotiations regarding the protection of biological materials under the Convention on Biodiversity, and it has pressed for reform of the TRIPS agreement to require disclosure of the origin of genetic resources.[160] It also supported Brazil's initiative to create a new development agenda in the World Intellectual Property Organization, and it reached out to African countries to help block initiatives that would have led to stronger intellectual property constraints on them.

The explosion of the AIDS crisis provided leverage for India and other developing countries to press for the loosening of TRIPS requirements and enhance access to medicines, including through the issuance of compulsory licenses. India was a leader of developing countries in WTO negotiations that, in 2001, gave rise to the Doha Declaration on TRIPS and Public Health, the adoption of a waiver in August 2003, and the subsequent amendment to the TRIPS agreement in 2017. The amendment enables any member country to export pharmaceutical products under a compulsory license issued by a country facing "a national emergency or other circumstances of extreme urgency," although the conditions of the waiver remain stringent and contested.[161] Indian companies are well-positioned to export drugs to other countries issuing such licenses, and India itself issued a compulsory license and threatened to issue others to induce decreases in domestic prices.[162] The mere threat of a compulsory license can have a powerful effect, bolstered by the actual issuance of one.

---

[158]   Omar Ramon Serrano Oswald and Mira Burri, "India, Brazil, and Public Health: Rule-Making through South-South Diffusion in the Intellectual Property Rights Regime?," *Regulation & Governance* (2020).

[159]   Peter Drahos, "The Jewel in the Crown: India's Patent Office and Patent-based Innovation," in *Intellectual Property Policy Reform: Fostering Innovation and Development*, eds. Christopher Arup and William van Caenegem (Cheltenham: Edward Elgar Publishing, 2009), 80–100.

[160]   Ibid., 94. To revive discussions in the WTO on the problem of bio-piracy and the linkage of the TRIPS agreement with the Convention on Biodiversity, the government organized a major conference in Geneva in June 2018 with the South Centre and the Centre for WTO Studies. Press Release, Press Information Bureau, Government of India, *International Conference on the TRIPS CBD Linkage 7–8 June 2018 in Geneva* (May 30, 2018).

[161]   The waiver applies to Art. 31(f) of the TRIPS agreement, which provides, "such use shall be authorized predominantly for the supply of the domestic market of the Member authorizing such use."

[162]   Tricia Olsen and Aseema Sinha, "Linkage Politics and the Persistence of National Policy Autonomy in Emerging Powers: Patents, Profits, and Patients in the Context of TRIPS Compliance," *Business and Politics* 15, no. 3 (2013): 323–356. Since India did not grant pipeline patents, however, it had to deal with fewer patented medications than Brazil.

Although the "waiver" had less of a formal legal effect because of its stringent conditions and US pressure on third countries, the normative debate around the issue catalyzed mobilization among international organizations, NGOs, and country health officials that facilitated increased exports of Indian generics. In other words, the mobilization around the waiver arguably helped protect, entrench and expand India's generics trade, which US and EU pharmaceutical companies would like to see diminished.[163] Even if countries do not grant formal legal "waivers" and compulsory licenses, law still can have a powerful effect in catalyzing social movements, shaping social norms, and affecting government practices.

In parallel, key Indian domestic court cases support India's generic drug policies that are important not only for its trade, but also domestically and transnationally as a model. In 2014, the Supreme Court dismissed an appeal filed by Bayer concerning India's first grant of a compulsory license, which was widely reported around the world and provided an example for others.[164] Indian stakeholders also have creatively used US law to support greater access to generic medicines domestically in ways that can be taken up by other countries. In a 2008 case, *Roche* v. *Cipla*, an Indian court denied Roche's demand for injunctive relief against Cipla, a generic producer, by creatively citing a US case, *eBay* v. *MercExchange*, and a non-precedential US Federal Circuit decision that noted public health concerns. It did so in a way arguably no US court would have used, and in support of the generic sector.[165]

India again worked closely with the generic sector in successfully settling a WTO claim against the European Union in the *EC – Drug Seizure* case.[166] European governments (and in particular the Netherlands) seized seventeen consignments of Indian generic drugs from cargo planes being refueled at European airports when the generics were destined for countries in Africa and South America.[167] A number of Indian industry associations, including Pharmexil and FICCI, worked with the government to assess the facts, WTO legal claims, and negotiating strategies before the government commenced consultations with the European Union. The Department of Commerce evaluated the credentials and relevant expertise of foreign experts and Indian law firms before engaging Venugopal and US law professor Frederick Abbott.[168] It then commenced formal

[163] Ahlam Rais, "India Retains 'World's Leading Generics Exporter' Spot," Process Worldwide, November 13, 2017.
[164] The case involved NATCO, a generic Indian pharmaceutical company. The Supreme Court decided against Bayer because it failed to provide access to a cancer medication at an affordable price. *Bayer Corporation v. Union of India & Ors.* (Special Leave Petition No. 30145/2014).
[165] Kapczynski, "Harmonization and Its Discontents," 1607.
[166] WT/DS408/1 (May 19, 2010).
[167] Kher, "India's Trade Disputes," 29.
[168] This procedure is explained in the written response given by the Trade Policy Division of the Ministry of Commerce & Industry, *Information Sought Under RTI Act, 2005 Seeking Information Pertaining to DS-408, Involving India before the Dispute Settlement Body (DSB) at the World Trade Organization (WTO)* (New Delhi: Ministry of Commerce & Industry, 2012).

WTO consultations that enhanced its leverage in negotiating a favorable settle-ment with the European Union.[169] When the European Union subsequently proposed a trademark law in 2015 authorizing customs officials to seize goods in transit on grounds of suspected trademark violations, India immediately responded with support from Pharmexcil and other industry associations.[170] The European Union repealed the regulations in question and has not seized Indian drugs since then.[171]

In sum, the TRIPS agreement constitutes a US and European export of domestic laws and policies that had dynamic effects within India. The agreement catalyzed change in Indian industry, Indian institutions, and Indian professions. Yet India has used TRIPS flexibilities to tailor its patent law to its development context in ways that recursively serve as a model for other countries. Although civil society activists critique the Indian state for not going further in exploiting TRIPS flexibilities, the government has taken many initiatives to shape the meaning and practice of TRIPS norms in light of the demands of competing factions within India. The transnational legal order for patent rights remains contested. By building legal capacity and coordinating with private lawyer expertise, India has shaped the legal order to defend and advance its constituents' interests, while those interests clash and change in light of the trans-national context.

V. TRANSNATIONAL LEGAL ORDERING OF INVESTMENT LAW: INDIA'S SHIFTING POSITION

India became an increasingly important capital importer and exporter in parallel to its liberalization of trade. Its annual inbound foreign direct investment jumped from US$ 2 billion in 1995 to US$ 37.3 billion by 2018, while its annual outbound foreign direct investment rose from US$ 119 million in 1995 to US$ 14.5 billion by 2018, as Figure 5.3 shows. Singapore became its largest source of inbound invest-ment and its largest destination of outbound investment, reconfirming its status as the "gateway to India." Overall, India remains a larger importer of foreign capital given its huge internal market, though its companies increasingly engage in outbound investment.

As with trade law, India initially was a rule taker as it signed investment law agreements based on the models of European capital-exporting countries. It signed its first bilateral investment treaty (BIT) with the United Kingdom in 1994, the same year that it concluded the agreement establishing the WTO. The UK BIT served as a kind of template for those that followed, covering agreements between

---

[169] Interviews with FICCI representative and private lawyers, New Delhi, January 2012.
[170] Asit Ranjan Mishra, "India Opposes Proposed European Trademark Rules," *Livemint*, October 14, 2015.
[171] The EU regulations were (EC) 207/2009 and (EU) 2015/2424 permitting the seizure of drugs in transit.

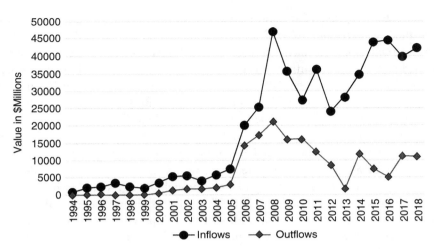

FIGURE 5.3 India's FDI inflows and outflows (US$)[172]

India and 84 other countries.[173] Between 1994–2003, India entered into 56 BITs, and then another 28 through 2014.

In 2003, India created its first model BIT, which was lean and reflected its 1994 agreement with the United Kingdom.[174] The model was entitled an "Agreement for the Promotion and Protection of Investments," and its preamble set forth the objective of "fostering greater investment by investors" and was silent about state regulatory prerogatives. Substantively the model included broad, open-ended provisions on the definition of investment ("every kind of asset"), "fair and equitable treatment," expropriation (which included regulatory measures having an equivalent effect), and national treatment and most-favored nation obligations (which contained no modifier limiting the obligation to treatment in "like circumstances"). These open-ended provisions, taken from the UK BIT, effectively delegated to arbitral panels the ability to develop a pro-investor jurisprudence with little guidance.

As with trade law, India enhanced its legal capacity in investment law after finding itself on the defensive. After an important investor case against it in 2011, the government faced a backlash, spurring it to reevaluate all of its existing investment

172   Sources: Reserve Bank of India, Annual Report, *Foreign Direct Investment Flows to* India (August 29, 2018), https://rbi.org.in/Scripts/AnnualReportPublications.aspx?Id=1249; Department of Economic Affairs, *Overseas Direct Investment,* https://dea.gov.in/overseas-direct-investment; United Nations Conference on Trade and Development, *Country Facts Sheets 2019 (India),* https://unctad.org/sections/dite_dir/docs/wir2019/wir19_fs_in_en.pdf.

173   Prabhash Ranjan and Pushkar Anand, "The 2016 Model Indian Bilateral Investment Treaty: A Critical Deconstruction," *Northwestern Journal of International Law and Business* 38, no. 1 (2017): 1.

174   Aniruddha Rajput, "India's Shifting Treaty Practice: A Comparative Analysis of the 2003 and 2015 Model BITs," *Jindal Global Law Review* 7 (2016): 201–226.

agreements.[175] In 2015, after considerable consultation among government minis-tries, the private sector, and civil society, India adopted a new model BIT. In this way, it aimed to play a proactive role in shaping its investment accords, including in the regional economic partnership agreements that it is pursuing. In the process, it provided a new model, potentially shaping international investment law's contours.

The 2011 case that catalyzed India's reevaluation of its BITs was *White Industries Australia Limited* v. *The Republic of India*.[176] In *White Industries*, an Australian company claimed damages from the delay of Indian courts in the enforcement of a commercial arbitral award. The key question was whether the claim involved an investment or a commercial dispute. India would have won the case under the Australia-India BIT but for the importation, through the BIT's most-favored nation clause, of a provision of the latter BIT. Through this clause, the arbitral tribunal "incorporated" a provision from the India-Kuwait BIT providing that each state must grant "effective means of asserting claims and enforcing rights." The arbitral tribunal found that the court delays constituted a violation of this provision and awarded the investor AU\$4,085,180 in damages, plus interest and costs. The Indian media widely covered the case. A slew of new foreign investor filings ensued against Indian regulatory measures, including following an Indian Supreme Court ruling that canceled spectrum and telecom licenses that were auctioned amid a corruption scandal. Indian civil society groups protested, critical commentary proliferated, and the Indian Parliament held hearings, spurring intensive internal government debate.[177]

Critics pressed the government to reevaluate the provisions it had cavalierly accepted in earlier investment agreements, and the government responded. In July 2012, the Committee of Secretaries decided that investment dispute notices should be handled through the mechanism of an Inter-Ministerial Group headed by the Department of Economic Affairs of the Ministry of Finance. The government created a standing group chaired by the Cabinet Secretary to assess all of India's investment treaties. It was a major enterprise, which was relatively transparent and consultative, as the government engaged with industry and civil society groups. The government eventually prepared a draft model BIT that received extensive com-mentary, including a full analysis by the Law Commission of India and comments from the business community that maintained that the draft had gone too far in restricting investor protections. During this process, the government also consulted

[175] In the late 1990s, India was involved in an investment dispute with Enron, a US-based energy corporation, concerning its failed investment in the Dabhol power project in Western India, but it was settled out of court. Ronald J. Bettauer, "India and the International Arbitration: The Dabhol Experience," *George Washington International Law Review* 41, no. 2 (2009): 381–387.

[176] *White Industries Australia Limited* v. *The Republic of India*, Final Award, UNCITRAL (November 30, 2011).

[177] Kavaljit Singh and Burghard Ilge (eds.), *Rethinking Bilateral Investment Treaties – Critical Issues and Policy Choices* (New Delhi: Both Ends, Madhyam, Centre for Research on Multinational Corporations, 2016).

four international organizations, the New York based law firm Curtis, Mallet-Prevost, Colt & Mosle LLP, and an international think tank.[178] The government eventually removed some of the more restrictive changes in its initial draft before publishing the new Model BIT in December 2015.

India's model BIT serves as a template for its renegotiation of its existing BITs as well as for future BITs.[179] In general, the model BIT is much more protective of state regulatory and judicial sovereignty. Its preamble sets forth an object and purpose that balances investor protection rights with developmental and regulatory concerns, "seeking to align the objectives of Investment with sustainable development and inclusive growth." It limits the scope of coverage of foreign "investment" by excluding portfolio investments, sovereign debt, and ordinary commercial contracts. Procedurally, it requires investors to exhaust domestic remedies for at least five years before commencing arbitration. Substantively, it limits the reach of investor protections that arbitral tribunals have interpreted broadly, and it creates public policy exceptions modeled on WTO law.[180] It also sets forth complementary obligations of investors, including to comply with host state law, although it curtailed the extent of the obligations included in the earlier draft following push-back from Indian investors and legal consultants.

In parallel, the Modi government terminated sixty-nine of India's eighty-four extant bilateral investment treaties to spur their renegotiation. For its remaining BITs, it requested formal joint interpretive statements to remove ambiguities from open-ended provisions.[181] Although India's BITs continue under their terms before the terminations take effect, India has staked out a new position that implicates the future transnational legal ordering of cross-border investment. While others have yet to adopt India's model, India's position has further delegitimized the mainstream Western approach to BITs and thus opened space for consideration of new alternatives.[182]

---

[178]   Mihaela Papa and Aditya Sarkar, "Rising India in Investment Arbitration," in *The Indian Legal Profession in the Age of Globalization: The Rise of the Corporate Legal Sector and Its Impact on Lawyers and Society*, eds. David Wilkins, Vikramaditya Khanna, and David Trubek (Cambridge: Cambridge University Press, 2017), 705–733.

[179]   Model Text for the Indian Bilateral Investment Treaty (2015); James Nedumpara, "India's Trade and Investment Agreements," in *Reconceptualizing International Investment Law from the Global South*, eds. Fabio Morosini and Michelle Ratton Sanchez Badin (Cambridge: Cambridge University Press, 2018).

[180]   For example, it turns the broad "fair and equitable treatment" clause into a narrower customary international law minimum standard of treatment, while limiting the full protection and security clause. It circumscribes the definition of indirect expropriations. It eliminates the most-favored nation clause and restricts the national treatment clause to situations of "like circumstances" while carving out sector-specific exemptions. And it excludes umbrella clauses that incorporate contract claims.

[181]   Ranjan and Anand, "The 2016 Model BIT." India has signed Joint Interpretative Statements with two countries, Bangladesh and Colombia, which includes clarification of the standard for assessing "fair and equitable treatment."

[182]   We thank Anthea Roberts, a participant in the UNCITRAL working group reform process, for this formulation.

In the process, India developed internal legal capacity in investment law that builds from and complements what it developed in trade law. In 2017, it created the Centre on Trade and Investment Law within CRIT, which hires and provides internships to young Indian international lawyers and periodically consults with outside counsel. As litigation continues under India's existing BITs, the government and private sector are developing expertise that they can deploy to adapt the regime over time. This expertise helps India proactively shape the renegotiation and formal interpretation of its BITs.

India increasingly links investment agreements with trade agreements in broader "economic cooperation" and "economic partnership" agreements that integrate trade in goods, services, and investment. This is particularly important for the government's Look East/Act East policy with its Asian neighbors. In negotiating the investment chapter for the Regional Cooperation Economic Partnership, for example, India advanced its 2015 Model BIT. In contrast, India remains wary of multilateral processes for developing investment law with the Global North. It has been largely successful in forestalling investment law negotiations at the WTO. And within the United Nations working group in UNCITRAL, which is assessing reform of the investment law regime, India has been notably silent and cagey, as if reflecting internal divisions within it.

Through its adoption of a new prototype for the negotiation, renegotiation, and interpretation of its investment agreements, India nonetheless is contributing to the shaping of the transnational legal ordering of investment law. The 2015 Model BIT provides a template not only for India's negotiations. It also includes provisions for consideration by other countries that wish to rein in the expansive scope of investment law as interpreted in investor-state arbitrations and thus better protect the state's right to regulate in light of development and public welfare concerns.[183] Even if no other country adopts India's particular hybrid approach as a model, India's position has further destabilized what had been a mainstream Western approach. Other large developing countries are following a similar path in reconsidering and terminating existing BITs, such as Indonesia and South Africa. India's example reinforces their decisions. The Indian model BIT provides one more example of how capital importing countries can insert safeguards in BITs, such as through requiring the exhaustion of local remedies.[184] As developing (and developed) countries weigh the pros and cons of signing and revising BITs, India's actions contribute to the delegitimization of the status quo, opening space for new alternatives.

---

[183] Nedumpara, "India's Trade and Investment Agreements."

[184] Robert Howse, "International Investment Law and Arbitration: A Conceptual Framework," *International Law and Litigation* (Hélène Ruiz Fabri ed., 2019), Studies of the Max Planck Institute Luxembourg for International, European and Regulatory Procedural Law, Vol. 15 (Nomos, Baden-Baden, Germany) (2017): 363–446.

VI. CONCLUSION

To return to this book's three questions, India invested significantly in building trade law capacity in response to pressure from WTO litigation. To do so, it changed and transformed itself internally. In the process, it recursively enhanced its ability to shape the international legal order for trade.

The United States and Europe were the primary creators of the international trade and investment legal orders. Yet, although first on the defensive, India gradually built legal capacity to defend its interests in a system characterized by asymmetric power favoring those not only with greater economic leverage but also with greater technical and legal resources. International trade and investment law privilege the value of legal and economic expertise in national trade, investment, and regulatory policy.

The trade regime catalyzed the development of new legal capacity within the Indian state and pressed the Indian bureaucracy to become more transparent and open to greater input from the private sector. In the process, trade and investment law-related expertise diffused outside the state's administrative services. The government created new specialized think tanks while also outsourcing work, directly and through its think tanks, to the Indian private sector. Through the ensuing public–private partnerships, the government enhanced its ability to prepare and defend claims, analyze potential claims, provide the analytic backdrop to assess and develop negotiating positions, tailor the implementation of international economic law requirements, and consider new domestic policy initiatives in light of them. India transformed itself along multiple dimensions within the constraints of its institutional heritage in order to engage with the international economic law order.

Through these internal changes, the government positioned itself to participate recursively in the shaping of that legal order through negotiations, litigation, and practice. It continues to participate in the development of international economic law bilaterally, regionally, and multilaterally. Although much less prominently than China, India too is shaping the future ecology of the transnational legal order for trade and broader economic relations.

6

How China Took on the United States and Europe at the WTO

With *Henry Gao*

In joining the World Trade Organization in December 2001, China assumed vast legal commitments that significantly affected its internal laws and institutions. Western countries hoped to transform China and integrate it into a liberal, capitalist global economy.[1] Many of China's leaders aimed to use the process for internal reform as well. Nonetheless, they wished to do so on their own terms, and they faced considerable opposition internally. The government invested massively in developing legal capacity, including to adjust to WTO requirements that the United States had pressed upon it. In the process, China learned how to defend its interests through the WTO and to use the rules against the United States and the European Union. China's responses affected US and European perceptions of the legal order, and the US reaction, in turn, has eroded it. As China grew economically and benefitted from liberalized trade, as the 2008 financial crisis humbled American-style neoliberalism and raised China's profile, and as President Xi assumed power and favored a growing role for the state and state-owned enterprises, what had seemed a tough deal for China in its WTO Accession Protocol increasingly appeared to many in the United States to be unfair to the United States.

WTO rules played into law and policy developments in China involving political and professional contests, including between market liberalizers and neo-Maoists.[2] Officials had to manage and respond to domestic political backlash that China had "sold out" its interests by making such concessions.[3] Leftist scholars and activists

---

[1] For example, President Clinton stated, "[by] joining the WTO, China is not simply agreeing to import more of our products; it is agreeing to import one of democracy's most cherished values: economic freedom. The more China liberalizes its economy, the more fully it will liberate the potential of its people – their initiative, their imagination, their remarkable spirit of enterprise. And when individuals have the power, not just to dream but to realize their dreams, they will demand a greater say." Clinton's Speech on China Trade Bill, March 9, 2000.

[2] On the neo-Maoist left, Jude Blanchette, *China's New Red Guards: The Return of Radicalism and the Rebirth of Mao Zedong* (Oxford: Oxford University Press, 2019), 84 (a movement "that saw global conspiracies of Western domination, the infiltration of China and the party by traitors and 'hostile forces,' and a belief in an inevitable and unavoidable conflict with the United States").

[3] Interview with high-level official, May 2012; Margaret Pearson, "China in Geneva: Lessons from China's Early Years in the World Trade Organization," in *New Directions in the Study of China's*

"framed the WTO as part of a 'soft war' waged by Western powers, particularly the United States and United Kingdom, to pry open China's markets for the benefit of Western corporations, and ultimately to 'advance neo-colonialism and to control the entire world'."[4] Reformers, in contrast, used international legal norms as leverage to advance their internal policy goals.

As China developed legal capacity to handle WTO issues, it became enmeshed in transnational legal processes. These processes spurred changes and transformations in government, academia, law firms, and business. Key parts of the Chinese government and Chinese stakeholders became embedded in transnational legal processes of international economic integration, which included a binding international dispute settlement process that was new to China.

From the perspective of transnational legal ordering, international trade law involves not just law at the international level but dynamic interactions within states, between states, and with international organizations that implicate international, national, and local law and practice. The international trade regime affected institutions and professions within China along multiple dimensions, including within government, academia, law firms, business, and private trade associations. To implement its WTO obligations, China made sweeping changes in its legal system. The Chinese government took novel steps to spread understanding of WTO law and dispute settlement throughout society in ways that helped legitimate international trade litigation and domestic legal change. Investment in teaching and research on WTO law brought new approaches such as the case method for the study of law. By contributing to the opening of the economy, and by subjecting internal governance to external accountability norms and processes, the WTO increased the overall prominence of the legal profession within China. Yet, to preserve its unique political and economic system, China also introduced initiatives that, in the view of many in the United States and Europe, violate WTO disciplines either in letter or in spirit. China aimed to shape the understanding and flexible application of WTO legal norms for its model of state capitalism, affecting US perceptions of the system's legitimacy and relevance. This chapter addresses the WTO context while the following one assesses China's initiatives under President Xi that could give rise to a broader Sino-centric legal order alongside the multilateral one, building from infrastructure finance, a web of trade and investment agreements, and indigenous innovation policies in which intellectual property plays a supporting role.

Without building strong capacity in WTO law, China's growing clout in the WTO would not have been possible. In turn, the United States would not have viewed WTO negotiating principles of reciprocity and the WTO dispute settlement system with its Appellate Body as significant constraints on US trade policy. How did

---

    Foreign Policy, eds. Alastair Iain Johnston and Robert Ross (Stanford: Stanford University Press, 2006), 242, 246.
4   Blanchette, *China's New Red Guards*, 66.

China, a country with an anti-legalist, Confucian tradition not known for lawyering, a country also facing considerable language barriers in an organization where English is the de facto governing language, build its trade law capacity? What broader effects did those efforts have for Chinese institutions, professions, and practices? And what were the implications for the multilateral trading system?

I. CHINA'S CHALLENGES IN JOINING THE WTO

A. *China's Challenges*

While China was one of the founding members of the General Agreement on Tariffs and Trade formed after World War II, it withdrew after the communist revolution in 1949 and did not play any role in the multilateral trading system. It sought to resume its membership in 1986,[5] but it then took fifteen years for China to be accepted back into the system. Unlike other WTO members, China had no experience with GATT and WTO law, whether in terms of the WTO committee system or litigation. Moreover, it had not participated in litigation before international courts as litigation was at odds with Chinese state and business norms for dispute resolution. China, in short, faced daunting challenges in joining the WTO's legalized and judicialized system. In order to join the organization, China had to agree to a stringent accession protocol in November 2001. To start, it had to make deep tariff cuts for imports, and it agreed to significantly liberalize services trade, in each case by far more than any other emerging economy.[6] For trade in goods, it agreed to reduce its average bound tariff to 10 percent by 2008, with an average of 9.1 percent for industrial products and 15.8 percent for agricultural products. In comparison, Brazil agreed to an average bound tariff of 31.4 percent (30.8 percent for industrial and 35.5 percent for agricultural goods) and India an average bound tariff of 49 percent (34.7 percent for industrial and 114.2 percent for agricultural goods). In contrast, however, the United States had agreed to average bound tariffs of 3.5 percent (3.3 percent for industrial and 4.8 percent for agricultural goods) and the European Union to 5.5 percent (3.9 percent for industrial and 15.9 percent for agricultural goods).[7]

---

[5]   China was an original member of the GATT in 1948, but the Kuomintang government in Taiwan, which occupied the Chinese seat at that time, withdrew from the GATT in May 1950. For more details on the legal controversy surrounding the withdrawal and the history of the accession process, Henry Gao, "China's Participation in the WTO: A Lawyer's Perspective," *Singapore Year Book of International Law* 11 (2007): 41–48. China sought to rejoin the GATT in the 1980s when the reformist Zhao Ziyang was China's Premier.

[6]   Nicholas Lardy, *Integrating China into the Global Economy* (Washington, DC: Brookings Institution Press, 2002), 33–35, 66–75.

[7]   World Trade Organization, International Trade Center, United Nations Conference on Trade and Development, *World Tariff Profiles 2009* (2009), 2–18 (these reflect initial bindings at the time of accession).

China further agreed to eliminate state monopolies on imports and exports, to open its economy to competition, and to overhaul its laws, regulations, procedures, and administrative and judicial institutions across all levels of government. It agreed that all regulations affecting trade would be nondiscriminatory and that government standard setting would be transparent and based on international standards.[8] It is committed to stringent intellectual property protection,[9] and independent review by judicial or administrative tribunals of all trade-related administrative actions.[10] And it agreed to grant greater rights to other WTO members against China, and reduced China's rights against them, compared to standard WTO rules. For example, as a condition to accession, China agreed not to apply export taxes (except as scheduled) and granted other WTO members the right to treat China as a "nonmarket economy" in their anti-dumping investigations for a fifteen-year period, and to use alternative benchmarks in their subsidy and countervailing duty investigations of Chinese products. It thus made it easier for countries to impose antidumping and countervailing duties against Chinese products. These provisions, which did not apply to other WTO members, raised charges that China's Accession Protocol was an unequal treaty mirroring China's earlier history of "unequal treaties" with Western powers.[11]

The country started the complicated process of revising its laws before it formally joined the WTO pursuant to a bilateral agreement with the United States on November 15, 1999. The United States wielded significant leverage since it was the gatekeeper to China's WTO accession. To implement the bilateral agreement and China's subsequent WTO commitments, the government established an "Office for the Clean-up of Laws and Regulations" on December 1, 1999, under the auspices of the Ministry of Commerce (then named MOFTEC, or Ministry of Foreign Trade and Economic Cooperation).[12] The "clean up" operation was immense, involving bureaucrats at all levels, from the central government to provincial and local ones. The office first focused on the "clean up" of laws and regulations at the central level, starting with MOFTEC and expanding to other Ministries. The office then turned to provincial and local regulations. It classified laws and regulations into one of four categories: regulations "to be kept," "to be revised," "to be abolished," and "to be reenacted." Overall, the office reports that it oversaw the "cleaning up" of more than 3,000 laws and regulations, including around 1,150 at the central government level, in order for China to meet its WTO commitments.[13] The office completed its work

---

[8]　GATT Articles III and X, *The TBT Agreement, The SPS Agreement.*

[9]　TRIPS Agreement; Andrea Wechsler, "China's WTO Accession Revisited: Achievements and Challenges in Chinese Intellectual Property Law Reform," in *European Yearbook of International Economic Law*, eds. Christoph Herrmann, Markus Krajewski, and Jörg Philipp (Heidelberg: Springer-Verlanger, 2012), 125.

[10]　Article 2(D)1, *China's Protocol of Accession.*

[11]　Julia Qin, "WTO-Plus Obligations and their Implications for the World Trade Organization Legal System – An Appraisal of the China Accession Protocol," *Journal of World Trade* 37 (2003): 483.

[12]　"Zhang Yuqing Interview," in *Rushi Shinian Fazhi Zhongguo* [10 Years in the WTO, Rule of Law in China], eds. Lu Xiaojie, Han Liyu, Huang Dongli, Si Xiaoli, and Yang Guohua (2011), 6–7.

[13]　Ibid., 6–11.

in around two years, constituting arguably the largest, condensed exercise of law-making and law revision in China's (and perhaps the world's) history. Pause for a moment and think counterfactually if this were demanded of the United States: It is inconceivable that the United States would revise its laws to such an extent upon signing a treaty and joining an international organization. Rather, WTO law largely reflected existing US law.

Although there was significant debate in government about the terms of China's accession, after China joined the WTO, the government launched a campaign to generate enthusiasm in the country regarding its accession.[14] The government sponsored numerous WTO-related initiatives, such as the establishment of WTO centers around the country. Thousands of seminars were held and books published on WTO law, arguably constituting more publications on the WTO than the total published elsewhere in the world combined.[15] Scores of Chinese officials, judges, and scholars came to the United States for training in WTO law, and scores of experts went to China to teach WTO law under technical assistance and capacity-building initiatives.[16] In 2003, the government even organized a national contest regarding knowledge of the WTO in which over five million people reportedly participated. The final session broadcast like a game show on China Central Television, and the winner was flown to Geneva to visit the WTO and meet with its Director-General.[17] Such popular participation in learning technical international law rules is unheard of and, we imagine, would be the envy of international law enthusiasts around the world. The government trumpeted China's joining the WTO as leverage to carry out market-oriented reforms, and further China's integration in the global economy and global institutions. The United States and European Union likewise hoped that China's accession would further China's transformation into a market economy, and to encourage it to move towards a liberal democracy.

---

[14]   Pearson, "China in Geneva;" Yang Guohua, "China in the WTO Dispute Settlement: A Memoir," *Journal of World Trade* 49, no. 1 (2015): 1, 3. Stories of common peoples' interests in the WTO in China are legion. To give an example, Peter Hessler's popular book *Oracle Bones* frequently refers to the excitement of China's joining the WTO among the people he encounters. At one point, Hessler meets a photographer on a bridge on the Yalu River in the town of Yabaolu across from North Korea who "kept bringing up the WTO. I asked him why he was so interested. 'The newspapers say that if we join the WTO, we'll have more foreign visitors coming to China', he explained. 'And of course if China's economy improves, then there will be more Chinese tourists coming here, too. So it has an effect on me'." Peter Hessler, *Oracle Bones: A Journey through Time in China* (New York: HarperCollins, 2006), 67.

[15]   Julia Qin, "Trade, Investment and Beyond: The Impact of WTO Accession on China's Legal System," *China Quarterly* 191 (2007): 720.

[16]   Guohua, "A Memoir," 1, 3–5; Asian Development Bank, *Technical Assistance to the People's Republic of China for WTO Membership and Foreign Trade Reform* (2001).

[17]   Zhenyu Sun, "China's Experience of 10 Years in the WTO," in *A Decade in the WTO: Implications for China and Global Governance*, eds. Ricardo Meléndez-Ortiz, Christophe Bellmann, and Shuaihua Cheng (Geneva: ICTSD Programme on Global Economic Policy and Institutions, 2011), 12.

B. *The WTO's Significance for China*

Economic development is critical for the Chinese government, which hopes to avoid being mired in a "middle-income trap" where the country is less competitive in low-wage production (because wages have risen) and unable to compete in high-value-added markets.[18] Trade (imports plus exports) soared to around 65 percent of China's gross domestic product in 2006 from 24 percent in 1990, before declining to 38 percent by 2018 as a huge Chinese middle class formed and China's domestic market grew.[19]

Managing its trade relations is crucial not only for China's economic development but also for its political stability. China has a strong state under an authoritarian (formally Marxist) government. The Chinese state invests significantly in industrial policies, ranging from direct state ownership to state subsidization of economic sectors, including (as alleged by the United States and European Union) through state bank financing at lower than market rates, state company selling manufacturing inputs at less than market value, and a state innovation policy that discriminatorily promotes indigenous research and development to upgrade China's economy.[20] Law and lawyers play increasingly important roles in this mixed economy, whether one views it as "socialist with Chinese characteristics," "capitalist with Chinese characteristics," or simply "state capitalism."[21] Although many commentators maintain there has been a turn away from law in general,[22] business, investment, and trade law flourish, creating new career opportunities for lawyers.[23]

Joining the WTO was part of, and contributed to, a broader "opening up" process in China in which law and lawyers play a growing role in commercial transactions and dispute settlement, both internally and externally. By 2018, the Chinese legal bar had over 300,000 members and the judiciary had over 200,000 judges.[24] This is a remarkable

---

[18]   Randall Peerenboom and Tom Ginsburg, *Law and Development of Middle-Income Countries: Avoiding the Middle-Income Trap* (Cambridge: Cambridge University Press, 2014).

[19]   The World Bank, "Merchandise Trade (% of GDP)," *The World Bank*, https://data.worldbank.org /indicator/NE.TRD.GNFS.ZS (accessed January 22, 2020).

[20]   Chapter 7, this book; David Wertime, "It's Official: China is Becoming a New Innovation Powerhouse," *Foreign Policy*, February 7, 2014.

[21]   Compare Yasheng Huang, *Capitalism with Chinese Characteristics: Entrepreneurship and the State* (Cambridge: Cambridge University Press, 2008); *Law and Economics with Chinese Characteristics: Institutions for Promoting Developing in the Twenty-First Century*, eds. David Kennedy and Joseph Stiglitz (Oxford: Oxford University Press, 2015); Branko Milanovic, *Capitalism Alone: The Future of the System that Rules the World* (Cambridge: Harvard University Press, 2019). China formally revised its constitution to call itself a "socialist market economy" in 1993, just as negotiations for the WTO's creation were being completed.

[22]   Compare Carl F. Minzner, "China's Turn against Law," *American Journal of Comparative Law* 59 (2011): 935; Randall Peerenboom, *China's Long March Toward Rule of Law* (Cambridge: Cambridge University Press, 2002).

[23]   Sida Liu, David Trubek, and David Wilkins, "Mapping the Ecology of China's Corporate Legal Sector: Globalization and its Impact on Lawyers and Society," *Asian Journal of Law and Society* 3 (2016): 2273–2297.

[24]   Ji Li, *Power, Law, and Justice in China* (Cambridge: Cambridge University Press, forthcoming) (manuscript on file).

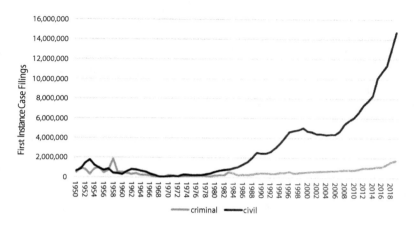

FIGURE 6.1 Number of first instance case filings in China (1950–2019)[25]

change given that the legal profession was almost wiped out during the Cultural Revolution. The use of courts for dispute settlement in China skyrocketed. The number of civil claims filed at first instance soared from 62,000 in 1969 (during the Cultural Revolution), to 2.4 million in 1990, to 6 million in 2010, and to almost 15 million in 2019. China's economic opening, the increased role of markets and commercial law, and rising expectations among the populace help explain these changes.

In parallel, lawyers play an increasingly significant role in China's outbound commercial relations, including for its Belt and Road Initiative, as addressed in Chapter 7. China's joining the WTO and its experience in the organization helped catalyze and significantly contributed to these economic, institutional, and professional changes within it. International trade law, in short, had huge implications for the Chinese economy, the Chinese government, and Chinese law and lawyers.

By 2009, following the global financial crisis, the continued rise of China as an economic power, and the significant strengthening of China's legal capacity to defend its interests in WTO dispute settlement and negotiations, the US–China relationship had dramatically changed.[26] China began to increasingly assert itself as a rival to the United States and European Union. It had little to learn from them after their economic governance models lost credibility during the 2008 Great Recession. By 2010, China had become the world's second largest economy, surpassing Japan.[27]

[25]   Ibid. (citing Report on China Law Development and China Statistics Yearbook).
[26]   Martin Jacques, *When China Rules the World: The End of the Western World and the Birth of a New Global Order* (East Rutherford: Penguin, 2009); Ho-fung Hung, *The China Boom: Why China Will Not Rule the World* (New York: Columbia University Press, 2016).
[27]   The World Bank, "The World Bank in China: Overview," *The World Bank*, www.worldbank.org/en/country/china/overview (accessed February 16, 2019). David Barboza, "China Passes Japan as Second-Largest Economy," *New York Times*, August 15, 2010, B1, www.nytimes.com/2010/08/16/business/global/16yuan.html?pagewanted=all&_r=0 (accessed February 16, 2019).

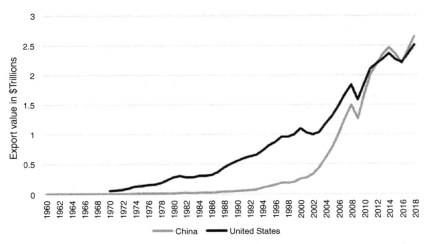

FIGURE 6.2 Comparison of exports between China and the United States[28]

By 2013, it became the world's largest trader in goods, surpassing the United States, while its internal market grew at even a faster rate than its exports. As Figure 6.2 shows, Chinese trade soared after China joined the WTO in 2001, reflecting huge transformations in China's economy and the accompanying role of Chinese lawyers. Forecasters predict that China will surpass the United States as the world's largest economy within a decade.[29] In law and development circles, one heard of a new "Beijing consensus" as displacing, or at least rivaling, the neoliberal "Washington consensus."[30] By 2018, the rest of the world was more connected through trade with China – which is the top importer for twice as many countries as the United States (61 vs. 30) – enhancing China's influence.[31] This reduced the clout of the United States and European Union in the WTO, which represented well over half of the GDP and trade of all other WTO members combined until China joined.[32]

To participate effectively in the multilateral trading system, China invested in building legal capacity. Only then could it attempt to shape the interpretation of WTO law to better protect its access to foreign markets and defend its domestic

[28] World Bank, Exports of goods and services (current US$) – United States, China, https://data .worldbank.org/indicator/NE.EXP.GNFS.CD?locations=US-CN.
[29] Pankaj Ghemawat and Thomas Hout, "Can China's Companies Conquer the World," *Foreign Affairs* 25 (2016): 86–98.
[30] John Williamson, "Is the 'Beijing Consensus' Now Dominant?," *Asia Policy* 13 (2012): 1; Stefan Halper, *The Beijing Consensus: Legitimizing Authoritarianism in Our Time* (New York: Basic Books, 2012).
[31] Cent. Intelligence Agency, *Imports – Partners*, The World Factbook www.cia.gov/library/publica tions/the-world-factbook/fields/403.html; Cent. Intelligence Agency, *Exports – Partners*, The World Factbook www.cia.gov/library/publications/the-world-factbook/fields/241.html.
[32] John Barton, Judith Goldstein, and Richard Steinberg, *The Evolution of the Trade Regime: Politics, Law, and Economics of the GATT and the WTO* (Princeton: Princeton University Press, 2006), 13.

trade-related policies. Most of its initial programs focused on building the capacity of government officials, but gradually the government turned toward enhancing the capacity of nongovernmental actors since it realized that private actors play important roles at the WTO, particularly in dispute settlement.[33] By 2006, within five years of its accession, China emerged from being a reluctant participant that tried to avoid WTO litigation to become an active and formidable player that used the system to defend its interests. China's joining the WTO and its building of trade-related capacity contributed to changes within China, which in turn affected the transnational legal order for trade.

II. BUILDING A TRADE LAW COMMUNITY IN CHINA

A. *Building Trade Law Capacity in Government*

Even before its accession to the WTO, the Chinese government realized that its lack of legal capacity could be a major challenge. For example, in early 2002, President Jiang Zemin stated that it was inevitable that China would suffer losses in WTO dispute settlement due to its unfamiliarity with WTO rules.[34] To prepare China for its post-accession challenges, Jiang urged the government to prioritize the development of a team of professionals well versed in WTO rules, including experts on international trade policy, trade law, trade negotiations, and antidumping investigations. Pursuant to the high-level exhortations, central, provincial, and local government departments invested significantly in WTO-related capacity-building initiatives, expanding the role for lawyers.

In the central government, the State Council and the Central Committee of the Communist Party of China issued a joint Notice on China's WTO Accession to all Ministries and provincial governments on November 20, 2001, in which they called for Party organs and government organizations at all levels to strengthen the study of WTO rules and the training of WTO experts.[35] Many ministries restructured their internal organization in preparation for the upcoming accession. They worked with MOFTEC to "clean up" laws and regulations to meet China's new obligations and ensure that new laws and regulations comply with WTO rules.

---

[33] Gregory Shaffer, *Defending Interests: Public-Private Partnerships in WTO Litigation* (Washington, DC: Brookings Institution Press, 2003).

[34] Jiang Zemin, "Zai Jilie de Guoji Jingzheng zhong Zhangwo Zhudong [Seize the Initiative amidst Intense International Competition]," in *Jiang Zemin Wenxuan: Disan Juan [Selected Works of Jiang Zemin: Volume III]* (Beijing: Foreign Languages Press, 2006), 455.

[35] Zhonggong Zhongyang Bangongting, "Guowuyuan Bangongting Guanyu Woguo Jiaru Shijie Maoyi Zuzhi Youguan Qingkuang de Tongbao [Announcement by the General Office of the Central Committee of the Communist Party of China and the General Office of the State Council on China's Accession to the WTO]," *Zhongbanfa*, November 20, 2001. Within the Chinese system, the State Council is the Central Government, headed by the Premier.

The government reorganized its lead ministry for international trade and renamed it the Ministry of Commerce (MOFCOM). MOFCOM has a Janus-faced role of looking inward and outward. Internally, MOFCOM oversees China's compliance with its WTO obligations. Externally, MOFCOM protects China's trading interests abroad, including before the WTO. It staffs China's mission to the WTO, which is the largest in Geneva with a delegation of over twenty individuals.[36] By Janus-faced, we do not mean that MOFCOM is "insincere," but rather that, in having to look both inwards and outwards, MOFCOM experiences pressure toward compliance so as not to open China to legal challenge when it pursues claims against others.

Following China's accession, MOFCOM (then named MOFTEC) established two new Departments to address WTO matters which likewise have two-sided missions: the Department of WTO Affairs and the Fair Trade Bureau. Internally, the Department of WTO Affairs reviews draft Chinese legislation and policy to ensure they are WTO consistent.[37] Externally, it represents China in WTO negotiations, WTO trade policy reviews, and before WTO committees, where it is responsible for notifying new and amended Chinese regulations as required under WTO agreements.[38] The Fair Trade Bureau plays the same dual role regarding the application of import relief laws, both in China where it conducts investigations of foreign products, and outside of China where it follows investigations of Chinese products. These roles likewise enhance the departments' sensitivity to the importance of Chinese compliance with WTO commitments since it needs credibility when pressing other countries to meet their commitments toward China.[39]

MOFCOM has a separate Department of Treaty and Law (DTL) that is responsible for legal issues in China's international economic relations and handles cases before the WTO dispute settlement system. In 2001, MOFCOM created a Division on WTO law within DTL to handle WTO disputes.[40] It established a second DTL Division on WTO Law in 2009 when China faced a slew of new disputes. The total number of DTL officials dedicated to WTO litigation increased from five to nine.[41]

---

[36] Based on personnel identified as working on WTO issues in the WTO Directory. The mission, housed in a beautiful building on Lake Geneva, is by far the nicest of all missions to the WTO. Based on the author's years of interviews.

[37] MOFCOM, Zhuyao Zhineng [Main Functions], *Ministry of Commerce of the People's Republic of China: Department of WTO Affairs (China WTO Notification and Inquiry Center)*, June 23, 2015, http://sms.mofcom.gov.cn/article/gywm/200606/20060602467456.shtml; Interview with official, Beijing, July 20, 2016; interview with former MOFCOM official, Beijing, July 22, 2016.

[38] Ibid. Li Chengang, "Zhongguo Canyu Shimao Zuzhi Zhengduan Jiejue Shijian Gaishu [Overview of China's Participation in WTO Dispute Settlement Practices]," in *Shimao Zuzhi Guize Boyi: Zhongguo Canyu WTO Zhengduan Jiejue de Shinian Falu Shijian [Gaming with WTO Rules: China's Ten Years' Experience in WTO Dispute Settlement Practices]*, ed. Li Chengang (Beijing: The Commercial Press, 2011), 14–15.

[39] Interviewees noted how the WTO has helped to discipline the government's application of anti-dumping law in China. Interview with partner, Beijing law firm, June 11, 2014.

[40] Chengang, *Overview*, 15.

[41] Ibid., 27.

These officials work with China's diplomats responsible for WTO dispute settlement in China's WTO mission in Geneva, so that China has around a dozen officials specializing in WTO dispute settlement in total. China's WTO dispute settlement team enhanced lawyers' roles in China's international trade relations.

The GATT requires WTO members to take "reasonable measures" to ensure local compliance with GATT obligations.[42] China's central government has used this provision to try to assert greater control over local actors, which generally is a challenge.[43] The central government aimed to spur local government officials to become familiar with WTO rules. In February 2002, two months after China's formal WTO accession, the central government held a one-week training course for senior officials at the Provincial and Ministerial Level.[44] The lecturers included President Jiang and Premier Zhu Rongji, as well as high-level officials from MOFCOM and other ministries, highlighting the political importance that the central government wished to convey. The training course explained the main rules in the WTO to senior officials and reminded them that all new laws and regulations needed to be consistent with WTO requirements.

After the training course, many provinces drafted Plans of Action in response to China's WTO accession.[45] A key component was to strengthen trade law capacity. To achieve this objective, local governments established what they called "WTO Centers," analogous to, but much more ambitious than, India's "WTO cells." Funded by the local governments, these centers are semigovernmental institutions that conduct WTO-related training, research, and outreach activities. In the two to three years before and after China's WTO accession, the centers were the favorite pet projects of ambitious local officials who established them across the country. In 2019, the Shanghai center employed about forty professionals and the Shenzhen center about thirty.[46]

The centers served important internal and external roles. Internally, when a local government passed a regulation, it was to consult with the local WTO center to confirm that the regulation is WTO consistent, and amend it as needed.[47] This process aimed to embed the international rules within internal policy making. Externally, the centers were to provide information to companies to help them address trade barriers, such as antidumping and countervailing duty investigations, and seizures of goods on intellectual property grounds. As Chinese companies moved up the value chain and produced technology-intensive goods, intellectual

---

[42] GATT Article XXIV.12.

[43] Pittman Potter, "China and the International Legal System: Challenges of Participation," in *China's Legal System: New Developments, New Challenges*, ed. Donald C. Clarke (Cambridge: Cambridge University Press, 2008), 145, 150.

[44] Sun Zhenyu, *Rineiwa Kongzong Suiyue [Busy Years in Geneva]* (Beijing: Ren Min Chu Ban She, 2011), 37.

[45] *Zhongguo Jiaru Shijie Maoyi Zuzhi Guoduqi Beijing Xingdong Jihua [Action Plan for Beijing during China's Transition Period in the WTO]*, ed. Zhang Mao (Beijing: Social Science Literature Publishing House, 2003).

[46] Interviews in Shanghai and Shenzhen Centers, June 2014 and email confirmation in April 2020.

[47] Interview at Shenzhen WTO Affairs Center, June 13, 2014.

property issues became more salient, such as under US Section 337 pursuant to which US customs seizes imported products that allegedly violate US intellectual property rights.[48] The centers also helped MOFCOM prepare an annual trade barriers report regarding measures that Chinese exporters face. It was modeled after the annual US National Trade Estimates Report on Foreign Trade Barriers, once more illustrating the influence of US models in transnational legal ordering.[49]

When China first joined the WTO, WTO matters represented the cutting edge for policy and the leadership spurred officials to exhibit WTO awareness.[50] The WTO "craze" faded, in part because of the turn away from multilateral trade negotiations to bilateral and regional ones, and in part because of disenchantment with the WTO given the widespread use of antidumping and other measures against Chinese products.[51] Most provincial and local governments quietly abandoned their WTO centers so that by 2014 only the WTO centers in Beijing, Shanghai, and Shenzhen remained active.[52] These centers broadened their mandates to encompass bilateral and plurilateral trade and investment agreements. For example, in 2012, the Shanghai center established an Institute of Global Trade and Investment under its auspices,[53] and it played an important supporting role in the creation of the China (Shanghai) Pilot Free Trade Zone, which experimented with trade and investment liberalization. In addition, while in the early years, the majority of the Shanghai center's staff had a legal background and focused on WTO implementation, a growing proportion of the staff began to have an economic background and provided economic analysis to support bilateral and plurilateral trade and investment negotiations as part of China's new initiatives addressed in Chapter 7.[54]

The US election of President Trump and the US-launched trade war deepened these trends. Nonetheless, cloaking its national interest within a commitment to the multilateral rules-based trading system and standing with other countries to oppose US unilateralism and protectionism strengthened China's international position politically. In January 2020, China formed an alliance with the European Union, Australia, Brazil, Canada, Mexico, and others to develop an interim WTO appeals mechanism after the US blockage of the Appellate Body in December 2019, which the group formalized in March 2020.[55] These countries remain wary of China's rise and many are skeptical of its commitments. Nonetheless, China is better positioned in aligning itself with international organizations such as the WTO that the United States threatens to abandon.

[48]   Ibid.
[49]   Interview with member of Shanghai WTO Center, June 12, 2014.
[50]   Interview with lawyer, Shanghai, June 12, 2014.
[51]   Interview at Shenzhen WTO Affairs Center, June 13, 2014.
[52]   Interview with member of Shanghai WTO Center, June 12, 2014.
[53]   Shanghai's WTO Affairs Consultation Center, "About the Center," *SCCWTO*, www.sccwto.org /introduce?locale=zh-CN.
[54]   Interview with member of Shanghai WTO Center, June 12, 2014.
[55]   Philip Blenkinsop, "EU, China and 14 others agree to stop-gap fix for WTO crisis," *Reuters*, March 27, 2020.

B. *Building Expertise in Academia, WTO Centers, and Think Tanks*

In addition to boosting WTO-related capacity within central, provincial, and local governments, the central government took steps to build the capacities of other actors and incentivize them to invest in developing expertise in WTO law. Through these initiatives, WTO legal norms diffuse. The capacity-building initiatives spanned academia, law firms, private businesses, and industry associations. We start with academia, which illustrates the implications for Chinese legal study, research, and practice in international economic law.

China's government exercises great influence in academia, in particular through its funding of research. With the government's promotion of the WTO's importance for China, WTO law became a popular subject and discipline in Chinese universities. In 2000, the year before China joined the WTO, the government made International Economic Law (which includes WTO law) a mandatory subject on the national bar exam.[56] China's Ministry of Education included International Economic Law (and thus WTO law) as one of sixteen mandatory courses for all Chinese law schools.[57] Between 2007 and 2014, almost two-thirds of all funded research proposals were for international economic law topics.[58]

As a result, in most of the more than six hundred law schools in China, there is at least one professor who claims to specialize in WTO law, a much greater number and percentage than in the United States where the study of WTO law has waned.[59] Because of the concentration of universities in major cities, the most reputable centers for WTO teaching and research are in cities such as Beijing, Shanghai, Guangzhou, Chongqing, and Xiamen. Many of these specialists teach in the traditional elite law schools, the so-called "Five Institutes and Four Departments," which refers to the five independent law institutes and four law departments in comprehensive universities when the government restructured higher education institutions in 1952. In addition, the government established two foreign trade institutes in Beijing in 1951 and Shanghai in 1960, respectively, under the auspices of the trade ministry. These elite schools have multiple professors who teach international trade law, including specialized seminars on WTO law and specific topics such as WTO dispute settlement, trade in services, and the WTO Agreement on Trade-Related Aspects of Intellectual Property Rights.

---

[56]   Ministry of Justice, "Lvshi Zige Kaoshi Banfa [Rules on Lawyer's Qualification Exam]," Art. 16, Order 61, July 26, 2000.

[57]   Ministry of Education, "Putong Gaodeng Xuexiao Benke Zhuanye Mulu he Zhuanye Jieshao [Overview of the Catalogue of Majors for Institutions of Higher Education]," *Ministry of Education of the People's Republic of China*, 67, 2012, www.moe.edu.cn/s78/A08/A08_gggs/s8468/201212/t20121218_181006.html.

[58]   Anthea Roberts, *Is International Law International?* (New York: Oxford University Press, 2017), 216–217 (Figure 17).

[59]   Interview with law professor, Beijing, July 25, 2016. Compare Roberts, *Is International Law International?*, 224 (international law occupying a peripheral place in the US academy).

Most WTO scholars in China are graduates from these elite law schools, and the leading ones couple their degrees with overseas experience. The foreign study and experience of China's WTO scholars exemplify the transnational nature of this legal field.[60] Each of the eight Chinese academics on China's Indicative List of WTO Panelists for WTO disputes had either studied overseas or been visiting scholars abroad.[61] More broadly, over 40 percent of international law academics have received at least one law degree outside the country.[62]

Professors teaching WTO law in China have spearheaded use of the case study method in China. China is a civil law country where judges do not create jurisprudence, and it thus has been difficult to adopt the case law method in Chinese law schools. The WTO legal field, however, is completely different. By the start of 2020, WTO panels and the Appellate Body had issued 258 panel reports and 145 Appellate Body reports that built an elaborate, evolving jurisprudence to create "legitimate expectations" among the WTO's member governments and traders and other stakeholders within them.[63] To teach WTO law, Chinese professors thus included cases in the advanced curriculum.

In 2007, the Ministry of Education of China launched a comprehensive teaching reform plan to improve the teaching quality in Chinese universities. One important component of the plan was to develop "Bilingual Courses" that can "substantially improve the English levels of college students in their areas of studies and enhance their capacities to conduct research in English."[64] Among law school subjects, WTO law was considered one of the few that are most suitable for teaching in English. Many law schools thus began to offer courses on WTO law in English in order to build students' English language capacity. In turn, this development helped professors and students become more familiar with foreign scholarship on WTO law.

[60] The transfer and China's pragmatic adaptation of legal ideas has parallels with China's receipt and pragmatic adaptation of economic ideas . Julian Gewirtz, *Unlikely Partners: Chinese Reformers, Western Economists, and the Making of Global China* (Cambridge: Harvard University Press, 2017). More broadly, China became the largest sender of law students (as well as visiting students) to the United States. Paul Musgrave, "Universities Aren't Ready for Trade War Casualties," *Foreign Policy* (May 19, 2019) ("Chinese visitors account for one-third of the foreign undergraduates and graduate students studying in the United States").

[61] Because of the large number of cases in which China is a party, only one Chinese has served on a panel, Mr Zhang Yuqing, who was a member of an *EC – Bananas* compliance panel. European Communities – Regime for the Importation Sale and Distribution of Bananas, Recourse to Article 21.5 of the DSU by the United States," *Constitution of the Panel, Note by the Secretariat*, WT/DS27/84, August 13, 2007.

[62] Anthea Roberts, "Cross-Border Student Flows and the Construction of International Law as a Transnational Legal Field," in *The Globalization of Legal Education: A Critical Perspective*, eds. Bryant Garth and Gregory Shaffer (on file) (typically an advanced degree such as an LLM or PhD).

[63] Appellate Body Report, "Japan-Taxes on Alcoholic Beverages," WTO/DS8, July 11, 1996, 10, 11. This number does not include separate decisions regarding the amount of time for compliance and actual compliance, and three arbitrations.

[64] Ministry of Education and Ministry of Finance, "Guanyu Shishi Gaodeng Xuexiao Benke Jiaoxue Zhiliang yu Jiaoxue Gaige Gongcheng de Yijian [Advice on the Implementation of the Project on Quality of College Teaching and Teaching Reform in Higher Education]," *Jiaogao*, January 22, 2007.

To build students' understanding of WTO rules, MOFCOM organized the China WTO Moot Court Competition with two of China's elite law schools, China University of Politics and Law, and Southwest University of Political Science and Law.[65] The competition, which is conducted in English and simulates WTO panel procedures, aims to "promote the training and selection of [China's] personnel for WTO negotiations and dispute settlement." The first competition was held in Beijing in November 2012, and it drew teams from eight universities from four cities. The number of teams doubled to sixteen in 2013 and rose to eighteen in the ensuing years. The panelists include Chinese trade lawyers, professors, and MOFCOM officials that handle WTO cases. MOFCOM officials and the private lawyers use the opportunity to identify and recruit young talent.[66]

The study of WTO case law can have broader implications on the formation of legal professionals in China, especially those who will enter commercial practice, but also for those who enter government or become judges. When graduates work in ministries outside of MOFCOM, not only does basic knowledge of WTO law diffuse through the government, but MOFCOM has interlocutors in other ministries acquainted with WTO legal rules and principles. Such diffusion of expertise facilitated compliance with China's WTO commitments and potentially deeper socialization processes regarding trade law principles and legal reasoning.

A senior MOFCOM official stressed to us how the judges of the Supreme People's Court know WTO law.[67] Although the Supreme People's Court rejected proposals that WTO law should be directly applicable before Chinese courts, their rules provide that Chinese law is to be interpreted where possible to comply with WTO requirements.[68] Chinese courts have referenced WTO law in a number of decisions.[69]

---

[65] It is "the first Moot Court Competition officially sponsored by a Ministry" in China, revealing the importance that the government has given to WTO law and dispute settlement. Nankai University, "Nankai Daibiaodui Huode Shoujie Quanguo WTO Moni Fating Jingsai Jijun [Nankai Team Won Third Place in the first National WTO Moot Court Competition]," *Nankai News Network*, December 6, 2012.

[66] Interview with lawyer, Beijing, June 11, 2014.

[67] Interview with official at MOFCOM Research Institute, July 20, 2016. For example, Cao Jianmin, a well-known WTO scholar and former President of the East China University of Politics and Law, served as Deputy President of the Supreme People's Court and President of the Supreme People's Procuratorate. Similarly, in 2015, the government appointed WTO scholar Liu Jingdong from the Institute of Law at the China Academy of Social Sciences to be the Deputy Presiding Judge for the Fourth Division on Civil Cases of the Supreme People's Court of China.

[68] Article 9 of the Supreme People's Court's Regulations on Issues Concerning the Trial of Administrative Cases Relating to International Trade provides, "[i]f there are two or more reasonable interpretations for a provision of the law or administrative regulation applied by a peoples court in the hearing of an international trade administrative case, and among which one interpretation is consistent with the relevant provisions of the international treaty that the PRC concluded or entered into, such interpretation shall be chosen, unless China has made reservation to the provisions." Congyan Cai, "International Law in Chinese Courts," *American Journal of International Law* 110 (2016): 269, 275–277.

[69] Ibid., 286–287.

Although, unlike Brazil, China did not create an internship program in its Geneva mission, it often includes Chinese law professors in its delegations to WTO hearings before panels and the Appellate Body and they take these experiences back home with them. A law professor attending an Appellate Body hearing, for example, emphasized how quickly and repeatedly the legal issues arose, reflecting more of an "inquisitorial process" involving "common law" reasoning. From the experience of the hearing, he highlighted how "the training of our students should be harder, should be tougher."[70] Another law professor attending a WTO hearing noted that the experience gave him a completely new perspective of the WTO that he brings to his classroom. Now he gives factual scenarios to his students and lets them work through the facts while studying the WTO background rules on their own.[71]

The experiences of Chinese trade law professors abroad shape their teaching. As one law professor noted in 2014, "more and more professors in China are trained in the United States," many of whom take a course in international trade law, and these experiences could have significant effects over the next ten to twenty years for law teaching in China.[72] Many of these academics stress that much is at stake in the study of the WTO in China, both for the multilateral trading system and internally within China.[73] The mandatory study of WTO law in Chinese law schools fostered transnational processes that affect legal training.

To promote research on WTO issues, the government supported the creation of several WTO research associations. The oldest is the Chinese Society of International Economic Law, which was established in 1984 by Professor Yao Meizhen from Wuhan University[74] and later led by Professor Chen An from Xiamen University.[75] When China joined the WTO, the government established the WTO Law Research Society under the auspices of the China Law Society, and it appointed Sun Wanzhong, a former Director-General of the Office for Legislative Affairs at the State Council, as its first President. Two years later, MOFCOM established the China Society for World Trade Organization Studies.[76] China's first ambassador to the WTO, Sun Zhenyu, took the helm in 2011, and the Society became quite active, organizing many training courses and research projects.

---

70 Interview with Chinese law professor, Beijing, June 11, 2014.
71 Interview with two Chinese law professors, Beijing, June 11, 2014.
72 Interview with Chinese law professor, Beijing, June 11, 2014.
73 Interview with group of Chinese law professors, Beijing, July 27, 2016.
74 Wang Chuanli, "Yao Meizhen yu zhongguo Guoji Jingjifa [Yao Meizhen and international Economic Law in China],"*Wuda Guojifa Pinglun [Wuhan University International Law Journal]* 18, no. 1 (2016): 15.
75 Chinese Society of International Economic Law, "Xuehui Jianjie [About the Society]," *CSIEL*, 2014, www.csiel.org/about.aspx?baseinfoCateID=72&baseinfo_Id=72&CateId=72&ViewCateID=72.
76 China Society for World Trade Organization Studies, "Jianjie, Zongzhi ji Zhuyao Zhineng [Introduction, Objectives and Main Functions]," *Ministry of Commerce of the People's Republic of China*, October 17, 2013, http://cwto.mofcom.gov.cn/article/about/201310/20131000353150.shtml.

In addition to the formal research societies, entrepreneurial individuals established informal networks to exchange views on WTO law. Yang Guohua, now a law professor at Tsinghua University, established an email list entitled "Academic Circle on WTO" and a WeChat group named "Rule of Law Utopia" when he was Deputy Director-General of DTL in MOFCOM. Most of China's leading WTO scholars are members of these groups, and they often engage in heated discussions on cutting-edge issues in WTO law.

In parallel, when the WTO Secretariat launched a WTO Chairs Programme in 2010, it selected the Shanghai Institute of Foreign Trade (which changed its name in 2013 to Shanghai University of International Business and Economics) as one among fourteen centers worldwide. The program aims to enhance knowledge of the WTO and the international trading system among academics and policymakers in developing countries through curriculum development, research, and outreach by universities and research institutions. As of 2019, the Shanghai team consisted of five professors and around twenty full-time faculty and researchers spanning two schools – the WTO Chair Institute-China and the School of Trade Negotiations – which, in turn, link with researchers in other faculties. The institute covers WTO dispute settlement and trade policy review, and it provides translation services for MOFCOM. These initiatives illustrate the broad transnational ties of WTO researchers in China, linking with the WTO secretariat as well as other Geneva-based organizations.

Chinese law firms and MOFCOM occasionally seek advice from Chinese law professors on international trade matters. They initially did so on an ad hoc basis where an individual official knew a law professor. This practice gradually became institutionalized after MOFCOM organized regular seminars on current WTO cases. The exchanges helped the government tap into academic expertise, and helped the academics keep abreast of legal developments. A Chinese academic specializing in WTO law, for example, was part of the legal support team for the US-China "phase 1" agreement in relation to the trade war.[77]

In addition to its consultations with academics, MOFCOM runs a formal secondment program for law professors, which it started in 2011.[78] Under the program, MOFCOM selects young academics from elite law schools around the country and assigns them to the Department of Treaty and Law. During their one-year stint, the professors are treated as MOFCOM staff members and conduct research on legal issues and participate in all aspects of the WTO dispute settlement process. MOFCOM invited law professors to observe WTO hearings in Geneva as members of the Chinese delegation. It also invited them to hear presentations at MOFCOM by foreign lawyers who handle China's WTO cases.[79] These experiences help orient their research and pedagogy.

---

[77] Email from Chinese academic, March 20, 2020.
[78] Interview with two Chinese law professors, Beijing, June 11, 2014.
[79] Interview with US lawyer, Washington, DC, December 19, 2014.

The rise of Chinese nationalists under President Xi,[80] the US trade war launched in 2018, and the US neutering of the WTO Appellate Body, raise questions regarding the future of such transnational processes in Chinese academia regarding WTO law. However, as Chapter 7 shows, trade, investment, and cross-border private law remain central to China's ambitions, which have helped spur Chinese legal education on transnational dispute settlement. China aims to build on and repurpose Western models for legal education to enhance its sphere of influence. As Anthea Roberts writes,

> Top Chinese law schools are beginning to offer LLM programs in English designed to attract students from around the world. The Chinese government is offering tens of thousands of scholarships to Chinese universities to foreign students, scholars, and diplomats, including a significant number to individuals coming from Africa. These efforts represent an attempt by China to build up its soft power by sensitizing foreign students to Chinese views, customs, and preferences, and to cultivate professional and personal networks that will carry on into the future.[81]

In Shenzhen, which serves "as a principal gateway for China's Belt and Road Initiative" and aspires to be "China's Silicon Valley," China created the Peking University School of Transnational Law, linked to China's leading research university – Bei-da, Peking University. The school, which offers both a Chinese Juris Master and a traditional English-language US Juris Doctor degree in a four-year program, has focused research and teaching on the hybrid transnational legal approaches that Chinese firms employ for China's Belt and Road Initiative.[82] In particular, the school seeks scholars who are able to address "the legal systems of major Belt and Road countries" for "transactions and commercial dispute resolution involving non-Western parties." In reflection of the school's name, first-year students take a year-long course in "Transnational Legal Practice."

C. *Building Trade Law Expertise in Law Firms*

Litigation in the WTO is a highly specialized activity that has spurred governments to hire and work with legal professionals, and in particular WTO law specialists in private law firms.[83] Given the stakes for China's development policy, the government hired the world's best trade lawyers to defend it, who were in US and European

[80] Blanchette, *China's New Red Guards*, 128 (quoting a neo-Maoist military propagandist saying, American agents are "entering China's top think tanks and guiding the country toward low-skilled labor and economic colonization. This is an attempt to get China to enter the global economic system they themselves lead").

[81] Roberts, "Cross-Border Student Flows and the Construction of International Law as a Transnational Legal Field."

[82] Philip J. McConnaughay and Colleen B. Toomey, "China and the Globalization of Legal Education: A Look into the Future," in *The Globalization of Legal Education: A Critical Perspective*, eds. Bryant Garth and Gregory Shaffer (on file).

[83] Shaffer, *Defending Interests*.

law firms. In parallel, it worked to foster the development of internal expertise within Chinese law firms. It did so by having a Chinese law firm work with a foreign law firm in all but one of the first twenty-eight cases that China faced before WTO panels.[84] As one US lawyer working for China stated, China has been "smart" in its dual use of foreign and domestic lawyers, which facilitates "technology transfer."[85] Over time, lawyers in Chinese private law firms developed significant WTO law-related expertise.

The development of the international trade and business law fields in China is a phenomenon that flourished after the WTO's creation. As the *China Youth Daily*, a major national newspaper, lamented in late 2001, "Chinese lawyers familiar with international law, international trade law and WTO rules are extremely rare."[86] For China to effectively engage with WTO law, including for the preparation and defense of its own regulations, it needed Chinese legal professionals to enhance their competency in English and in trade law.

China's accession to the WTO was a catalyst for developing the Chinese legal profession more generally, thereby facilitating transnational legal ordering.[87] To promote such development, the Ministry of Justice issued an Opinion on "Accelerating the Reform and Development of the Legal Profession after China's Accession to the WTO" in August 2001.[88] The ministry noted, "Chinese lawyers are weak in handling international legal business, and China lacks talents who can excellently handle foreign-involved legal services, and the lawyers' competitive capacity in the international legal service market are weak." It stressed:

> We should improve the continuing education of the practicing lawyers, strengthen the education and training of the lawyers in respect of newly arising economic and legal knowledge, scientific and technological knowledge, and foreign language ability. We should open various training avenues, select excellent talents to accept trainings abroad, and meanwhile take corresponding measures to guarantee those

---

[84]   For example, in the 2014 *China – Rare Earths* case, the government worked with the US law firm Sidley Austin, together with the Chinese law firm AllBright.

[85]   Interview with US lawyer, Washington, DC, December 19, 2014.

[86]   "Yang Lushi Qiangtan Zhongguo Zhan Bentu Lushi: Shuilai Da WTO Guansi [Foreign Lawyers Entering China to Compete with Local Lawyers: Who will Litigate the WTO Cases?]," *Zhongguo Qingnian Bao [China Youth Daily]*, December 10, 2001 (also lamenting that "there are only about 2,000 lawyers in the whole country who can use English fluently to negotiate deals and sign contracts with foreign clients").

[87]   Sida Liu, "The Changing Role of Lawyers in China: State Bureaucrats, Market Brokers, and Political Activists," in *The New Legal Realism: Studying Law Globally*, eds. Heinz Klug and Sally Engle Merry (Cambridge: Cambridge University Press, 2016): 180–198 ("after joining the WTO, more than a hundred new foreign law offices were established in Beijing and Shanghai, which significantly intensified the competition in the corporate law market. While elite Chinese corporate law firms grew into megafirms with hundred or even thousands of lawyers, foreign law offices also localized by employing Chinese lawyers and developing localized expertise on practicing Chinese law").

[88]   Ministry of Justice, "Opinions of the Ministry of Justice on Accelerating the Reform and Development of the Legal Profession after China's Accession to the WTO," *Sifatong*, March 8, 2001 (translation by LawinfoChina, a legal database run by Peking University).

lawyers selected for overseas studies will come back to China to provide services. We should do our utmost to make the quantity and quality of China's foreign-involved lawyers reach a level in line with the demand of China's market economic construction and development by the year 2010.

It was a policy paralleling the country's initiatives for building indigenous technology (Chapter 7) through massive investment, cross-border exchange, and considerable "imitation" – including learning through "copying" and "pasting."[89]

In the area of trade law, MOFTEC and its Department of Treaty and Law took the lead in building the trade bar's capacity. In June 2000, the DTL organized a delegation to attend a training course in Washington D.C.[90] The delegation included officials from the main ministries handling economic issues and legislative bodies, scholars from universities and research institutes, and practicing lawyers, all selected by DTL. The course was taught at Georgetown University Law Center by Professor John Jackson, widely referenced in China as the "father of the WTO."[91] The course was a great success and many participants became leading figures on WTO law issues in China, such as Dr. Yang Guohua who would become lead counsel in many of China's WTO cases as Deputy General-Counsel at DTL.

Although the government always hired foreign lawyers to be best represented in WTO cases, it also wished to build the capacity of Chinese law firms.[92] From its very first case, the government deliberately hired domestic private law firms to work with the foreign firms. In the early years, the government selected ten Chinese law firms and tried to groom them for WTO work by having them provide support to the foreign law firms, and work alone with the government (without foreign assistance) on third-party submissions.[93] For example, in its first case, the *US-Steel Safeguard* case initiated in 2002, China hired the French law firm Gide Loyerette as its counsel, together with four domestic private law firms to assist in the background.[94] Most of these Chinese firms were boutique law firms with trade remedies practices.

Over the past decade, however, all but one of the original ten discontinued their WTO litigation practices, although domestic trade remedies practices continued to prosper. In 2016, only the mega-firm King & Wood Mallesons, among the original firms, continued to handle WTO dispute settlement for the government, along with four other firms: Zhong Lun; Jincheng, Tongda & Neal; AllBright; and Gaopeng & Partners. When one compares these two groups of law firms, the new firms are much

---

[89]   Interview with lawyer in Chinese law firm, Beijing, June 11, 2014.
[90]   Chengang, *Overview*, 15.
[91]   An Chen, *The Voice from China: An Chen on International Economic Law* (New York: Springer, 2013), 248 (Jackson as the "Father of the WTO"); Guohua, "A Memoir," 4 ("Jackson as famously called the 'Founding Father of the GATT/WTO'").
[92]   Chengang, *Overview*, 27.
[93]   Interview with official in MOFCOM, December 2013.
[94]   Chengang, *Overview*, 27.

larger, include some of the largest law firms in China, are "full-service" firms, engage younger lawyers with experience abroad, and are based in Beijing.[95]

These larger law firms have the resources to support a WTO legal practice, as their corporate practices generate sufficient surpluses. Although WTO work remains much less lucrative than these firms' other practice areas, maintaining a WTO practice enhances the prestige of the firm since it involves representing the Chinese government. On the practical side, working on these cases helps the big law firms maintain "guanxi" (good connections) with MOFCOM, which in addition to its jurisdiction on trade issues is entrusted with regulatory powers over commercially important areas such as the approval of foreign investment and the enforcement of China's competition laws. While different divisions within MOFCOM handle these issues, building "guanxi" with DTL officials through WTO cases makes it easier for the law firms to contact officials in other divisions. Navigating WTO law mixes with traditional Chinese ways of doing business.

These Chinese law firms have also generated work related to WTO law that has broader implications within China, as well as for the international trading system. As the former DTL Deputy Director-General Yang Guohua writes, "Chinese lawyers have grown up to provide WTO legal services not only to MOFCOM in WTO disputes, but also to other government agencies and companies."[96] The most clearly linked area is trade remedy practices, which reflect a legalization of Chinese import relief practices. These law firms also have expanded into other related areas, such as international investment law, international commercial arbitration, foreign project investment under the Belt and Road Initiative, and bilateral and plurilateral trade agreements, addressed in Chapter 7.[97]

D. *Development of Trade Law Expertise in Companies and Trade Associations*

Thirty years ago, most Chinese companies were not only state owned; they were arms of Chinese ministries and local governments. Today, state-owned enterprises have become corporatized and many have shares listed on stock exchanges.[98] Although private companies produce more than 60 percent of the country's GDP, the larger ones all have Communist Party representatives and committees within

---

[95]   In 2019, for example, King & Wood Mallesons had over two thousand lawyers in twenty-seven offices around the world.

[96]   Guohua, "A Memoir," 11.

[97]   Interview with lawyer in major Beijing law firm, June 8, 2014; interview with lawyer Beijing, July 27, 2016; telephone interviews with senior partners in Beijing law firms, March 20, 2020.

[98]   Curtis Milhaupt and Wentong Zheng, "Reforming China's State-Owned Enterprises: Institutions, Not Ownership," in *Regulating the Visible Hand?: The Institutional Implications of Chinese State Capitalism*, eds. Benjamin L. Liebman and Curtis J. Milhaupt (Oxford: Oxford University Press, 2015), 175, 182.

them, designed to exercise oversight.[99] Chinese companies are thus generally much more deferential to state officials than their counterparts in the United States, Europe, Brazil, and India.[100] Many private Chinese companies, especially those that are small or not well connected, find that government officials are difficult to approach. They thus have not developed a habit of hiring law firms to lobby and work with the government on trade disputes, and they have been further reluctant on account of the firms' fees.[101] In antidumping cases, many Chinese companies, in addition, face collective action problems to organize and defend themselves.

Following China's accession to the WTO, there were signs of change, as large Chinese companies and independent trade associations became more willing to hire trade lawyers and defend their interests as partners with the government. Larger Chinese companies increasingly hired in-house counsel, including trade lawyers. In addition, some small and medium-sized companies created industry associations independent of the Chinese state to work with private law firms on foreign and domestic antidumping investigations that eventually can (and did) lead to WTO cases. Both initiatives represent major changes in China and reflect a relative turn of Chinese companies to engage trade lawyers, thus supporting transnational legal ordering.

Chinese Companies' In-house Counsel

Before China's accession to the WTO, Chinese companies also faced significant trade barriers abroad. Most of them chose to abandon the foreign market rather than fight in a foreign legal procedure. Following China's accession, in order to help Chinese companies to understand and benefit from WTO rules, the government launched extensive education campaigns, which were conducted by WTO Centers established around the country.

Larger Chinese companies independently saw the need to develop trade-related legal capacity from their experience with foreign antidumping and other measures. They built in-house expertise, including in import relief, intellectual property, customs, export control, trade facilitation, and investment law. For example, by 2018, the Chinese technology giant Huawei had around five hundred lawyers in the legal department at its headquarters in Shenzhen, of whom around 55 to 60 percent

---

[99] Nicolas Lardy, *The State Strikes Back: The End of Economic Reform in China* (Washington DC: Peterson Institute for International Economics, 2019), 2; Mark Wu, "The WTO and China's Unique Economic Structure," in *Regulating the Visible Hand?: The Institutional Implications of Chinese State Capitalism*, eds. Benjamin L. Liebman and Curtis J. Milhaupt (Oxford: Oxford University Press, 2015), 313, 330–331.

[100] Milhaupt and Zheng contend that "state capitalism as practiced in China today is largely synonymous with state capture . . . . Large firms in China – whether SOEs, privately owned enterprises (POEs), or ambiguous mixtures of state and private ownership – survive and prosper precisely *because* they have fostered connections to state power." Milhaupt and Zheng, "Reforming China's State-Owned Enterprises."

[101] Scott Kennedy, *The Business of Lobbying in China* (Cambridge: Harvard University Press, 2005) (noting some changes, including in light of China's joining the WTO).

were intellectual property specialists.[102] This number does not include lawyers in its foreign affiliates of whom there were around thirty in Western Europe.[103] In addition, from 2013–2018, Huawei hired as its Vice-President and Head of Trade Facilitation and Market Access an American lawyer who formerly served as Chairman of the American Chamber of Commerce in Brussels.[104]

Building in-house trade law expertise takes time and resources that most Chinese small and medium-sized enterprises cannot afford. To encourage more Chinese companies to bring their problems to the government, MOFCOM introduced a Foreign Trade Barrier Investigation mechanism in 2002, which was modeled after US Section 301 legislation and the European Union's Trade Barrier Regulation.[105] However, companies only formally invoked it in two cases in the first twelve years, the first involving a 2004 investigation regarding Japanese import quotas on laver (seaweed) that was successfully settled, and the second regarding US subsidies in the renewable energy sector initiated in 2012. A main reason Chinese private companies did not use it is that traditionally they lacked access to the government. Thus, when they encountered trade barriers, they resolved the problem by shifting their exports elsewhere or by switching to other products.

Because the formal Foreign Trade Barrier Investigation mechanism was rarely used, MOFCOM introduced an informal alternative around 2005. This approach – nicknamed the "Quadrilateral Coordination" mechanism – involves the cooperation of four parties: the central government, local government, industry association, and individual companies.[106] Under it, industry associations play a key role as the bridge between private companies and the government, thus resolving private companies' concerns about access. But to act effectively, industry associations would have to enhance their trade law capacity and their independence.

New Independent Industry Associations Organized for Trade

Historically, industry associations have not been independent of the government in China. Rather, they were established by and affiliated with functional Ministries in

---

[102]   Interview with James Lockett, formerly of Huawei, March 23, 2020. These are estimates. By lawyers, we mean legal professionals with law degrees. Compare a post on BRC job search, *Exclusive Recruitment, Huawei Legal Department*, July 28, 2018, https://posts.careerengine.us/p/5b5b98562451b570012d5359 (stating "Established in 1995, Huawei's Legal Department has 700+ employees worldwide, 300+ legal employees (including 170 local foreign lawyers), and 300+ intellectual property employees," by which it probably references patent and trademark experts).

[103]   The Legal 500, "In conversation: Jan Bredehöft, head of legal Germany, Huawei Technologies," summer 2018, www.legal500.com/gc-magazine/interview/in-conversation-jan-bredehoft-head-of-legal-germany-huawei-technologies/.

[104]   Personal website of James Lockett, "Overview," *Lockett-International*, www.lockett-intl.com/about_james.

[105]   Henry Gao, "Taking Justice into Your Own Hand: The Trade Barrier Investigation Mechanism in China," *Journal of World Trade* 44 (2010): 633–659.

[106]   Henry Gao, "Public-Private Partnership: The Chinese Dilemma," *Journal of World Trade* 48 (2014): 983.

particular domains, which were separate from MOFTEC (MOFCOM's predecessor). These associations, moreover, had no expertise on foreign trade issues. To address this problem, MOFTEC created in the late 1980s seven trade associations for importers and exporters of products, divided into broadly defined sectors.

Although these trade associations have closer links with MOFCOM, they still are ineffective in assisting most Chinese companies. Because they are established by the government, and not by the companies themselves, they are rather bureaucratic and irresponsive to the companies' needs and demands. Many companies rarely turn to them for help since the companies view them as associations that govern them, rather than serve them. As one lawyer told us, "the trade association is a second government . . . . This is central planning."[107]

After China's Foreign Trade Law liberalized trading rights in July 2004, private firms could directly conduct international trade. To protect their interests, they began to form independent industry associations. This represented a significant institutional development in China, which resulted from its integration in the global economy. Private firms do so to overcome collective action problems and better address the informational demands for defending (as well as avoiding) trade disputes. These private associations better respond to company interests because their scope of coverage is very narrow and tends to cover just a single product or several closely related products. For example, there are trade associations for fasteners, for parasols, and for cigarette lighters. Such high degree of product specialization facilitates their ability to identify specific trade measures affecting the industry, such as antidumping investigations. Moreover, these industry associations locate in the cities and counties where the industry operates, as in provinces such as Zhejiang and Guangdong. Most importantly, because these industry associations are formed on the companies' own initiatives, they are more responsive to the companies' needs and demands, and the companies are more comfortable approaching them when the companies encounter trade barriers. To help their members address trade barriers, the private industry associations hire personnel with trade law expertise, train existing staff, and work with government trade departments and private law firms in individual cases.

The European Union's 2007 antidumping investigation of Chinese iron and steel fastener imports illustrates the proactive role that local industry associations can play.[108] In that case, the Jiaxing Fasteners Export and Import Industry Association helped fight the EU investigation at every step of the process. It helped complete the EU questionnaires and worked with lawyers to challenge the EU measures before EU courts, a WTO panel, and the Appellate Body.[109] The association engaged in

[107] Interview with lawyers from Beijing law firm, June 10, 2014. Milhaupt and Zheng, "Reforming China's State-Owned Enterprises," 196 ("the industrial associations actively supervise the operations of firms in the respective industries and have retained much, if not all, of the power exercised by their state predecessors").

[108] Gao, "Public-Private Partnerships," 993–996.

[109] WT/DS397/AB/R (July 15, 2011); WTDS397/AB/RW (January 18, 2016) (Art. 21.5).

extensive lobbying efforts. Its representatives went to Brussels to meet with Commission officials and work with other stakeholders, such as European importers, distributors, and downstream industries, to lobby against the EU investigation. After the Commission imposed antidumping duties, the association pressed MOFCOM to initiate an antidumping investigation against EU producers as retaliation, and to file a WTO complaint that led to the Appellate Body ruling against the European Union. It also convinced the government to challenge the European Union's compliance with the Appellate Body's findings.

This arrangement involved public–private coordination comprised of the central government, local government, industry association, individual companies, and private lawyers. As one Chinese lawyer told us, he learned how US trade associations operate when he worked in Washington D.C. with a US law firm. Now in China, he advises his clients to form industry-developed coalitions with a secretariat to defend themselves against foreign antidumping proceedings.[110] Such arrangements once more represent a form of borrowing from US practice.

In addition to assisting companies in individual cases, new industry associations provide other trade-related services, such as the creation of Foreign Trade Pre-Warning Centers. These Centers monitor trade data in a particular sector and alert companies when they identify risks of impending trade barriers. First pioneered in Zhejiang Province, more than one hundred pre-warning centers had sprouted around the province by late 2011.[111] Linking more than 6,000 companies in sectors ranging from textiles and clothing, to steel, consumer electronics, and agricultural products, the centers cover every major regional economic block in the province. On average, every center has two full-time staff. They distribute pre-warning information to companies through newsletters, websites, bulk text message broadcasts, and instant messaging programs. In 2010, the centers in Zhejiang sent more than half a million pre-warning messages through websites and text messages. Based on the experience in Zhejiang, associations in other provinces established similar pre-warning centers.

It remains a much greater challenge to form independent industry associations in China than in Brazil and India. A Chinese lawyer who earlier worked for a law firm in the United States notes three particular challenges.[112] First, "the mentality in China" differs because the firms are so focused on competing against each other in foreign markets that they have trouble cooperating in foreign antidumping investigations. They generally have difficulty overcoming collective action problems. Second, the firms lack faith that WTO law can help them gain real market access following a WTO case, given the drawn-out legal procedures and weak remedies, including no retrospective remedies in WTO law, complemented by a protectionist

---

[110]   Interview with lawyer, Shanghai, June 11, 2014. These clients often are small and medium-sized companies that produce consumer items, such as footwear and bedroom furniture.
[111]   Gao, "Public-Private Partnerships," 1002–1003.
[112]   Interview with lawyer, Shanghai, June 11, 2014.

turn in the United States and elsewhere. Third, creating ad hoc coalitions is much more difficult in China because they invite closer scrutiny by the Chinese government. There is thus less of a bottom-up push from Chinese industries to organize collectively, hire lawyers, bring matters to MOFCOM, and challenge foreign measures, compared to Brazil.[113] Nonetheless, the development of independent industry associations for trade matters represents a significant development in China, constituting both an offshoot of, and further conduit for, transnational legal ordering. These associations continue to help businesses navigate import barriers to Chinese products in the United States, Europe, and around the world.

III. TRANSNATIONAL LEGAL ORDERING OF TRADE POLICY

A. WTO Negotiations

In WTO negotiations, China deliberately kept a low profile in its first years as a WTO member. During the early days of the Doha Round, China contended that it made such huge commitments in its Accession Protocol that its market access commitments already exceeded what other emerging economies were being asked to make.[114] Early on, at the 2003 ministerial meeting in Cancun, China joined the G-20 group in supporting the Brazil-India initiative on agricultural subsidies and safeguards, but it did not play an active role. It likewise joined the G-33 of developing countries, led by India, but only provided "support from behind," happily "leaving the leadership role to India and Brazil."[115] As China grew economically, however, the United States pressed China to be more engaged. It invited China to join what had expanded from a G-4 and G-6 to become the G-7 inner group of WTO members at the July 2008 Mini-Ministerial negotiations in Geneva.[116] It urged China to be "more responsible" and make greater concessions in key industrial sectors.[117]

Yet, China wanted to protect its policy space to upgrade its economy through state intervention and state subsidies. China thus rather supported broader developing country coalitions that refused to make greater concessions. With developing countries, China pointed to the mandate of the Doha round pursuant to which "developing countries" were to receive *"special and differential treatment"* in "all elements of the negotiations," which was a longstanding GATT and WTO negotiating

---

[113] Ibid.

[114] Henry Gao, "China's Ascent in Global Trade Governance: From Rule Taker to Rule Shaker, and Maybe Rule Maker?," in *Making Global Trade Governance Work for Development*, ed. Carolyn Deere-Birkbech (Cambridge: Cambridge University Press, 2011), 156–167.

[115] Kristen Hopewell, *Clash of Powers: US-China Rivalry in Global Trade Governance* (Cambridge: Cambridge University Press, 2020), 37 (citing interviews in Geneva and New Delhi).

[116] Paul Blustein, *Misadventures of the Most Favored Nations: Clashing Egos, Inflated Ambitions, and the Great Shambles of the World Trade System* (New York: Public Affairs, 2009), 13, 262–263.

[117] Henry Paulson, *Dealing with China: An Insider Unmasks the New Economic Superpower* (New York: Hachette, 2015), 398 ("want China to play a bigger, more responsible leadership role in international groups like the World Trade Organization").

principle.[118] In this way, China could bide its time and preserve the status quo. Time was on its side given that the United States and Europe were bound by much greater tariff commitments. China thus felt little need to be proactive in negotiations.

The United States became increasingly frustrated. It contended that China was hiding behind its self-designated developing country status while becoming an economic powerhouse. China responded that, despite its economic growth, it remained a developing country given the huge number of Chinese who remain poor, especially in rural areas, and the much lower rate of China's per capita income.[119] Moreover, such self-designation was a longstanding GATT and WTO convention, as even South Korea and Singapore continued to claim such status until they relinquished it in 2019 under US pressure for future negotiations.[120] In parallel, China worked hard to win friends with developing countries by not only supporting their positions in Geneva, but also providing foreign aid and investment, and sponsoring WTO technical assistance programs that they sought, such as a new WTO training program for them.[121] Developing countries were thus wary of frontally challenging China.[122]

In addition, China was able to take advantage of a second traditional WTO negotiating principle, which is that negotiations should be based on *"reciprocity."* Under the reciprocity principle, if a country, such as the United States, requests tariff concessions of another country, such as China, it must "pay" for them by providing a substantially equivalent level of concessions in return. For GATT negotiations, this principle was combined with the *"principal supplier rule,"* where major traders negotiate bilaterally, the results of which are then multilateralized through the most-favored-nation principle. The United States had insisted on the reciprocity and principal supplier rules, which became "foundational" for GATT lawmaking.[123]

---

[118]   In 1965, the parties added Part IV of the GATT that provided, "The developed countries do not expect reciprocity for commitments . . . of less developed contracting parties." GATT article XXXVI.8. In the WTO, see Doha Declaration, para. 13 on agriculture, and para. 16 on non-agricultural products.

[119]   China's per capita income was just fifteen percent of that of the United States in 2017, according to World Bank data. It is this combination of China's economic size and its level of development in per capita times that Hopewell calls the "China paradox," which has been so disruptive of the WTO regime. Hopewell, *Clash of Powers*, 29.

[120]   Singapore announced in September 2019 that it will "not seek special and differential treatment in ongoing and future negotiations at the WTO." Channel News Asia, "Singapore supports update of WTO rules, will not use special provisions for developing nations: Chan Chun Sing," September 18, 2019. South Korea maintained that status until 2019, mainly to protect its rice farmers. Jane Chung and Joori Roh, "South Korea to Give Up Developing Country Status in WTO Talks," *Reuters*, October 25, 2019.

[121]   Under the program, China provides five intern positions at the WTO per year "to help recent graduates and young professionals from least-developed countries and developing countries increase their understanding of the WTO and of trade law, international economics and international relations in general." WTO, "The China WTO accession internship programme," at www.wto.org /english/thewto_e/acc_e/pillar1_e.htm.

[122]   Hopewell, *Clash of Powers*, 85.

[123]   Rorden Wilkinson and James Scott, "Developing Country Participation in the GATT: A Reassessment," *World Trade Review* 3 (2008): 473–510, 486. As a result, the GATT and WTO were viewed as a bundle of bilateral contracts.

These negotiating practices once more reflected US law, in this case the 1934 Reciprocal Trade Agreements Act in which Congress defined US negotiating authority for the GATT.[124] At the time, these two negotiating principles served to exclude developing countries because developing countries lacked important markets with which to "pay" for US concessions of interest to them. As Nicolas Lamp writes, "the overarching effect of the two exclusionary moves that marked the origins of the GATT was to universalize the principles and practices of US lawmaking."[125] Paradoxically, however, because of these longstanding practices, the United States lacked negotiating leverage over China (as well as other major emerging economies) during the Doha round because US average bound tariffs were already at 3.5 percent, while Chinese average bound rates were 10 percent. The United States thus wanted China (and other emerging economies) to "catch up" and agree to greater tariff cuts than the United States in order to create more balance.[126]

In key negotiating meetings in 2008 and 2011, the United States pressed for "sectoral" tariff cuts pursuant to which China and others were to make greater concessions in key sectors, such as for chemicals, industrial machinery, and electronics and electrical products. The United States pressed for zero percent tariffs in such sectors to ensure that emerging economies (and particularly China) made market access commitments that would ensure greater balance.[127] China with Brazil and India, however, resisted and maintained that, under the US approach, they would be making a "disproportionate effort" that is inconsistent with the principle of reciprocity, not to mention that of "special and differential treatment" under the Doha mandate.[128] Technically, China, along with Brazil and India, was correct. Yet, from the US perspective, the deal that China reached when it joined the WTO in 2001 looked much worse as China became the world's largest trader. The United States thus maintained that China was not assuming obligations "commensurate" with its role in the global economy.[129] China had become the primary US concern.

In 2015, the United States extended its demand that China "catch up" in the area of agricultural subsidies. China had committed to a de minimis exemption for agricultural domestic support at 8.5 percent in its Accession Protocol, which was less than the 10 percent applied to developing countries, but more than the 5 percent

[124] Nicolas Lamp, *Lawmaking in the Multilateral Trading System* (2013), 27–36 (thesis on file).
[125] Ibid., 36.
[126] Report by the Director-General on His Consultations on NAMA Sectoral Negotiations, TN/C/14, April 21, 2011, para. 8, 12.
[127] Blustein, *Misadventures*, 253 ("Most important, Washington was demanding that the round include 'sectoral' deals – special accords in which a handful of key countries would reduce tariffs to zero, or very close to zero, in individual sectors").
[128] Report by the Director-General on His Consultations on NAMA Sectoral Negotiations, TN/C/14, April 21, 2011, para. 13 (referencing balance, proportionality, and the Doha mandate); and Lamp, *Lawmaking*, 61–62. Brazil and India, in turn, also feared that if they made such concessions, it would trigger a new onslaught of Chinese imports.
[129] The President's 2011 Trade Agenda, United States (2011) ("asking these emerging economies to accept responsibility commensurate with their expanded roles in the global economy").

applied to the United States and Europe.[130] China's agricultural production had grown massively since 2001 and so had the value of its domestic agricultural subsidies, such that China had become the world's largest provider of domestic agricultural support, as well as the world's fourth largest exporter.[131] Once again China refused to make these concessions, in this case on the grounds that it needed to develop its poorer rural regions (including politically sensitive regions such as Xinjiang) and thus better manage mass urbanization, and ensure food security.[132] Once again it invoked the principle of special and differential treatment as a developing country. Similarly, under the reciprocity principle, if the United States demanded more from China, the United States would have "to pay" by making its own concessions. In the realm of agriculture, US concessions were of relatively little value to China.[133]

In sum, China used traditional WTO negotiating principles of reciprocity and special and differential treatment to thwart US pressure on it to commit to greater market access, which created US disenchantment with the WTO system. Since 2015, China played a somewhat more proactive role in making proposals in WTO negotiations, but they did not involve new tariff or subsidy commitments.[134] Beginning in 2016, it advanced new proposals on investment facilitation and e-commerce, and it helped initiate the establishment of a Trade and Investment Working Group.[135] For WTO insiders, however, China has not stepped up to assume the leadership role in the WTO that the United States once held, and it is not prepared to do so, especially in terms of granting greater market access.[136] Rather, China appears to have been biding its time in a mercantilist manner, and is simply not ready to lead an organization whose predominant focus has been trade liberalization.

---

[130] I thank Nicolas Lamp for this point.
[131] Hopewell, *Clash of Powers*, 64. China similarly has the world's largest fishery fleet, which it massively subsidizes (such as through fuel subsidies) but defends on development grounds. It thus has blocked a US initiative to curtail fisheries subsidies, which it tried to link to US concessions on antidumping rules that it knew the United States would not accept. Ibid., chapter 3.
[132] Xianjing is a major producer of cotton.
[133] Hopewell, *Clash of Powers*, 80–83.
[134] Henry Gao, "From the Doha Round to the China Round: China's Growing Role in WTO Negotiations," in *China in the New International Economic Order: New Directions and Changing Paradigms*, eds. Lisa Toohey and Jonathan Greenacre (Cambridge: Cambridge University Press, 2015), 94–96.
[135] Marcia Don Harpaz, "China and the WTO: On a Path of Leadership?," in *Handbook of the International Political Economy of China*, ed. Ka Zeng (Northampton: Edward Elgar Publishing, 2019), 260–280.
[136] Interviews with officials at WTO, Geneva, July 9–11, 2019. In a related vein, a lawyer who long worked inside a major Chinese company stated that China's refusal to agree to negotiate a reduction in its tariffs during the Doha round "was a PR disaster for China," and that this "left MOFCOM dangling," but it was imposed by the National Development and Reform Commission and Finance Ministry, which were more powerful. Telephone interview, March 23, 2020.

B. *Litigation*

In WTO dispute settlement, China started passively. In the first few years, it tried to avoid WTO litigation by settling every WTO complaint brought against it.[137] As a Chinese official working on WTO matters confirmed in 2003, "China is uncertain about the DSU . . . . People in government do not like to bring cases [and] they also fear the U.S. bringing cases against them."[138] Thus, the official said, in line with "Asian values," "you negotiate over disputes; you do not litigate." In the meantime, however, the government invested in learning about the dispute settlement process through attending proceedings as a third party before every WTO panel from August 2003 to 2006. In the words of another official, China was learning from "the example of the United States and E.U."[139]

After learning how the dispute settlement system operated, the government became more active as a litigant, first as a respondent and then as a complainant in its disputes with the United States and European Union.[140] Starting with the *China-Auto Parts* case in 2006, China no longer favored settling claims over litigating them, but instead strove to raise strong defenses in almost every case through substantive and procedural arguments. In 2008, its litigation strategy became more aggressive, as it advanced creative interpretations of China-specific commitments in its Accession Protocol to reduce asymmetries. It also started bringing cases against the United States and European Union as a complainant. As an official told us, these changes represented a "transformation for China from the perspective that litigation is not the goal" to one where "we now accept that multilateral dispute settlement process is an appropriate channel for resolving disputes . . . . Although many in government feel shocked that we are a defendant in an international court, and still think that litigation is not good, which is a reflection of our heritage, our culture, we now accept it."[141] The official thought "highly of the system" because it ultimately makes it "easier to settle" disputes thanks to the third-party ruling.

By the end of 2019, China was the WTO's third most active party in dispute settlement (after the United States and European Union), as well as the third most active third party (after Japan and the European Union), even though it joined the WTO seven years after the organization's creation. Figure 6.3 shows China's annual and cumulative number of cases as a respondent and complainant through 2019, as it became a repeat player.

[137] Henry Gao, "Aggressive Legalism: The East Asian Experience and Lessons for China," in *China's Participation in the WTO*, eds. Henry Gao and DonLewis (London: Cameron May Ltd., 2005), 315–351.

[138] Interview with official in Chinese mission, Geneva, May 25, 2012 (referencing the WTO Dispute Settlement Understanding). As another official remarked seven years earlier, "it is contrary to Chinese philosophy and culture" to litigate. If you litigate against a friend, then they "will no longer be a friend." Interview with official in Chinese mission, Geneva, July 12, 2005.

[139] Interview with official in Chinese mission, Geneva, July 12, 2005.

[140] Gao, "China's Ascent in Global Trade Governance," 167–172.

[141] Interview with official in Chinese mission, Geneva, May 25, 2012.

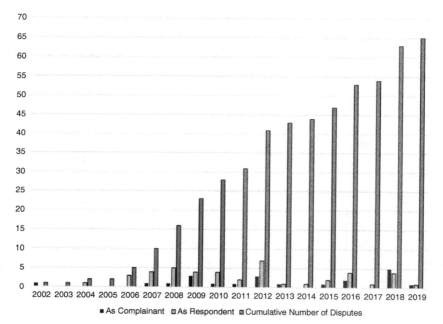

FIGURE 6.3 China as complainant and respondent in WTO dispute settlement (2001–2019)[142]

In WTO dispute settlement, MOFCOM involves lawyers from the beginning of formal consultations. It does so because the consultations can be helpful in gathering information to help prepare a case or defense. Once MOFCOM determines that a WTO complaint will be litigated, it starts the process of selecting outside law firms by asking firms to submit bids. In formulating their bid, the firm provides, along with its fee schedule, a twenty-to-fifty-page memorandum analyzing the legal issues.[143] In deciding whom to select, MOFCOM considers both the quality of the memorandum and the fees.[144]

Since no Chinese law firm had any experience in WTO dispute settlement, MOFCOM turned to foreign law firms for representation when China began to litigate WTO disputes rather than settle them. While the Chinese government is generally wary of involving foreign lawyers in other areas, and although there initially was some internal debate, the government continues to hire foreign law

---

[142] WTO, Disputes by Member, www.wto.org/english/tratop_e/dispu_e/dispu_by_country_e.htm, accessed May 25, 2020.

[143] Interview with lawyer in major Beijing law firm, June 8, 2014 and with official from MOFCOM Research Institute, July 20, 2016.

[144] One participating lawyer stressed that "the government picks on the strength of the analysis, not just on the price." Interview with lawyer in major Beijing law firm, June 8, 2014.

firms for WTO litigation.[145] Li Chengang, former Director-General of DTL who then became an Assistant Minister at MOFCOM, justified the decision by noting that WTO litigation is a highly specialized activity that requires significant legal skills, and that this strategy has proven effective for long-time GATT/WTO Members such as Japan, India, and Brazil.[146] In response to concerns that foreign lawyers might be untrustworthy, his former colleague Yang Guohua noted, the "lawyers provide professional legal services. They will do their best no matter which country they work for .... As a client, all we care about is their capabilities to provide professional services."[147] In the process, they also facilitate legal technology transfer since the government always hires a Chinese law firm to work in parallel.

When WTO members bring complaints against China, China relies primarily on foreign counsel for its defense because of their greater familiarity with WTO jurisprudence and courtroom advocacy.[148] In these cases, the foreign law firm takes primary responsibility for the legal analysis, while the Chinese firm assists primarily with the factual presentation of the relevant Chinese measures. A Chinese lawyer quips, "the Chinese law firm collects the ingredients, while the foreign law firm cooks them into a dish."[149] The foreign law firms can (and often do) hire and pay higher salaries to employ Chinese lawyers to do this analysis in parallel, but the government insists that a Chinese law firm be included. In the process, the foreign law firms grant access to the Chinese lawyers to their WTO databases and the WTO submissions that they used in previous cases. From this experience, Chinese lawyers learn significant legal skills involved in building and defending WTO cases.[150]

In terms of being a complainant, China has only filed WTO complaints against the United States (sixteen cases) and the European Union (five cases) through the start of 2020. In these cases, MOFCOM hires an American or European law firm not only because of their WTO expertise but also because they understand the trade laws and practices in their home jurisdictions.[151] In contrast, for other countries, China has used informal, political mechanisms to resolve its trade disputes. It has either acquiesced to their protectionist policies to retain good relations (such as with developing countries), used more coercive responses (such as tit-for-tat import relief measures against the other country's imports), or otherwise settled them politically.

[145] Interview with former official of Department of Treaty and Law, June 9, 2014.
[146] Chengang, *Overview*, 27.
[147] Yang Guohua, "Zuihao de Lushi (The Best Lawyers)," in *Women Zai WTO Da Guansi [Litigating in the WTO]*, eds. Yang Guohua and Shi Xiaoli (Beijing: Intellectual Property Publishing House, 2015), 146.
[148] Only the United States, European Union, Brazil, Canada, Mexico, Guatemala, and Japan had filed complaints against China as of January 2020.
[149] *Transcript of the High-Level Forum on Litigating in the WTO, in Litigating in the WTO*, 174 (Yang Guohua & Shi Xiaoli eds., 2015) (translated into English by the authors).
[150] Interview with lawyer, Beijing, June 11, 2014.
[151] As explained by a senior MOFCOM official, "we hire Washington D.C. lawyers in cases against the U.S., and Brussels lawyers in cases against the E.U." Interview, December 2013.

As Ji Li writes, norms on litigiousness still matter, such that China is less likely to bring a case against another state with non-litigious norms.[152] Moreover, China can use carrots and sticks to resolve disputes with weaker parties.

For WTO complaints that do not proceed to litigation before a panel, the government hires only Chinese law firms, and, in the process, helps train Chinese lawyers. It likewise hires only Chinese law firms when China is a third party before a WTO panel, except in rare cases involving systemic issues that are important to China. One Chinese lawyer active in WTO cases worked with the government in about a dozen cases in which China was a third party between 2003 and 2008, including a number of subsidy cases involving the United States, European Union, Canada, and Korea, an area in which Chinese practices would subsequently be challenged before the WTO.[153] He stressed how "being a third party was important for capacity building. I saw and studied how others would write submissions, develop arguments; in some cases, I could see how a party participated in oral hearings, such as before the Appellate Body." As another attorney stated, "we copied, we learned, we pasted. As an entrepreneurial saying goes (in Chinese), creation starts from imitation."[154] The lawyer "loved" to see how "legal" the WTO work was. Through these processes of public–private partnership in WTO litigation, the government helped build expertise to defend Chinese interests, as well as to bring international trade law home.

Even in cases where it is a third party, however, the government may be quite demanding. To submit a bid to represent China in such cases, a Chinese law firm may again write up to thirty to fifty pages of legal analysis.[155] The case *EU-Antidumping Measures on Biodiesel* brought by Argentina, for example, was of systemic importance for China because it involved the use of surrogate prices from third countries in antidumping calculations. This practice favors the finding of dumping, and, where dumping is found, inflates antidumping margins. It is often used against Chinese imports. China submitted a fifty-page submission in support of Argentina's arguments.[156] Because of the case's systemic importance, the government hired a US law firm (Sidley Austin) and a Chinese law firm (Zhong Lun) for the third-party submission and the WTO hearings. Argentina won the case establishing precedent to China's benefit.

To help them understand the Chinese measures at issue, the foreign law firms sometimes request meetings with the relevant government agencies responsible for the measure, which MOFCOM helps to arrange and coordinate. Initially, many

---

152   Ji Li, "The Impact of Chinese Legal Reform on WTO Dispute Resolution," in *China's Socialist Rule of Law Reforms under Xi Jinping*, eds. John Garrick and Yan Chang Bennett (New York: Routledge, 2016), 167, 171–173 (setting forth a "norm-based theory" and noting non-litigious strategies in disputes with Korea and Japan).

153   Interview with lawyer in major Chinese law firm, Beijing, June 8, 2014.

154   Interview with lawyer in Chinese law firm, Beijing, June 11, 2014.

155   Interview with official from MOFCOM Research Institute, July 20, 2016.

156   Interview with lawyer, Beijing, July 27, 2016.

ministry officials were annoyed by the meetings and regarded the foreign law firms as troublemakers. However, after MOFCOM explained to them that the meetings help the law firms better understand and defend the Chinese measures before the WTO, ministry officials softened their attitude and became more accommodating. For example, in the *China-IPR* case, lawyers met with the Ministry of Public Security, as well as the Supreme People's Court because the US challenge raised issues of judicial interpretation of Chinese law and judicial practice.[157]

For the panel hearings in Geneva, MOFCOM typically sends the largest delegations of any WTO Member. The Chinese delegation includes MOFCOM officials, lawyers from both foreign and domestic law firms, representatives from the relevant ministries, and possibly also industry association representatives and academics. Unlike some WTO Members such as Japan and the United States, which always keep the private lawyers outside of the panel hearing room, MOFCOM had no reservation about bringing the foreign lawyers into the hearing and having them make China's oral arguments and answer the panel's questions.

Chinese officials and lawyers have spoken about a potential new stage in which Chinese firms become solely responsible for China's WTO cases.[158] In the 2012 case of *US-Antidumping Measures on Shrimp and Diamond Sawblades from China*, a Chinese law firm assumed the role of lead counsel, but the United States did not defend itself because the case involved Appellate Body precedent that the United States no longer challenged.[159] In any case, lawyers in China have gained substantial expertise to advise the Chinese government and companies on trade law matters.

Impact on Jurisprudence

Through its investments in developing trade law expertise, China became a formidable opponent of the United States and European Union in WTO litigation. Within a decade of its accession, China established itself as a "repeat player" that could strategize to "play for rules" by shaping their meaning in WTO jurisprudence.[160] As Mark Daku and Krzysztof Pelc show statistically through textual analysis, "across a single decade, China effectively doubled its average level of influence over panel and AB rulings,"[161] affecting the meaning of WTO legal norms. US perceptions of the WTO legal order correspondingly changed.

---

[157] Interview with lawyer in major Beijing law firm, June 8, 2014.

[158] Interviews with MOFCOM official, Beijing, June 9, 2014; and with lawyer, Beijing, June 11, 2014.

[159] WT/DS422/R (July 23, 2012). The case regarded the US practice of "zeroing" in antidumping calculations during a period in which the United States was revising its regulations to comply with earlier Appellate Body rulings. Interview with lawyer with major Beijing law firm, July 23, 2016.

[160] Joseph Conti, "Learning to Dispute: Repeat Participation, Expertise, and Reputation at the World Trade Organization," *Law & Social Inquiry*, 35 (2010): 625–662.

[161] Mark Daku and Krzysztof J. Pelc, "Who Holds Influence Over WTO Jurisprudence?," *Journal of International Economic Law* 20, no. 2 (2017): 233–255, 250.

Through its WTO complaints, China began to shape WTO jurisprudence to constrain US and EU discretion in imposing protection against Chinese imports, which created consternation in Washington D.C. In a series of cases, China successfully challenged US and EU antidumping and countervailing duty measures that provided protection to US and European import-competing industries. Notably, China repeatedly and successfully challenged the US practice of double counting injuries to US industries through combining relief from antidumping and subsidy investigations to increase duties.[162] Perhaps most importantly, it successfully challenged the US definition of a "public body" that the US Commerce Department used to find that Chinese state-owned enterprises subsidized other Chinese producers by providing inputs at below market rates, and thereby apply countervailing duties against Chinese products. The Appellate Body found that Chinese state-owned enterprises are not "public bodies" unless they exercise "government functions," and thus their actions are not subject to the WTO Agreement on Subsidies and Countervailing Measures unless this is shown.[163] This decision was of great importance for China since Chinese state-owned enterprises monopolize key utilities such as electricity, oil, and water, and control key sectors such as banking, telecommunications, and steel, and allegedly provide inputs at below market prices.

In addition, China benefitted from earlier cases brought by India and others that challenged the practice of zeroing in antidumping calculations, which involves discounting (setting at zero) any negative price comparisons between foreign domestic prices and foreign export prices. In this way, US authorities could inflate dumping margins, or find dumping where otherwise there would be none, to better protect domestic industry. China successfully challenged the United States' ongoing use of these practices under revised methodologies.[164]

China likewise successfully challenged EU and US practices of using surrogate, third-country data in import relief cases to inflate antidumping duties on Chinese products.[165] These complaints were highly politically sensitive for China, the United States, and the European Union because they implicated US and EU treatment of China as a "non-market economy" for purposes of antidumping calculations. The United States and European Union apply the nonmarket economy label to justify using third-country prices in assessing whether China dumps products in their markets so that they can raise tariffs to counter such dumping. If the United States

---

[162] WT/DS379/AB/R (March 25, 2011); WT/DS449/AB/R (July 7, 2014).

[163] WTO Doc. WT/DS379/AB/R (March 11, 2011); USTR Statement Regarding WTO Appellate Body Report in Countervailing Duty Dispute with China, Office of US Trade Representative (March 17, 2011) ("'I am deeply troubled by this report', said United States Trade Representative Ron Kirk. 'It appears to be a clear case of overreaching by the Appellate Body. We are reviewing the findings closely in order to understand fully their implications'"); WT/DS437/AB/R (December 18, 2014).

[164] WT/DS422/R (July 23, 2012); WT/DS471/AB/R (May 23, 2017).

[165] China challenged the use of third-country data in 2009 and 2010, giving rise to WT/DS397/AB/R (July 28, 2011); and WT/DS405/R (February 22, 2012).

or European Union uses prices from Singapore (as a surrogate for Chinese domestic prices), for example, it can more easily find lower priced or below cost sales in the United States and Europe.[166] The United States and European Union use these methodologies to raise antidumping duties to prohibitive levels (such as over 500 percent) and effectively block market access to Chinese products.[167] In December 2016, China launched systemic claims against the United States and European Union concerning provisions of their laws "pertaining to the determination of normal value for 'non-market economy' countries in antidumping proceedings involving products from China."[168] After the WTO panel issued an interim report which reportedly ruled against China on most points, China suspended the case in June 2019 to avoid having the decision published.[169] Regardless of the rationale of the panel decision, a loss in the case fueled China's suspicion that it was being treated unequally in light of political pressure. USTR Robert Lighthizer had stated that "I have made it very clear that a bad decision with respect to the non-market economy status of China . . . would be cataclysmic for the WTO."[170]

---

[166]   For example, the European Union used Singapore prices in an antidumping case involving television sets from China, and the United States used Portuguese prices in an antidumping case involving crayfish. Le Thi Thuy Van and Sarah Y. Tong, "China and Anti-Dumping: Regulations, Practices, and Responses," *EAI Working Paper No. 149*, Singapore 2009, footnote 55 (on E.U. use of Singapore); Department of Commerce, "International Trade Administration, Notice of Preliminary Results of Antidumping Duty New Shipper Administrative Reviews: Freshwater Crawfish Tail Meat From the People's Republic of China," 66 FR 18604, April 10, 2001.

[167]   For examples of exorbitant US antidumping duties imposed against Chinese products through using third country prices, Len Bracken, "U.S. Hits Chinese Melamine With 500 Percent Tariffs," *Bloomberg International Trade Representative*, January 7, 2016 ("The U.S. is imposing antidumping duties and countervailing duties on melamine exports from China that add up to at least 507.65 percent."); Brian Flood, "Chinese Fertilizer Will Face Massive Duties," *Bloomberg International Trade Representative*, February 16, 2017 ("[T]he imports will face antidumping duties of 493.46 percent, and anti-subsidy duties of 206.72 percent, in line with rates previously calculated by the Commerce Department."); Brian Flood, "Chinese Roadbuilding Products to Face Stiff Duties," *Bloomberg International Trade Representative*, February 9, 2017 ("The decision means that the imports will face antidumping duties of up to 372.81 percent and anti-subsidy duties of up to 152.50 percent, based on a previous Commerce Department ruling."); Brian Flood and Rossella Brevetti, "Commerce Assigns Duties on Cold-Rolled Steel," *Bloomberg International Trade Representative*, May 19, 2016 ("Commerce found dumping margins of 71.35 percent for Japan and 265.79 percent for China. It found a subsidy rate of 256.44 percent for China.").

[168]   WTO DS 515 and DS 516. These cases involve Art. 15(a)(ii) of China's Protocol of Accession, which permits WTO Members to treat China as a "non-market economy" and thus use prices from surrogate third countries for the determination of normal value for a fifteen-year period, which expired on December 11, 2016, pursuant to Article 15(d) of the Accession Protocol. China only had a panel created in its complaint against the European Union, and not against the US.

[169]   Communication from the Panel, WT/DS516 (June 17, 2019). Bryce Baschuk, "China Loses Market-Economy Trade Case in Win for EU and U.S., Sources Say," *Bloomberg*, April 23, 2019. It is unclear whether the ground of the Panel's decision was the continued validity of the rest of Section 15 despite the expiration of 15(a)(ii), or relevant provisions in the Antidumping Agreement, such as the language on "particular market situation" under Article 2.2. Henry Gao and Weihuan Zhou, "The End of WTO and the Last Case?," *East Asia Forum*, July 10, 2019.

[170]   Shawn Donnan, "Trump Trade Tsar Warns against China 'Market Economy' Status," *Financial Times*, June 22, 2017.

Through its WTO complaints, China nonetheless was able to challenge and legally constrain US and EU administrative practices that increase protection against Chinese imports. The individual cases involved billions of dollars of Chinese imports. For example, just one of the products (rubber pneumatic tires) covered in one case (DS379) against the United States involved over US$ 17 billion dollars in imports.[171] Similarly, one case against the European Union regarding steel fasteners (DS397) involved almost US$ 5 billion dollars of imports.[172] In 2019, China received permission to impose US$ 3.6 billions in sanctions against the United States for failure to comply with an Appellate Body ruling, which constituted the third highest award in WTO history.[173]

Most importantly, these cases created de facto precedent regarding the legality of US and EU antidumping and countervailing duty methodologies that potentially affect all trade from China, which respectively totaled US$ 462.8 billion of imports into the United States and US$ 368 billion of imports into the European Union in 2016.[174] Following these cases, the United States and European Union changed their administrative regulations, but these regulations, too, are subject to challenge.[175] Moreover, these decisions affect negotiating leverage. If the United States would like to revise WTO texts to permit these practices, it will have to give China and other countries something in return under traditional WTO negotiating principles. The extent of US trade with China potentially affected by antidumping and countervailing investigations, and US reactions to these losses, compared to earlier losses in WTO disputes, highlight the United States' sense of vulnerability to Chinese legal challenges.

C. *Implementation and Policy Space*

The WTO and international trade law generally represent a significant shift in Chinese views about "sovereignty," because China has submitted to binding dispute

[171] WTO Dispute Data, www.wtodisputedata.com/data (follow the "Download" link under "Disputed Product Imports" to view the dataset using Stata) (listing bilateral imports of Chinese rubber pneumatic tires into the US totaling $17,125,810,660 from 1996 to 2010 – an average of $1,141,720,710 per year).

[172] Ibid. (listing bilateral imports of Chinese steel fasteners into the European Union totaling $4,945,502,110 from 1996 to 2010 – an average of $329,700,140 per year).

[173] Brendan Murray, "China Wins WTO Case to Sanction $3.6 Billion in U.S. Trade," *Bloomberg*, November 1, 2019 (the case involved the US practice of zeroing).

[174] 2016: U.S. Trade in Goods with China, Foreign Trade, www.census.gov/foreign-trade/balance/c5700.html; *EU-China: Trade in Goods*, European Commission Trade, http://ec.europa.eu/trade/policy/countries-and-regions/countries/china/ (click on icon for "table view") (figures converted from euros to U.S. dollars).

[175] Implementation of Determinations Under Section 129 of the Uruguay Round Agreements Act: Certain New Pneumatic Off-the-Road Tires; Circular Welded Carbon Quality Steel Pipe; Laminated Woven Sacks; and Light-Walled Rectangular Pipe and Tube From the People's Republic of China, 77 Fed. Reg. 52,683-02 (August 30, 2012); Commission Implementing Regulation (EU) 2016/278, Repealing the Definitive Anti-Dumping Duty Imposed on Imports of Certain Iron or Steel Fasteners Originating in the People's Republic of China, as Extended to Imports of Certain Iron or Steel Fasteners Consigned from Malaysia, Whether Declared as Originating in Malaysia or Not, 2016 O.J. (L 52) 1.

settlement and formally complied with rulings against it.[176] It has done so because the government views trade, economic globalization, and the development of international economic institutions to be in China's interest. Nonetheless, there are those who have seen WTO law and litigation as a force that must be contained for China to pursue its development goals through state planning and others who have seen the WTO as a force for liberalization and the rule of law in China's domestic governance.[177]

As with any country, there are divisions within China about how to approach WTO law, litigation, and implementation. As an EU embassy official in Beijing stated, "there is no one China. It's not one country ... Central agencies vary. Provincial and local governments vary."[178] These internal divisions are reflected in struggles "between pro-trade departments such as MOFCOM and more conservative ministries."[179] The divisions explain why MOFCOM had other ministries' officials involved in WTO hearings because it believed their participation would help facilitate eventual acceptance and compliance with WTO rulings.[180] When asked about the most difficult challenge that the Chinese mission faces, one Chinese diplomat in Geneva responded, "We don't wish to arouse anxieties at home; we thus prepare information for the media; we give a view of the positive side of dispute outcomes; we try to mitigate so it does not become a difficult political issue."[181] In engaging in capacity-building efforts, MOFCOM simultaneously engaged in constituency building.

MOFCOM is the key intermediary between the WTO and national ministries engaged in domestic policy.[182] Its WTO departments are the "watch dogs" for China's compliance.[183] A routine part of MOFCOM's work, in the words of a former Deputy Director General of its Treaty and Law Department is "to check the WTO consistencies of the draft documents from both the other departments of MOFCOM and different ministries ... Normally my colleagues and I would send back our feedbacks to the drafters and meetings would be held when necessary."[184] MOFCOM's authority is thus critical for China's implementation of WTO law,

---

[176] Maria Adele Carrai, *Sovereignty in China: A Genealogy of the Concept since 1840* (Cambridge: Cambridge University Press, 2019), 204–212 ("entering the WTO ... constituted a major exception to its usual rejection of international institutional scrutiny"); Weihuan Zhou, *China's Implementation of Rulings of the World Trade Organization* (Oxford: Hart Publishing, 2019).

[177] Interview with former MOFCOM official, July 22, 2016.

[178] Interview with Delegation of EU, Beijing, July 30, 2016.

[179] Xiaowen Zhang and Xiaoling Li, "The Politics of Compliance with Adverse WTO Dispute Settlement Rulings in China," *Journal of Contemporary China* 23 (2014): 143, 158. One practitioner stated, "MOFCOM always stands on the liberal side." Interview with senior partner, Beijing, July 25, 2016.

[180] Interview with professor at UIBE, July 21, 2016.

[181] Interview with former Ambassador, June 10, 2014.

[182] Interview with official at MOFCOM Research Institute, July 20, 2016.

[183] Yang Guohua, "WTO and Rule of Law in China: A View Based on Personal Experience," *Global Trade and Customs Journal* 11 (2016): 1, 3.

[184] Ibid., 3.

and, more deeply, for the permeation of WTO legal norms in the mentalities and practices of Chinese government officials and private actors. The impact of the decline and collapse of WTO Appellate Body authority remains to be seen, but it is nonetheless important to understand the processes through which WTO dispute settlement had an impact, as well as the limits of that impact, within China.

MOFCOM's handling of WTO cases helped it build a professional reputation among China's ministries and thus enhanced its relative authority in inter-ministerial discussions.[185] As one senior official noted, "during their meeting with other ministries, they [MOFCOM officials] will explain why a measure is inconsistent with WTO rules. When their view is affirmed by the WTO, the MOFCOM gains more respect from the other ministries."[186] As a leading private lawyer confirmed, MOFCOM has involved affected ministries from the start of a WTO case so that, when China loses a WTO case, "the affected ministry will understand the fact that the measure is not WTO consistent."[187] Especially in the early days, "China brought huge delegations to Geneva because it brought in the agencies to show the process is fair and that China is going to lose, which would make acceptance of the rule of law and compliance easier."[188] Chinese lawyers saw a positive effect in that ministry officials "start to care about WTO rules because once they were being sued in the WTO they start to think that 'this is for real!'"[189] As one stated, "my observation is that through the experiences gained from these years, people become more and more serious about WTO law when they formulate the measures or policies."[190]

This experience implicated many government ministries, as well as local government. For example, the *China-Raw Materials* case involved the Ministry of Land and Resources, the Ministry of Environmental Protection, and the powerful National Development and Reform Commission. A lawyer notes how MOFCOM also works with local governments regarding their subsidy policies. If local subsidies are found to be WTO-inconsistent and the local government does not comply, the policies "can escalate to the State Council."[191] Different ministries now call the lawyer "periodically to ask random questions to see if an initiative is ok under WTO rules." The value of WTO litigation, in other words, is not just winning a case, but socializing a ministry to take account of WTO law,[192] leading to the settlement of the legal norms in practice.

---

[185]   As a Chinese lawyer notes, "MOFCOM has built up a reputation as a professional in this area." Interview with partner at major Beijing law firm, June 8, 2014.
[186]   Interview with MOFCOM official, Beijing, December 2013.
[187]   Interview with partner at major Beijing law firm, June 8, 2014.
[188]   Interview with partner, Washington, DC, December 19, 2014.
[189]   Ibid.
[190]   Interview with partner at major Beijing law firm, June 8, 2014. Another practitioner spoke of being consulted by a Chinese ministry as to whether its proposed new regulations are valid under WTO law, which constitutes "a different language" in China now. Interview with Senior Partner, Beijing, July 25, 2016.
[191]   Interview with partner at major Beijing law firm, June 8, 2014.
[192]   Interview with senior partner, Beijing, July 25, 2016.

The use and acceptance of WTO litigation and its implications for Chinese law and regulatory practice became somewhat normalized within China, as reflected in the 244 cases in which China participated through 2019 as a party or third party.[193] The former Deputy Director-General of MOFCOM's Treaty & Law Department underscores how this "was unprecedented in its [China's] legislative history in the sense of amending its laws according to international rules" following an international court ruling.[194] China, for example, complied with the *China-Raw Materials* and *China-Rare Earths* decisions because, in a Chinese official's words, "the Ministries see the WTO as a just process."[195] The official contended, "this is such an important progress;" it helps one "envisage the rule of law in China." Another MOFCOM official thus contended that the WTO has been a "pioneering area in China for the rule of law."[196] Similarly, one legal academic speculated that among the reasons MOFCOM created secondment programs for Chinese law professors to assist it on WTO matters is that the professors can become supporters of MOFCOM's efforts in China on WTO-related matters, thereby helping with China's compliance with its WTO commitments.[197]

Many of the Chinese practitioners we met said that they are trade liberals and believers in the WTO. They thus have clear predilections about the role of markets and law in society. Their hope is that WTO law can seep into the practices of local governments and firms. They stressed how far China has come in relation to its past. One told us that he "can't believe how much freer is China today, where one can be sarcastic, ironic and criticize the government on trade law issues, at least privately."[198] China still has much to learn regarding the WTO, he said, but things are getting better. As regards trade law and policy, he emphasized:

> "I am a person who lived through the time of the Cultural Revolution. I was in China from the worst time and now, and I can say that it's not easy progress to become what China is today ... We went through lots of ups and downs, suffered a lot .... And now I see the people, news, criticism, comments, journalists. It's unbelievable. From your perspective it might be normal, but for me it's really unbelievable. ... Now we can criticize the government, comment on the policies, talk about WTO law. It really changed a lot."

Yet, as time passed, more Chinese officials and stakeholders became skeptical and some disillusioned about the WTO, even before the Trump administration's 2018 launch of a trade war. Some disenchantment stemmed from China learning how to

---

[193] This figure is as of January 1, 2020.

[194] Guohua, "A Memoir," 11–12. The United States, however, lost on its key enforcement claims, which made it much easier for China to comply. Cui Huang and Wenhua Ji, "Understanding China's Recent Active Moves on WTO Litigation: Rising Legalism and/or Reluctant Response?," *Journal of World Trade* 46 (2012): 1303.

[195] Interview with MOFCOM official, June 9, 2014.

[196] Interview with official at MOFCOM Research Institute, July 20, 2016.

[197] Interview with two law professors, Beijing, June 11, 2014.

[198] Interview with law partner, Beijing, June 9, 2014.

play the legal game and limit the impact of losses in WTO cases. As MOFCOM official Ji Wenhua noted after watching the tactics of others at the WTO, "we should try to employ some [such] strategies, including resorting to *sophistry* and *delay tactics*."[199] In the early years, China knew nothing about internal WTO processes and took the Trade Policy Review Mechanism (TPRM) quite seriously. But, over time, the government saw that other WTO Members took little heed of the TPRM process.[200] For reformers in China, this realization adversely affected attitudes and decision making within China's ministries. For example, China has export restrictions on around two hundred products. When it lost the *China – Raw Materials* case regarding export restrictions on ten raw materials,[201] the United States asked China to remove all of China's restrictions.[202] Instead, the Chinese government removed only those restrictions that the WTO decision specifically enumerated, and it waited to be sued, possibly after full WTO litigation, before removing others.[203] In other words, it engaged in second-order compliance with the specific Appellate Body ruling, and not first-order compliance with the rules as applied to Chinese measures.[204]

Even before the trade war, WTO law was perceived as less important in China for multiple reasons, including because the dispute settlement system could be gamed and thus was seen as less constraining, because trade negotiations turned to other venues, and because foreign political leaders espoused economic nationalism that targeted China. A leading Chinese WTO law academic noted that, as a result, "fewer students are interested in the WTO than in earlier years."[205] This attitudinal change poses a challenge for reform advocates using WTO law to foster domestic change in China. Since "each national and local agency must know WTO law" in order to "know if a violation might occur," if WTO law is deemed less important to study, such knowledge will diminish within functional ministries and local administrative bureaucracies in adopting and implementing new regulations.[206]

---

[199]　Gao, "Public-Private Partnerships," at 169.

[200]　Interview with two professors, Beijing, July 28, 2016.

[201]　WT/DS394/AB/R (February 22, 2012). The raw materials were bauxite, coke, fluorspar, magnesium, manganese, silicon carbide, silicon metal, yellow phosphorus, and zinc.

[202]　Interview with two professors, Beijing, July 28, 2016.

[203]　This led the US and others to file new complaints in 2012 in DS432 (regarding tungsten and molybdenum), and in 2016 in DS508 (regarding various forms of antimony, cobalt, copper, graphite, lead, magnesia, talc, tantalum, and tin).

[204]　Compare Zhou, *China's Implementation*; Timothy Webster, "Paper Compliance: How China Implements WTO Decisions," *Michigan Journal of International Law* 35 (2014): 525, and Timothy Webster, *China's Implementation of WTO Decisions*, in *China in the International Economic Order: New Directions and Changing Paradigms* (Lisa Toohey, Colin Picker, and Jonathan Greenacre 2015), 98, 110–111 (noting that China's compliance record is better than that of the United States and European Union, and that "China has made major revisions to its domestic legal system in order to comply with the DSB rulings, [and] . . . typically within the reasonable period of time in which it agreed to do so").

[205]　Interview with law professor, Beijing, June 11, 2014.

[206]　Interview with former official of Department of Treaty and Law, Beijing, June 9, 2014.

With the consolidation of power of President Xi, China enhanced state-owned enterprises as central pillars for China's economic strategy, and market-oriented reforms declined in importance.[207] Even though the WTO somewhat empowered MOFCOM in inter-ministerial relations, MOFCOM is a much less powerful ministry than others, such as the Ministry of Finance and the National Development and Reform Commission, and WTO divisions within MOFCOM are now viewed as lower in the MOFCOM hierarchy.[208] For those developing China's version of state capitalism, such as at the National Development and Reform Commission (NDRC), WTO rules did not seem too constraining given the case-by-case nature of their application, the difficulty of developing factual evidence regarding Chinese subsidies and market access barriers, the advantage of procedural delay given the lack of retrospective remedies, and the possibility of restricting compliance to narrow issues and thus not implicating China's state capitalist model.

For some, China only uses trade lawyers in WTO litigation to legitimate its policies and thus its model of state capitalism.[209] Where China loses a case, it formally complies, but it does so to a minimal extent in ways that continue to deny market access and pose no threat to its broader policies – giving rise to charges of Chinese "paper compliance."[210] This spurs US charges that the WTO system is not working for China because China's form of state capitalism is at odds with the spirit of the WTO system.[211] From this perspective, China's use of lawyers permits it to appeal to having a law-abiding nature, while avoiding the changes that the United States argues are required for China to comply with the spirit of a liberal trade legal order.

Although WTO legal disputes are less important in China today, the WTO nonetheless served as a catalyst for reformers within China in the development of legal institutions and the disciplining of central, regional, and local decision makers to be more responsive to the WTO's legal constraints, including WTO requirements for transparency, judicial review, and nondiscrimination. In 2014, the State Council again passed a notice calling on all Chinese ministries to ensure that new Chinese trade-related laws and regulations, including those passed at the sub-central level, comply

---

[207]   Elizabeth Economy, *The Third Revolution: Xi Jinping and the New Chinese State* (Oxford: Oxford University Press, 2018). As a Chinese lawyer euphemistically concluded, "the atmosphere in China on the WTO is not as good as when China joined." Interview with former official of Department of Treaty and Law, Beijing, June 9, 2014. Another said, "these are difficult times." In a similar vein, another stated, "I think it is a really hard moment." Interview with partner, Beijing law firm, July 29, 2016. Compare Lardy, *The State Strikes Back*, with Nicholas Lardy, *Markets over Mao: The Rise of Private Business in China* (New York: Columbia University Press, 2014) (for a more optimistic view written a few years earlier).

[208]   Interview with two law professors, Beijing, July 28, 2016.

[209]   Compare Ian Hurd, *How to Do Things with International Law* (Princeton: Princeton University Press, 2017), 131 ("By presenting acts as lawful, governments seek the political legitimation that comes from behaving legally in a rule-of-law setting").

[210]   Webster, "Paper Compliance."

[211]   Mark Wu, "The 'China, Inc.' Challenge to Global Trade Governance," *Harvard International Law Journal* 56 (2016).

with WTO requirements through a procedure administered by MOFCOM's Department of WTO Affairs.[212] MOFCOM also helps oversee compliance with China's other external trade commitments, such as under the so-called "phase 1" Economic and Trade Agreement with the United States, although that agreement raises concerns about consistency with WTO rules.[213] Differing views and responses to the WTO – and trade law more broadly – continue to compete in China. In any case, lawyers are used, and those lawyers have worked with the Chinese government and Chinese enterprises, implicating transnational legal ordering and China's ability to take on the United States and European Union before the WTO and in trade governance more broadly.

D. *Transnational Legal Ordering of Protectionism: Import Relief*

WTO import relief law catalyzed the development of new institutions, norms, and practices in China, just as in Brazil and India. Chinese state officials and private lawyers handle both foreign import relief investigations against Chinese exports, and internal investigations against foreign imports. This area of law did not exist until 1996 so that there were no antidumping lawyers in China. China only launched its first trade remedy case in 1997 when Chinese lawyers on behalf of a group of Chinese newsprint manufacturers submitted a petition to MOFTEC to commence an antidumping investigation.[214] The case heralded the legalization of Chinese import relief administration and the development of China's import relief bar. The government official who handled the investigation, Mr. Wu Xiaochen, later became a leading private trade lawyer at the Hylands Law Firm and wrote a book *Antidumping Law and Practice of China.*[215]

---

[212]   The rules provide: "Any regulations and documents related to trade in goods, trade in services and trade-related intellectual property, either by ministries under the State Council or by local governments ... must be in compliance with the WTO Agreement, its Annexes and subsequent agreements, and China Accession Protocol and Working Party Report." State Council, "Guowuyuan Bangongting Guanyu Jinyibu Jiaqiang Maoyi Zhengce Hegui Gongzuo de Tongzhi [State Council Rules on Further Strengthening Trade Policy Compliance Practice]," June 17, 2014. A Chinese official claimed that this shows China's commitment to WTO compliance through transforming decision making by central and sub-central government units in China to conform with WTO law. Interview with official at MOFCOM Research Institute, Beijing, July 20, 2016. Case discussed in Guohua, "WTO and Rule of Law."

[213]   Weihuan Zhou and Henry Gao, "US-China Phase One Deal: A Brief Account," *Regulating for Globalization Blog*, January 22, 2020.

[214]   Wang Qinhua, "Zhongguo Duiwai Fanqingxiao de Zhuangkuang ji Anli [China's Antidumping Experience and Cases]," in *Fanqingxiao Yingdui Zhidao [How to Deal with Antidumping]*, eds. Wang Qinhua and Zhang Hanlin (Beijing: People's Press, 2004), 28–29.

[215]   Ding Purple, "93 Jie Xiaoyou, Sifeng Lushi Shiwusuo Hehuoren Wu Xiaochen: Yi Shisan Nian, Sishi qi Fanqingxiao An [Wu Xiaochen: Class of 93 Alumni and Partner at Sifeng Law Firm: Thirteen Years, Forty Antidumping Cases]," *University of International Business and Economics School of Law*, http://law .uibe.edu.cn/OutListContent/index.aspx?nodeid=109&page=ContentPage&contentid=2300. Mark Wu, "Attacking with a Borrowed Sword: The Rise of Trade Remedies Law in China," *Harvard Globalization Lawyering and Emerging Economies China Series Working Paper* (2015).

Within government, China created a new Fair Trade Bureau within MOFCOM that has internal and external responsibilities regarding antidumping, subsidy, and safeguards law (collectively known as import relief law). Internally, the bureau conducts import relief investigations of foreign products, administering these laws. Externally, it follows foreign import relief investigations of Chinese products, which is critical because China is subject to more foreign investigations and measures than any other country.[216] In this way, the bureau differs from the US Department of Commerce and the EU trade directorate that largely let companies fend for themselves in foreign antidumping and countervailing duty investigations. In contrast, MOFCOM's Fair Trade Bureau spends much of its time helping Chinese exporters in foreign proceedings, including through bilateral bargaining.[217] In particular, MOFCOM always pays the lawyers' fees in foreign countervailing duty investigations to defend Chinese interests.[218] Since most WTO disputes brought by China involve foreign import relief measures, the Fair Trade Bureau must keep abreast of WTO jurisprudence in this area. This dual internal-external role can socialize the Fair Trade Bureau in its application of China's import relief laws, facilitating transnational legal ordering. While antidumping law did not exist in China in 1996, by 2018, around fifty officials specialized in this area.[219]

The practice has since flourished in China, which has become one of the world's largest users of antidumping measures. After China joined the WTO and as Chinese officials became more familiar with this legal tool, a growing number of Chinese lawyers specialized in antidumping law, as depicted in Figure 6.4. This represents a form of legalization of import relief that empowers private and state-owned companies to trigger a government investigation through a petition, starting a formal legal process in which lawyers represent both sides. China now uses antidumping law frequently against the United States and Europe, allegedly at times in a tit-for-tat fashion as a "retaliatory" response to US and EU investigations.[220] As in the West, it is the primary area of practice in trade law in China through which lawyers can build expertise in an active sector of WTO law. Although the practice slightly declined in China following the 2008 financial crisis, it remains highly institutionalized, representing a transnational legal order for import relief law that builds from Western models and is subject to international discipline under WTO rules, namely the WTO Antidumping Agreement. A former member of the WTO secretariat noted how Chinese officials "used the WTO to

---

[216]   MOFCOM, "Main Functions."
[217]   Interview with lawyer in major law firm, Beijing, June 10, 2014.
[218]   Interview with lawyer formerly in Department of Treaty and Law, Beijing, June 8, 2014.
[219]   Email exchange with Yu Shengxing, a leading Chinese antidumping practitioner, in April 2019.
[220]   USTR, *2019 USTR Report on China's WTO Compliance* (March 2020) ("China has made a practice of launching AD and CVD investigations that appear designed to discourage its trading partners from the legitimate exercise of their rights under WTO rules"); Mark Wu, "Antidumping in Asia's Emerging Giants," *Harvard International Law Journal* 53 (2012): 101 (earlier contesting this finding regarding China, but arguing it is true regarding India).

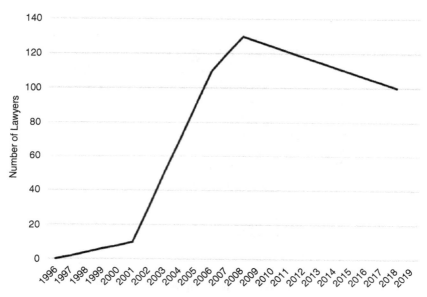

FIGURE 6.4 The development of China's antidumping bar[221]

bring the rule of law to China" in import relief matters, which was a "huge sea change for the Chinese" who now "have keen lawyers" and "solid investigative authorities" to handle import relief claims.[222]

Chinese law firms represent both the Chinese petitioner and the foreign companies in these cases. From 2003 to 2010, China implemented 122 antidumping measures and was the world's largest user after India.[223] Since 2010, although the number of antidumping measures initiated by China dropped, the country still remained one of the main users along with India and Brazil.[224]

As Chinese law firms built expertise in this area, they increasingly represented Chinese companies and trade associations in foreign antidumping and other import relief investigations as well.[225] They often work closely with MOFCOM and industry associations to help overcome collective action problems.[226] They typically work

---

[221] Authors' estimate based on interviews with trade remedies lawyers in China. The numbers are not exact but reflect the average change in numbers between the years 1996, 2001, 2006, 2008, and 2018. We include the figure to illustrate visually the rapid growth of this specialized area of practice following China's accession to the WTO in 2001.

[222] Interview, June 29, 2017.

[223] Wu, "Antidumping in Asia's Emerging Giants," 101.

[224] World Trade Organization, "Anti-dumping Measures: By Reporting Member 01/01/1995-31/12/2015," WTO, www.wto.org/english/tratop_e/adp_e/AD_MeasuresByRepMem.pdf.

[225] One practitioner noted that the firm had represented Chinese firms in antidumping proceedings in the United States, European Union, Argentina, Brazil, Egypt, India, Mexico, South Africa, and Turkey. Interview with Senior Legal Counsel, Beijing, July 26, 2016.

[226] Interview with lawyer, Shanghai, June 12, 2014.

with foreign law firms in foreign administrative processes, but sometimes they do the work alone for Chinese clients. One of the leading practitioners, Mr. Pu Ling-chen of Zhong Lun law firm, returned to Beijing after over twenty years in Brussels where he had received a law degree at Free University of Brussels, interned for the European Commission, and practiced antidumping work with law firms from the United States and the United Kingdom. He often defends Chinese clients in import relief investigations directly before EU administrative bodies even though based in Beijing.[227] Once more, China had built legal capacity, transformed its institutions domestically, upgraded its profession, and used this legal capacity to defend Chinese interests.

IV. CONCLUSION

More than any other country in our study, China illustrates the critical role of legal capacity, the broad domestic implications of transnational legal ordering processes, and the recursive impacts of these changes on the international trade legal order. Building trade law capacity in the legal profession and among firms to use WTO rules served the dual purpose of changing Chinese domestic institutional practices and advancing national interests within the global economy. By investing in human capital to build legal capacity, China enhanced state capacity to challenge the United States and Europe in WTO dispute settlement and other trade fora, in turn affecting the transnational legal order for trade. In parallel, through these processes, the WTO helped advance the position of trade legal norms in China's economic governance, increasing the role of law and lawyers. Compared to the baseline where China started, the country significantly opened its economy, integrated into the global economy, and invested in the diffusion of trade law norms. China's accession to the WTO illustrates how a government that fiercely resists any external intervention into domestic affairs embraced international economic law for its own ends within the broader transnational context.

Transnational legal processes involve conflicts within states as well as between states, and these different sets of conflicts interact. Bringing China into the WTO was about more than just opening its market. It involved processes of transnational legal ordering that had broad implications along multiple dimensions for government institutions, the role of markets, the development of professions, and normative frames in which government accountability is assessed. It involved internal Chinese contests over the direction of China's economic policy conducted within the context of an international legal regime. As Mark Wu writes, "[e]conomic reformers, led by Premier Zhu, utilized the WTO accession process to push their

---

[227] Similarly, another Chinese attorney told us he was about to go to India for an optical company to represent it in an antidumping case there. Interview with lawyer, Beijing, June 11, 2014.

agendas. WTO commitments served as a means to lock in desired reforms of China's economic structure."[228] Some even viewed the WTO in quasi-constitutional terms regarding its impact on Chinese public law. Tom Ginsburg writes, "[t]he WTO became, in essence, an amendment to the Chinese constitution. Internal forces wished to 'lock in' commitments before they could be whittled away at the local level, and third-party monitoring, locked in by international agreements, provided the mechanism."[229] The WTO, in other words, was more than just about international law and compliance with it; it was about trans-national legal ordering.

Yet, China also fiercely defended its model of state capitalism, which it enhanced following President Xi's assumption of power, while it "revived Maoist tools of governance."[230] Simultaneously, China continued to express its commitment to the multilateral trade legal order, which it saw as benefiting China. The earlier extensive changes to Chinese laws and the process of promoting consistency with WTO rules, in other words, did not represent an abdication of sovereignty, but rather a means for Chinese officials to achieve internally contested goals of economic and governmental reform to advance the government's version of state capitalism within a broader transnational context.

China's successful deployment of legal capacity in WTO litigation did not fit well with the United States. Many in the US political establishment began to view China's joining the WTO as a bad bargain given China's economic rise, the surge in Chinese imports into the United States, and WTO constraints on the US ability to raise protective tariffs. As a result, the United States became less committed to upholding the international trade legal order and pressed for its fundamental reform. China's successful adaptation to WTO law, in other words, paradoxically called into question US commitments to the trade legal order that the United States had created, as Chapter 8 addresses. Already by 2008, the WTO became less central to international trade law as countries turned to negotiating bilateral and plurilateral

---

[228] Wu, "The WTO and China's Unique Economic Structure," 313, 344–345. As President Jiang Zemin noted in the speech he gave at the WTO Seminar for Provincial-level Officials on February 25, 2002, "The accession to the WTO demands major changes in the ways the economy is managed by our governments at all levels. We shall further adjust and improve our modus operandi and legal system to meet the demands of the socialist market economy in accordance with the general rules of the market economy." Zemin, *Jiang Zemin Wenxuan: Disan Juan [Selected Works of Jiang Zemin: Volume III]*, 454.

[229] Tom Ginsburg, "The Judicialization of Administrative Governance: Causes, Consequences and Limits," in *Administrative Law and Governance in Asia*, eds. Tom Ginsburg and Albert H. Y. Chen (Abingdon: Routledge, 2009), 10. One Chinese academic went so far as to affirm, "I was optimistic about China's joining the WTO ... and the impact of legal reasoning [from engaging with the WTO] – that once the skill was mastered it would teach people to be rational, and once rational, they would manage their rights and obligations, ... and this is the beginning of the rule of law." Interview with professor, July 25, 2016.

[230] Blanchette, *China's New Red Guards*, 139.

trade agreements. As a result, the WTO is best viewed as part of a broader ecology of international trade law involving increased geopolitical rivalry between the United States and China. It is here that China has made its most dramatic moves in shaping the international economic legal order, offering a new model for trade governance. Chapter 7 shows how.

7

A New Chinese Economic Law Order?

With *Henry Gao*

Building from its success in taking on the United States and Europe in the WTO, China followed the United States and European Union in turning to bilateral and plurilateral trade and investment agreements. Yet, it did so with a new vision of placing itself at the center of the transnational legal ordering of trade, finance, and investment in Asia and beyond. Through webs of finance, trade, and investment initiatives involving memoranda of understanding, contracts, and trade and investment treaties, China is incrementally developing a new, decentralized model of economic governance.[1] This model combines private and public international law in transnational legal ordering imbued with Chinese characteristics. It builds from existing Western models, but it repurposes them. It uses law to help manage the risks to its outbound investment and trade. In the process, China could create a vast, Sino-centric, regional order in which the Chinese state plays the nodal role.

The Chinese model for international economic law reflects a component of China's internal development in the 2000s, which supplemented economic reform and liberalization with state-led infrastructure development. The approach starts with the financing of infrastructure through Chinese state-owned banks as part of China's Belt and Road Initiative, involving telecommunications networks, roads, airports, and ports, which Chinese companies construct using Chinese standards. These projects enable China to export its excess capacity of steel, concrete, and other products. They also open new markets for Chinese products generally. They are supported by private law contract and dispute resolution. This comprises the key private international law component of China's economic law model, albeit one that is state-led.[2] China then complements these initiatives with bilateral investment and free trade agreements that assure preferential access for Chinese goods, services, and capital. This web of agreements comprises the public international law

---

[1] The model is decentralized in that it does not deploy an international organization, while at the same time it is Sino-centric. We use the term "model" in terms of patterns. In this way, we contrast China's approach to what was termed the "Washington consensus."

[2] Put simply, private international law addresses agreement by cross-border commercial contract, while public international law addresses agreement by treaty.

component of its approach. In parallel, China massively subsidizes technological innovation to reduce reliance on Western technology, while encouraging Chinese state-owned and private companies to acquire advanced technology abroad, luring Chinese scientists who study abroad to return to China, and enhancing the role of intellectual property within China. This component involves Chinese domestic law, but its aim and effect are transnational in scope. Here, too, China builds from and repurposes Western legal models. In complement, China develops relations with local political and economic elites where it can leverage the draw of its lending, foreign aid, and huge internal market for their exports.

China implements these initiatives gradually and pragmatically to learn from trial and error, analogous to the country's internal development model, reflected in the popular adage attributed to Deng Xiaoping – "crossing the river by feeling the stones."[3] But now, Chinese state-owned and private enterprises are internationalized and integrated within Sino-centric global production chains. It is a hub and spokes model, with China as the hub.[4] These initiatives are reshaping the ecology of the international trade legal order. Their development will depend on political and economic contests within China regarding policy formation and implementation and the response to these initiatives abroad, in each case involving competition among factions. Collectively, these internal, external, and international contests will shape the future of the transnational economic legal order.

One of the central takeaways from this chapter is that the US-launched trade war will not – contra President Trump – "be easy to win."[5] China has developed close economic ties with countries around the world such that by 2018 it was the largest importer for twice as many countries as the United States.[6] It has thus diversified its trade so that it is less subject to US leverage, and other countries will have little economic interest in significantly decoupling from China. While the United States may press a few countries not to use or rely on certain high-tech Chinese products on security grounds (such as Huawei's 5G telecommunications infrastructure), these countries will be tempted to develop ways to do so if Chinese companies' products are superior and better bargains; otherwise, their economies will be prejudiced because of the adverse effects on those relying on such technology. At the same time, some countries may enhance safeguards to reduce strategic vulnerabilities that could arise from overreliance on products from China, as the European Union has signaled.

---

3   Ezra F. Vogel, *Deng Xiaoping and the Transformation of China* (Cambridge: Harvard University Press, 2011), 2.
4   As noted by Alba, Hur, and Park, the hub and spokes model is a framework that has been used to analyze trade agreements since the 1970s. Joseph Alba, Jung Hur, and Donghyun Park, "Do Hub-and-Spoke Free Trade Agreements Increase Trade? A Panel Data Analysis," ADB Working Paper Series on Regional Economic Integration, no. 46 (April 2010) (answering positively).
5   Ana Swanson, "Trump Calls Trade Wars 'Good' and 'Easy to Win'," *New York Times*, March 2, 2018.
6   Cent. Intelligence Agency, "Imports – Partners," *The World Factbook*, www.cia.gov/library/publications/the-world-factbook/fields/403.html (last visited September 23, 2019); Cent. Intelligence Agency, "Exports – Partners," *The World Factbook* (61 vs 30).

In this chapter, we first lay theoretical ground for understanding China's approach (Section I). We then examine China's export of a state-led, infrastructure-based development model (using private international law tools) (Section II), complemented by its construction of a web of free trade and investment agreements (using public international law components) (Section III), together with an indigenous innovation policy (grounded in domestic law with a transnational ambition) (Section IV). We show how these distinct initiatives link to constitute a major development in the changing ecology of the transnational legal ordering of trade and economic relations (Section V).

I. MIMICKING WHILE REPURPOSING: THE EVOLVING ECOLOGY OF TRANSNATIONAL LEGAL ORDERING

China's model is not completely new. It has its forbearers with those of former colonial empires that built ports, railroads, roads, and bridges around the world to extract natural resources and create new markets for their manufactured products. As in those earlier times, China will encounter local resistance, while working with local allies to create economic ties to advance its interests. Westerners made their fortunes in the process, as will many Chinese today.

Similarly, neither does China offer a completely new model of finance, trade, and investment law norms and institutions since it borrows heavily from Western models. China's model *mimics and repurposes* Western laws and institutions.[7] China is developing new institutions and structures that build from and interact with existing ones as part of transnational legal ordering, such as the WTO for trade, ICSID for investment arbitration, the World Bank for finance, the London Commercial Court for transnational contract disputes, and various other Western institutions for intellectual property. China is mimicking these institutions with its own while repurposing them to advance its interests in ways that are more accommodating of state sovereignty and state involvement in the economy, and less demanding in terms of domestic social regulation and the use of judicialized dispute settlement.

---

[7] Compare Ivan Krastev and Stephen Holmes, *The Light That Failed: Why the West is Losing the Fight for Democracy* (New York: Pegasus Books, 2020) (on China's successful form of borrowing); Zachary Elkins and James Melton, "The Content of Authoritarian Constitutions," in *Constitutions in Authoritarian Regimes*, eds. Tom Ginsburg and Alberto Simpser (Cambridge: Cambridge University Press, 2014), 141 (on mimicking and repurposing constitutions); and Tom Ginsburg, "Authoritarian International Law," *American Journal of International Law* 114 (April 2020): 221–260. This dynamic parallels the concept of "selective adaptation" that scholars used earlier to address China's internal law reforms, but it also differs because of these Chinese initiatives' external dimension. Pitman B. Potter, "Globalization and Economic Regulation in China: Selective Adaptation of Globalized Norms and Practices," *Washington University Global Studies Law Review* 2 (2003): 119–150. In part, China is mimicking and repurposing because it has been reluctant to engage in new lawmaking, and because it is not in the position to create a wholly new international economic law regime.

In contrast to a liberal model of development grounded in private enterprise and market competition, the Chinese model emphasizes the key role played by government planning and industrial policy, involving massive investment in infrastructure. As the Chinese economy grew increasingly strong, China gained confidence in its economic model and started to promote it as an alternative to development models advocated by US-dominated Bretton Woods institutions that rely on private property, markets, and a non-interventionist state. Several Chinese initiatives illustrate China's approach, especially the Belt and Road Initiative, which it complements with new development finance institutions and trade and investment agreements. Through them, China seeks to develop new markets for Chinese products governed through a combination of contracts and treaties, backed by new dispute resolution mechanisms. They spur economic integration that creates new ties with Beijing, providing Beijing with greater leverage politically.[8]

In law and development circles, this model is often referenced as the "Beijing model" or "Beijing consensus," constituting a rival to the so-called neoliberal "Washington consensus," as summarized in Table 7.1.[9] Western analysts originally coined the term, but the Chinese government then adopted it under a new name, the "China Model."[10] The government initially was cautious and emphasized that China would not export its model or ask other countries to replicate it.[11] Yet, as China gained confidence, President Xi Jinping predicted that the Chinese Model would have increasing influence around the world.[12]

These models are archetypes and involve ideological contestation within countries, including within China. With Xi's consolidation of power and the US frontal challenge to China, however, these two models have gained greater salience.

China is not aiming to displace existing institutions such as the WTO and World Bank. Rather, China supports the WTO and Bretton Woods institutions, which have served it well. Indeed, it aims to take greater leadership roles in them, as well as within United Nations economic law institutions. Chinese nationals head four UN specialized agencies, while no other country leads more than one, and a Chinese

---

[8] Nadège Rolland, *China's Eurasian Century? Political and Strategic Implications of the Belt and Road Initiative* (Washington, DC: National Bureau of Asian Research, 2017), 181 (giving examples of Mongolia, Norway, and South Korea).

[9] John Williamson, "Is the 'Beijing Consensus' Now Dominant?," *Asia Policy* 13 (2012): 1–16; Matt Ferchen, "Whose China Model is it Anyway? The Contentious Search for Consensus," *Review of International Political Economy* 20, no. 2 (2013): 390–420.

[10] Joshua Cooper Ramo coined the term in 2004. Joshua Cooper Ramo, *The Beijing Consensus: Notes on the New Physics of Chinese Power* (London: Foreign Policy Centre, 2004); Maurits Elen, Interview: Joshua Cooper Ramo, *The Diplomat*, August 10, 2016.

[11] "Xi Jinping Chuxi Zhongguo Gongchandang yu Shijie Zhengdang Gaoceng Duihuahui Kaimushi bing Fabiao Zhuzhi Jianghua" ("Xi Jinping Attended the Opening Ceremony of the Dialogue between China Communist Party and World Political Parties and Delivered the Keynote Speech"), December 1, 2017, Xinhua News, www.xinhuanet.com/politics/2017–12/01/c_1122045499.htm.

[12] Xi Jinping, "Guanyu Jianchi he Fazhan Zhongguo Tese Shehui Zhuyi de Jige Wenti" ("Several Issues on Adhering to and Developing Socialism with Chinese Characteristics"), in Qiushi, March 31, 2019, www.xinhuanet.com/2019–03/31/c_1124307481.htm.

TABLE 7.1 *Comparison of Washington Consensus and Beijing Consensus*[13]

	Washington Consensus	Beijing Consensus
Political system	Liberal democracy	Authoritarian government
Economic development model	Laissez-faire market economy with little government intervention, such as industrial policy	Industrial policy with heavy state intervention; state-owned firms for critical sectors
Trade and investment policies	Open economy with little restriction on foreign trade and investment	Limited opening with many express or de facto restrictions on foreign trade and investment
Foreign policy	Promotion of liberal, democratic, market ideals	Noninterference, sovereignty and self-determination
Doctrinal rigidity	Rigid regarding legal prescriptions in terms of rights	Non-prescriptive ideologically; experiment through trial and error

national was a leading candidate to head the World Intellectual Property Organization.[14] Nonetheless, China's model represents a different one than the liberal, multilateral, law-centered model built by the United States and Europe after World War II and expanded and solidified after the Cold War. Unlike the US and European models, China's is based not on transplants from its domestic laws but rather on development policies grounded in infrastructure and innovation, supported by memoranda of understanding, contracts, and treaties. As a former member of the Ministry of Commerce told us, China is well-positioned since it "is in the middle between the West and developing countries," and it can point to its own "gradual learning and legal experimentation."[15] Moreover, China's model, led by an

[13] This compilation builds from our own observations as well as works in the broader literature, such as Peterson Institute for International Economics, "Interview Transcript with John Williamson," *Beijing Consensus Versus Washington Consensus?*, November 2, 2010; Yasheng Huang, "Debating China's Economic Growth: The Beijing Consensus or The Washington Consensus," *Academy of Management Perspectives* 24, no. 2 (2010): 31–47; Yang Yao, "Beijing Consensus Or Washington Consensus: What Explains China's Economic Success?," *Development Outreach World Bank* (2011); Keun Lee, Mansoo Jee, and Jong-Hak Eun, "Assessing China's Economic Catch-Up at the Firm Level and Beyond: Washington Consensus, East Asian Consensus and the Beijing Model," *Industry and Innovation* 18, no. 5 (2011): 487–507; Randall Peerenboom, "China and the Middle-Income Trap: Toward a Post Washington, Post Beijing Consensus," *The Pacific Review* 27, no. 5 (2014): 651–673.

[14] Chinese nationals lead the Food and Agricultural Organization (FAO), the International Telecommunications Union (ITU), the UN Industrial Development Organization (UNIDO), and the International Civil Aviation Organization (ICAO). Michael McCaul, "The United States Can't Cede the U.N. to China," *Foreign Policy*, September 24, 2019. The United States organized a campaign to block China's candidate to lead WIPO. Nick Cumming-Bruce, "U.S.-Backed Candidate for Global Tech Post Beats China's Nominee," *New York Times*, March 4, 2020.

[15] Telephone interview, March 22, 2020.

authoritarian state, is less transparent and thus more attractive to authoritarian regimes. Formal law and formal dispute settlement play reduced roles and are displaced by soft law (set forth in memoranda of understanding) and informal state-to-state and private negotiation to resolve disputes. The approach has parallels to what contract law scholars theorize as "relational contracts" under which the ongoing relationship is more important for the contracting parties than formal legal commitments.[16] They do so in the shadow of China's increased economic clout and thus of power asymmetries. As Tom Ginsburg writes, it is a legal order grounded more in "coordination" (of policy and commercial relations) than in "commitment" (in terms of legal rights).[17]

Two complementary theoretical ways of viewing China's initiatives are in terms of "layering" and "ecologies" of transnational legal ordering. The concept of *"layering"* captures how new structures are built on previous ones as part of institutional change.[18] China's initiatives do not create a new, comprehensive, alternative model of economic law. They rather layer on top of existing international trade, investment, and development finance institutions. The concept of *"ecologies"* captures how actors interact, coexist, cooperate, and compete in complex processes within and between institutions that shape institutional development over time.[19] As Susan Block-Lieb and Terence Halliday write, "global lawmaking should not begin with an IO [international organization] as the unit of analysis, but with the sea in which it swims."[20] China's initiatives dynamically form part of a complex ecology of international economic institutions that coexist, complement, cooperate, and compete to shape norms and normative ties. They complement existing international institutions in which China aims to play a leading role, while building parallel Chinese-led institutions that interact with existing ones, just as is the case with US, European, Brazilian, and Indian trade and investment initiatives.

In this way, China's approach to economic order can be viewed as both linked to the status quo while also (at least potentially) offering a revisionist model.[21] China projects itself as a keen supporter of the WTO and the multilateral system, and, in this sense, as a status quo power. In parallel, however, China aims to end US and

---

[16] Stewart Macaulay, "Non-Contractual Relations in Business: A Preliminary Study," *American Sociological Review* 28 (1963): 55; Ian Macneil, *The Relational Theory of Contract: Selected Works of Ian Macneil* (London: Sweet & Maxwell, 2001).

[17] Ginsburg, "Authoritarian International Law."

[18] Jeroen van der Heijden, "Institutional Layering: A Review of the Use of the Concept," *Politics* 31, no. 9 (2011): 9–18; Kathleen Thelen, *How Institutions Evolve: The Political Economy of Skills in Germany, Britain, the United States and Japan* (Cambridge: Cambridge University Press, 2004), at 35.

[19] Susan Block-Lieb and Terence Halliday, *Global Lawmakers: International Organizations in the Crafting of World Markets* (Cambridge: Cambridge University Press, 2017); Gregory Shaffer and Mark Pollack, "Hard vs Soft Law; Alternatives, Complements, and Antagonists in International Governance," *Minnesota Law Review* 94 (2010): 706.

[20] Lieb and Halliday, *Six Faces of Globalization: Who Wins, Who Loses, and Why It Matters*, at 31.

[21] Jacques deLisle, "China's Rise, the U.S., and the WTO: Perspectives from International Relations Theory," *Illinois Law Review Online* (2018): 57–71.

European dominance in the WTO, while building institutions and transnational economic ties that collectively can be viewed as revisionist of the existing order in a broader ecological sense. In the process, China's initiatives provide it with *options* (or hedges) that facilitate ongoing economic order, supported by law, if the multi-lateral system continues to erode or even implode. China thus reserves the option of going either way, whether to be a status quo or a revisionist power.[22]

China has labeled its foreign policy a vision of "a community of shared future for mankind," which President Xi Jinping first announced at the 70th Session of the UN General Assembly in 2015,[23] and then reiterated at the United Nations Office at Geneva in 2017.[24] These pronouncements offer little new in substance, as they emphasize mutual respect and inclusive development, which repeats the position China has taken since its announcement with India of the Five Principles of Peaceful Co-existence in the 1950s. In parallel, however, there is an internal Chinese literature viewing a Sino-centric order as a modern analogue to the traditional conception of Chinese *Tianxia*, or "All Under Heaven" world system, which has China at the center.[25] For some, calls for deference toward China at the center of the region recall China's historical "tributary system," as well as Japan's efforts to create a "Greater East Asia Co-Prosperity Sphere" in the run-up to World War II,[26] together with the US Monroe Doctrine applied to Latin America and the Caribbean.[27]

Instead of building from official Chinese discourse about its foreign economic policy, we develop, from a range of sources, our own construction of how these disparate Chinese initiatives can fit together to form a decentralized Sino-centric

---

[22] We thank Jacques deLisle for this point.

[23] Working Together to Forge a New Partnership of Win-win Cooperation and Create a Community of Shared Future for Mankind, Statement by H. E. Xi Jinping, President of the People's Republic of China, At the General Debate of the 70th Session of the UN General Assembly, New York, September 28, 2015, available at https://gadebate.un.org/sites/default/files/gastatements/70/70_ZH_en .pdf.

[24] Work Together to Build a Community of Shared Future for Mankind, Speech by H. E. Xi Jinping, United Nations Office at Geneva, Geneva, January 18, 2017, available at http://iq.chineseembassy.org /eng/zygx/t1432869.htm.

[25] Nadège Rolland, "China's Vision for a New World Order," *NBR Special Report* #83 (National Bureau of Economic Research, January 2020), 30–34, 50–51 (citing a range of contemporary Chinese thinkers).

[26] David Kang, *East Asia before the West: Five Centuries of Trade and Tribute* (New York City: Columbia University Press, 2010), 3 (the tribute system continued until the Opium War and the onslaught of Western colonialism, with China "clearly the dominant military, cultural, and economic power in the system"). Chinese leftists deploy rhetoric regarding China's history to critique liberal democratic values and the institution of judicial review in support of authoritarianism. Sebastian Veg, "The Rise of China's Statist Intellectuals: Law, Sovereignty, and 'Repoliticization'," *The China Journal* 82 (2019): 23–45. Interestingly, this vision resonates with the increased popularity among leftist intellectuals in China of the Nazi legal theorist Carl Schmitt, including Schmitt's concept of the *Großraum* ("great space") as a regional order. Ryan Mitchell, "The Decision for Order: Chinese Receptions of Carl Schmitt Since 1929," *Journal of Law and International Affairs* 8, no. 1 (2020): 181–263.

[27] "John Bolton and the Monroe Doctrine," *The Economist*, May 19, 2019.

order that complements, competes with, and reorients the existing international economic law order. What we are describing is not a neatly coherent, centralized order that reflects a new Chinese theoretical model for global governance. Much of China's approach for economic law order is fragmentary. Its signature Belt and Road Initiative is an amalgam of multitudinous projects. What we aim to capture is the incremental evolution of a Chinese economic order comprised of webs of agreements under the Belt and Road Initiative, supported by bilateral trade and investment agreements, which, in turn, are linked to China's indigenous innovation policy with its transnational ambitions.

Philip Jessup theorized the combination of private international law, public international law, and "other law" addressing transnational problems as "transnational law."[28] China's approach combines these tools pragmatically and strategically. Yet, when viewed in combination, China's initiatives involve more than transnational problem-solving through law. They aim to create order, a transnational economic order supported by law, with China at the hub.[29] As we will see, China's approach does not involve deep integration of norms (thus differing from the Western liberal model), but nonetheless aims at a type of transnational order, supported by law, that permeates states through creating close ties with government and business leaders.

II. EXPORTING THE CHINESE DEVELOPMENT MODEL ABROAD: FINANCING INFRASTRUCTURE

A. *Belt and Road Initiative*

First proposed by President Xi Jinping in 2013, the Belt and Road Initiative (BRI) ambitiously aims to develop new markets, enhance the security of China's access to resources, and facilitate the internationalization of the Renminbi (China's currency), while building new institutions and governance mechanisms.[30] It is

---

[28] Philip Jessup, *Transnational Law* (New Haven: Yale University Press, 1956) (defining "transnational law" in functional terms as "all law which regulates actions or events that transcend national frontiers," which includes public international law, private international law, and "other rules which do not wholly fit into such standard categories").

[29] Compare Jessup's analysis with that of Terence Halliday and Gregory Shaffer on "transnational legal orders." Terence Halliday and Gregory Shaffer, *Transnational Legal Orders* (Cambridge: Cambridge University Press, 2015); and Gregory Shaffer and Carlos Coye, "From International Law to Jessup's Transnational Law; from Transnational Law to Transnational Legal Orders," in *The Many Lives of Transnational Law: Critical Engagements with Jessup's Bold Proposal*, ed. Peer Zumbansen (Cambridge: Cambridge University Press, 2020), 126–152.

[30] Julian Chaisse and Mitsuo Matsushita, "China's 'Belt and Road Initiative: Mapping the World Trade Normative and Strategic Implications," *Journal of World Trade* 52, no. 1 (2018): 163. It also enables China to diversify its investment of its foreign exchange reserves away from low-yield US government bonds. Tom Miller, *China's Asian Dream: Empire Building Along the New Silk Road* (London: Zed Books, 2017), 32. In the process, China aims to be a leader in the development of a central bank digital currency, while proceeding cautiously. Chen Jia, "China Promotes Global Digital Fiat Currency Standardization," *China Daily* (December 8, 2018). However, BRI contracts generally use the

predominantly a private international law model based on contract and contract dispute resolution that paradoxically is state-led.[31] Formally, the BRI's objectives are to build five types of links among countries lying along BRI industrial corridors: (1) to enhance "policy coordination"; (2) to improve infrastructure "connectivity"; (3) to reinforce "unimpeded trade"; (4) to move forward with "financial integration"; and (5) to create "people-to-people bonds."[32] In this way, China can create a network of "strategic partnerships" grounded in economic ties that enhance regional and global economic integration, increase economic reliance on China, and further Chinese influence.[33] Some of these projects facilitate China's projection of military strength, including by providing the Chinese navy with access to deep water ports and, through them, protect trade routes to and from China.[34] More generally, China aims to project soft (and thus "smart") power through such financing (backed by contract), which is not subject to the conditionalities imposed by the West.[35] Many countries viewed such exercise of power, at least for a time, as subtler than that of the United States, which difference became even more salient under the Trump administration's "America First" policies.[36]

Internally, the BRI is very much a project associated with President Xi.[37] It is coordinated by a steering group, which is chaired by a Vice Premier and housed in the National Development and Reform Commission (NDRC), which is central to

US dollar for payment because of its stability and liquidity. Telephone interviews with internal and external counsel for Chinese state-owned enterprises. March 20, 23, 27, and 30, 2020.

[31] Interestingly, Chinese state-owned enterprises appear to use better drafted, international-style contracts than Chinese private companies. Mathew Erie, "Chinese Law and Development," *Harvard International Law Journal* 62 (2021): 60.

[32] National Development and Reform Commission, "Ministry of Foreign Affairs, and Ministry of Commerce of the People's Republic of China," *Vision and Actions on Jointly Building Silk Road Economic Belt and 21st-Century Maritime Silk Road*, State Council, 2015.

[33] Joshua Meltzer, "China's One Belt One Road Initiative: A View from the United States," *Brookings Report*, June 19, 2017.

[34] Francisco Jose Leandro, "The OBOR Global Geopolitical Drive: The Chinese Access Security Strategy," in *The Belt and Road Initiative: Law Economics and Politics*, eds. Julien Chaisse and Jedrzej Gorski (Leiden: Brill Nijhoff, 2018), 90 (citing the teachings of US Rear Admiral Alfred Thayer Mahan, Leandro writes, "a global maritime trade network will naturally develop an immense sea power"); Bruno Macaes, *Belt and Road: A Chinese World Order* (London: Hurst, 2019), 72; "The best offence is a good defence," *The Economist*, September 28, 2019, 81.

[35] Compare Axel Dreher, "IMF and Economic Growth: The Effects of Programs, Loans, and Compliance with Conditionality," *World Development* 34, no. 5 (May 1, 2006): 769–788; Erica R. Gould, "Money Talks: Supplementary Financiers and International Monetary Fund Conditionality," *International Organization* 57, no. 3 (Summer 2003): 551–586; Randall W. Stone, "The Scope of IMF Conditionality," *International Organization* 62, no. 4 (Fall 2008): 589–620.

[36] Compare, for example, China's "win-win" slogan with "America First." Kristen Hopewell, *Clash of Powers: US-China Rivalry in Global Trade Governance* (Cambridge: Cambridge University Press, 2020).

[37] Baogang He, "The Domestic Politics of the Belt and Road Initiative and its Implications," *Journal of Contemporary China*, 28, no. 116 (2019), 180–195. The BRI, in part, was a strategic response to the Obama administration's "pivot to Asia" in order to protect its interests in the region. Rolland, *China's Eurasian Century?*, 114–119.

China's industrial policy and strategy. The NDRC and China's Ministry of Foreign Affairs and Ministry of Commerce officially co-lead the BRI at the central level. This structure indicates that trade with the BRI countries is now part of the broader foreign policy framework of China and coordinated by overall state planning. In parallel, provincial bodies help mobilize the BRI, since part of the core strategy is to bolster economic growth in China's poorer regions, such as in the west and south-west, including Xinjiang.[38] China's state-owned enterprises are central to carrying out the initiative, particularly for the building of infrastructure.

The BRI comprises the land-based Silk Road Economic Belt, which links China with Europe through Central and Western Asia, and the sea-based 21st Century Maritime Silk Road, which connects China with Southeast Asian countries, Africa, and Europe. The initiative covers at least sixty-five countries in three continents, with a total population of around 4.4 billion, or 63 percent of the world population.[39] These countries account for 29 percent of global GDP and 23.4 percent of global merchandise and services exports. The project often has been compared with the post-World War II Marshall Plan by the United States, adopted as a response to the Cold War with the Soviet Union,[40] but the BRI dwarfs it in size, and now represents a Chinese response to its intensifying Cold War with the United States. The Marshall Plan provided only US$13 billion to six European countries, which is equal to US$150 billion today.[41] In contrast, the estimated price tag for the BRI is at least 1 trillion (and potentially many trillion) US dollars.[42] Given the lack of transparency, it is impossible to know the exact figure, but it appears large and looming. As Mathew Erie writes, although there is a certain amount of Chinese campaign-style boosterism to the BRI, the US and EU response to the BRI of creating their own "policy imitations" suggests that they recognize its impact.[43]

China is building the BRI through packages of bilateral arrangements and agreements. They involve customs clearance, investment promotion and facilitation, trade

---

[38] He, "The Domestic Politics;" Rolland, *China's Eurasian Century?*, 181 (China's infrastructure building was not only "a tool to stimulate growth in times of financial and economic crises but also . . . a way to consolidate the central government's control over the country's remote frontiers").

[39] China has not officially confirmed the number of BRI countries or the criteria for identifying them, but at least sixty-five countries (including China) are commonly acknowledged to be BRI countries. Lutz-Christian Wolff, "China's 'Belt and Road' Initiative – An Introduction," in *Legal Dimensions of China's Belt and Road Initiative*, eds. Lutz-Christian Wolff and Chao Xi (Hong Kong: Wolters Kluwer, 2016), 8. In March 2019, Italy signed an MOU on the joint construction of the BRI with China, becoming the first G7 country to do so. Xinhua, China, "Italy Sign BRI MoU to Advance Connectivity," March 25, 2019.

[40] Benn Steil, *The Marshall Plan: Dawn of the Cold War* (Oxford: Oxford University Press, 2018).

[41] Gwynn Guilford, "Don't Be Fooled by China's Grand Plan to Rule the World," *Quartz*, December 1, 2017.

[42] Jonathan Hillman, "How Big is China's Belt and Road?," *Center for Strategic and International Studies*, April 3, 2018. The projected BRI and the Marshall Plan, however, are more comparable in size in terms of the percentage of China's and the United States' GDPs at the respective times.

[43] Erie, "Chinese Law and Development," [11, 40]. For example, the United States established a new International Development Finance Corporation in 2019.

and investment treaties, dispute resolution mechanisms, visa agreements, memoranda on standardization, special economic zones, special tax regimes, academic and student exchanges, and so forth.[44] Each economic corridor in the BRI adopts a different package, subject to local negotiations and adaptation to different geopolitical conditions, but the modalities are similar.[45]

This building of infrastructure facilitates trade, investment, and migration that have complementary effects. Chinese individuals migrate to BRI countries and become entrepreneurs, forming a networked Chinese diaspora around the world that further facilitates trade and investment with China. To give one example, analysts estimate that about a million Chinese have "ventured to Africa over the past two decades to seek their fortunes."[46] As a forerunner of these processes, the town of Prato, Italy, the center of the Italian textile industry, became dominated by Chinese entrepreneurs and workers making apparel with the "made in Italy" label for global markets.[47] In 2019, Italy joined the BRI pursuant to a Memorandum of Understanding with China in the hope that Chinese state-owned entities can help develop Italian ports, further facilitating such transnational processes.[48]

The BRI is not just about hard infrastructure, but also about electronic commerce, facilitating trade of Chinese products. Alibaba Cloud is growing faster than Amazon outside of their home markets, and it benefits from its dominance of China's internal market, which is the largest e-commerce market in the world. Hoping to leverage BRI-spurred economic growth and ensuing consumer demand into a "One Belt, One Road, One Cloud" future, Alibaba has been aggressively promoting its Electronic World Trade Platform (eWTP) concept.[49] It launched its "Enabling E-commerce" initiative along with the WTO and the World Economic Forum (WEF) in late 2017.[50] Through Alibaba, China is once more not only coordinating with but also layering upon the work of existing international public and private institutions, such as the WTO and WEF.

---

[44]   Silk Rhodes, "Why China is Lavishing Money on Foreign Students," *Economist*, January 26, 2019, 36 ("numbers of foreign students grew fourfold in 2004–2016; student numbers from BRI-related countries expanded eightfold," rising to 61 percent of those on Chinese government scholarships). On university exchanges, Rolland, *China's Eurasian Century?*, 64–66.

[45]   Leandro, "The OBOR Global Geopolitical Drive," 88. On different economic corridors, Rolland, *China's Eurasian Century?*, 72–85.

[46]   Emily Feng and David Piling, "The Other Side of Chinese Investment in Africa," *Financial Times*, March 26, 2019.

[47]   Sylvia Smith, "The Italian Fashion Capital Being Led by the Chinese," *BBC*, February 12, 2013.

[48]   Stuart Lau, "Italy May Be Ready to Open up Four Ports to Chinese Investment Under 'Belt and Road Initiative'," *South China Morning Post*, March 19, 2019; Jason Horowitz, "A Forgotten Italian Port Could Become a Chinese Gateway to Europe," *New York Times*, March 18, 2019.

[49]   Parag Khanna, *The Future is Asian: Commerce, Conflict, and Culture in the 21st Century* (New York: Simon & Schuster, 2019), 189; Henry Gao, "Digital or Trade? The Contrasting Approaches of China and US to Digital Trade," *Journal of International Economic Law* 21, no. 2 (2018): 308–310.

[50]   WTO, "WTO, World Economic Forum and eWTP Launch Joint Public-Private Dialogue to Open Up E-commerce for Small Business," December 13, 2017.

In parallel, China is developing free trade zones in the Chinese interior and in BRI countries so that Chinese firms may expand their global trade and production networks.[51] Within China, the country established new pilot free trade zones in 2017 in Chongqing, Henan, Hubei, Shaanxi, and Sichuan. They are different from the first batch of Chinese free trade zones, especially the one in the Pudong district of Shanghai, which experimented with trade and investment liberalization and reducing government red tape. These early free trade zones served as laboratories and "test beds for domestic economic reforms" to pioneer market liberalization in order to attract foreign and domestic investment, integrate into global value chains, and enhance export-led growth.[52] The Shanghai free trade zone was the first to apply a "negative list" approach to investment approvals so that all investments are automatically permitted, except in sectors explicitly restricted. These zones facilitated technology transfer to Chinese industry through emulation, spillovers, and, for some, theft, in turn spurring competition and internal Chinese R&D spending.[53] This legal experimentation illustrates how transnational legal ordering processes within China helped integrate its economy with the global economy.

In contrast, these new free trade zones are strategically selected to develop the poorer Western provinces and to link them with BRI countries, which in turn develop free trade zones linked to China.[54] For example, the ones in Chongqing and Sichuan serve as key nodes in the China–Europe Railway Express, which reaches into Europe, while the one in Shaanxi is crucial in linking China with central Asian states.[55] Within BRI countries, the Chinese government worked with state-owned companies to finance and build huge industrial parks in new "economic and trade cooperation zones." Chinese lawyers have advised on the drafting of other country's laws for "special economic zones," building from China's domestic experience.[56] As a Chinese lawyer from a major Beijing law firm told us, "we did research how China did it, starting with Shenzhen at the end of the 1970s . . .. For all

---

[51] Justin Yifu Lin, "'One Belt and One Road' and Free Trade Zones: China's New Opening-Up Initiatives," *Frontiers of Economics in China* 10, no. 4 (2015): 585.

[52] Barry Naughton, *The Chinese Economy: Adaptation and Growth* (Cambridge: MIT Press, 2018), 427.

[53] For example, the largest sector for US investment was information and communications technology companies. Ibid., 435.

[54] These duty-free zones provide for zero percent tariffs and eased customs administration, and thus different treatment compared to the rest of the country. They thus aim to attract investment to take advantage of lower input costs. Tom Miller, *China's Asian Dream: Empire Building Along the Silk Road* (London: Zed Books, 2017); National Development and Reform Commission, *Vision and Actions*.

[55] Chongqing and Chengdu, the capital of Sichuan Province, has more trains than all other Chinese cities with China–Europe Railway Express. See Zhang Zhi, "China-Europe Railway Express Sped Up: Several Cities Rushed to Launch, Chongqing, Chengdu, Xi'an are in the Top Three [Zhongou Banlie Jiasupao: Duodi Qiangkai, Chongqing Chengdu Xi'an Weilie Qiansanjia]," *China Times*, August 2, 2019, https://finance.sina.com.cn/roll/2019-08-02/doc-ihytcerm8069823.shtml

[56] Telephone interview, Chinese senior partner at major law firm, March 20, 2020; Erie, "Chinese Law and Development," [62] (citing 2019 interview with Vietnamese lawyer regarding Chinese assistance with Vietnam's law).

of those major economic zones, we showed how it evolved from symbolic regulation to a practical set of rules to help investors make investments. From this research, we can help tell our counterparts what lessons China learned."[57] By January 2019, China announced that it had built eighty-two such zones within BRI countries with total investment of US$ 29 billion.[58] By building key infrastructure like roads and ports, and helping to revamp customs processes in these countries, these projects help achieve key BRI objectives, such as facilities connectivity and increased trade.

These initiatives benefit from legal infrastructure in terms of soft law agreements, contracts, and dispute resolution mechanisms, although that infrastructure is more flexible than Western models.[59] Companies typically conduct BRI projects under the umbrella of a Memorandum of Understanding between China and the receiving country, complemented by public and private contracts.[60] The projects focus on infrastructure-building, including roads, rail, ports, airports, pipelines, electrical power plants, and telecommunications. They catalyze different forms of public–private partnerships between the state, state-owned enterprises, and private companies. The intertwined nature of large private enterprises and the Chinese party and state facilitate these partnerships.[61] Chinese firms, financed by loans from state-owned banks, such as the China Development Bank and the Export-Import Bank of China, undertake the projects.[62] By 2017, China's Xinhua News Agency noted that state-owned enterprises at the central level (as opposed to the provincial level) alone had already participated in more than 1,700 BRI projects.[63] Chinese state-owned and

---

[57] Telephone interview, March 20, 2020.

[58] Ministry of Commerce Press Office, *2018 nian Shangwu Gongzuo Nianzhong Zongshu zhi san: Yidai Yilu Jingmao Hezuo Chengxiao Xianzhu* (2018 Year-end Summary for Commerce Works, No. 3: Significant Achievements in Belt Road Initiative Economic and Trade Cooperation), December 27, 2018.

[59] Erie, "Chinese Law and Development," [12] (citing a workshop in Shanghai where a UK lawyer advocated that China use its leverage to impose "a standard agreement" for Chines loans, while Chinese lawyers retorted that China prefers dialogue under the principle of "non-intervention").

[60] Maria Adele Carrai, "It is Not the End of History: The Financing Institutions of the Belt and Road Initiative and the Bretton Woods System," in *The Belt and Road Initiative*, eds. Julien Chaisse and Jędrzej Górski (Leiden: Brill Nijhoff, 2018), 107–145.

[61] As Milhaupt and Zheng write, "the boundary between state and private ownership of enterprise is often blurred in contemporary China." Curtis Milhaupt and Wentong Zheng, "Beyond Ownership: State Capitalism and the Chinese Firm," *Georgetown Law Journal* 103 (2015): 665, 671. The large private companies themselves are required to include a Communist party committee to ensure good relations with authorities. Mark Wu, "The China Inc. Challenge to Global Trade Governance," *Harvard International Law Journal* 57 (2016): 282–284.

[62] Most of the financing is provided by Chinese banks. China created a Silk Road Fund in 2014 under the central bank, the People's Bank of China. China is now the world's largest creditor, surpassing the IMF and World Bank. Sebastian Horn, Carmen Reinhart, and Christoph Trebesch, "China's Overseas Lending," *KIEL Working Paper* 5 (No. 2332, June 2019).

[63] Xinhua, "Zhongyang Qiye Jiji Canyu 'Yidai Yilu' Jianshe, Shezu chao 1700 ge Xiangmu (Central SOEs Actively Participating in BRI Construction, Involved in over 1700 Projects)," *Xinhua News Agency*, December 23, 2017. The numbers should be read with some scepticism given that companies may label BRI projects to signal loyalty to President XI given that this is his favoured policy initiative. Tanner Greer, "One Belt, One Road, One Big Mistake," *Foreign Policy*, December 6, 2018.

private firms are well-positioned to engage in BRI projects because they are supported by state subsidies – including export credits provided below OECD-prescribed minimum rates[64] – and they coordinate with state authorities to obtain government procurement contracts. Analysts estimate that around 89 percent of the contractors of BRI projects funded by Chinese banks have been Chinese companies.[65]

Private Chinese external and in-house lawyers play major roles in BRI contracts. State-owned enterprises have created large in-house legal departments consisting of dozens of lawyers, with lawyers also in their many foreign affiliates. Some of these lawyers trained in the United States. The founder of the legal department of the huge outbound Chinese construction company China Machinery Engineering Corporation, for example, graduated from Harvard Law School.[66] These in-house lawyers work with outside Chinese law firms, international law firms, and local law firms in BRI countries to do due diligence, draft memoranda of understanding, and write and negotiate engineering, procurement, and construction contracts, and operation and management agreements, as well as joint ventures and corporate organizational documents for special purpose vehicles. These contracts are of an "international" nature, and counsels build them from models that they have used in the past.[67]

Critically, China exports Chinese *standards* through the BRI, challenging US and European dominance in standard setting. Standards can be viewed as a form of soft law that fall within what Jessup called "other law" in his concept of transnational law because they are not clearly captured within the categories of private and public international law. It is an area that legal scholars often ignore because the standards often are not legally binding (formally), although they may be directly incorporated through contracts (such as in an annex), and they can have major regulatory impacts in practice.[68] China has established national standards that it requires manufacturers

---

64 China is by far the world's largest provider of export credits, which it extends through China Eximbank, China Development Bank, and Sinosure. It uses these export credits to support BRI infrastructure projects, including for the priority sectors in its advanced manufacturing initiatives, such as the advanced information and communications technology of Huawei and rail transport around the world. In the process, China is undermining the OECD Arrangement on Officially Supported Export Credits, a US initiative created in 1978 to discipline countries' provision of export credit. Hopewell, *Clash of Powers*, chapters 4 and 5.

65 "Gateway to the Globe," *Economist*, July 28, 2018, 15.

66 CMEC references itself as a "window to the world" company. Telephone interview with in-house legal counsel, March 30, 2020.

67 Telephone interviews with practicing lawyers and in-house counsel at a major Chinese state-owned enterprise and a major Chinese private enterprise, March 20, 23, 27, and 30, 2020.

68 Ibid. Erie, in contrast, categorizes "standards" as a "nonlaw" mechanism, but, in doing so, he notes Chinese legislation on standards and the chapter on "legal liability" in that law, as well as the fact that BRI loans and contracts at times address the use of Chinese standards, which has given rise to litigation. Moreover, China first established its standard setting body as part of its accession to the WTO, again illustrating the links with law. Erie, "Chinese Law and Development," [52–54]. Compare Harm Schepel, *The Constitution of Private Governance: Product Standards in the Regulation of Integrating Markets* (Oxford: Hart Publishing, 2005).

and service providers to use when entering China's market. In turn, Chinese companies use these standards when exporting goods and services abroad.[69] Given the size of China's market, China can use domestic standard setting to provide a competitive advantage for Chinese companies in its internal market. And given the number of infrastructure projects abroad that China finances, China is well positioned to shape international and regional standards in practice, such as for infrastructure.

When Chinese firms like Huawei build telecommunication and other infrastructure projects in BRI countries, they use Chinese standards rather than Western ones, and they want to internationalize them. In this way, the Chinese can gradually shape the adoption of Chinese standards through practice in many regions in the world, establishing facts on the ground with increased market share.[70] As in-house counsel of a large Chinese state-owned enterprise told us regarding a contract for building a rail system in South America, the client initially wanted the company to follow Spanish/European standards, but when it became aware of the quality of Chinese rail standards, it "accepted them." The Chinese lawyer's experience was that "even five or ten years ago it was impossible to accept the Chinese standard, but now it is different, and more and more countries will accept Chinese standards."[71] Through network effects, the standards can become dominant over time. Some of these standards contain patented technology and intellectual property so that not only will Chinese companies have a first mover advantage, but they also can receive royalties under contracts, including from other companies that bid for BRI projects.[72]

Most worryingly for the United States, China appears to have the lead in developing 5G (fifth generation) wireless technology standards, where Huawei seeks dominance.[73] 5G technology could fundamentally change the economy as well as everyday life, unleashing new competition for technological leadership.[74] As an April 2019 report of the US Defense Innovation Board warns, "The country that owns

---

[69] Andrew Polk, "China Is Quietly Setting Global Standards," *Bloomberg*, May 7, 2018.

[70] China also attempted this strategy in the early 2000s when it announced that companies had to use its Wi-Fi standard called WAPI for products sold in China, but at the time it was in a weaker position. It backed down under pressure from the United States and Japan, and a network of companies and Chinese exporters critical to global value chains. Han-Wei Liu, "China Standard Time: The Boundary of Techno-Nationalism in Megaregionals," in *Governing Science and Technology under the International Economic Order*, eds. Shin-yi Peng, Han-Wei Liu, and Ching-Fu Lin (Cheltenham: Edward Elgar, 2018), 114–138.

[71] Telephone interview, March 20, 2020.

[72] Peter Yu, "Building Intellectual Property Infrastructure Along China's Belt and Road," *University of Pennsylvania Asian Law Review* 14 (2019): 275–325.

[73] Alan Beattie notes that "Ren Zhengfei, the founder of Huawei, told the FT this month that it was seeking dominance in the internet of things sector, using China's large manufacturing sector to develop chips and software for companies to connect factory floors to the internet." Alan Beattie, "How the US, EU and China Compete to Set Industry Standards," *Financial Times*, July 23, 2019.

[74] 5G wireless technology expands capacity, enhances the speed of information flows, reduces latency for near-real time communication, and transforms scalability for new services. Klint Finley, The WIRED Guide to 5G, *Wired*, December 18, 2019.

5G will own many of these innovations [such as for autonomous vehicles and the Internet of Things] and set the standards for the rest of the world . . . . That country is currently not likely to be the United States."[75] China's lead in this area implicates developments in critical fields such as artificial intelligence, robotics, and smart manufacturing – the so-called Internet of Things involving sensors and data collection in an increasingly digitalized, data-driven global economy.[76] Chinese companies are becoming increasingly competitive in these areas, potentially giving Chinese innovators and vendors a critical advantage in multiple product fields.[77]

For China, standard setting is another part of "the strategic game among big powers … over system design and rule making."[78] China is investing major resources in developing transnational standards through domestic and international bodies as a complement to its BRI initiatives. In 2018, China launched "China Standards 2035," a strategic scheme overseen by a revamped agency – the Standards Administration of China – to encourage indigenous innovation under Chinese party-state guidance.[79] Its aim is to set standards in emerging, cutting-edge industries. Internationally, China has dramatically increased its leadership positions in international standard-setting bodies across councils, technical management boards, technical committees, sub-committees, and working groups. It volunteers regularly to host standards meetings and provide secretariat services. The past president of the International Standardization Organization (ISO) (from 2015 to 2017) was Chinese as is the current president of the International Electrotechnical Committee (IEC) (from 2020 to 2022). To give one example of its international engagement, China and Chinese companies are working to shape UN facial recognition standards in the International Telecommunication Union.[80] China

---

75 Milo Medin and Gilman Louie, *The 5G Ecosystem: Risks & Opportunities for DoD* (Arlington: Defense Innovation Board, April 2019), 7.

76 Gregory Shaffer, "Trade Law in a Data-Driven Economy: A Call for Modesty and Resilience," in *Reconfiguring International Economic Law in an AI Era*, eds. Shin-yi Peng, Ching-Fu Lin and Thomas Streinz (Cambridge: Cambridge University Press, 2021).

77 The US–China Security Review Committee writes, "[Beijing's] efforts may lock in Chinese preferences for standards in IoT and supporting infrastructure sooner rather than later, as nascent IoT and 5G standards exist in a fragmented and complex standards-setting environment." John Chen et al., "China's Internet of Things," *Research Report Prepared on Behalf of the U.S.-China Economic and Security Review Commission*, October 2018, 1.

78 Emily de La Bruyere and Nathan Picarsic, "China's next plan to dominate international tech standards," *TC*, April 11, 2020.

79 Bjorn Fagerstern and Tim Ruhlig, "China's Standard Power and Its Geographic Implications for Europe," *Swedish Institute of International Affairs*, February 2019. The People's Daily reported, citing President Xi, "Whoever sets the standard has the right to speak; whoever holds the standard has the commanding heights." Tian Shihong, "Kaichuang Woguo Biaozhunhua Shiye Xin Jumian" ("Create a new situation in China's standardization cause"), *People's Daily*, September 6, 2016, http://theory .people.com.cn/n1/2016/0906/c40531-28693273.html (also noting the importance of combatting protectionism through standards).

80 Anna Gross and Madhumita Murgia, "Chinese Tech Groups Shaping UN Facial Recognition Standards," *Financial Times* (December 1, 2019) (noting that "China's influence in drafting and setting the standards at the UN has grown").

could even create its own standard-setting body for Asia and BRI partner countries if it does not get its way in international standard-setting bodies – a strategy paralleling its development of new international development banks.

For transnational dispute settlement, BRI contracts generally provide for arbitration to be held in hubs outside of China, such as Singapore for contracts in Asia, and London and Paris for contracts in Africa and South America.[81] In 2018, China established the China International Commercial Court under the Supreme People's Court as a new place for BRI-related dispute settlement, although foreign contracting parties generally do not agree to dispute settlement within China so that the court so far remains largely symbolic.[82] Formally the new international commercial court is regarded as a division of the Supreme People's Court and, as such, its decisions are final and not subject to appeal. This court has two branches based in Shenzhen and Xi'an.[83] It reflects once more a form of mimicking while repurposing a Western legal model, that of the Commercial Court in London – which Singapore had earlier adopted in 2013 with the Singapore International Commercial Court. However, in the case of the new Chinese court, unlike in Singapore, the regulations require that judges be "able to use at the same time Chinese and English as their work languages." Moreover, in practice, unlike in Singapore, China has appointed exclusively Chinese judges to the court,[84] who are assisted by an advisory Expert Committee with predominately non-Chinese experts, thus repurposing the model with Chinese characteristics. By the end of 2018, the China International Commercial Court announced that it had accepted a variety of cases involving foreign and Chinese companies.[85]

These developments form part of an ongoing shift toward Asia as a center for transnational dispute settlement (whether through arbitration or special international commercial courts),[86] with China aiming to play a more important role.

[81] Telephone interviews with SOE in-house legal counsel, March 30, 2020; former internal lawyer with Huawei, March 23, 2020; and external counsel for three major Beijing law firms, March 20 and March 27. These interviewees all noted that Hong Kong is less frequently used because it is increasingly viewed as a part of China. The governing law is either local law or the law of a neutral third country, at times linked to the country's colonial heritage. Parties use mediation more for technical disputes, which involves engineers. If the dispute is not resolved, then arbitration is most common. Interview with in-house legal counsel in major state-owned enterprise, March 30, 2020.

[82] Telephone interviews with practicing lawyers and in-house counsel at a major Chinese state-owned enterprise and a major Chinese private enterprise, March 20, 23, 27, and 30, 2020. One lawyer noted that the court can be used for enforcement of foreign judgments and arbitral awards. Interview, March 23, 2020.

[83] Mathew Erie, "The China International Commercial Court: Prospects for Dispute Resolution for the 'Belt and Road Initiative'," *ASIL Insights* 22, no. 11 (2018). Both branches are under the guidance of the Fourth Civil Division of the Supreme People's Court.

[84] China International Commercial Court, "Judges," *Supreme People's Court of the People's Republic of China*. Erie, "China International Commercial Court."

[85] China International Commercial Court, "The International Commercial Court of the Supreme Court has Accepted a Number of International Commercial Dispute Cases," *Supreme People's Court of the People's Republic of China*.

[86] Mathew S. Erie, "Legal Hubs: The Emergent Landscape of International Commercial Dispute Resolution," *Virginia Journal of International Law* 60 (2020): 225.

These new Chinese and Asian institutions, together with Asian professional networks using them, compete to offer services for transnational dispute resolution that, in the process, they will shape over time. There thus will be pressure on the China International Commercial Court to be highly professional like the London and Singapore models if it is to succeed. Ultimately, the China International Commercial Court's use will depend on parties' bargaining power, the court's reputation for expertise and impartiality, and the relationship of the host country with China.

The BRI's exact size and scope are unclear given China's lack of transparency. There are risks that come with such a lack of transparency. China already must manage the risk of domestic credit crises resulting from state banks' extension of low-interest loans to state-owned enterprises, the terms and accounting for which are opaque.[87] By exporting this domestic state-led, private-law development model to countries governed by unstable and corrupt regimes, China raises new debt exposure not only for the recipient countries, but for China itself. Backlash against Chinese debt obligations has intensified in recipient countries, especially following leadership changes (such as in Malaysia, Pakistan, and Sri Lanka). Criticism of Chinese "debt-trap diplomacy" is rising, even though China has shown flexibility in renegotiating loans, more so than Western hedge funds that buy distressed debt.[88] Nonetheless, if projects foreclose and credit collapses, President Xi's "China Dream," externalized as part of the country's "Go Out" strategy, risks becoming a nightmare.[89]

B. *Asian Infrastructure Investment Bank and New Development Bank*

Throughout the 2000s, the United States blocked any increase in China's shareholding and voting rights in the World Bank and International Monetary Fund that would reflect China's growing importance in the global economy.[90] Because of its frustration, and to help finance regional infrastructure more broadly, China officially proposed the creation of the Asian Infrastructure Investment Bank (AIIB) in 2013. The fact that it proposed both the AIIB and the BRI in 2013 suggests a coordinated strategy to enhance Chinese influence regionally and globally. China signed a Memorandum of Understanding in Beijing to create the AIIB in 2014 and AIIB operations started in 2016. The United States opposed the bank's

[87] Victor Shih, "Financial Instability in China: Possible Pathways and Their Likelihood," *Merics China Monitor* (October 20, 2017).

[88] Compare "Remarks by Vice President Pence on the Administration's Policy Toward China," *Foreign Policy*, October 4, 2018; Agatha Kratz et al., "New Data on the Debt Trap Question," *Rhodium Group*, April 29, 2019; Chas Freeman, "On Hostile Coexistence with China," *Remarks to the Freeman Spogli Institute*, May 3, 2019.

[89] Greer, "One Belt, One Road, One Big Mistake."

[90] Martin A. Weiss, "Asian Infrastructure Investment Bank (AIIB)," *Congressional Research Service*, 7-5700, February 3, 2017.

creation and lobbied countries not to join it. However, in a diplomatic triumph for China and defeat for the United States, the AIIB grew to 100 members by 2019, including all major developed countries other than the United States and Japan.[91]

While the AIIB started as a Chinese initiative and China is the largest shareholder with around a 27 percent voting share, China has tried to play down its influence as the membership of the AIIB expanded to include major Western countries. The Chinese government has made clear that the projects funded by the AIIB will not be limited to countries in the BRI. However, most of the approved projects have been in BRI countries, as the BRI is already vast and expanding.[92] To alleviate governance concerns, China has tried to assure that the AIIB follows "best practices" (i.e. those of the Western-controlled multilateral development banks), and the AIIB's lending practices to date confirm this policy. For example, the AIIB largely borrows its safeguards and operating procedures from other multilateral development banks, and most of its initial projects have been co-financed with them. The AIIB emphasizes that "our core principles are openness, transparency, independence and accountability and our mode of operation is 'Lean, Clean and Green'."[93] China wishes to develop a reputation as a responsible leader of a multilateral development bank, and it knows that civil society will scrutinize the bank's operations.

Nonetheless, the AIIB is controlled by China, has permanent headquarters in Beijing, and is run by a Chinese president. Its first president, Mr. Jin Liqun, previously served as chairman of China's first joint venture bank and chairman of the Supervisory Board of China's sovereign wealth fund.[94] Indeed, the AIIB is under greater de facto day-to-day control of China than the World Bank of the United States. Unlike the World Bank, the AIIB's directors are based in their home countries, not at bank headquarters, and they are required to meet only every three months. Although all AIIB projects through 2018 were approved by the board, the bank's Accountability Framework Regulation permits delegation of project approval to the bank's President. The AIIB's President and staff in Beijing thus potentially can exercise greater autonomy.[95]

The AIIB represents another form of mimicking while repurposing a Western model – the Bretton Woods development finance model. Just as the World Bank has served to advance US policy goals, the AIIB should advance China's. However, the

---

91   The United Kingdom, for example, resisted US entreaties, negotiated in secret with China, and gave the Obama administration 24 hours' notice before joining the AIIB.

92   The largest borrower from the AIIB has been India, which China views as part of the BRI, even though no formal MOU has been signed. Xinhua, Which Are the Countries on the BRI? [Yidai Yilu Yanxian Guojia Douyou Naxie?], October 25, 2019, available at www.imsilkroad.com/news/p/76186.html; Krzysztof Iwanek, "Fully Invested: India Remains the China-led AIIB's Biggest Borrower," *The Diplomat*, September 6, 2019.

93   AIIB, "Our Founding Principles," *Asian Infrastructure Investment Bank*, www.aiib.org/en/about-aiib /index.html.

94   Weiss, "AIIB."

95   Daniel C. K. Chow, "Why China Established the Asia Infrastructure Bank," *Vanderbilt Journal of Transnational Law* 49 (2016): 1255.

mechanisms will be different. The United States used the World Bank and International Monetary Fund to require legal reforms in line with American style capitalism. They did so through leverage provided under structural adjustment programs and through IMF surveillance policies that include Reports on the Observance on Standards and Codes (known as ROSCs) regarding good institutional practices.[96] Over time, the Bretton Woods institutions reduced their focus on funding basic infrastructure and rather emphasized creating a legal framework that would help attract private investment.

In contrast, the main reason for the AIIB's establishment is to finance infrastructure projects in the region, thus including countries covered by the BRI. This lending, in turn, helps develop new export markets for Chinese products. Beijing can use the AIIB to finance infrastructure that can be built by Chinese state-owned enterprises and private companies using Chinese standards. Even if companies from third countries win the contracts, the infrastructure facilitates the trade of Chinese products, such that the lent money can come full circle. Although the AIIB will not require legal reforms and will be governed under the principle of "non-interference," it offers further means to integrate economies into China's economic sphere. It helps foster ties with interest groups in regional neighbors, enhance China's place in global governance, and develop China's reputation as a responsible steward of economic globalization and development policy. The AIIB, in complement to the BRI, conveys China's soft power, providing a symbol of Chinese leadership in regional governance.[97]

China has complemented the AIIB with the creation of the New Development Bank (formerly called the "BRICS Development Bank"), which is headquartered in Shanghai. The New Development Bank has a capital of $100 billion and its shares are equally divided between the five BRICS countries (Brazil, Russia, India, China, and South Africa), who have equal voting rights in selecting its projects. In addition, China has many other channels to finance overseas infrastructure projects, such as through China's state-owned banks, which have provided the vast bulk of its development lending.

These Chinese-led development banks provide developing countries with new sources of finance, ones that are linked with Beijing instead of Washington, and that funding comes without political conditions to adopt neoliberal policies. In the

---

96 Although the World Bank did not apply substantive policy conditions for assistance in its early days, this changed first with the structural adjustment policies of the 1980s and then with the turn to governance policies in the 1990s. *The World Bank: Its first half century*, eds. Devesh Kapur, John Lewis, and Richard Webb (Washington, DC: Brookings Institution, 1997). Chow, "Why China Established," 1277–1279 (on World Bank conditions regarding privatization; deregulation; private property rights, intellectual property rights; tax reform; and market-determined interest and exchange rates); Weiss, "AIIB," 4.

97 For this reason India has expressed great wariness of the Belt and Road Initiative, even though it is the largest recipient of AIIB-financed projects. Enda Curran, "The AIIB: China's World Bank," *Bloomberg*, August 6, 2018.

process, these banks' operation creates leverage that can enhance China's role in the Bretton Woods institutions. The US Congress's approval to increase China's voting rights in the IMF and World Bank came *only after* the AIIB's formation. The AIIB works with the World Bank and so it currently operates as a complement within the existing international economic order – a form of institutional layering in the order's evolving ecology. The AIIB is quite useful to China in the context of the trade war, for it conveys a reputation of China as a responsible global leader. Outside the United States and Japan, the rest of the world has embraced this Beijing-based institutional development.

III. DEVELOPING A WEB OF FREE TRADE AND INVESTMENT AGREEMENTS

A. *Free Trade Agreements*

To complement these initiatives as part of its development and broader strategy, China is creating a web of trade and investment agreements that grant it preferential access to foreign markets. This public international law component once more forms part of the evolving ecology of the international trade and investment legal orders. It borrows from Western models but is tailored to advance China's interests. Unlike the US model for free trade agreements and bilateral investment treaties where the United States insists on using a common US template to address behind-the-border issues, Chinese free trade agreements do not aim to change internal governance systems.

China turned to such agreements around a decade after it joined the WTO. At the 18th Party Congress in 2012, President Hu emphasized that the "implementation of the FTA [free trade agreement] strategy shall be further accelerated." In response, the State Council issued several Opinions on Accelerating the Implementation of the FTA Strategy in 2015, which laid out a comprehensive blueprint for China's trade agreement strategy in complement to its broader private law-oriented finance-trade-investment model under the BRI.[98] As of June 2020, China had signed free trade agreements with thirteen countries, including South Korea and Australia in 2015.[99] In addition, it had launched trade negotiations with six others,[100] as well as

---

[98] State Council, "Several Opinions on the Acceleration of the Implementation of the FTA Strategy (Guowuyuan guanyu Jiakuai Shishi Ziyoumaoyiqu Zhanlue de Ruogan Yijian)," *Guofa* (2015) No. 69, Beijing: Chinese Government Network.

[99] China has agreements with Chile (November 2005), Pakistan (November 2006), New Zealand (April 2008), Singapore (October 2008), Peru (April 2009), Costa Rica (April 2010), Iceland (April 2013), Switzerland (July 2013), South Korea (June 2015), Australia (June 2015), Georgia (May 2017), Maldives (December 2017), and Mauritius (October 2019).

[100] It had launched negotiations with the Gulf Cooperation Council (April 2005), Norway (September 2008), Sri Lanka (September 2014), Israel (March 2016), Moldova (March 2018), and Panama (July 2018).

a trilateral agreement with South Korea and Japan. In 2002, it concluded its first free trade agreement with the ten-member Association of Southeast Asian Nations (ASEAN), and in 2003, it formalized Closer Economic Partnership Arrangements with Hong Kong, and Macau.[101] It aimed to expand these agreements through negotiating a Regional Comprehensive Economic Partnership that would comprise fifteen Asian countries, of which China already had a free trade agreement with all but Japan. Overall, China envisages over fifty free trade agreements as part of its implementation of the BRI.[102] These agreements bolster China's status as a hub for global and regional value chains.

China (at least initially) negotiated these agreements incrementally by starting with an agreement on trade in goods and then expanding it to cover services after commitments on goods are substantially implemented.[103] It has complemented these agreements with an investment agreement that facilitates further economic integration. For example, the China–ASEAN Agreement on Trade in Goods entered into force in 2005, while the Agreement on Trade in Services became effective in 2008. Then, in 2009, the two parties signed an Agreement on Investment. Similarly, China signed its agreement on trade in services with Pakistan four years after the parties signed their agreement on trade in goods. Developed countries, however, can press China to enter agreements for goods and services simultaneously, which is one reason China's negotiation with Australia took ten years to complete.[104]

These free trade agreements are narrower in scope compared to those of the United States, European Union, and Japan. In line with China's policy emphasis on non-interference in internal regulatory affairs and respect for sovereignty, the agreements do not require new rules for regulatory issues, such as labor and environmental protection, or competition policy. China prefers to address these issues, if demanded by trading partners, in standalone side agreements or Memoranda of Understanding.[105]

China, nonetheless, has used these free trade agreements to establish rules and precedents regarding its treatment as a market economy.[106] This treatment is

---

[101] In turn, Hong Kong concluded a free trade and investment agreements with ASEAN in November 2017, providing further bridges between them.

[102] Carrai, "It Is Not the End of History."

[103] Henry Gao, "Selected Issues in TPP Negotiations and Implications for China," in *Regional Cooperation and Free Trade Agreements in Asia*, eds. Jiaxiang Hu and Matthias Vanhullebusch (Leiden: Brill Academic Publishers, 2014), 77–98.

[104] These agreements can contain provisions designed to advance particular Chinese sectors, such as services commitments in the agreements with Australia and New Zealand relating to Chinese cooks and tour guides.

[105] Henry Gao, "China's Evolving Approach to Environmental and Labour Provisions in Regional Trade Agreements," *ICTSD Blog*, August 25, 2017.

[106] Henry S. Gao, "China's Ascent in Global Trade Governance: From Rule Taker to Rule Shaker, and Maybe Rule Maker?," in *Making Global Trade Governance Work for Development*, ed. Carolyn Deere-Birkbeck (Cambridge: Cambridge University Press, 2011), 153–180.

important for antidumping calculations, where the United States and European Union use constructed data from other markets to determine if Chinese products are being sold at less than fair value, resulting in higher antidumping tariffs imposed on Chinese products. China has insisted on the recognition of its market economy status as a precondition for virtually every free trade agreement that it has signed. However, even though eighty-one countries have formally recognized China as a market economy, the United States, European Union, and Japan have refused to grant it this status, based on their interpretations of the relevant WTO Agreements and China's Accession Protocol.

The biggest among China's trade agreements is the Regional Comprehensive Economic Partnership (RCEP), which promises to create the largest free trade area in the world. The agreement is between fifteen Asian countries: the ten members of ASEAN plus Australia, China, Japan, New Zealand, and South Korea. The parties launched negotiations in November 2012 to cover trade in goods and services, investment, and intellectual property protection, and signed it in November 2020 (after India dropped out the year before).[107] Even without India, the RCEP constitutes the largest free trade bloc in the world, covering around 30 percent of global GDP, and about 27 percent of global merchandise trade.[108] The Obama administration's pivot to Asia and its driving the negotiation of a Trans-Pacific Partnership (TPP) that excluded China accelerated RCEP negotiations.

Although India's withdrawal diminished the agreement's geographic scope, it facilitated conclusion of a more ambitious agreement. Tariffs are to be reduced to 0 percent on about 90 percent of tariff lines, implemented over different time periods to accommodate member sensitivities regarding products from particular RCEP partners. In addition, and importantly, RCEP creates common rules of origin that are relatively liberal, which will facilitate the ability of regional and global supply chains to benefit from the tariff cuts.[109]

Although many Western commentators assumed that China drove RCEP negotiations, in practice, it assumed a low profile. Formally, the RCEP's Guiding Principles and Objectives explicitly state that "negotiations for the RCEP will recognize ASEAN Centrality in the emerging regional economic architecture," a point on which ASEAN insisted. Given ASEAN's historical and current problems with China, it is not surprising that ASEAN insisted on being recognized as taking

---

[107]   Regional Comprehensive Economic Partnership, *Guiding Principles and Objectives for Negotiating the Regional Comprehensive Partnership.*

[108]   World Bank GDP (Current US$), at https://data.worldbank.org/indicator/NY.GDP.MKTP.CD?locations=AU-BN-KH-CN-ID-JP-LA-MY-MM-NZ-PH-SG-KR-TH-VN-1W (November 22, 2020) (29.4 percent in nominal terms and 30.4 percent in PPP terms). Were India to have joined RCEP, these countries would have accounted for almost half of the world's population, around 33 percent of global GDP in nominal terms (and 37 percent in PPP terms), and about 30 percent of global merchandise trade.

[109]   Unless otherwise specified, the rules of origin only require 40 percent of the value of components to be sourced within RCEP member countries, or a change in tariff heading. RCEP, chapter 3.

the lead. However, ASEAN is a weak regional institution with no uniform agenda. Thus, the "ASEAN Centrality" principle made it difficult to conduct negotiations. Moreover, even if China wished to drive and dominate the negotiations, it has to contend with Japan (the world's third largest economy), followed by South Korea and Australia, as significant countervailing economic powers. Thus, the principle of ASEAN Centrality represents a compromise.

In addition, there remains significant rivalry among RCEP members. The relation between South Korea and Japan is charged with longstanding conflict, going back to Japan's annexation of South Korea in the first half of the twentieth century. The two have been negotiating a free trade agreement for almost fourteen years with no conclusion in sight.[110] China has conflicts with many RCEP members regarding its claims in the South China Sea.[111] Adding to the problem is the wide disparity of the parties' development levels, which delayed agreement on a common approach to negotiations.

Due to these challenges, expectations regarding an ambitious RCEP remained low. Because some of the parties are concerned about liberalizing services and investment, and about imposing new requirements on intellectual property and competition policy, these areas involved fewer major new commitments.[112] Moreover, the agreement did not address behind-the-border regulatory issues such as labor rights, environmental protection, and state-owned enterprises. If subsequently addressed, provisions will likely be couched in soft, best-endeavor language, and be excluded from dispute settlement, consistent with the "ASEAN way."[113] The agreement even permitted discriminatory treatment among its members, such as through different tariff schedules applying to different countries, since this approach was the only way the parties could address each other's "various sensitivities and interests."[114]

In sum, the RCEP and China's bilateral trade agreements offer a paradigm that is more sensitive to national sovereignty than US agreements. They leave more room for policy space, including through provisions providing for special and differential

---

[110] Asia Regional Integration Center, *Japan-Republic of Korea Free Trade Agreement (JKFTA)*, 2003.

[111] It also shared a militarized and disputed border with one RCEP party (India), although India dropped out of the RCEP in 2019 because of concerns over China's trade dominance.

[112] As Peter Yu notes, many of the parties to the RCEP are also parties to the TPP (Australia, Japan, New Zealand, and almost half of ASEAN), and China increasingly has viewed benefits from intellectual property protection, such that norms are converging in Asia. Peter Yu, "TPP, RCEP and the Future of Copyright Normsetting in the Asia-Pacific," in *Making Copyright Work for the Asian Pacific? Juxtaposing Harmonisation with Flexibility*, eds. Susan Corbett and Jessica Lai (Canberra: ANU Press, 2017), 19–46. The intellectual property chapters in China's free trade agreements are growing in scope, from no mention in China's 2008 agreement with Singapore to over 3,000 words in China's 2013 agreement with Switzerland. Yu, "Building Intellectual Property Infrastructure Along China's Belt and Road," 281.

[113] Banyan, "Getting in the Way," *Economist*, May 17, 2014.

[114] RCEP, "Joint Leaders' Statement on the Regional Comprehensive Economic Partnership," *Vientiane: Lao PDR*, September 8, 2016.

treatment and other flexibility mechanisms. For many development economists, such an approach is better because it is more flexible for development policy, including industrial policy.[115] Although other analysts stress the need for binding commitments on behind-the-border issues to facilitate global supply chains,[116] these supply chains already have flourished among RCEP countries. They have done so even though the utilization rate by business of preferential tariff rates in Asian free trade agreements has been low.[117]

B. *Network of Bilateral Investment Treaties*

China complements its trade agreements with an even broader network of bilateral investment treaties. In total, China has signed 125 bilateral investment treaties, with 107 in force, and an additional twenty-three treaties with investment provisions, of which nineteen are in force.[118] That is more than any other country except Germany. Its partners include all major economies in the world except the United States. In 2008, the United States and China commenced negotiation of an investment treaty, but it was put on hold because of rising geopolitical tensions between them. In contrast, the European Union and China concluded a Comprehensive Agreement on Investment in late December 2020, subject to ratification.

Chinese investment agreements incrementally have built from Western models, such as through acceptance of investor–state dispute settlement, but China is developing them pragmatically and is including "soft law" alternatives for dispute resolution, such as mediation. China's investment treaty negotiations with the European Union and United States, in turn, are linked to internal Chinese reform initiatives. As one interviewee noted, "it is not by chance that in July 2013, the United States and China jointly announced that they would agree to negotiate" an invest-ment treaty that covers all sectors, unless specifically excluded, and in the following month, China's State Council announced the approval of investments on such basis in a free trade zone in Shanghai as a "trial."[119]

China has significantly changed its approach to bilateral investment treaties over the past three decades. When China first signed investment agreements, it was an

---

[115] Dani Rodrik, *Straight Talk on Trade: Ideas for a Sane World Economy* (Princeton: Princeton University Press, 2017).

[116] Richard Baldwin, "21st Century Regionalism: Filling the Gap Between 21st Century Trade and 20th Century Trade Rules," *World Trade Organization: Economic Research and Statistics Division,* May 23, 2011.

[117] Just more than 30 percent of ASEAN-China trade purportedly used preferential rates under the ASEAN-China free trade agreement. Pasha Hsieh, "Against Populist Isolationism: New Asian Regionalism and Global South Powers in International Economic Law," *Cornell International Law Journal* 51, no. 3 (2018): 683–729. This figure could improve in light of RCEP's harmonized rules of origin.

[118] UNCTAD, "China: Bilateral Investment Treaties (BITs), Investment Policy Hub," *Investment Policy Hub* (visited October 8, 2020).

[119] Telephone interview, March 20, 2020.

importer of foreign direct investment, and was correspondingly wary of making extensive investment commitments backed by international dispute settlement. As Figure 7.1 shows, China's joining the WTO in 2001 almost immediately had a huge impact on incoming investment into China, as multinational firms increasingly used China for their global supply chains. However, it was only around 2005 that China's outbound investment began to take off, soaring particularly in the wake of the global financial crisis of 2007–2008. Correspondingly, China's investment agreements became more protective of outbound investors.

The 1998 investment treaty with Barbados heralded a new Chinese approach that granted foreign investors access to investor–state arbitration under the agreement establishing the International Centre for Settlement of Investment Disputes.[120] Since around 2008, a new generation of Chinese bilateral investment treaties emerged with two new features. First, they included a national treatment obligation pursuant to which the state cannot favor domestic enterprises, subject to exceptions for existing measures.[121] Second, the new agreements expanded the scope of ICSID investor–state arbitration to cover all investment disputes.[122]

These changes reflect China's shift from being the world's largest destination of foreign direct investment – it surpassed the United States in 2003, two years after joining the World Trade Organization[123] – to becoming one of the world's major capital exporting nations. In 1999, China launched its "Going Global" (or "Go Out") policy, where it encouraged Chinese firms to invest abroad.[124] The results were impressive. Whereas China was the world's top destination for foreign direct investment between 1990 and 2015, by the end of that period, it also had become one of the world's primary foreign investors. In 2001, outward Chinese foreign direct investment constituted only 15 percent of China's inbound investment. By 2016, Chinese outward foreign direct investment substantially surpassed it, although it plunged starting in 2018 – especially in the United States – because of rising trade tensions, enhanced US and European investment scrutiny of Chinese acquisitions on national security grounds, and new Chinese restrictions on outbound capital, followed by the COVID-19 pandemic.[125]

China's investment strategy takes two dominant forms. As part of China's Go Out policy, the government encouraged Chinese state-owned and private enterprises to acquire advanced technology through acquisitions of companies in the United

[120] Axel Berger, "The Politics of China's Investment Treaty-Making Program," in *The Politics of International Economic Law*, eds. Tomer Broude, Marc L. Busch, and Amelia Porges (Cambridge: Cambridge University Press, 2011), 162–185.

[121] China's agreement with Mexico provides an example. UNCTAD, *China-Mexico Bilateral Investment Treaty*, 2008, Article 3.

[122] UNCTAD, *China-Germany Bilateral Investment Treaty*, 2003, Article 9.

[123] Sandra Poncet, "Inward and Outward FDI in China," in *China and the World Economy*, eds. David Greenaway, Chris Milner, and Shujie Yao (London: Palgrave Macmillan, 2007), 112–134.

[124] Naughton, *The Chinese Economy: Adaptation and Growth*, 446.

[125] UNCTAD, *World Investment Report 2016* (ranking China first for inward FDI between 1990 and 2015, and noting China reaching parity by 2014); Khanna, *The Future is Asian*, 164 (noting 90 percent drop of Chinese investment in the United States in 2018).

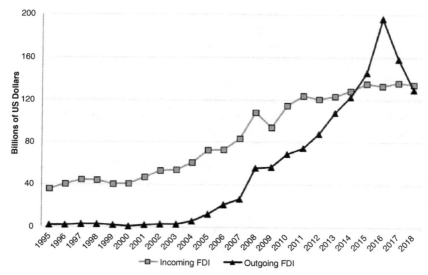

FIGURE 7.1 China's incoming and outgoing foreign direct investment[126]

States, Europe, and other developed countries. In parallel, it encouraged such companies to invest in developing countries, including as part of the BRI, particularly in infrastructure and resource extraction projects. The first type of investment largely involves corporate acquisitions and the second greenfield foreign direct investment. The total value of outbound Chinese investment became greater in developed countries given the cost of major acquisitions, although Chinese investment plummeted in the United States after the US-launched trade war. For example, China National Chemical Corp bought the Swiss-based Syngenta for US$43 billion in 2017 (the largest acquisition to date), which is critical for China's ambitions in agricultural biotechnology.[127]

China's investment in BRI countries nonetheless continued to grow, increasing Chinese demands for investment protection. In 2017, Chinese firms signed 7,217 new project contracts in BRI countries, with a total contract volume of US $144.3 billion, constituting 54.4 percent of its total foreign project contracts.[128] Since many BRI countries pose high political and economic risks, China and Chinese companies need to find ways to protect their investments, including

---

[126] Sources: Incoming FDI: MOFCOM Report on Foreign Investment in China (2017–2018), UNCTAD World Investment Report (2008, 2002, 2000); China News; Outgoing FDI: MOFCOM Report on Development of China's Outbound Investment (2018); UNCTAD World Investment Report (2002, 2000).

[127] United States Trade Representative, *Section 301 Report*, August 24, 2018, 126.

[128] Business Administration in Kazakh, "China's Investment Cooperation with Countries Along the 'Belt and Road' in 2017," *Ministry of Commerce of the People's Republic of China*, March 5, 2018, www.mofcom.gov.cn/article/i/jyjl/e/201803/20180302717955.shtml.

through bilateral investment treaties, which complement commercial arbitration and other mechanisms.[129]

By 2018, China was viewed as a "status quo" country favorable to the existing global investment law regime, as opposed to a "transformational" one proposing new models, as in the case of Brazil and (to a mixed extent) India.[130] From their international trade law experience, some Chinese trade specialists believe that China should look favorably on an appellate process for investor–state dispute settlement. As one of our interviewees working with the government observed, China has often fared better challenging US import relief measures before the WTO Appellate Body than before ad hoc panels, and it takes note that the United States has never lost before ad hoc panels in investor–state dispute settlement under NAFTA and other treaties (where there is no appellate mechanism).[131] Within the United Nations working group in UNCITRAL assessing the reform of the investment law regime, China has stressed that the inconsistency and incorrectness of arbitral decisions "were problems in the system and that the existing mechanisms of review (annulment and judicial review) were inadequate."[132] On these grounds, it supports consideration of "a permanent appellate mechanism as a reform proposal."[133] In sum, China found that the investment protection models developed in the West suited it for protecting its own outbound investments and expressed support for their further judicialization. Nonetheless, China's investment agreements are still more respective of state sovereignty than US and European ones, and China is likely to rely much more on soft forms of dispute resolution in practice, such as pre-arbitration consultation and mediation, given its aim to build cooperative, cross-border ties.[134]

IV. THE TRANSNATIONAL LEGAL ORDER FOR INTELLECTUAL PROPERTY RIGHTS AND CHINA'S INNOVATION STRATEGIES

As part of its strategy to expand trade and investment through the BRI, the government also has massively supported Chinese technological development. China already deemed it risky to rely on Western technologies before the United States launched

---

[129] Senior Chinese officials, such as former MOFCOM Vice Minister Wei Jianguo, suggested that China expedite the signing of BITs with BRI countries in 2015. Interview, "Former Deputy Minister of the Ministry of Commerce: One Belt," *21st Century Business Herald*, March 31, 2015, http://finance .sina.com.cn/china/20150331/015921847760.shtml.

[130] Fabio Morosini and Michelle Ratton Sanchez Badin, "Reconceptualizing Investment Law from the Global South," in *Reconceptualizing Investment Law from the Global South*, eds. Fabio Morosini and Michelle Ratton Sanchez Badin (Cambridge: Cambridge University Press, 2017), 35; Congyan Cai, "Balanced Investment Treaties and the BRICS," *AJIL Unbound* 112 (2018): 217–222 (China having more "balanced" approach than other BRICS).

[131] Interviews with a lawyer in a major Chinese law firm working with the government, July 23, 2016 and March 20, 2020.

[132] Anthea Roberts, "UNCITRAL and ISDS Reforms: Moving to Reform Options ... The Politics," *EJIL: Talk!*, November 8, 2018.

[133] Anthea Roberts and Taylor St. John, "UNCITRAL and ISDS: Chinese Proposal" *EJIL: Talk!*, August 5, 2019.

[134] Ibid.

a trade war, and it has been encouraging indigenous innovation through government subsidies complemented by enhanced intellectual property protection. Yet unlike the United States and European Union, China is not an evangelist pressing countries to change their intellectual property laws and practices. Rather, China has gradually and pragmatically enhanced its own internal intellectual property system by adopting and repurposing Western models with the aim of becoming a world leader in developing new technologies. These technologies will be critical for the BRI, including through standards used for infrastructure projects, which in turn create corridors for exporting Chinese manufactured products that use advanced technologies such as robotics and artificial intelligence. This section first addresses China's long and contentious relationship with the United States over intellectual property and its internal development of intellectual property laws and institutions. It then assesses China's strategic plan to develop indigenous technology, reduce dependence on the West, and become a world technological power at the cutting edge of the next industrial revolution.

A. *From a Western Transplant to Indigenous Innovation*

China's relationship with intellectual property law is intricately linked to its relationship with the United States. In 1979, China entered into a bilateral agreement with the United States regarding intellectual property protection in the context of their trade relations, following which China joined the World Intellectual Property Organization (in 1980), enacted new patent, copyright, and trademark laws (between 1982 and 1984), and acceded to the Paris Convention for the Protection of Industrial Property (in 1984).[135] The United States continued its pressure on China to recognize US intellectual property, placing the country on its "Priority Watch List" for allegedly unfair trade practices, and threatening sanctions, which helped spur China's adoption of its 1990 copyright law. China took further steps to avoid sanctions by signing a Memorandum of Understanding Between China and the United States on the Protection of Intellectual Property in 1992, which catalyzed further amendments to Chinese laws and regulations.[136] Most notably, as part of its accession to the WTO in 2001, China agreed to the WTO Agreement on Trade Related Aspects of Intellectual Property Rights, complemented by further commitments in its Working Party Report, which included fifty-five paragraphs on intellectual property.[137] This marked a tectonic shift in China's intellectual property rights regime, and it ushered in new domestic institutional development.[138] At this time, transnational legal ordering was top-down for China, as

---

[135]   Peter K. Yu, "From Pirates to Partners: Protecting Intellectual Property in China in the Twenty-First Century," *American University Law* 50, no. 1 (2000): 131, 136.

[136]   Ibid., 140–142.

[137]   World Trade Organization, *Report of the Working Party on the Accession of China*, WT/ACC/CHN/49, Oct. 1, 2001, paras. 251–305.

[138]   Andrea Wechsler, "China's WTO Accession Revisited: Achievements and Challenges in Chinese Intellectual Property Law Reform," in *European Yearbook of International Economic Law*, eds. Christoph Herrmann, Markus Krajewski, and Jörg Philipp (London: Springer Nature, 2012), 125.

China was pressed to adopt Western legal norms.[139] Although China was in the process of becoming a manufacturer of the world, the technology came from abroad and the royalties flowed there.

After China joined the WTO, the United States pressured China to comply with its new WTO commitments. US private associations, such as the Business Software Alliance working with International Data Corporation, found that China had a piracy rate of 90 percent in the mid-2000s.[140] In 2007, the United States brought a WTO complaint against China for failing to comply with its commitments under the TRIPS agreement and the Accession Protocol. China invested significant resources in defending the case, whose outcomes were largely a draw.[141]

Countries are best positioned to resist what they view as impositions by foreign powers at the enforcement stage. Although the TRIPS agreement provides for protection and enforcement of intellectual property rights, it also contains ambiguities and exceptions. China took advantage of them to defend its interests, while also turning a blind eye to infringements, in part because it lacked administrative capacity at the local level, but mainly because it had less interest in enforcement given its other priorities.[142]

The TRIPS agreement, combined with China's Accession Protocol to the WTO, nonetheless had major implications in China, as it created new opportunities for transnational legal ordering that catalyzed stakeholders in China, including the government and private actors, triggering top-down and bottom-up processes. Developments in China were not simply foreign "transplants." From a top-down vantage, the government has been trying to create its own domestic "indigenous innovation" policies, to the consternation of the United States and Europe. It invested significant resources in developing new intellectual property institutions to support such innovation, including specialized courts and specialized judges for intellectual property disputes. From a bottom-up perspective, Chinese individuals invested in new careers, including as attorneys, patent and trademark agents, patent examiners, and bureaucratic agency and judicial

---

139 William P. Alford, *To Steal a Book is an Elegant Offense: Intellectual Property Law in Chinese Civilization* (Stanford: Stanford University Press, 1995), 30–55 (on transplants and how the Chinese "learned the law at gunpoint").

140 Yu, "From Pirates to Partners," 2.

141 In 2009, the panel found China did not properly dispose of goods seized by customs and that it improperly denied copyright protection to works that had yet to be authorized for publication or dissemination. These were matters that were of minor importance and China forthwith revised its copyright law to comply with the decision. China was victorious on two more important issues, its threshold for criminalization of IP infringement and its disposal of infringing goods through means other than auctions. Panel Report, *China – Measures Affecting the Protection and Enforcement of Intellectual Property Rights*, WT/DS362/R, Mar. 20, 2009, DSR 2009:V, 2097.

142 Peter K. Yu, "TRIPS and its Achilles' Heel," *Journal of Intellectual Property Law* 18 (2010–2011): 479, 495–496; Kenneth Guang-Lih Huang, Xuesong Geng, and Heli Wang, "Institutional Regime Shift in Intellectual Property Rights and Innovation Strategies of Firms in China," *Organization Science* 28, no. 2 (2017): 355, 358. Kristie Thomas, *Assessing Intellectual Property Compliance in Contemporary China* (London: Palgrave Macmillan, 2017).

officials.[143] Chinese companies hired and worked with these individuals. In parallel, domestic constituencies that embraced intellectual property protection and became rights holders engaged in information campaigns and enforcement actions.[144] They worked to shape public awareness and attitudes towards intellectual property, including among new generations of Chinese. As the Chinese became wealthier, consumers became more interested in consumer protection, such as against trademark fraud. WTO law supported this dynamic development of transnational legal ordering over the governance of intellectual property that shaped state institutions and professions in China, which, in turn, interacted with new constituent demands.

Remedies for violations of intellectual property rights were initially weak in China. Over time, China enhanced them, including because of pressure from domestic stakeholders. In 2000 and 2001, China amended its patent, copyright, and trademark laws to provide for injunctive relief for the first time, which parties increasingly used.[145] Although the United States criticized China's criminal laws for lacking sufficient power to deter violations, China expanded the list of criminal intellectual property offences and granted more enforcement powers to criminal courts.[146] At the local level, administrative agencies were to enforce intellectual property rights, but courts also played an increasing role through criminal penalties and by allowing litigants to protect their rights against infringements by actors operating outside of local jurisdictions.[147] As part of the so-called "phase 1" US–China Economic and Trade Agreement of January 2020, China agreed to further increase enforcement together with penalties "as an interim step" through applying them "at or near the statutory maximum," followed by new legislation that will increase civil and criminal law penalties, complemented by new commitments to lower the threshold for criminal enforcement.[148]

These changes required considerable institutional development. Analysts now consider China's State Intellectual Property Office (SIPO) to be "in the top tier of patent offices that will dominate the emerging system of global patent administration."[149] The number of patent examiners in SIPO soared from around

[143] A separate profession of patent agents and trademark agents developed which is in competition with IP lawyers for business. Sida Liu, "The Changing Role of Lawyers in China: State Bureaucrats, Market Brokers, and Political Activists," in *The New Legal Realism*, eds. Heinz Klug and Sally Engle Merry, vol. 2 (Cambridge: Cambridge University Press, 2016), 181.

[144] Thomas, *Assessing Intellectual Property Compliance*, 139.

[145] Ibid., 91.

[146] Ibid., 146.

[147] Susan Finder, "The Protection of Intellectual Property Rights through the Courts," in *Chinese Intellectual Property Law and Practice*, eds. Mark A. Cohen et al. (Alphen aan den Rijn: Kluwer Law International, 1999), 165, 255.

[148] Economic and Trade Agreement between the Government of the United States of America and the Government of the People's Republic of China, signed on January 15, 2020. Article 1.22 addresses enforcement, Art. 1.27 addresses interim and subsequent steps regarding penalties, and Art. 1.7 addresses the threshold for criminal enforcement.

[149] Peter Drahos, *The Global Governance of Knowledge: Patent Offices and Their Clients* (Cambridge: Cambridge University Press, 2010), 233.

400 in 1996[150] to around 5,000 in 2009[151] to over 11,400 in 2017.[152] China is now the largest issuer of patents in the world, surpassing the United States.[153] In 2017, it ranked second in terms of international patent applications and third in terms of international trademark registrations.[154] The bulk of these patents are weak utility and design patents (as opposed to invention patents) filed in response to university, career, and other state-driven incentives, and are soon abandoned to avoid filing fees.[155] Yet, although China is still playing catch-up, its ambitions are grand.

At the judicial level, China created specialized intellectual property divisions within courts and, in 2014, specialized intellectual property courts in Beijing, Shanghai, and Guangzhou.[156] These courts have directly applied the TRIPS agreement in dozens of private disputes.[157] In 2015 alone, these specialized courts concluded 9,872 cases.[158] In 2018, China created new tribunals for defined technology-related intellectual property matters in ten provinces and two additional cities around the country, while stripping some Chinese courts of jurisdiction over these matters.[159] It also established a specialized intellectual property court of appeal at the national level to foster uniform jurisprudence in intellectual property law.[160] Housed in the Supreme People's Court and headed by one of its Vice-Presidents, the new court has heard all appeals against patent-related decisions from lower courts since January 1, 2019.[161] It is expected that appeals on other intellectual property cases, such as copyright and trade secrets, also will be made to the new court.[162] Paradoxically, China "has emerged as the world's

[150] Sha Shu, "Jiedu Zhongguo Zhuanli Shenchayuan (Decoding Chinese Patent Examiners)," *China Intellectual Property*, no. 9, www.chinaipmagazine.com/journal-show.asp?665.html.

[151] "Guojia Zhishi Chanquanju Zhongguo Zhuanli Shenchayuan Naxie Shier (The Stuff on Patent Examiners at SIPO)," *China IP News*, June 13, 2010, http://ip.people.com.cn/GB/11872843.html.

[152] State Intellectual Property Office of the P.R.C., *Annual Report*, 43, 2016, www.sipo.gov.cn/gk/ndbg/2016/201705/P020170505541250020396.pdf.

[153] World Intellectual Property Organization, "Who Filed the Most PCT Patent Applications in 2017?"

[154] "Who Filed the Most Madrid Trademark Applications in 2017?," *World Intellectual Property Organization*, www.wipo.int/export/sites/www/ipstats/en/docs/infographic_madrid_2017.pdf; "Who Filed the Most PCT Patent Applications in 2017?," *World Intellectual Property Organization*, www.wipo.int/export/sites/www/ipstats/en/docs/infographic_pct_2017.pdf.

[155] Lulu Yilun Chen, "China Claims More Patents Than Any Other Country—Most Are Worthless," *Bloomberg*, September 26, 2018 (noting China's three categories of patents).

[156] Thomas, *Assessing Intellectual Property Compliance*, 143 (on specialized courts).

[157] *See* Congyan Cai, "International Law in Chinese Courts during the Rise of China," *American Journal of International Law* 110 (2016): 269, 286–287.

[158] Thomas, *Assessing Intellectual Property Compliance*, 144.

[159] Covington, *Establishing 15 IP Tribunals Nationwide, Chinese Courts Further Concentrate Jurisdiction over IP Matters*, March 15, 2018.

[160] People's Court News Media Corporation, "The Supreme People's Court Issued the 'Regulations on Certain Issues of the Intellectual Property Tribunal," *Supreme People's Court*, December 28, 2018, www.court.gov.cn/zixun-xiangqing-137461.html.

[161] The Beijing News, "The Supreme Law Intellectual Property Court Unveiled the Relevant Cases in Accordance with the Law," *Tencent*, January 1, 2019, https://new.qq.com/omn/20190101/20190101A0FHFB.html.

[162] Guo Liqin, "SPC Establishes IP Court, Paving the Road for a Uniform National Appeal Court," *Yicai*, October 23, 2018, www.yicai.com/news/100045081.html.

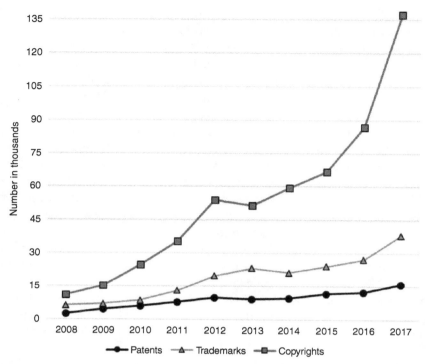

FIGURE 7.2 Intellectual property cases in Chinese courts[163]

most litigious country in the intellectual property area," with 16,010 new patent cases, 37,946 new trademark cases, and 137,267 new copyright cases reportedly filed in 2017, as captured in Figure 7.2.[164]

In international negotiations, China has been a status quo country on intellectual property issues.[165] Unlike Brazil and India, it has not actively contested the international intellectual property regime, and it has not issued (or threatened to issue) a compulsory patent license, such as for essential medicines. It also is the only BRICS country to agree to prohibit parallel imports of products that businesses can use to evade intellectual property protection. In this sense, China has largely mimicked and built upon Western laws and institutions. However, China repurposed them as part of its broader international goals. China now seeks to be

---

[163] Sources: The Supreme People's Court of China: Intellectual Property Protection by Chinese Courts (2010–2014, 2016), State Intellectual Property Office of China: Intellectual Property Rights Protection in China (2015, 2017), and People's Court Daily [Renmin Fayuan Bao].

[164] Supreme People's Court of the People's Republic of China, The Status of Judicial Protection of Intellectual Property Rights in Chinese Courts (2017) 2 (2018); Yu, "Building Intellectual Property Infrastructure Along China's Belt and Road," 313.

[165] Omar Serrano, "China and India's Insertion in the Intellectual Property Rights Regime: Sustaining or Disrupting the Rules?," *New Political Economy* 21, no. 4 (2016): 343–364.

a technological leader, such as in biotechnology, harnessing its large market and huge public and private investment in research and development as part of its indigenous innovation policies. It has worked with the World Intellectual Property Organization to support the enhancement of intellectual property protection abroad through its Belt and Road Initiative.[166]

B. *China's Challenge: Indigenous Innovation Policies*

Although China's intellectual property laws developed from transplants from the West, it adapted them into a national asset that is critical for its development model and global ambitions. As in the United States, the private sector, seeking economic rents through the monopoly power that intellectual property provides, helps drive intellectual property protection. Yet government technocrats are in much greater control of intellectual property policy in China than in the United States, and their focus is on innovation and economic development. Since the mid-1990s, China has actively used industrial policy to promote the development of high-tech and other key industries.[167] To avoid dependency on Western firms and subjection to leverage from the United States, China launched initiatives to encourage indigenous innovation, or what it called "independent intellectual property."[168] The government wished to shift the country's logo from "made in China" to "created in China." It particularly wished to become dominant in cutting-edge technology. The US-launched trade war increased its urgency.

The development of a strong intellectual property rights regime is an important component of China's innovation initiatives. In February 2006, the State Council issued "The National Medium- and Long-Term Plan for the Development of Science and Technology (2006–2020)," which stressed the need to build "innovative capacity" to become "an economic power." To encourage "indigenous innovation," the Plan stressed the need to "further perfect the nation's IPR system and create an agreeable legal environment that respects and protects IPR, increase public awareness of IPR, uplift the nation's IPR management level, enhance IPR protection, and crack down on various IPR piracy activities according to law."[169]

---

166 China National Intellectual Property Administration, "The 2018 High-Level Conference on IP for Countries along Belt and Road highlights Inclusiveness, Development, Cooperation, Mutual Benefit" (2018), at http://english.sipo.gov.cn/news/officialinformation/1131332.htm.

167 Sebastian Heilmann and Lea Shih, "The Rise of Industrial Policy in China, 1978–2012," *Harvard-Yenching Institute Working Paper Series* (2013): 1–24; Jean-Christophe Defraigne, "China's Industrial Policy," *Europe China Research and Advice Network (ECRAN)* (2014).

168 State Council, *Outline of the National Intellectual Property Strategy* (2008), stressing the concept of *zizhu zhishi chanquan*, which can be translated as "independent intellectual property". Peter Yu, "When the Chinese Intellectual Property System Hits 35," *Queen Mary Journal of Intellectual Property* 8 (2018): 3–14.

169 The full text is available at www.itu.int/en/ITU-D/Cybersecurity/Documents/National_Strategies_Repository/China_2006.pdf ("[d]espite the size of economy, our country is not yet an economic power primarily because of our weak innovative capacity").

In line with the Plan, patent filings soared in China (Figure 7.3). In the 1997–2011 period, patent filings in China increased by 3,245 percent. In 2019, China for the first time surpassed the United States as the top source of international patent applications filed through the Patent Cooperation Treaty, a rise of over 200-fold in just twenty years.[170] Huawei Technologies remained the world's leading filer of international patent applications for the third consecutive year and three other Chinese companies were in the top ten.[171] Among educational institutions, four Chinese universities appeared in the top ten filers in 2019, while there were none prior to 2018. Although the bulk of Chinese patents remain weak (for the reasons noted earlier), there is a concerted effort to enhance quality and strengthen protection, as reflected in increases in patent litigation (Figure 7.2) and royalty flows to China (Figure 7.4).[172]

China's development of intellectual property protection now forms part of its strategy to make China a global leader in innovation. Changes in China's five-year plans over time reflect China's shift in emphasis in its development strategy. Innovation rose from a relatively marginal focus in the 10th Five-Year Plan in 2001 when China joined the WTO to a dominant focus in its 13th Five-Year Plan in

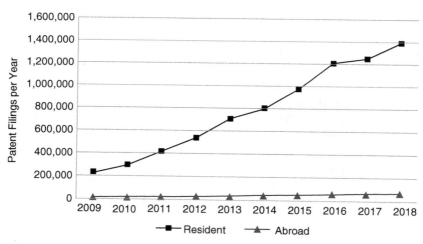

FIGURE 7.3 Patent filings by China[173]

[170] World Intellectual Property Organization, "China Becomes Top Filer of International Patents in 2019 Amid Robust Growth for WIPO's IP Servicers, Treaties and Finances, April 7, 2020.
[171] Ibid; Yu, "Building Intellectual Property Infrastructure Along China's Belt and Road," 275–325.
[172] Richard McGregor, *The Party: The Secret World of China's Communist Rulers* (New York: HaperCollins, 2010), 26–27, 72; Lily H. Fang, Josh Lerner, and Chaopeng Wu, "Intellectual Property Rights Protection, Ownership, and Innovation: Evidence from China," *The Review of Financial Studies* 30, no. 7 (2017): 2448, 2450 ("[E]ven among the most prolific Chinese patent filers, 81% do not have U.S. filings, and over 90% do not have Japanese or European filings.").
[173] Source: WIPO, "Statistical Country Profiles: China," www.wipo.int/ipstats/en/statistics/country_pro file/profile.jsp?code=CN.

2016.[174] In 2015, China launched its "Made in China 2025" policy to upgrade Chinese industry, which posed a new threat to Western technological dominance.[175] It did so through a combination of massively subsidizing domestic innovation, supporting acquisition of foreign firms and technology, and obtaining foreign technology through other means, from scouring open source materials to outright theft.[176]

Building from Germany's "Industry 4.0" project and US industry's "Industrial Internet" initiatives, the Made in China 2025 plan aims to link big data, automated analytic tools, and wireless sensor networks with industrial equipment for "smart manufacturing." It listed ten priority sectors – advanced information and communications technology; advanced automated machine tools and robotics; aerospace and aeronautics; high-tech shipping; rail transport; new energy vehicles; power equipment; agricultural machinery; new materials; and advanced medical devices and pharmaceuticals. These industries form part of what is envisaged as a fourth industrial revolution, which builds from digitalization, cloud computing, and other new technologies that are critical for efficiency, quality control, and product responsiveness. China's ability to collect data on its 1.4 billion citizens offers it a strategic advantage.

The plan set targets for China to become "self-sufficient" by raising the domestic content of core components and materials from below 20 percent in 2018 to 40 percent by 2020 and 70 percent by 2025.[177] It represents a new form of import substitution policies (grounded in local content targets), but with the further aim for China to obtain a "world-leading" position by 2049.[178] This symbolically important date coincides with the one-hundredth anniversary of the Chinese communist revolution. The policy complements the BRI, which is to be "a high-tech road" using Chinese technology.[179]

---

174 Thomas, *Assessing Intellectual Property Compliance*, 158 (noting mentions rising from twenty-six in its tenth Five-Year plan for 2001–2005; thirty-one in its 11th Five-Year plan; forty-nine in its 12th Five-Year plan; and seventy-one in its 13th Five-Year plan for 2016–2020).

175 *Notice on Issuing "Made in China" 2025*, State Council, Gua Fa [2–15] No. 28, May 8, 2015. Jost Wubbekke et al., *Made in China 2025: The Making of a High-tech Superpower and Consequences for Industrial Countries* (Berlin: Merics, 2016).

176 Andrew B. Kennedy and Darren J. Lim, "The Innovation Imperative: Technology and US-China Rivalry in the Twenty-First Century," *International Affairs* 94 (2018): 553 (categorizing in terms of "making," "transacting," and "taking").

177 According to a survey by the Chinese Ministry of Industry and Information Technology in 2018 covering 30 large firms and 130 critical basic materials, China lacks 32 percent of the key materials and relies on imports for another 52 percent of the materials. People's Network, "Deputy Minister of the Ministry of Industry and Information Technology: 32% of the 130 Key Basic Materials are Still Blank in China" [Gongxinbu Fubuzhang: 130 duozhong Guanjian Jichu Cailiao Zhong, 32% zai Zhongguo reng Kongbai], *The Paper*, July 17, 2018, www.thepaper.cn/newsDetail_forward_2271086.

178 Office of the United States Trade Representative, "Findings of the Investigation into China's Acts, Policies, and Practices Related to Technology Transfer, Intellectual Property, and Innovation Under Section 301 of the Trade Act of 1974," *Office of the United States Trade Representative*, March 22, 2018, 16.

179 Wang Yiwei, *The Belt and Road Initiative: What Will China Offer the World in its Rise* (Beijing: New World Press, 2016), 12.

258 The Cases of Brazil, India, and China

These policies entail long-term strategic planning, public goal setting, public–private coordination and mobilization, and massive state funding at the central and local levels through low-interest loans, capital injections, and other subsidies. To move up the value chain of production, China subsidizes high-tech sectors through new funding mechanisms such as the Advanced Manufacturing Fund and the National Integrated Circuit Fund.[180] It uses government procurement and licensing procedures to favor Chinese companies and facilitate Chinese "absorption and re-innovation" of foreign technology in support of Chinese self-sufficiency and economic dominance in these sectors.[181] It encourages private and state-owned companies to invest in foreign countries, and it financially supports their external acquisitions, so that they gain access to advanced technology, such as for the next generation of semiconductors.[182] In addition to direct acquisitions, China supports investment abroad in industrial parks and joint laboratories for research and development, and seeks to hire talent away from foreign companies.[183] In parallel, the government supports and encourages investment in high-tech startups, both in China and abroad, often linked to universities.[184] By 2018, the number of Chinese startups valued at over US$ 1 billion, known as "unicorns," was roughly the same as in the United States, and China could soon surpass it.[185] The government aims to stimulate policy innovation through experimentation at the central, provincial, and local levels, including through pilot projects.[186] In sum, the Middle Kingdom wants to avoid the middle-income trap and move up the value chain of production.[187] To do so, it massively supports investment in developing and acquiring advanced technologies. As depicted in Figure 7.4, China has significantly closed the gap with the United States in terms of royalty flows. While US companies received approximately 26.8 times the royalties of Chinese companies in 1998, the difference narrowed to just 1.8 times in 2017.

China's practices spurred a severe response from the United States, as well as defensive reactions in other advanced economies that will shape the future of the

---

[180] Wubbekke et al., "Made in China 2025," 7.

[181] Office of the USTR, *Section 301 Report*, 30 .

[182] Josh Horwitz, "Why the Semiconductor is Suddenly at the Heart of US-China Tech Tensions," *Quartz*, July 24, 2018.

[183] Office of the USTR, *Section 301 Report*, 79, 143, 181.

[184] Ibid., 143; Lee et al., "China's Economic Catch-Up," 494 ("the direct involvement of academic institutions in industrial business is called 'forward engineering'").

[185] The Economist, "The Geography of Technology," *Economist*, September 1, 2018, 22. Given the incentives for companies to claim they are technology-related in order to obtain subsidies, it is difficult to determine the number of these that are high-tech startups.

[186] Wubbekke et al., "Made in China 2025," 23–24.

[187] The controversial term "Middle Kingdom [Zhongguo]" has been used by China as a self-reference since the Zhou Dynasty three thousand years ago. Literally it means "the country at the centre [of the world]," and it reflects China's pride as the chosen country. See Wang Erh-min, "The Origin of the Name 'Zhongguo' and its Modern Interpretation [Zhongguo Mingcheng Suyuyan jiqi Jindai Quanshi]," in *Studies on History of Modern Chinese Thoughts [Zhongguo Jindai Sixiangshi Lun]*, ed. Wang Erh-min (Taipei: Huashi Publishing, 1977), 441–480.

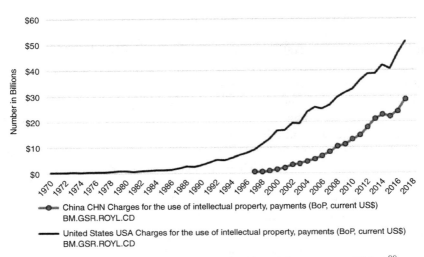

FIGURE 7.4 Royalty flows over time: The United States versus China[188]

international economic law order. Already the 2006 Plan for indigenous innovation was controversial, with some observers calling it a "blueprint for technology theft on a scale the world has never seen before."[189] In March 2018, the Office of the United States Trade Representative issued a 182-page Section 301 report that accused China and Chinese companies of appropriating US technology and intellectual property.[190] The Section 301 report recognized that China's ambitious "Made in China 2025" project aims to make China a global leader in strategic advanced technology industries. The United States raised four main accusations against China. First, it accused China of using investment authorizations and joint ventures to force US companies to transfer their technology to Chinese companies as a condition for gaining access to China's market. Second, and relatedly, it accused China of using its complex, multi-tiered administrative licensing regimes to force de facto technology transfer, thereby discriminating against US firms in favor of local ones. Third, it challenged state support of acquisitions of US technology from US companies as unreasonable and a threat to US technological leadership. Fourth, it accused China's People's Liberation Army and Chinese companies of cyber theft of sensitive commercial information, including by leveraging government intelligence for commercial gain. In each case, it highlighted the central role of not only the

[188] The World Bank, "Charges for the Use of Intellectual Property, Payments (BoP, Current US$) – China, United States," *World Bank DataBank*, https://data.worldbank.org/indicator/BM .GSR.ROYL.CD?locations=CN-US.
[189] James McGregor, *China's Drive for "Indigenous Innovation": A Web of Industrial Policies* (Washington, DC: U.S. Chamber of Commerce, 2010), 4.
[190] Office of the USTR, *Section 301 Report*.

Chinese state but also the Chinese Communist Party which is the ultimate power within the state.

In parallel, Europe and other advanced economies heightened review and restrictions on Chinese acquisition of high-tech companies and their technology.[191] The United States joined forces with the European Union and Japan to form a common front against Chinese practices that favored Chinese state-owned and private companies, including regarding technology licensing and transfers.[192] Under pressure from the United States and others, the Chinese government and media stopped referencing the plan under the "Made in China 2025" moniker. But China's ambitions to shift toward a high-tech, high productivity economy through public–private coordination continue.

Western concerns are not just economic. They are also strategic, including because some of this technology has military uses that could threaten US supremacy.[193] Were China to get the upper hand in core network technologies like 5G, it would not only access valuable data but also be better positioned to breach the integrity of networks that are central to modern economies. Similarly, were China to control the cobalt industry, which is required for most modern electronics, then "entire industries could come under the control of a rival geopolitical power."[194] These technologies and materials implicate economic supremacy and national security. The United States, in response, turned to shielding its technology through a combination of investment controls, export controls, prosecutions, and other sanctions, intended to stifle China's rise.[195]

Pursuant to the Section 301 investigation, the United States raised tariffs on $50 billion of Chinese imports in two tranches in July and August 2018, then another $200 billion in September, and threatened to cover all Chinese imports. In parallel, the United States filed a WTO complaint against China's discriminatory technology licensing requirements, which facilitates the transfer of foreign technology to their Chinese joint-venture partners.[196] Going further, the United States issued an arrest warrant for Huawei Technologies' chief financial officer Meng Wanzhou, the

[191]   Nikkei, "Chinese M&A Deals Face Wall as US and Europe Guard Tech," *Nikkei*, June 19, 2018 (referencing tightened national regulations and an EU framework for screening foreign direct investment in EU members, which entered into force in 2019).

[192]   USTR, *Joint Statement on Trilateral Meeting of the Trade Ministers of the United States, Japan, and the European Union*, September 25, 2018.

[193]   The Made in China 2025 plan promotes the "two-way transfer between military and civilian technologies." Anthea Roberts et al., "Geoeconomics: The Chinese Strategy of Technological Advancement and Cybersecurity," *Lawfare*, December 3, 2018 (quoting the plan).

[194]   James McBride, "Is 'Made in China 2025' a Threat to Global Trade," *Council on Foreign Relations*, August 2, 2018.

[195]   Anthea Roberts, Henrique Choer Moraes, and Victor Ferguson, "Toward a Geoeconomic Order in Trade and Investment," *Journal of International Economic Law* 22 (2019): 655 (on "shielding" and "stifling").

[196]   *China – Certain Measures Concerning the Protection of Intellectual Property Rights, Request for Consultations by the United States*, IP/D/38; WT/DS542/1, March 26, 2018.

daughter of the company's founder, who was apprehended in December 2018 while she was changing flights in Canada, for dodging US sanctions against Iran and for the theft of technology.[197] Then, in August 2020, the administration announced it would ban the use of popular Chinese apps such as TikTok and WeChat.[198] These actions were shots across the bow to counter China's ambitions.

Once more, US threats could induce Chinese reforms to crack down on cyber theft, remove discriminatory aspects of its technology licensing regime, and eliminate provisions that the United States claims entail "forced technology transfers" to a joint venture partner as part of investment approvals – what others call "trading market for technology."[199] For example, China's new Foreign Investment Law enacted in 2019 contained provisions that prohibit forced technology transfer, provide better intellectual property protection for foreign investors, and grant pre-establishment rights for investors. The 2020 US–China Economic and Trade Agreement formalized these changes as treaty commitments, together with other provisions that China had already codified regarding trade secrets and others that it was contemplating but had yet to enact.[200] Yet, what matters will not be formal law – which is subject to interpretation in implementation or malign neglect – but actual practice. The "phase 1" deal called for greater enforcement, but as Figure 7.2 shows, trends in China already move in this direction, and, in any case, statistics on "number of enforcement actions" can be easy to game.[201]

China remains far behind the United States, Europe, and Japan in technology. To the extent that Made in China 2025 is only a top-down project based on quantitative targets and campaigns leading to inefficient spending and accrued debt, and does not harness bottom-up forces, it could lead to overcapacity and increased credit risks to the Chinese economy. Thus, in the end, it may not compete successfully with the more bottom-up, dynamic capitalist system of Silicon Valley and the West. But in that case, one might ask, why not let the two systems compete instead of imposing a US "market economy" model on China?

The underlying tensions and conflict now appear destined to continue, especially given the dual use and critical network aspects of many leading technologies. They

[197] Kate Conger, "Huawei Executive Took Part in Sanctions Fraud, Prosecutors Say," *New York Times*, December 7, 2018.

[198] James Palmer, "Why Is the United States Effectively Banning WeChat and TikTok?," *Foreign Policy*, August 7, 2020.

[199] The concept of "forced technology transfer" is contentious because companies agree to it as part of their investment into China. They could forego investing if they found the arrangement to be contrary to company interests. Daniel Gros, "Are China's Trade Practices Really Unfair?," *Project Syndicate*, December 5, 2018; Lee et al., "China's Economic Catch-Up," 493.

[200] Chapter 1 of the agreement addresses "Intellectual Property," and Chapter 2 "Technology Transfer."

[201] Mark Cohen, the first IP attaché at the U.S. embassy in Beijing, concludes, "The situation was predictable: late-term administrations may ... be tempted to condone campaign-style IP enforcement, which can generate impressive enforcement statistics but have limited deterrence or long-term sustainability." Mark Cohen, "The Phase 1 IP Agreement: Its Fans and Discontents," *China IPR*, January 21, 2020.

are "geoeconomic" in nature in that economic and political security concerns and rivalry become salient.[202] The US ban on the sale of parts and software to the Chinese telecommunications giant ZTE in April 2018 on national security grounds, which all but shut down the company, and the US placement of Huawei and other Chinese companies on the Entity List for export controls in 2019 and 2020, which effectively can blacklist them, illustrate the risks to China of its technological lag. Following the direct intervention of President Trump, the ban was lifted after ZTE paid a US$1 billion fine, and the United States has deployed the Entity List as a bargaining chip that can be modified or tailored to permit critical sales. Yet, for China, the threats make clear its need to develop its innovation policy so that its companies no longer depend on foreign technology.

V. A CHANGING TRANSNATIONAL ECONOMIC LAW ORDER

When China joined the WTO in 2001, it was a recipient of legal norms largely designed by the United States that were incorporated into the world trading system. It became a diligent student of that system and gradually and increasingly engaged with it to defend its interests, as Chapter 6 showed. As China grew economically more powerful, it gained confidence in its own pragmatic economic model, and it recursively began to challenge the US-led legal order with new initiatives. Domestically, it aimed to boost economic growth through state-led industrial policy, increasingly carried out by reorganized state-owned enterprises, as well as private companies linked more closely with the party and the state.

Although China officially recognizes the importance of the WTO, and occasionally even holds itself out as the champion of the multilateral trading system,[203] China has been quietly expanding its network of strategic partnerships and bilateral agreements behind the scene (just as have the United States and European Union), which expands its options if the multilateral system collapses. Incrementally and pragmatically, it is developing a form of trade and economic law governance that puts state-led finance and state-subsidized infrastructure development, combined with domestic innovation policy, at the center. In the geoeconomic competition of the 21st century, it offers a rival model of economic integration and governance.

China's approach is unlike the US and European models, which build regional and global rules and institutions based on legal templates and transplants of domestic laws.[204] China's model builds from pragmatic, incremental development policy grounded in infrastructure development, innovation, and webs of memoranda of

---

[202]   Roberts et al., "Toward a Geoeconomic Order."
[203]   President Xi's Speech at the World Trade Forum, Davos, Switzerland, January 17, 2017.
[204]   For a classic account of economic integration through law in terms of different states of integration from a free trade area to a customs union to a common market to an economic union, which would be reflected in the trajectory of the European Union, Bela Balassa, *The Theory of Economic Integration: An Introduction* (London: Palgrave, 1963), 1–3.

understanding, contracts, and treaties. China is exporting a developmental model through the Belt and Road Initiative, facilitating some relocation of labor-intensive sectors abroad while Chinese industry moves up the value chain of production. It is a model that offers an alternative to US-built and US-dominated institutions. It builds from, and layers on, existing international economic law and institutions as part of the changing ecology of international economic governance involving increasing geoeconomic competition between China and the United States.

China is not abandoning institutions such as the WTO. Rather, it is positioning itself as their defender while combatting Western dominance within them. In parallel, it is creating new options for itself and other countries by fashioning a network of infrastructure projects with supporting treaties and institutions that, in combination, are creating a Sino-centric transnational legal order for trade and investment. China and Chinese professionals now draw from the trade-related legal capacity and different dimensions of institutional change that they built and adapted for the WTO system (Chapter 6). In sum, China has mastered the rules of the game in the WTO while building a new Sino-centric order in parallel. For China, it is not a question of either-or, but each at once.

As the WTO's authority declines, China's development of a new Sino-centric economic order assumes greater salience. Indeed, while analysts earlier found that the WTO constituted an indirect "amendment to the Chinese constitution," China directly incorporated the Belt and Road Initiative into the Constitution of the Communist Party of China in October 2017.[205] The two Chinese constitutions are distinct, one for the state and one for the party, with the latter clearly becoming most important under President Xi. In each case, the analysis captures transnational links between domestic and international economic governance. With the former, the link involved a Western-driven international institution (the WTO) implicating internal Chinese governance. With the latter, the link involves internal Chinese governance implicating international legal ordering (the BRI). The shift in these links reflects the interaction of changes within China and the transnational legal ordering of trade and investment.

The Belt and Road Initiative represents an open architecture since any country can join it, in contrast to the US and European club model. Under the club model, the United States and European Union aim to build new rules through excluding those outside of the club, only to invite them subsequently on their terms.[206] That was the model for the GATT and then the WTO with its "single package" of

[205] Compare Tom Ginsburg, "The Judicialization of Administrative Governance: Causes, Consequences and Limits," in *Administrative Law and Governance in Asia*, eds. Tom Ginsburg and Albert H. Y. Chen (Abingdon: Routledge, 2009) 10 (on the WTO and the Constitution of the People's Republic of China); and Macaes, *Belt and Road*, 41 (on the Belt and Road Initiative and the Constitution of the Communist Party of China).

[206] Robert Keohane and Joseph Nye, "Between Centralization and Fragmentation: The Club Model of Multilateral Cooperation and Problems of Democratic Legitimacy," *John F. Kennedy School of Government Harvard University Faculty Research Working Papers Series* (2001).

agreements incorporating intellectual property and trade in services. China joined the WTO and its covered agreements without having negotiated them and, in addition, had to make China-specific commitments. Similarly, it is the model for the US network of bilateral trade and investment agreements built on common US templates, as well as the abandoned TPP. Were China to have joined the TPP, it would have had to agree to terms already in place and likely once more had to make additional commitments. The European Union long epitomized the club model by requiring massive internal legal and institutional changes for countries to join it.

In contrast, under the Chinese model, international law plays more of a background and complementary ordering role involving "soft" mechanisms of coordination through Memoranda of Understanding and informal state-to-state negotiation to resolve disputes, as in a "relational contract" arrangement, but operating in the shadow of China's economic and political clout.[207] Under such an arrangement, the ongoing relationship is more important for the parties than the formal legal commitments; the contract serves as a coordinating device that the parties can adjust and work around as new challenges arise in their commercial relationship. In this way, China hopes to build ties with political and economic leaders and "shift the center of geopolitical gravity away from the US and back to Eurasia."[208] Under the Belt and Road Initiative and China's web of trade and investment treaties, China is largely mimicking and repurposing Western models of contract, commercial arbitration, investment protection, and trade liberalization, while building on Western norms of intellectual property protection through patents, copyrights, and trademarks. However, the repurposed model is based not on a neoliberal one grounded in legal commitments as much as a state-led, pragmatic, coordinative governance model.

In complement to the Belt and Road Initiative, China has spent massively on innovation through a broad range of policies to support the development and acquisition of advanced technologies, including through enhanced intellectual property protection that once more builds from Western models for Chinese purposes. It is seeking to make a "great leap forward" to become a "manufacturing superpower" and an "internet superpower" through state-led and state-coordinated innovation policies. In this way, it can be at the forefront of a fourth industrial revolution that combines big data, automation, and new technologies critical for advanced manufacturing.

Although China's free trade and investment agreements started as rather modest, innocuous deals, when these agreements are coupled with the development of the

---

[207]   As a Beijing law professor told Shaffer, "the BRI is still a political initiative rather than a rule-based, rule-of-law one." Telephone interview, March 22, 2020. On relational contracts, Macaulay, "Non-Contractual Relations;" Macneil, *The Relational Theory of Contract*.

[208]   Yiwei, *The Belt and Road Initiative* (a book by a Chinese professor at Renmin University in Beijing that reflects views from China's leadership). Shambaugh views China as building a "parallel global institutional architecture to the postwar Western order," such as through the Asian Infrastructure Investment Bank based in Beijing. David Shambaugh, *China's Future* (Hoboken: John Wiley & Sons, 2016), 162–163.

Belt and Road Initiative through state-backed loans, investments, and construction projects, one detects the rise of a new transnational order based on premises different from the traditional US-centric Washington consensus. As for development assistance, the Chinese model (when using its own development banks) removes the stringent good-governance conditions attached to loans granted by international development banks. In the area of trade agreements, although China calls for the substantial reduction of trade barriers on goods, commitments on services tend to be rather shallow, while environmental protection and labor rights are left out.[209] The Chinese agreements also tend to avoid new issues, such as US-sought disciplines on state-owned enterprises and competition, or substantive rules governing the digital sphere (such as banning data localization requirements). As to investment, China has abandoned its earlier position of resisting investor–state arbitration and begun to grant more substantive rights to investors, such as pre-establishment rights and the use of "negative lists" (where investments in all sectors are permitted unless specifically listed). This policy change contrasts with the growing resistance to investor protection in developed countries, and it reflects China's shifting position from a major recipient to among the world's largest providers of outbound investment.

When it comes to values, the Chinese trade law model formally can be viewed as "value-free" and "non-ideological" since it purports to be non-intrusive in domestic economic governance – reflecting the Bandung principles of "non-interference," "sovereignty," and "self-determination." It can thus be contrasted with the labor, human rights, and environmental prescriptions included in US and EU trade agreements and the conditionalities set forth in loans from US and European-dominated Bretton Woods institutions. As a high-level WTO official states, "the U.S. also sold ideals, while China is only selling stuff; they are merchants, not missionaries."[210] This is not to say that the Western model was centered only on values as opposed to interests, since the United States and Europe always have pursued their interests. Nonetheless, under China's model, there is no promulgation of particular values such as human rights and democracy, or of a particular role for government in the market.[211]

---

[209] China's potential role in environmental governance is more a function of its goal to be a global leader in clean energy technologies rather than environmental law.

[210] Interview, Geneva, July 5, 2017.

[211] Compare Samuel Huntington, *The Clash of Civilizations and the Remaking of the World Order* (New York: Touchstone, 1996) (the United States is "a missionary nation," proselytizing "Western values"); Graham Allison, "China vs America: Managing the Next Clash of Civilizations," *Foreign Affairs*, September/October 2017, 83–84 (contrasting China's focus on "order"); Samm Sacks, "Beijing Wants to Rewrite the Rules of the Internet," *The Atlantic*, June 18, 2018. Nadège Rolland presents a table contrasting the characterization of the Chinese model focused on development, value-free policies, sovereignty, internal uniformity, and state-led policy, to a Western model based on democracy, individualism, liberalism, external harmonization, and rules. Rolland, *China's Eurasian Century?*, 130. In the Chinese model, China is clearly "uncomfortable with the idea of democratization" that it rejects as "Western values," and more comfortable working with authoritarian leaders that demand non-interference in domestic affairs. Ibid., 180.

However, China too is espousing values when it uses terms such as "mutual respect," "win-win development," and "harmony" as part of a "community of shared destiny," as it aims to accommodate and shield authoritarian rule from internal and external critique.[212] Its conditions require others to recognize China's internal sovereignty, and, in particular, political recognition of its "One-China" policy and silence on the "three T's" (Taiwan, Tibet, and Tiananmen), repression of Muslims in Xianjing, and any other Chinese internal policies. These agreements can serve, in parallel, to support authoritarian leaders to China's liking, who, in turn, defer to China. Authoritarian governments are keen to adopt Chinese practices to control the internet and ensure public order, such as through data localization requirements, cybersecurity laws, and the adoption of Chinese surveillance and censoring technology. In exchange, they will permit Chinese companies to collect data on their citizens that the companies can use and market to provide themselves with an edge in the data-driven economy. China is investing significantly to exercise greater discursive power in defining sovereigntist norms for the international system, especially to combat what it views as Western ideologies of liberal democracy and civil and political rights that the United States has deployed to uphold US predominance "on the global stage" and to place the Chinese government on the defensive, both internationally and internally.[213] China aims to "break the Western moral advantage" and to focus on "development rights," which implicitly takes account of its successful developmental model.[214]

Nonetheless, despite expending significant resources on developing Confucius institutes and diffusing official views through the global media, including through free provision of the English language editions of the *China Daily*, the *Global Times*, and other publications, China is not winning the soft power game. China's hardline positions regarding the "South China Sea," Hong Kong, Xianjing, and other issues have triggered a decline of external public perceptions of China in other countries.[215] As regards deliberations in the WTO, in the words of a WTO insider, China can be "tone deaf."[216] It can go through the motions of consultations to search for "consensus," but there is no sense that it has "heard other parties." "One cannot just bring practices that work in Beijing to Geneva and be successful." The United States may have lost soft power under the Trump administration, but China has yet to harness it convincingly.

The question arises whether countries considered to be US allies must choose between China and the United States in their economic relations. These policy choices will engage constituencies within countries in their own internal political

---

212 William Callahan, "China's 'Asia Dream': The Belt Road Initiative and the New Regional Order," *Asian Journal of Comparative Politics* 1 (2016): 226, 231–232.
213 Rolland, "China's Vision," 26.
214 Ibid., 5–6, 35 (citing Li Ziguo).
215 Laura Silver, Kat Devlin, and Christine Huang, "People Around the Globe are Divided in their Opinions of China," *Pew Research Center*, September 30, 2019.
216 Interview, Geneva, June 29, 2017.

struggles, which, in turn, will shape the future of the transnational legal order for trade. The United States is expending significant political, economic, and diplomatic capital to counter the Chinese-led economic order which it, at times, appears to view as an existential threat. In 2018, Vice President Pence gave a major speech on China, dubbed the equivalent of the Truman Doctrine on containment of the Soviet Union. Pence wished to rally allies to isolate and combat China's authoritarianism, mercantilism, and aggression, including its so-called "debt-trap diplomacy" and "Orwellian system premised on controlling every aspect of human life."[217] Secretary of State Michael Pompeo followed with what the Trump administration billed as a "major China policy statement" on the China "threat" to the American "way of life" at the Nixon library in July 2020.[218] The United States renegotiated NAFTA to include a provision permitting it to withdraw from the agreement if a partner pursues an agreement with a "non-market country," which clearly targets China. The United States would like to extend this condition through agreements with others.[219]

The United States might be more successful with its immediate neighbors, but even they do not view this provision as a significant constraint on expanding trade relations with China where tariff rates are already low. Moreover, US allies in Asia, Latin America, and even Europe are pursuing free trade and investment agreements with China. Chile – arguably the US top economic law ally in Latin America – already has a free trade and investment agreement with China. Greece, Italy, and Luxembourg have formally joined the BRI. Most countries continue to work with Huawei, despite considerable US pressure, although there are signs of change in some OECD countries. The economies of US allies in Asia, such as Australia, Singapore, and South Korea, depend on good relations with China. To quote conservative Prime Minister Scott Morrison, Australia aims to "maintain our unique relationships with the United States, our most important ally, and China, our comprehensive strategic partner, in good order, by rejecting the binary narrative of their strategic competition and instead valuing and nurturing the unconflicted benefit of our close association" with both.[220] While some in the United States will contend that countries working with both orders are "non-aligned" (recalling the rhetoric of an earlier era), third countries wish to retain a political alliance with

---

[217] The Hudson Institute, "Remarks by Vice President Pence on the Administration's Policy Toward China," *The White House*, October 4, 2018.

[218] Michael Pompeo, "Communist China and the Free World's Future," U.S. Department of State, July 23, 2020.

[219] Office of the United States Trade Representative, *United States–Mexico–Canada Agreement*, Chapter 32, Article 10 (2018). Ironically, through the 2020 US–China Economic and Trade Agreement, the United States was the first among the three countries to fall under this clause. China's purchase commitments for agricultural, energy, and other products (in chapter 6 of the agreement) should favor US over Canadian and Mexican producers, as might certain specific commitments China made (in chapter 3) to accept US agricultural products under its sanitary and phytosanitary regulations.

[220] Prime Minister of Australia, *Speech – Lowy Lecture "In Our Interest,"* October 3, 2019.

the United States while not severing their economic ties with China.[221] US allies resent being pressed to choose and will strive to avoid doing so.

China's hub-and-spokes system, combining private and public international law through loans, contract, and contract dispute resolution institutions, coupled with trade, and investment agreements, offers the potential of creating an expansive, cross-regional, informal, rival Sino-centric economic order. For this reason, it is illusory to think that the US-China trade war will "be easy to win."[222] Although commentators suggest that the trade war could split the world into competing trade blocs and a new geoeconomic variant of the Cold War, most countries will work to navigate the tensions between the United States and China so that they maintain strong economic ties with both. The difficulty of this navigation is particularly apparent in the European Union, which, in 2020, labeled China both "a cooperation partner with whom the EU has closely aligned objectives ... and a systemic rival promoting alternative models of governance."[223] Thus, if a new Cold War deepens, it will be quite different than that with the autarchic former Soviet Union. Such a scenario, nonetheless, could make an empty shell of the WTO-led multilateral trading system that the United States erected following the end of the (first) Cold War. The legal architecture for the global economy has shifted from a centralized legal order to a decentralized ecology of coexisting and competing transnational institutions.

---

[221] It is a "big ask" that would be very "painful," in the words of Singapore Prime Minister Lee Hsien Loong. Choo Yun Ting, "Asian Countries Would Be Very Unhappy If They Have to Choose between US and China: PM Lee Hsien Loong," *The Straits Times*, October 6, 2019.

[222] An American lawyer who worked for a large Chinese company told Shaffer that the American reaction to China "reminds me of the U.K. in the 1950s. The US is still thinking we are the colonial power. We wish to go back. It is a nostalgic and nationalist reaction that won't help us (the US) maintain our competitiveness." Telephone interview, March 23, 2020.

[223] European Commission and HR/VP contribution to the European Council, *EU-China — A strategic outlook* (March 12, 2019).

PART III

The Future of the Transnational Legal Order for Trade

8

Why the US Disenchantment? Managing the Interface

"Now the US has become a wrecking ball to the system," a WTO insider tells me. "It's like Gotham City where the Joker took over."[1] In the words of the European Union's ambassador to the WTO, the United States is "walking away from the system it largely built up itself; the architect of global governance is taking time off."[2] It is a sea change in Geneva and for the world.

To understand this change in the transnational legal order for trade, we must turn from these three emerging powers to their impact on trade politics and narratives within the United States. The links between the rise of emerging powers and US trade politics is highly contested, involving competing narratives and their policy repercussions. Nonetheless, there has been a general rhetorical shift in US politics on trade, the WTO, and its dispute settlement system, in particular because of China's rise, but also because of emerging economies generally. This shift facilitated the election in the United States of an economic nationalist whose administration became the "wrecking ball." The United States paradoxically became the revisionist power. It aimed to upend the trade legal order out of frustration with the constraints placed on it because of emerging powers' use of WTO rules and negotiating principles (Section I), which created opportunities for new, competing narratives in the United States about trade and investment (Section II), which helped catalyze new US trade strategies (Section III). Counterfactually, why else would the United States frontally challenge the WTO and its dispute settlement system? These changes raise the subsidiary questions of what's at stake (Section IV) and how to manage the interface between economic systems (Section V).

I. WHY THE US DISENCHANTMENT WITH THE WTO

Before we assess US disenchantment with the WTO, we make a broader point illustrated by a comparative one. The broader point is that state reactions to emerging

[1] Interview, Member of the WTO Secretariat, Geneva, June 30, 2017.
[2] Interview, EU Ambassador, Marc Van Heukelven, Geneva, June 30, 2017.

powers' impact on the WTO depend on their contexts. The discrepant responses of the United States and European Union illustrate the point. Both the United States and European Union were critical to the WTO's creation. Both saw their power decline economically and within the WTO. Both have been frustrated over similar issues that this section addresses. Yet, the European Union and United States responded to emerging powers' rise and effect on the WTO legal order in dramatically different ways. While the United States attacked the WTO and neutered its dispute settlement system, the European Union became its greatest defender. Because of the US response, the European Union's formation of alliances became much more complicated. On the one hand, it works with China, Brazil, and others to preserve WTO institutions. It even created a new coalition with China to save the WTO appellate process through creating an interim mechanism that, as of July 2020, had twenty-two members, in addition to the EU's twenty-seven members. On the other hand, the European Union joins forces with the United States and Japan to pressure China to rein in its form of state capitalism and state-led innovation policies.

This US–EU divergence raises the comparative question of why the European Union responded differently. The explanation becomes clearer when we address the competition between different narratives within the United States regarding economic globalization supported by WTO rules. For now, I highlight three reasons. First, the political reaction against trade arguably has been less severe in the European Union because inequality is less gaping there, in large part because European governments provide greater social safety nets and economic adjustment assistance for citizens.[3] Second, the political reaction has been starker in the United States because it is the geopolitical hegemon whose predominance China threatens. Although the European Union is an economic and regulatory power, it is not a military or geopolitical one. The European Union is thus less directly affected by a hegemonic transition in favor of China and other emerging powers. Third, historically and culturally, Europe experienced the Second World War in a much more searing way than the United States. The project of creating a European economic community historically is closely linked to ensuring peace in Europe through tying Germany into a broader economic community. Similarly, it is closely linked to creating a system of multilateral economic governance through the GATT and the WTO. The European Union's predecessor, the European Coal and Steel Community, was proposed just two years after the GATT's creation, and the European Union was formed just two years before the WTO. Multilateral economic governance and trade liberalization are thus a much greater part of Europe's identity, and European leaders have viewed them in security terms.[4] These

---

[3] For example, European flexicurity policies (especially in Scandinavia) combine labor market flexibility, lifelong learning, active labor market policy, and social security. Gregory Shaffer, "Retooling Trade Agreements for Social Inclusion," *University of Illinois Law Review* 1 (2019): at 23–24. Similar points could be made about Japan.

[4] I thank Anthea Roberts for stressing this point.

differences reinforce this book's argument that one cannot fully understand change at the international level without studying recursive interactions between the international and domestic planes that drive the settlement and unsettlement of transnational legal orders.

To turn to the United States, there are social and political divisions within it, just as in Brazil, India, and China, with which the transnational legal ordering of trade interacts. Its vehement response to the WTO in large part is tied to the election of an economic nationalist in an extremely close vote.[5] Nonetheless, US dissatisfaction with the WTO preceded President Trump and will continue after him. First, even before his upset election over Hillary Clinton, many US officials felt that the market access that the United States and China provide had become unbalanced, especially given China's emergence as a global trading power. As Chapter 6 addressed, because US bound tariff rates are substantially lower than China's, the Obama administration pressed China, along with Brazil and India, to cut their tariffs in key industrial sectors, preferably to (or near) zero percent, in order to ensure better symmetry. Yet, under traditional GATT negotiating principles of reciprocity, the United States would have to "pay" to obtain these "concessions" through making new market access commitments of an equivalent amount. The United States, however, lacked negotiating leverage because US tariffs were already low. To US consternation, China, Brazil, and India referenced not only the traditional GATT reciprocity principle but also the principle of special and differential treatment for developing countries, which the Doha round mandate explicitly incorporated. Through invocation of these principles, they thwarted US pressure for them to "catch up" by making greater market access commitments, and the United States walked away from the negotiating round. As the case studies show, enhanced trade policy capacity within state institutions and the private sector was critical for their strengthened roles in these negotiations.

Second, in parallel, China and other emerging powers deployed trade law capacity to use the WTO dispute settlement system to challenge politically sensitive US practices under WTO law. In particular, they successfully challenged US use of "trade remedy" laws to constrain the US ability to raise tariffs and protect US industry from foreign import competition in line with WTO rules. The WTO Appellate Body interpreted the applicable legal provisions "to clarify" their meaning, as provided in Article 3 of the WTO Dispute Settlement Understanding, and it was persuaded by complainant countries' legal arguments in a series of cases. In total, over 38 percent of Appellate Body decisions issued through 2019 concerned antidumping, countervailing duty, or safeguard claims, which rises to 51 percent

---

5   President Trump won by less than 80,000 votes combined in the states of Michigan, Pennsylvania, and Wisconsin, representing 0.06 percent of the 137 million votes cast in the national election, which tipped the US Electoral College in his favor. In contrast, Hillary Clinton won the popular vote by nearly 2.9 million votes, or 2.1 percent of the popular vote. Had Clinton been elected president, US policy would have been much less nationalist and much more globally engaged.

when including subsidies claims.[6] Many of these decisions spurred vociferous US protests that the Appellate Body had exceeded its authority and exhibited anti-US bias.[7] Social scientists view these laws, in part, as providing political safety valves that afford protection and adjustment for import-competing industries, while maintaining support for the overall trading system, although the diagnostic rationale for the laws is disputed. The United States found it particularly difficult to apply these laws to China given Appellate Body interpretations of WTO requirements, fueling further political backlash within the United States.

Here are three examples of ambiguous technical provisions in WTO agreements applying to import relief law where the Appellate Body rendered decisions against US practices and in favor of China and other WTO members. First, Article 17.6 of the WTO Agreement on Antidumping provides that "where the [WTO] panel finds that a relevant provision of the Agreement admits of more than one permissible interpretation," it shall defer to the national authority's interpretation "if it rests upon one of those permissible interpretations." This sentence was included on US insistence. Yet, that same provision also provides, on the insistence of the European Union, that "the panel should interpret the relevant provisions of the Agreement in accordance with customary rules of interpretation of public international law," for which, according to a civil law approach, there is only one correct interpretation. Second, Article 2.4 of that agreement provides that "a fair comparison" shall be made between "export" and "normal" prices to determine if there is dumping, without any provision clarifying whether the longstanding US practice of "zeroing" is prohibited because it does not constitute a "fair comparison." And third, the WTO Agreement on Subsidies and Countervailing Measures provides, in Article 1, that the agreement applies to "a financial contribution by a government or any public body," without defining what is a "public body," and, in particular, whether the term encompasses a state-owned enterprise. In each case, the United States lost the interpretative contest.

The United States was much more critical of Appellate Body decisions on import relief measures than Europe, arguably (once more) because the United States lacks a comparable social safety net and adjustment programs, such that import relief laws play a more politically salient role in offering protection from imports that can trigger job losses and suppress wages. As a WTO high-level secretariat official noted, "the United States has always pushed the window on antidumping," but it "is not developing other political safety valves such as trade adjustment, unlike Europe."[8] US politics, reflecting a dominant "market" ideology, constrained US expansion of domestic assistance and retraining programs and use of WTO flexibilities to protect

---

[6] Author's count.

[7] The United States lays out its array of charges against the Appellate Body in United States Trade Representative, *Report on the Appellate Body of the World Trade Organization* (February 2020), 81–120.

[8] Interview, Secretariat Official, Geneva, June 29, 2017. Another high-level WTO official told me, "the biggest problem is that no one in the US wants to spend money on labor market adjustment." Interview, Geneva, June 29, 2017.

vulnerable communities. Had the United States responded to the trade liberalization that it advocated with a more expansive social safety net and greater trade adjustment assistance, the transnational legal order for trade would likely be more stable today.[9] Once more, US domestic law interacted with international trade law, but this time in terms of what the United States did not do. Because the United States failed to respond *recursively* to international trade law by enhancing the US social safety net and trade adjustment programs to ensure more equally distributed benefits from trade, it created opportunities for a political candidate advocating protectionist policies – a self-proclaimed "tariff man."[10]

Third, WTO rules do not cover issues that were not contemplated when the WTO was created in 1995, over a quarter of a century ago. In the words of the European Union's ambassador to the WTO, "the WTO is an aging bedrock that has difficulty modernizing."[11] For example, many find that WTO rules have not adequately addressed new technologies important for US and European trade. Thus, when China introduced regulations that require companies to use local servers and hand over source code, WTO rules were unhelpful to combat these restrictions. Moreover, although China's Accession Protocol prohibited "forced technology transfer" through government licenses, most of these transfers occur in the context of joint venture negotiations that are required for a foreign company to operate in many sectors in China. These "private" negotiations are not covered in WTO agreements, but rather were the subject of a US–China bilateral investment treaty negotiated during the Obama administration, which the Trump administration abandoned.[12]

Fourth, the United States complains that WTO rules are currently "not sufficient" to address the state's intrusive role in China's economy, which violates the spirit of the WTO's "open, market-oriented approach."[13] In this vein, Mark Wu argues that WTO rules are inadequate because they were designed for countries with market economies, whereas the Chinese government intervenes massively through formal and informal state command.[14] President Xi's policies of strengthening China's state-owned

9   Edward Alden, *Failure to Adjust: How Americans Got Left Behind in the Global Economy* (Lanham: Rowman & Littlefield, 2016).
10 Natasha Bach, "Trump Warns China He is a 'Tariff Man' if Trade Negotiations Falter," *Fortune*, December 4, 2018.
11 Interview, Ambassador Van Heukelven, June 30, 2017.
12 Alan Sykes, "The Law and Economics of 'Forced' Technology Transfer (FTT) and its Implications for Trade and Investment Policy (and the U.S.-China Trade War)," Stanford Law Paper Series No. 544 (2020).
13 USTR, *2017 USTR Report to Congress on China's WTO Compliance* (January 2018), 2; USTR, *2019 USTR Report to Congress on China's WTO Compliance* (March 2019), 6; Ambassador Dennis Shea, "The WTO: Looking Forward," *Center for Strategic and International Studies*, October 12, 2018, www.csis.org/events/wto-looking-forward ("We need to recognize that the economic system of China is not compatible with the WTO norms;" and "the WTO as currently constituted is not equipped to deal with China").
14 Mark Wu, "The 'China, Inc.' Challenge to Global Trade Governance," *Harvard International Law Journal* 57 (2016): 261–324; Mark Wu, "The WTO and China's Unique Economic Structure," in *Regulating the Visible Hand?: The Institutional Implications of Chinese State Capitalism*, eds. Benjamin L. Liebman and Curtis J. Milhaupt (Oxford: Oxford University Press, 2015), 350 ("The

enterprises exacerbated these concerns. For example, the WTO Appellate Body found that state-owned enterprises may be deemed "public bodies" under the WTO Agreement on Subsidies and Countervailing Measures only if they exercise government functions, citing public international law texts on state responsibility in support. However, even Chinese state-owned enterprises without explicit governmental authority are often required to provide loans and promote the development of particular economic sectors. Although the 2015 Guiding Opinions on Deepening SOE Reform stipulates that state-owned enterprises shall "serve the national strategy and implement national industrial policy,"[15] in many cases, the government is not transparent so that it can be difficult to prove particular state-owned enterprises are acting as public bodies. Some commentators contend that existing WTO provisions are sufficient to challenge Chinese policies, but the United States never brought broad cases against Chinese practices, and rather turned to unilateral action.[16]

Fifth, the United States contends that China violates basic rule-of-law norms that limit its ability to challenge Chinese practices. For example, it maintains that China punishes firms that cooperate with the United States in bringing WTO cases.[17] It also charges that China files tit-for-tat antidumping investigations against its firms when it commences an investigation of Chinese products.[18] It likewise finds that China's law and regulatory practices are so nontransparent that it is extremely costly, if not impossible, to build a factual case for many WTO complaints. The Chinese government's aim, it maintains, is to undermine enforcement of WTO rules against China. Chinese officials deny such practices, but others claim that China's coercive and non-transparent practices violate the spirit of WTO law.

Finally, security concerns further beset the US-China trade relationship because China has massively subsidized research and development in leading industries, some of which could be used for military purposes, threatening US military dominance in Asia. Even besides technology's dual use, China's rise in leading sectors threatens US economic dominance, which – the United States contends – has a security dimension, including because they grant access to data on US citizens. These changing economic and strategic contexts shape debates over US trade and investment policy, such that US officials now claim that WTO rules asymmetrically

---

Party-state's desire to preserve its unique political economy is threatening to shatter the liberal [WTO] project of building a strong multilateral trading regime. In the end, both cannot stand").

[15] Central Committee of the Communist Party of China, State Council, "Guiding Opinions on Deepening SOE Reform," *China Government Network*, August 24, 2015, www.gov.cn/zhengce/2015–09/13/content_2930440.htm (accessed on February 22, 2020).

[16] Jennifer Hillman, "The Best Way to Address China's Unfair Policies and Practices Is through a Big, Bold Multilateral Case at the WTO," testimony at Hearing on US Tools to Address Chinese Market Distortions, US-China Economic and Review Security Commission, June 8, 2018; Weihuan Zhou and Henry Gao, "China's SOE Reform: Using WTO Rules to Build a Market Economy," *International and Comparative Law Quarterly*, 68, no. 4 (2019): 977–1022.

[17] Informal discussions with US and European officials and practicing lawyers.

[18] USTR, "In Annual Report, Decries China's Retaliatory Use of Trade Remedies," *Inside U.S. Trade*, January 9, 2017.

help China. As a result, the Trump administration maintained that permitting China's entry into the WTO on the terms agreed was a mistake.[19]

II. COMPETING NARRATIVES ABOUT TRADE AND INVESTMENT IN THE UNITED STATES

These US frustrations with China's and other emerging powers' use of WTO law combined with structural changes that affected US legal, economic, and strategic dominance. Together they catalyzed shifts in US domestic narratives about trade that facilitated the election of an economic nationalist (Donald Trump) over an establishment candidate (Hillary Clinton). In their work, Anthea Roberts and Nicolas Lamp identify a series of narratives about economic globalization in "the West."[20] Most of the examples come from the United States given the US challenge to the WTO and its importance for economic globalization's future. Four narratives gained salience in US political discourse that present major challenges to the establishment narrative about trade's benefits: an economic nationalist narrative; a geoeconomic narrative; an inequality narrative; and a resilience narrative. Contests between these narratives will shape international economic law's future. As Pierre Bourdieu wrote, "the specifically symbolic power to impose the principles of the construction of reality – in particular, social reality – is a major dimension of political power."[21]

The Trump administration trumpeted an *economic nationalist narrative*, viewing trade and investment as a zero-sum game that "pits workers in developed and developing countries against each other." It contended that those foreign workers are "stealing" American jobs and that those countries are "cheating" such that tariffs must be raised in response.[22] President Trump's rhetoric that the United States is losing, and China is not only winning but "raping" the United States in trade, popularized these concerns.[23]

With China's rise, this account has been complemented by a strategic, *geoeconomic narrative* regarding the relation of trade and investment to security concerns.[24] Geoeconomics refers to the role that security concerns, rivalry, and conflict play in

---

[19] USTR, 2017 *Report to Congress On China's WTO Compliance* (January 2018), 2 ("the United States erred in supporting China's entry into the WTO on terms that have proven to be ineffective in securing China's embrace of an open, market-oriented trade regime").

[20] Anthea Roberts and Nicolas Lamp, *Six Faces of Globalization: Who Wins, Who Loses, and Why It Matters* (Cambridge: Harvard University Press, 2021).

[21] Pierre Bourdieu, *Outline of a Theory of Practice* (Cambridge: Cambridge University Press, 1977), 165.

[22] Roberts and Lamp, *Six Faces*.

[23] Jeremy Diamond, "Trump: 'We Can't Continue to Allow China to Rape Our Country'," *CNN*, May 2, 2016.

[24] Compare Vice President Michael Pence, "Remarks by Vice President Pence on the Administration's Policy Toward China," *Hudson Institute*, October 4, 2018; Adam Beshudi, "Lighthizer: 'Made in China 2025' a Threat to Global System," *Politico*, November 6, 2017; Hal Brand, "Opinion, How China Went From a Business Opportunity to Enemy No. 1," *Bloomberg*, September 6, 2018.

trade and economic policy, where trade and investment measures can be wielded as weapons.[25] As China continues to grow at a more rapid pace than the United States, and as its industries threaten to become competitive in leading technologies, those adopting this view no longer see trade as a win–win proposition, but rather one that benefits China disproportionately. Moreover, they are concerned that sourcing goods from China can create dependencies that provide China with leverage and geopolitical tools, such as through Chinese-built 5G wireless telecommunications systems. In this way, the geoeconomic narrative has close links with the economic nationalist narrative in viewing the system as currently working in China's favor, and in calling for greater economic decoupling from China.

These two narratives became allied within the Trump administration. Commentators mocked Peter Navarro's book and movie *Death by China* when they appeared in 2011 and 2012, but the narrative has been successful politically.[26] Navarro became Director of the White House National Trade Council and then Director of Trade and Manufacturing Policy. His work depicts China as a predator and geostrategic threat to be countered, and the WTO as an impediment. Democrats declaim similar warnings of China's rise, creating bipartisan support to counter China.

A third, competing narrative – the *inequality narrative* – views trade and investment issues in distributional terms given the advantages that economic globalization has provided to capital in relation to the working and middle classes, furthering stark increases in inequality in the United States. Trade theory has long recognized that trade creates losers as well as winners. Economic globalization supported by international economic law created bargaining leverage for capital over labor, while constraining states' ability to tax mobile capital.[27] The impacts became more salient following the 2008 financial crisis. Although the effect on inequality arguably resulted more from technology and the free flow of capital than trade, trade was not innocent, and with the rise of global supply chains, the three are linked.[28]

---

[25]   Compare Edward Luttwak, "From Geopolitics to Geo-Economics: Logic of Conflict, Grammar of Commerce," *The National Interest* 20 (1990): 17, 19 (geoeconomics as "the admixture of the logic of conflict with the methods of commerce"); Robert D. Blackwell and Jennifer M. Harris, *War by Other Means* (Cambridge: Harvard University Press, 2016), 9 (geoeconomics as the "use of economic instruments to promote and defend national interests, and to produce beneficial geopolitical results"); Anthea Roberts, Henrique Choer Moraes, and Victor Ferguson, "Toward a Geoeconomic Order in Trade and Investment," *Journal of International Economic Law* 22 (2019): 655, 657 (using the term "to describe a macro level change in the relationship between economics and security in the regime governing international trade and investment").

[26]   Compare "Trade: Last Week Tonight with John Oliver," *HBO*, August 19, 2018, and Navarro's "Death by China: How America Lost its Manufacturing Base," April 10, 2016.

[27]   Dani Rodrik, *Straight Talk on Trade: Ideas for a Sane World Economy* (Princeton: Princeton University Press, 2017); Shaffer, "Retooling." Gabriel Zucman estimated that about 10 percent of global GDP (about $5.9 trillion) was parked in tax havens (with the vast majority of it unrecorded). Gabriel Zucman, *The Hidden Wealth of Nations: The Scourge of Tax Havens* (Chicago: University of Chicago Press, 2015).

[28]   Branko Milanovic, *Global Inequality: A New Approach for the Age of Globalization* (Cambridge: Harvard University Press, 2016); Mathew C. Klein and Michael Pettis, *Trade Wars are Class Wars:*

Empirical studies show that massive imports from China, in particular, increased risks to many communities in the United States and Europe.[29] The political fallout invigorated populist politics playing off nativist, racialized fears, and the loss of a sense of superior status in relation to others, such as foreigners, migrants, and citizens of color.[30]

From this vantage, as markets globalize, states need to ensure that the benefits of trade are broadly shared. US politicians on the political left, such as Bernie Sanders and Elizabeth Warren, stress that the majority of Americans' jobs have become more precarious and their wages stagnant, while the gap with wealthy "elites" has widened. In 2016, the share of US wealth of the bottom 90 percent of Americans fell to only 23 percent, the top 10 percent rose to 77 percent, and the top 1 percent soared to 38 percent, reaching levels of inequality not seen since the 1930s.[31]

These narratives are linked to structural changes that involve a *double-edged shift in inequality*. From a global perspective, trade simultaneously has reduced inequality between countries because of higher economic growth rates in Asia and the rise of a middle class in China and India, while it increased inequality within countries.[32] Inequality, in other words, is a function of what one does and where one does it. As a function of what one does, inequality has risen between capital and unskilled labor. As a function of where one does it, inequality has reduced as hundreds of millions have risen out of poverty, especially in Asia.[33] As Milanovic summarizes, "the great winners have been the Asian poor and middle classes; the great losers, the lower

---

How Rising Inequality Distorts the Global Economy and Threatens International Peace (New England: Yale University Press, 2020).

[29] David Autor, David Dorn, and Gordon Hanson, "The China Syndrome: Local Labor Market Effects of Import Competition in the United States," *American Economic Review* 103 (2013): 2121; Stefan Thewissen and Olaf van Vliet, "Competing with the Dragon: Employment Effects of Chinese Trade Competition in 17 Sectors Across 18 OECD Countries," *Political Science Research & Methods* 103 (2017): 1–18.

[30] Tom Jacobs, "Research Finds that Racism, Sexism, and Status Fears Drove Trump Voters," *Pacific Standards* (2018) (citing work of Diana Mutz and others); Daniel Trilling, "The Irrational Fear of Migrants Carries a Deadly Price for Europe," *Guardian* (2018); Adam Tooze, *Crashed: How a Decade of Financial Crises Changed the World* (New York: Penguin Books, 2018), 576 ("Even an issue such as trade was saturated with racial markers").

[31] Greg Leiserson et al., "The Distribution of Wealth in the United States and Implications for a Net Worth Tax," *Washington Center for Equitable Growth*, March 21, 2019 (citing author's calculations from Board of Governors of the Federal Reserve System, Survey of *Consumer Finances*; Lucas Chancel, "Ten Facts About Inequality in Advanced Economies," *WID.World, Working Paper No. 2019/15* (2019) (discussing trend of rising top 1 percent and falling bottom 90 percent); Emmanuel Saez and Gabriel Zucman, *The Triumph of Injustice: How the Rich Dodge Taxes and House to Make Them Pay* (New York: W.W. Norton & Company, 2019), 98, fig.5.3 (showing trend of rising top 1 percent and falling bottom 90 percent). They also note, "The United States is unique, among advanced economies, to have witnessed such a radical change in fortune." Ibid., 6.

[32] Milanovic, *Global Inequality*, 46–117.

[33] Over 850 million Chinese rose out of poverty in the last thirty-five years (to 25 million and declining) through trade-generated economic growth. "DataBank: Poverty and Equity," *The World Bank Group*, http://databank.worldbank.org/data/reports.aspx?source=poverty-and-equity-database (number of poor at $1.90 per day at 2011 PPP).

middle classes of the rich world."[34] Comparing the relative benefits from globalization in a graph produces Milanovic's famous "elephant curve": the elephant's large hump represents the lower and middle classes in Asia; its tail's dangling tip represents the world's poorest; the trough plummeting from the elephant's brow captures the lower and middle classes in rich countries; and the raised trunk reflects the top 1 percent of whom half are from the United States.[35]

This double-edged shift in inequality shaped political contests in the United States. On the one hand, *growing inequality within the United States*, accentuated after the global financial crisis of 2008, catalyzed a left-leaning politics that critiqued US trade deals for favoring corporations over workers. Bernie Sanders's attacks on Hillary Clinton's establishment positions on trade, such as her early support for the Trans-Pacific Partnership (TPP) as the "gold standard," arguably helped undercut traditional working-class support for her.[36] On the other hand, there is *declining inequality between the United States and China* (as well as other emerging economies), which created opportunities for those conveying nationalist positions, whether they take an economic populist or geoeconomic strategic slant.

A separate, but related narrative – a *resilience narrative* – stresses resilience's importance for a country to protect itself and its citizens from crises. It is related because the poor are most vulnerable when crises strike. The COVID-19 pandemic's upending of the global economy illustrates the point. The largely privatized US health-care system focused on short-term profits through outsourcing and lean, just-in-time delivery. As a result, hospitals lacked a stockpile of ventilators, masks, and other personal protective equipment, threatening health-care workers and impeding containment efforts after the virus spread. Likewise, data-driven industrialization and the so-called internet-of-things, such as driverless vehicles, raise risks of system integrity and sudden collapse that are linked to the geoeconomic narrative, as captured in debates over the adoption of 5G technology.[37] Economics, ecology, engineering, and psychology – from their different vantages – all stress the

---

[34] Milanovic, *Global Inequality*, 20.

[35] The biggest percentage gains from economic globalization were *not* the top one percent of the global population, but the middle classes in Asian economies, "predominantly China, but also India, Thailand, Vietnam and Indonesia." Milanovic, *Global Inequality*, 18. Milanovic calculates that these groups' income rose by about 80 percent between 1988 and 2008 (bettering the 66 percent increase of the top one percent), and they included 20 percent of the global population – individuals falling between the fortieth and sixtieth percentiles. In contrast, the lower and middle classes of developed countries did the worst during this period, with their incomes largely stagnant or increasing only slightly.

[36] Timothy Meyer and Ganesh Sitaraman, "Trade and the Separation of Powers," *California Law Review* 107 (2019): 583, 625.

[37] EU Coordinated Risk Assessment of the Cybersecurity of 5G Networks Report, October 8, 2019; Overview of Risks Introduced by 5G Adoption in the United States, July 31, 2019; Jan-Peter Kleinhans, "Whom to Trust in a 5G World?: Policy Recommendations for Europe's 5G Challenge," *Stiftung Neue Verantwortung*, December 2019.

importance of resilience.[38] Thus, it is argued, states and companies need to develop backup, modular, and exit systems involving redundant and diverse infrastructure to respond to the risks of system intrusions and breakdowns. From this vantage, regardless of whether geoeconomic conflict can be managed, societies should not be dependent on single sources of supply or single technological systems. Most starkly, combatting potentially catastrophic climate change calls for sustainable, resilient systems that reduce its risks, ranging from severe droughts and firestorms, to rising sea levels, mass migration, and economic and environmental collapse. Designing resilient systems comes with costs, but it protects societies from these catastrophic risks.

These particular narratives unfold differently in countries in light of their political, economic, and historical contexts. Although Europe experienced similar frustrations regarding the WTO as the United States, it reacted in a very different way, in part because European narratives have been less negative toward trade for the reasons discussed above. From the vantage of the inequality narrative, Europe is not beset by the same levels of inequality as the United States and generally provides more generous social safety nets and economic adjustment programs. In complement, from a geoeconomic perspective, Europe has viewed economic integration as a key part of its security, which catalyzed the European project and the European Union's creation.

Domestic narratives and political contests in powerful states recursively shape the trade legal order. It is the *indirect effects* of emerging powers' rise on politics and policy debates within the United States that will determine the trade legal order's future. These changes are not just *structural*. They manifested themselves through emerging powers' ability to cultivate and harness *trade law capacity* to defend and advance their positions in the WTO and its dispute settlement system, and to develop their own trade and investment initiatives outside of it, reducing US dominance in the system and constraining US options. This book recognizes that structural explanations are central to understanding current challenges to the international trade legal order, but these countries' development of trade law capacity is a necessary complement. It is the mechanism through which they were able to affect the rules of the game for trade and investment, which recursively helped spur changes in US politics, ensuing US challenges to the WTO, and, as a result, shifts in the ecology of the transnational legal ordering of trade and broader economic governance.

[38]　Ran Bhamra, Kevin Burnard, and Samir Dani, "Resilience: The Concept, a Literature Review and Future Directions," *International Journal of Production Research* 49 (2011): 5375 at 5386, 5393 (noting "the conceptual linkages between vulnerability, resilience and adaptive capacity"); Yossi Sheff, "Building a Resilient Supply Chain," *Harvard Business Review Supply Chain Strategy*, October 2005, 1; Jared Diamond, *Collapse: How Societies Choose to Fail or Succeed*, Revised Edition (New York: Penguin Books, 2011); Ian Goldin and Mike Mariathasan, *The Butterfly Defect: How Globalization Creates Systemic Risks, and What to Do about It* (Princeton: Princeton University Press, 2014).

III. US STRATEGIES IN THE WAKE OF EMERGING POWERS' RISE

US policymakers have debated what strategy the United States should adopt to revise and develop the rules of the game to address China. Under the Obama administration, the United States aimed to build coalitions of countries to set new rules through megaregional agreements, in particular the Trans-Pacific Partnership and the Transatlantic Trade and Investment Partnership. It aimed to "pivot to Asia" through new trade and investment partnerships. Many of the negotiated rules were tailor-made for China and directly responded to existing WTO jurisprudence favoring China.[39] For example, the TPP chapter on state-owned enterprises defined them according to their ownership, rather than in terms of the "exercise of government functions," contrary to the WTO Appellate Body's interpretation of WTO rules.[40] The TPP chapter generally required parties to ensure that they do not cause "adverse effects to the interests of another Party through the use of non-commercial assistance," which includes sales, services, grants, loans, and equity provided other than on a commercial basis.[41] The rules also updated trade rules regarding e-commerce. They prohibited forced localization of data and transfers of source code.[42] In each case, the TPP provisions reflected US positions, including where it did not prevail in WTO litigation or negotiations. The Obama administration lobbied for the TPP not only on economic grounds but also on strategic grounds to tie Asian economies more closely to the United States than China.[43]

The Obama administration hoped that the TPP would create a competitive negotiating environment that would draw other countries to join it on US terms so that their products would receive nondiscriminatory access to the US market, thus further broadening the rules' geographic reach. Because Vietnam would benefit through the TPP, the Philippines could feel pressure from Philippine producers to join and level the playing field for their products. Similarly, if Malaysia and other Southeast Asian countries would benefit, Thailand could feel pressure from Thai constituencies to accede. And if the Philippines and Thailand joined, the Indonesian government could feel constrained. In each case, these countries would have to agree to TPP rules that they did not participate in negotiating. Over time, to the extent that the TPP created significant benefits for members, China could feel pressure to join the club, which would create balanced market access for US companies. Indeed, factions within China looked favorably on joining the TPP and continue to contend that China should join its replacement, the Comprehensive and Progressive Agreement for Trans-Pacific Partnership.[44]

---

[39]   Daniel C. K. Chow, "How the United States Uses the Trans-Pacific Partnership to Contain China in International Trade," *Chicago Journal of International Law* 17 (2016): 370–402.

[40]   TPP, Article 17.1.

[41]   TPP, Article 17.6.

[42]   TPP, Articles 14.13 and 14.17.

[43]   Helene Cooper, "U.S. Defense Secretary Supports Trade Deal with Asia," *New York Times*, April 6, 2015 (treaty as important "as another aircraft carrier").

[44]   Amitendu Palit, *The Trans-Pacific Partnership, China and India: Economic and Political Implications* (New York: Routledge, 2014); Wang Huiyao, "China Should Join Trade Deal the U.S. Abandoned,"

Most dramatically, were the United States able to complete both the TPP and TTIP and expand their membership, then it even could try to merge the two agreements and withdraw from the WTO. The United States could thereby force China and the rest of the world to join the new organization if they wished to avoid discrimination against their products. It is through such processes that the Obama administration could shape the global legal order for trade and broader economic governance. In President Obama's telling words,

> America should write the rules. America should call the shots. Other countries should play by the rules that America and our partners set, and not the other way around. That's what the TPP gives us the power to do. . . . The world has changed. The rules are changing with it. The United States, not countries like China, should write them.[45]

That strategy would parallel the United States' earlier withdrawal from the GATT when it formed the WTO in 1995, such that other countries were forced to accept the full package of WTO agreements to maintain "most-favored-nation" trade relations with the United States. Once more, China would have to accept rules that the United States made and negotiate an accession protocol, possibly on discriminatory terms, to accede. In this vein, former Secretary of Treasury Henry Paulson wrote, "China is more likely to make the reforms necessary to join the TPP when it recognizes the danger of being excluded from it."[46]

However, both the political left and political right in the United States opposed the TPP out of concern that further economic liberalization (and accompanying regulatory rules) would again favor footloose multinational corporations to the detriment of US-based industry and US workers. After the election of President Trump, the United States took a different tack. It withdrew from the TPP, in part under the view that the TPP would be ineffective in shaping Chinese behavior. It turned to unilateral action.

When China did not capitulate, the Trump administration launched a trade war, raising average tariffs on Chinese imports from 3.3 percent in January 2018 to 21 percent by September 2019, and threatened others to pressure China to change its practices – as well as to reduce the US trade deficit, a pet peeve of President Trump's that trade policy cannot resolve.[47] In parallel, the United States tightened rules for foreign investment approvals and blacklisted or threatened to blacklist Chinese

Bloomberg Quint, June 26, 2020. Wang is President of the think tank Center for China and Globalization in Beijing, and is Counselor to the State Council, appointed by Premier Li Keqiang.

45 Barack Obama, "President Obama: The TPP Would Let America, Not China, Lead the Way on Global Trade," *Washington Post*, May 2, 2016; Michael Froman, "The Strategic Logic of Trade: New Rules of the Road for the Global Market," *Foreign Affairs* 111, November/December 2014.

46 Henry M. Paulson, *Dealing with China: An Insider Unmasks the New Economic Superpower* (New York: Hachette, 2015), 399.

47 Binyamin Applebaum, "On Trade, Donald Trump Breaks with 200 Years of Economic Orthodoxy," *New York Times*, March 10, 2016.

technology companies so that US companies cannot do business with them on national security grounds.[48] China retaliated by raising tariffs on US products to just over 21 percent, while lowering those for other countries to under 8 percent. Similarly, when the US administration prepared and implemented plans to increase protection against India's and Brazil's products, they drew countervailing plans to restrict US imports in retaliation.[49]

The United States and China reached a "phase 1" agreement in January 2020 that focuses, in particular, on intellectual property protection, containing rules that address China's alleged "forced technology transfers" as a condition for administrative licenses and joint venture approvals, and that require greater civil recourse and criminal enforcement against the theft of trade secrets, among other matters. There is little sign, however, that China will significantly curb the state's role in its economic development policy. Rather, China is diversifying its trade to other markets and striving to reduce its dependence on US technology, to the consternation of US high-tech companies. Now that the Trump administration abandoned the TPP, China is better positioned to take the lead in negotiating trade and investment arrangements governing Asian economic integration, such as through its Belt and Road Initiative and the Regional Comprehensive Economic Partnership agreement.

A new geoeconomic cold war has formed that involves much more than a trade war. This shift lies in large part through the reality of China's economic rise and its relation to technological change, connectivity, and systemic risks (illustrated by 5G communications infrastructure), and in part because of the US administration's rhetoric. Whether one believes that the rhetoric primarily captures reality, or that it is predominantly constructing reality (or whatever reality's and rhetoric's relative roles might be), the new narrative has become dominant in the United States. The Trump administration trumpeted economic security as part of national security.[50] It aimed to halt China's rise. And it found the WTO judicial system's independence too costly. The US response to China's rise, together with its imposition of tariffs on imports from its allies, is undermining the legal order that the United States created, reducing certainty and predictability, as well as trust in the United States.[51] The WTO's decline in authority plays out as other countries not only observe US tactics

---

[48]   In 2018, President Trump signed the Foreign Investment Risk Review Modernization Act, which granted new powers to the Committee on Foreign Investment in the United States (CFIUS) to block foreign investment, particularly from China, on national security grounds.

[49]   Chad Bown, "Trump's Mini-Trade War with India," PIIE, July 8, 2019; Nayanima Basu, "India Developing Strategy to Respond to Any U.S. Import Restrictions," *International Trade Reporter* 34 (2017); "Perdue, Fearing Retaliation, Says USDA Should Not Block Brazilian Beef," *Inside U.S. Trade's World Trade Online Daily News*, March 24, 2017.

[50]   "Promote Free, Fair, and Reciprocal Economic Relationships," in *National Security Strategy of the United States of America* (Washington, DC: The White House, 2017).

[51]   Jason Scott and David Rowman, "Trump Trade Snub Set to Boost China's Bid for its Own Asian Pact," 33 *International Trade Reporter* (BNA), 1638, November 17, 2016 (RCEP would give China "greater prestige in a region where it is seeking to displace U.S. influence").

in the trade war, but also deploy them in their own trade relations.[52] The increasing use of the geoeconomic narrative plays into a normative world where it gradually becomes normalized, with the result that issues can become less subject to scrutiny because they become matters of "common sense." Cold war tropes are an old concern of realists because their deployment can trigger overreactions with horrible consequences.[53]

China's and other emerging powers' successful use of WTO law and negotiating principles, in short, helped to spur the United States to challenge the legitimacy of the trade legal order that it had created. Under one scenario, the United States is attempting to revise and update trade and economic governance rules to maintain its hegemonic position. In the words of a Brazilian official, the United States would like "to rewrite the rules to guarantee more years of US dominance," of "US hegemony."[54] Its aim is to redesign the ground rules for WTO negotiations and to impose new substantive requirements. Procedurally, the United States wishes to terminate the WTO practice where a country can self-designate as a "developing country" and receive "special and differential treatment."[55] Substantively, it wants to rebalance commitments and rein in Chinese state capitalism, industrial subsidies, and the enhanced role of state-owned enterprises, among other goals. In this way, the United States hopes to compel the adoption of rules that advance its vision of international economic order. If this is correct, then the US strategy may be viewed as paralleling the US turn to unilateralism in the 1980s when it criticized the GATT, eventually leading to the creation of the WTO and the WTO's incorporation of trade in services, intellectual property protection, and binding dispute settlement.[56] The United States still wields structural power to attempt to shape the rules of the game, which the Biden administration can harness. Under another scenario, the United States is undermining the legal order it created so that balance of power, and not law, will be the dominant mechanism for ordering trade relations, and trade and investment will increasingly be viewed in zero-sum, geoeconomic terms, eroding international cooperation and trust. Whichever scenario prevails, the growing political and

52 A growing number of countries use national security rationales to justify trade measures, reflected in measures applied by Japan and Korea, the Ukraine and Russia, and the UAE and Qatar. Other countries do not mind the United States engaged in a trade fight with China, but they question why the United States also targets them. Interview, high-level official at WTO, Geneva, July 9, 2019.

53 Note the opposition, for example, of realists Hans Morgenthau to the Vietnam War, and Stephen Walt to the second Iraq war and to US hardline policy against Iran. Martin Weil, "Hans Morgenthau, Vietnam War Critic," *Washington Post*, July 21, 1980; Stephen Walt, *The Hell of Good Intentions: America's Foreign Policy Elite and the Decline of U.S. Primacy* (New York: Farrar, Strauss and Giroux, 2018).

54 Interview, July 11, 2019.

55 USTR Press Release, "Opening Plenary Statement of USTR Robert Lighthizer at the WTO Ministerial Conference," December 11, 2017; Communication from the United States, "An Undifferentiated WTO: Self-Declared Development Status Risks Institutional Irrelevance," WT/GC/W757/Rev.1, February 14, 2019.

56 Compare Thomas Bayard and Kimberly Ann Elliott, *Reciprocity and Retaliation in U.S. Trade Policy* (Washington, DC: Peterson Institute, 1994).

economic competition between the United States and China presents the greatest challenge for the maintenance of the multilateral trading system.

IV. WHAT'S AT STAKE?

As captured in these narratives about trade, much is at stake, including social welfare, economic development, distribution within and between countries, and world order and peace. With the fall of the Berlin Wall, collapse of the Soviet Union, and end of the Cold War, the predominant focus of trade and investment law and policy was economic, stressing how they increases a state's aggregate *social welfare*. International economics and trade law text books start with David Ricardo and his theory of comparative advantage, which shows how trade expands a country's consumption possibility frontier because its consumers' purchasing power goes further.[57] Its consumers can purchase more with their means. In parallel, more recent trade theory focuses on firms to show how trade enhances competition, which reallocates resources within a country to more productive firms, again benefitting consumers.[58] In both cases, to take from Adam Smith, trade and investment increase "the wealth of nations."

Yet, this view of their benefits is subject to significant caveats, which explains why much more is at stake, starting with the *distributional impacts* of trade and investment, as stressed in the inequality narrative. Economists always recognized that trade creates losers as well as winners within a country. Under neoclassical trade theory, the winners (export industries and consumers) gain more than the losers (import competing industries and their workers), so that it is in a country's interest to engage in trade while compensating or providing adjustment assistance to the losers. Yet, adjustment can be ineffective and compensation not forthcoming, catalyzing social backlash and undoing the social contract. The result has been trade and investment's contribution to a stark rise in inequality, especially within the United States, in favor of capital and skilled labor to the detriment of the middle and lower classes. From this perspective, it is not just China that benefits from US–China trade and investment, but also multinational companies, their management, and their shareholders, the largest number of which are based in the United States. A large percentage of Chinese exports to the United States are from multinational companies and the vast majority of the value added of those products came from foreign imports into China as part of global supply chains, with the largest amount from the United States.[59] Some Americans are thus benefitting, but the benefits are skewed.

[57] David Ricardo, *On the Principles of Political Economy and Taxation* (London: John Murray, 1817).
[58] Marc J. Melitz and Stephen J. Redding, "Heterogeneous Firms and Trade," in *Handbook of International Economics*, eds. Gita Gopinath, Elhanan Helpman, and Kenneth Rogoff, vol. 4 (Amsterdam: Elsevier, 2014), 1–54.
[59] Nicholas Lardy, "China's Weapons in a Trade War are Formidable," June 21, 2018 (87 percent of computers and electronics imported into the United States are produced by multinational companies); Neil C. Hughes, "A Trade War with China?," *Foreign Affairs* 84, no. 4 (July/August 2005): 94

In addition, as stressed by the geoeconomic narrative, *geoeconomic rivalry and security* concerns have become more salient with China becoming an economic power. When the United States was the world's sole hegemon and dominated global markets, there was little questioning whether trade could adversely affect US security interests. This narrative changed dramatically with China's rise, its threat to US technological leadership, and the electoral victory in the United States of "a tariff man." From a geoeconomic perspective, what matters are not the mutual gains from trade and investment but relative gains. The country's absolute welfare gains will be viewed as a strategic loss if the country is worse-positioned in relative terms. Thus, if China gains more than the United States from trade, then the United States might try to thwart China's gains even if it sacrifices its own citizens' economic welfare in the process. As a high-level official from Brazil states, "now the WTO is just a piece in a larger chess board."[60]

Variants of trade theory help explain these geoeconomic concerns about trade among rivals. In oligopolistic markets, a country can use trade policy measures, such as subsidies, to shift production from foreign to domestic firms. In such markets, domestic firms can then capture economic rents because they benefit from economies of scale while foreign firms encounter high start-up costs. As explained by *strategic trade* theorists, a government can thus create the comparative advantage theorized by Ricardo, including by subsidizing high value-added economic sectors that benefit its overall economy.[61] If chosen well, these policies can raise national economic welfare at another country's expense. The United States was concerned that Japan used these strategies during the 1970s, such as in the semiconductor industry.[62] Its chief concern now lies with China and China's massively subsidized indigenous innovation policies. China's rise recursively has emboldened the voices of those advocating a greater role for industrial policy to support and develop leading industries in the United States, such as through a "Green New Deal," as well as in Europe.

Relatedly, even under traditional trade theory, a country does not always benefit from trade. Where markets are "imperfect," countries can impose trade barriers to benefit themselves at other countries' expense. In the parlance of trade theory, where a country has a large market, it can impose tariffs that shift the *"terms of trade"* in its favor. If the exporting country's traders lower their prices to remain competitive, then the terms of trade shift in favor of the country imposing the tariff. China, India, and Brazil have large markets, and their tariffs can thus raise terms-of-trade

---

(around 60 percent of Chinese exports to the United States are from multinational companies and 80 percent of their value added came from foreign imports into China).

[60] Interview, July 11, 2019.
[61] Paul R. Krugman, "Is Free Trade Passé?," *Journal of Economic Perspectives* 1 (1987): 131–144.
[62] Laura d'Andrea Tyson, *Who's Bashing Whom?: Trade Conflict in High-Technology Industries* (New York: Columbia University Press, 1993).

concerns.[63] The Trump administration's tariffs, in theory, could shift the terms of trade against them, depending on the market. One of the core reasons for a trade agreement is to manage these reciprocal concerns to avoid a mutually destructive trade war.[64] Paradoxically, however, China's subsidies serve to increase US terms of trade in relation to China because they enhance US consumers' purchasing power, complicating policy analysis.

The view that the WTO legal regime is not compatible with China's economic system of state capitalism raises broader concerns for the prospects of *world order*. Legal order provided through the WTO, whatever its flaws, creates commercial predictability, stability of expectations for political officials, and a common language for deliberation and cooperation. That legal order, erected through US and European initiative following World War II, and deepened after the collapse of the Soviet Union, could decline and fall. Not long ago, the 2008 financial crisis struck the West. The crisis could have triggered global tit-for-tat protectionism, prolonging and deepening countries' economic straits, but the WTO successfully helped stabilize the global response.[65] Were there to be no multilateral organization to help coordinate a response, the next crisis could lead to greater conflict. A turn to bilateral deals and the potential formation of competing trading blocs do not bode well.

From the perspective of transnational legal order theory, the WTO's dispute settlement system is a critical governance institution for facilitating cooperation between states and fostering the permeation of common trade-related norms in law and practice within them. In the words of Alec Stone Sweet, WTO dispute settlement can be viewed as a "guarantor of reciprocity,"[66] a fundamental social mechanism for cooperation on which WTO rules are based. By attacking the WTO's legitimacy and reducing its authority, the United States is removing reciprocity guarantees and enhancing the prospect of conflict.

Economic nationalism is resurgent not only in the United States. When asked what is the greatest challenge that Chinese officials face regarding WTO dispute settlement, a high-level official responded that it is managing "Chinese

---

[63] Kyle Bagwell and Robert W. Staiger, "What Do Trade Negotiators Negotiate About? Empirical Evidence from the World Trade Organization," *American Economic Review* 101 (2011): 1238–1273 (empirically finding that the terms of China's accession to the WTO support their theory, in that the magnitude of China's tariff cuts rose proportionately with the ratio of other WTO Members' pre-negotiated import volumes to world prices).

[64] Kyle Bagwell and Robert Staiger, *The Economics of the World Trading System* (Cambridge: MIT Press, 2002), 3.

[65] *The Great Recession and Import Protection: The Role of Temporary Trade Barriers*, ed. Chad P. Bown (Washington, DC: The World Bank, 2011); Christina Davis and Krzysztof Pelc, "Cooperation in Hard Times: Self-restraint of Trade Protection," *Journal of Conflict Resolution* 61 (2017): 398–429.

[66] Alec Stone Sweet, "Judicialization and the Construction of Governance," in *On Law, Politics, & Judicialization*, eds. Martin Shapiro and Alec Stone Sweet (Oxford: Oxford University Press, 2002), 57.

nationalism."[67] In a subsequent discussion, that same official emphasized the broader importance of the WTO globally to "maintain peace and prosperity."[68] Under President Xi, nationalist forces have been emboldened and at times unleashed, which herald hazard when the next crisis hits.

The world earlier experienced the implications of US abandonment of an international institution, the League of Nations.[69] The GATT's creation in 1948 was based on learning from the experiences of the interwar period. The United States, and in particular its Secretary of State Cordell Hull, believed that "bilateralism and economic blocs of the 1930s, practiced by Germany and Japan but also Britain, were the root cause of the instability of the period and the onset of the war."[70] US elites believed that "long-term American prosperity required open markets, unhindered access to raw materials, and the rehabilitation of much – if not all – of Eurasia along liberal capitalist lines."[71] The order they built was based on negotiated rules and institutions supporting an open trade regime, grounded in collective decision-making. The WTO deepened this enterprise, backed by a compulsory, judicialized system for resolving disputes and interpreting ambiguous texts.

This could be a pivotal time for world order. As Richard Haass writes regarding the prospects for global cooperation following the coronavirus pandemic, "the more relevant precedent to consider may be not the period following World War II [after which the American-led legal order formed] but the period following World War I – an era of declining American involvement and mounting international upheaval."[72] During that interwar period, as a 1942 League of Nations report stated, "trade was consistently regarded as a form of warfare, as a vast game of beggar-my-neighbor, rather than as a cooperative activity from the extension of which all stood to benefit."[73] The memories of the interwar period and World War II have receded.

In the late 1990s and early 2000s, critiques of the WTO focused on issues of economic justice for developing countries. To respond to those critiques and create

---

67 Interview with high-level official, May 2012 (including both WTO and work on bilateral and plurilateral trade agreements). Compare Jude Blanchette, *China's New Red Guards: The Return of Radicalism and the Rebirth of Mao Zedong* (Oxford: Oxford University Press, 2019), 4.

68 Interview, June 10, 2014.

69 Gregory Shaffer and Michael Waibel, "The Rise and Fall of Trade and Monetary Legal Orders: From the Interwar Period to Today's Global Imbalances," in *Contractual Knowledge: One Hundred Years of Legal Experimentation*, eds. Gregoire Mallard and Jerome Sgard (Cambridge: Cambridge University Press, 2016), 289–323.

70 John Ikenberry, *After Victory: Institutions, Strategic Restraint, and the Rebuilding of Order after Major Wars* (Princeton: Princeton University Press, 2000), 176–177; Cordell Hull, *The Memoirs of Cordell Hull* (New York: Macmillan Co., 1948), 81 ("unhampered trade dovetailed with peace; high tariffs, trade barriers, and unfair economic competition, with war").

71 Melvyn P. Leffler, "The American Conception of National Security and the Beginnings of the Cold War, 1945–48," *The American Historical Review* 89 (1984): 346–381.

72 Richard Haass, "The Pandemic Will Accelerate History Rather Than Reshape It," *Foreign Affairs*, April 7, 2020.

73 League of Nations, Commercial Policy in the Interwar Period: International Proposals and National Policies, Official No: 1942.II.A.6.

consensus for a new round of trade negotiations, the Doha round was labeled the "Development Round." Now, questions of the justice of the international trade legal order are subsiding into more fundamental ones of order itself. Questions of justice and order, however, are linked since without order, justice claims have no firm ground on which to stand.[74] Much is in balance, including balance itself. In the words of the WTO Ambassador from New Zealand, David Walker, "we would like the sea around us to retain its name."[75]

These dimensions of what is at stake – social welfare, economic distribution, geoeconomic rivalry, and world order and peace – reciprocally affect each other. Concerns about fairness within states are easily reframed as concerns about fairness between states. Growing inequality within the United States fuels populist nationalist movements. These nationalist movements spur other nationalist responses and call into question the future of the legal order for trade and broader economic governance. The question becomes, in light of these challenges, how to manage the interface of different economic systems, and particularly China's form of state capitalism.

V. MANAGING THE INTERFACE OF ECONOMIC SYSTEMS

With the economic rise of China and other emerging economies, there will be growing tensions about how to manage the interface of countries' domestic policies. At this time, the key challenge is managing the relationship between the United States and China. For many commentators, the United States turned against China because China was to become a "market economy" and never did so.[76] China's form of state capitalism, it is argued, not only rigs the Chinese market, but global markets as well. China, from this perspective, defies the implicit "liberal understanding" of WTO law.[77] A common retort is that for the WTO and multilateralism to work, China must become "more like us" – with the US standing for "us."[78]

There are multiple problems with this account. First, it is revisionist history. Even though it may be the case that many in the West held this perception (perhaps out of genuine belief that China would naturally evolve toward a US-style capitalist system given its superiority), China never promised to adopt a particular mode of capitalism, and, after the 2008 financial crisis, it became increasingly wary of Western

---

[74] Steven Ratner, *The Thin Justice of International Law: A Moral Reckoning of the Law of Nations* (Oxford: Oxford University Press, 2016).

[75] Interview, Geneva, July 9, 2019.

[76] Kurt M. Campbell and Ely Ratner, "The China Reckoning," *Foreign Affairs*, March/April 2018. Compare President William Clinton, Speech on China Trade Bill at the Paul H. Nitze School of Advanced International Studies, March 9, 2000.

[77] Petros Mavroidis and Andre Sapir, "China and the World Trade Organisation: Toward a Better Fit," *Breugel Working Paper* (2019): 5; Mark Wu, "The China Inc. Challenge to Global Trade Governance," *Harvard International Law Journal* 57 (2016).

[78] Campbell and Ratner, "The China Reckoning"; Greg Brown, "China Should be More Like Us, Says David Petraeus," *Australian*, August 15, 2019.

models. Through its Accession Protocol, China agreed to stringent WTO rules, complemented by additional commitments that apply only to it, and it bound its tariffs at rates lower than any other emerging economy. That is all. It is true that the Xi administration enhanced the role of state-owned enterprises, including through consolidating them and bolstering the role of the Communist party through committees inside all companies.[79] But China made no greater commitment than to adhere to the WTO commitments that it made. This does not mean that the multilateral system currently provides an appropriate interface and that a new equilibrium between the trading system's main players is not needed. Yet, it does focus attention on the rules in place and new rules that should be considered.

Second, there is *no single way to structure economies* to pursue their development. The proper relation of the state and the market for development will always be uncertain and contentious. Traditionally, US policymakers trumpeted a US model in which the state plays a minimal role, although the United States has channeled massive assistance to industry, such as through the departments of defense, energy, and health.[80] China, in contrast, adopted a model of state capitalism in which capitalism thrives but the state remains prominent.[81] There is no one development model, and a plurality of models will make for a more resilient global economy. As a counterfactual, think if China had been "just like the United States" at the time of the 2008 global financial crisis, rather than providing a market of last resort when US-style capitalism imploded. What is needed is a multilateral framework that accommodates a diversity of models, with variation in response to domestic preferences, development contexts, and experimental strategies. Such an order should prohibit beggar-thy-neighbor policies while permitting countries to protect their social framework from the externalities of other countries' policies.

Trade liberals rightly lambast mercantilism for leading to losses in consumer welfare. Today the United States labels China as the arch-mercantilist, although the Trump administration at least rivaled it. Nonetheless, there are many different variations in the relation of the state and the market, and the market needs the state to function. What is frequently called mercantilism by free market advocates, Dani Rodrik points out, can be viewed in terms of different relations of the state and the market.[82] From this perspective, trade liberals focus on the demand/consumer side, arguing that a country's standard of living depends on what citizens may consume. China, in contrast, has focused on the production/supply side through tax incentives, low cost loans, and input subsidies, together with management of its currency. In the process, it has done well for Chinese citizens, while reducing prices

79   Nicholas Lardy, *The State Strikes Back: The End of Economic Reform in China?* (Washington, DC: Peterson Institute for International Economics, 2019).

80   Mariana Mazzucato, *The Entrepreneurial State: Debunking Public vs. Private Sector Myths* (Philadelphia, PA: Anthem Press, 2015 ed.).

81   Compare Wu, "China Inc."; Nicolas R. Lardy, *Markets Over Mao: The Rise of Private Business in China* (New York: Columbia University Press, 2014); and Lardy, *The State Strikes Back*.

82   Rodrik, *Straight Talk*, 135–136.

in the United States for US consumers. Yet, it also has helped catalyze growing inequality in the United States, as well as in China, since US capital has taken advantage of lower Chinese wages and production costs. The interface of the Chinese and American models, in the process, has led to increased domestic and international tensions that need to be managed carefully or both economies and their citizens will suffer.

Third, in the conventional American "free-market" narrative, the state and state-controlled enterprises are a drag on the economy, reducing economic efficiency.[83] Thus, over time, the United States should outperform China and have nothing to fear. Yet, the United States has lost confidence since the global financial crisis, and China's impressive economic performance highlights the question of the state's appropriate role in economic development. The best one can say is that there is room for experiment so that countries can learn from each other. The United States, for example, could learn from China and invest more in infrastructure, education, and basic research and development.[84] If the United States rather believes that tax cuts and trimming government are best to stimulate its economy in its rivalry with China, those are US domestic policy choices.

A related, and arguably even more difficult, challenge is that the world is experiencing a power transition as the US share of the global economy declines in relation to China's. It is an old story, giving rise to concerns of inevitable conflict between a rising and declining power that can lead to war – the so-called Thucydides trap.[85] When there is a single hegemon, then that hegemon is able to create and enforce rules for liberalized trade and investment, so that – per neoclassical economic theory – all countries benefit.[86] In contrast, when geopolitical tensions rise, contestants view outcomes in zero-sum terms where one wins and the other loses. Thus, countries rely less on law and more on geopolitical clout. From this perspective, the Trump administration – and perhaps both political parties in the United States – viewed the WTO's legal and judicial system as an unwelcome constraint in confronting China.

---

[83] Bown and Hillman write that "China itself would likely be the largest economic beneficiary to its own subsidies reform." Chad Bown and Jennifer Hillman, "WTO'ing a Resolution to the China Subsidy Problem," 22 *Journal of International Economic Law* (2019): 578, citing Lardy, *The State Strikes Back*.

[84] In OECD rankings, the United States declined from 16 to 25 in education and 14 to 19 in infrastructure between 2013 and 2019. *Global Innovation Index*, 2019. With irony, Rodrik notes Milton Friedman's characterization of the government as "the enemy" when proclaiming the magic of the market, pointing to what goes into the making of a pencil. Today, that pencil would be produced in China with its complex hybrid of state-led and market form of capitalism. Rodrik, *Straight Talk*, 131–132.

[85] Graham Allison, *Destined for War: Can America and China Escape Thucydides's Trap* (Boston: Houghton Mifflin Harcourt, 2017).

[86] Theorists in this vein include Robert Gilpin, *Global Political Economy: Understanding the International Economic Order* (Princeton: Princeton University Press, 2001); and Craig VanGrasstek, *Trade and American Leadership: The Paradoxes of Power and Wealth from Alexander Hamilton to Donald Trump* (Cambridge: Cambridge University Press, 2019).

China's rise and its organization of state capitalism, whatever China's initial commitments, are now a legitimate concern for the United States in terms of the shock China's exports had on workers in the United States, combined with geoeconomic challenges, particularly concerning the multiple uses of technology in a data-driven economy, as well as the implications for climate change. Trade-related distributional issues have become central to domestic politics and policy. New technologies play critical roles in the data-driven economy that WTO rules do not (at least clearly) cover. And global imbalances in the current (trade) account and capital (financial) account must be addressed.

These are key challenges of our time. The question becomes whether trade relations should be seen only in zero-sum terms or whether a common transnational legal order for trade is possible. In the former case, in Steve Bannon's terms, "there are two systems that are incompatible. One side is going to win, and one side is going to lose."[87] In the latter case, an order could provide governments with sufficient flexibility to organize markets in different ways while protecting themselves from the externalities of each other's actions, managing the rivalry between them, and cooperating over common concerns. China will not capitulate to US demands because US leverage is limited. Thus, the question arises – what outcome is possible besides radical decoupling into trade blocs that will be mutually harmful, involving ongoing economic warfare and risking even greater conflict? Can a system be devised that permits for the interface of their economic systems and defuses conflict? Is a common language available regarding fair competition that permits for difference and variation?

From this vantage, it can be asked whether the trade law system needs more law to address interface challenges, more discretion and flexibility to accommodate normative and institutional pluralism, or a combination of both? Many have contended that more law is needed, and indeed the United States has been pushing for more legal constraints on China's state development policies. The Obama administration created new rules for global trade through the TPP. The Trump administration then pursued commitments from China in these same areas through bilateral negotiations conducted in the context of a trade war, as reflected in the US–China "phase 1" deal.

Others, in contrast, contend that countries need to be constrained less by trade rules, leaving greater room for policy space for economic development and for protection of the domestic social contract. Rodrik, for example, calls for reweighing the scales between economic globalization and the nation-state, providing greater discretion for state policies.[88] I agree with Rodrik, while stressing the need for a combination of both more law and more policy discretion, thus requiring a key place for lawyers and legal capacity in designing such a system.

---

[87] Ana Swanson, "A New Red Scare is Reshaping Washington," *New York Times*, July 20, 2019.
[88] Rodrik, *Straight Talk*.

The trade regime needs to address these challenges. In particular, if the world is to maintain some form of stability and peace, US and Chinese forms of capitalism will need some form of interface. The alternative is prolonged economic conflict, and perhaps more, which could adversely affect needed global cooperation in other areas, such as to combat global warming, global pandemics, and global financial crises. That raises the question: what might be done within a framework of cooperation that both facilitates exchange and provides policy space to address social, developmental, and security concerns?

The response should be agreement on governing principles that accommodate different economic systems. The US–China Trade Policy Working Group has developed such a framework in broad terms. In the words of its Joint Statement, of which I am a signatory, a multilateral framework should be agreed that respects "each country's ability to design and implement its own domestic policies, to promote productive negotiations about how to share the benefits and minimize the harms that attend bilateral trade, and to facilitate fair competition in the multilateral sphere of international trade."[89]

Implementing this principle has two main components. On the one hand, countries should have the right "to design a wide variety of industrial policies, technological systems, and social standards." On the other hand, they should have the right to use tariff and non-tariff trade policies "to protect their industrial, technological, and social policy choices" in a manner that does not impose unnecessary or disproportionate impacts on foreign countries.[90] Both prongs are about policy space. China and other emerging economies would have the choice to organize their economies in different ways. However, China would recognize that those choices can affect constituencies in other countries. Countries would have the right to take proportionate measures to protect themselves and their domestic social bargains. Multilateral rules, in parallel, would prohibit beggar-thy-neighbor policies and be backed by binding dispute settlement.

This approach would retain a major role for multilateralism and the WTO. In theory, WTO rules already can be flexibly interpreted and applied in ways that generally accommodate this approach.[91] But it nonetheless would involve some tailoring of law through negotiations, coupled with an ethos that focuses on all stakeholders, and not just traders.

Not everything would have to be determined in the WTO. There is a place for bilateralism to manage conflicts so long as the bilateral arrangements do not prejudice third countries. There is also a broader place for institutional and normative pluralism within a common framework of multilateral rules.[92] China's Belt and

---

[89]   The US-China Trade Policy Working Group Joint Statement, "US-China Trade Relations: A Way Forward" (2019).

[90]   Ibid.

[91]   Gregory Shaffer, "Managing the Interface of U.S.-China Trade Relations" (2021) (on file).

[92]   Sonia Rolland and David Trubek, *Emerging Powers in the International Economic Order: Cooperation, Competition and Transformation* (Cambridge: Cambridge University Press, 2019).

Road Initiative and its web of trade agreements in Asia and beyond, Brazil's new investment model, and India's development of an "Act East" initiative (Chapters 4–7) reflect such institutional pluralism, as do parallel initiatives of the United States and European Union. The WTO Appellate Body went too far in refusing to recognize bilateral ex parte agreements.[93] If necessary, WTO rules should be clarified to accommodate them, possibly even permitting claims to be brought under them within its judicial order.[94] Yet, however organized, some sort of framework is needed to provide for a multilateral public order within which transnational legal ordering takes place.

Trade negotiations traditionally involve reciprocal bargaining to increase market access. In this way, they ratchet up trade liberalization over time. Yet, democratic governments are interested in more than just one-way trade liberalization. They also are concerned about policy space, including to address development, security, distribution, labor and environmental protection, and other values. Trade and investment negotiations can and should also involve reciprocal bargains over policy space to ensure democratic legitimacy and responsiveness.

As I have written elsewhere, one can envisage parallel trade negotiations over policy space between developed and developing countries.[95] The negotiations could involve the provision of greater policy space for developed countries to uphold the domestic social contract by protecting labor against social dumping, and greater policy space for developing countries to adopt experimental industrial policies to move up the value-added production chain. In this way, negotiations could address both the trade-labor problem involving the export of goods produced under working conditions that violate international norms, and the trade-development problem involving restrictions on industrial policies. Such a negotiation could give rise to a new trade and investment policy interface. In parallel, analogous institutional mechanisms and oversight procedures can be developed to address security concerns in ways that provide for appropriate flexibility,[96] as well as concerns over capital flows that drive trade imbalances.[97] The challenge with policy space is that it can impose significant externalities on outsiders. These externalities, however, can be subject to bargaining, as is the case with any rule. The challenge is to

---

93 Gregory Shaffer and Alan Winter, "FTA Law in WTO Dispute Settlement," *World Trade Review* 16 (2017): 303–326.

94 Michael Trebilcock, "Between Theories of Trade and Development: The Future of the World Trading System," *The Journal of World Investment & Trade* 16, no. 1 (2014): 122–140.

95 Shaffer, "Retooling." Compare Jean Pisani-Ferry, "Should We Give Up on Global Governance?," *Bruegel*, October 23, 2018 (need for a "critical multilateral base" with "a minimum set of universal principles and nimble global institutions," providing the GATT as an example).

96 J. Benton Heath, "The New National Security Challenge to the Economic Order," *Yale Law Journal* 129 (February 2020): 1020–1098.

97 One option is to tax capital inflows into the United States to help finance trade adjustment and other programs that benefit affected workers. Klein and Pettis, *Trade Wars are Class Wars*; Shaffer, "Retooling."

operationalize the concept of negotiating over policy space through new legal provisions while limiting the risks of protectionist abuse.

As part of that interface, a neutral, third-party dispute settlement system would need to be upheld as a guarantor of reciprocity. One alternative is to reestablish the WTO Appellate Body under existing rules, but the United States may be unwilling to pursue that option. The best argument against the previous Appellate Body model, as it was applied, is that the Appellate Body's normative power in interpreting ambiguous WTO rules was unchecked through a countervailing political process. WTO insiders long recognized the imbalance between judicial and political processes within the WTO.[98] Given the stalemate of WTO negotiating processes, the Appellate Body became more authoritative than WTO members in determining the meaning of global trade rules, because its decisions were automatically adopted (unlike political decisions that require consensus).[99] This imbalance raised legitimacy concerns.[100] Given the unlikelihood that countries will agree to be bound by more robust political processes involving voting, a call for strengthening WTO political processes will most likely fail. The only alternative for rebalancing is thus some retrenchment of judicial authority, while retaining an impartial, compulsory, and binding third-party dispute settlement mechanism, if possible – one which interprets rules in ways that are deferential to policy space wherever there is ambiguity. Even though a system of retrenched judicial authority is more favorable to powerful countries, it also could be more stable in the current geopolitical context by taking sovereignty concerns into greater account.[101]

These are politically challenging times. They present severe risks as well as opportunities. An improved interface is needed between different economic systems. What might be done in light of the stakes requires legal and institutional imagination. One option is to retool trade and investment agreements to address policy space, while providing for a more resilient global economy. A complementary option is to focus on problem-solving by building and enhancing structures to address mutual regulatory challenges, including through plurilateral agreements,

[98] This passage draws from Gregory Shaffer, "A Tragedy in the Making? The Decline of Law and the Return of Power in International Trade Relations," *Yale Journal of International Law* 44 (2018): 37–53. Compare Claus-Dieter Ehlermann and Lothar Ehring, "The Authoritative Interpretation Under Article XI:2 of the Agreement Establishing the World Trade Organization: Current Law, Practice and Possible Improvements," *Journal of International Economic Law* 8 (2005): 803.

[99] That is, positive consensus is required for political decisions in practice, but negative consensus applies to the adoption of Appellate Body reports. Put otherwise, in the words of USTR Lighthizer, the WTO has become "a litigation-centered organization," one in which the Appellate Body makes the final decision. "Lighthizer: WTO Becoming Too Focused on Litigation, Must Concentrate More on Negotiations," *World Trade Online* (December 11, 2017).

[100] Ehlermann and Ehring, "Authoritative Interpretation," 813 ("[I]f the legislative response ... is not available or not working, the independent (quasi-) judiciary becomes an uncontrolled decision-maker and is weakened in its legitimacy.").

[101] Erik Voeten, "International Judicial Independence," in *Interdisciplinary Perspectives on International Law and International Relations: The State of the Art*, eds. Jeffrey L. Dunoff and Mark A. Pollack (Cambridge: Cambridge University Press, 2012), 421–444.

which can lead to gains in regulatory protection and consumer welfare.[102] Lawyers and economists provided the intellectual constructs and designs for the existing trade legal order. John Maynard Keynes called lawyers the "poets" at Bretton Woods for their imagination in helping to craft the agreements.[103] Now economists and lawyers must do the same for the regime's redesign to save it from imploding. Yet, whether they will be empowered to do so depends on ongoing recursive dynamics between international and national law and politics.

---

[102] Bernard Hoekman and Charles Sabel, "In a World of Value Chains: What Space for Regulatory Coherence and Cooperation in Trade Agreements," in *Megaregulation Contested: Global Economic Ordering after TPP*, eds. Benedict Kingsbury, David Malone, Paul Mertenskotter, Richard Stewart, Thomas Streinz, and Atusuhi Sunami (Oxford: Oxford University Press, 2019), 271–239.

[103] John Maynard Keynes, *The Collective Writings of John Maynard Keynes*, 26: 102 (Donald Moggridge ed., 1980).

9

Conclusion: Going Forward

The US challenge to the legitimacy and efficacy of the international trade regime that it created, and emerging powers' defense of that regime, is a paradox that cuts across international relations theories. John Ikenberry, in his book *After Victory*, published a decade after the end of the Cold War and five years after the WTO's creation, asked this central political question: "What do states that have just won major wars do with their newly acquired powers." His answer was a legal one: they create the rules of the game. In this situation, he wrote, states "have sought to hold onto that power and make it last" through institutionalizing it.[1] He called the order that the United States created a "liberal hegemonic order" because other states consented to it in the context of American unipolar power, while the United States agreed to constrain itself under the rules to "make it acceptable."[2] Michael Zürn, in his theory of global governance, argues that such regimes endogenously create resistance because they are "embedded in a normative and institutional structure that contains hierarchies and power inequalities." He thus contends that "counter-institutionalization is the preferred strategy by rising powers."[3] And the realist Graham Allison, in his book *Destined for War*, writes, "Americans urge other powers to accept a 'rule-based international order'. But through Chinese eyes, this appears to be an order in which Americans make the rules, and others obey the orders."[4] To turn from international relations to sociologist Pierre Bourdieu's field theory, Bourdieu also finds that change within a field occurs through struggles where challengers employ "subversion" strategies to undermine the legitimacy of the status quo and *dominant groups deploy*

---

[1]   John Ikenberry, *After Victory: Institutions, Strategic Restraint, and the Rebuilding of Order after Major Wars* (Princeton: Princeton University Press, 2000), xi.

[2]   Ibid. John Ikenberry, "The Rise of China and the Future of the West: Can the Liberal System Survive?," *Foreign Affairs* 87 (2008): 23 ("Today's Western order, in short, is hard to overturn and easy to join").

[3]   Michael Zürn, *A Theory of Global Governance: Authority, Legitimacy & Contestation* (Oxford: Oxford University Press, 2019), 7, 17.

[4]   Graham Allison, *Destined for War: Can America and China Escape Thucydides's Trap* (Boston: Houghton Mifflin Harcourt, 2017), 147.

"conservation" strategies.[5] The paradox with the trade legal order is that, although Brazil and India initially resisted and complained about the WTO, they, along with China, became its defenders, while the United States, under the Trump administration, attacked it as illegitimate and neutered its dispute settlement system.[6] The United States became the revisionist power.

This book provides a legal explanation of the paradox, contending that structural changes alone do not explain shifts in the transnational legal ordering of trade. The structural changes manifested themselves through emerging powers' development and deployment of trade law capacity in the WTO. Legal capacity is a critical part of the larger story because it is the medium through which structural economic change becomes expressed in institutional terms.[7] Brazil's, India's, and China's development of trade law capacity translated these structural changes into institutional change. Through their deployment of legal capacity, they challenged the United States and helped shape the interpretation and development of the rules of the game, activating the structural changes that then became manifest within the WTO itself. This book documents these changes in the trade law field, which are becoming apparent in other areas of global governance where the United States complains of rising Chinese influence in UN bodies.

Power still matters for the effective development and harnessing of legal capacity. This book addresses three regional powers, and not developing countries generally. Most importantly, China's development of legal capacity had the greatest impact on the trade regime, which is why the book devotes two chapters to it, and why Chapter 8 focuses predominantly on the US rivalry with China. Yet, structural power also required investments in law. Counterfactually, why would actors have invested so much in legal capacity if it did not matter? If it were just cheap talk? These countries understood the importance of trade law capacity, which is why they invested in it, and continue to invest in it, even as the WTO declines in its authority.

This book empirically addressed three complementary questions regarding legal capacity, state transformation, and their implications for the trade legal order. To respond to them, the book assessed international and domestic institutional and legal analysis within a single analytic frame – that of transnational legal orders.[8] The

---

[5] Julian Go and Monika Krause, "Fielding Transnationalism: an introduction," *The Sociological Review Monographs* 64, no. 2 (2016): 6–30, 19. The same holds for Fligstein and McAdam's theory of "strategic action fields," which contrasts "incumbent" strategies to "defend the status quo," from those of "challenger groups" that "attempt to create new rules and a new order." Neil Fligstein and Doug McAdam, "Toward a General Theory of Strategic Action Fields," *Sociological Theory* 29 (2011): 1–26, 18.

[6] Although India objects more vociferously than Brazil and China to aspects of the WTO, as exemplified in the conclusion of the Trade Facilitation Agreement and its opposition to new initiatives on investment facilitation, it defends the WTO's dispute settlement system and multilateral governance of trade.

[7] I thank Joe Conti for this phrasing.

[8] Terence C. Halliday and Gregory Shaffer, *Transnational Legal Orders* (Cambridge: Cambridge University Press, 2015).

trade legal order sought to produce order in an issue area that actors construed as a problem, used law to address the problem, and was transnational in its geographic scope. It sought to produce *order* by creating shared norms and institutions regarding the regulation and conduct of trade that would orient social expectations, communication, and behavior within and between states. It was *transnational* in that it transcended and permeated national borders. And it was *legal* in that it adopted legal form to address the problems and because the norms directly and indirectly engaged international and national legal institutions. It was both fragile and dynamic. It is in the process of unsettling as actors cooperate, contest, and compete to reshape legal norms and practices at the domestic and international levels.

Many scholars called the order predominating at the end of the Cold War a constitutional one.[9] This vision of constitutional order focused on inter-state relations and politics, referring to "the 'governing' arrangements among a group of states, including its fundamental rules, principles, and institutions."[10] The concept of transnational legal orders, in contrast and in complement, captures the flow of legal norms and institutional forms and practices in which order depends on their permeation within national law, institutions, and practices. These developments, in turn, recursively affect the international legal order both directly in terms of substance, and indirectly through impacts within other states that can generate new challenges to the international legal order. The frame of transnational legal order thus examines the interaction between the international, the national, and the local, affecting the settlement, unsettlement, and change of legal norms and institutions. The significant changes in the state and markets in Brazil, India, and China cannot be understood outside of transnational legal ordering of which the WTO and webs of regional and bilateral trade and investment agreements form an integral part. Recursively, developments in the international trade and investment regime cannot be understood outside of the changes in these and other key countries. The international and national interact, intermesh, and shape each other. To understand these processes, one must open the black box of states and study developments and contests within them as well as between them.

For two decades, the transnational legal order for trade and investment largely worked as designed in line with the liberal hegemonic thesis. It became settled and institutionalized, and it had significant impacts around the world in inducing countries to transform their laws and institutions. Countries lowered tariffs, signed bilateral investment treaties based on US and European models, and enacted new

---

9   John H. Jackson, *The World Trade Organization, Constitution and Jurisprudence* (London: Royal Institute of International Affairs, 1998); Deborah Cass, *The Constitutionalization of the World Trade Organization: Legitimacy, Democracy, and Community in the International Trading System* (Oxford: Oxford University Press, 2005); Jeffrey Dunoff and Joel Trachtman, "A Functional Approach to International Consitutionalization," in *Ruling the World? Constitutionalism, International Law, and Global Governance*, eds. Jeffrey L. Dunoff and Joel P. Trachtman (Cambridge: Cambridge University Press, 2009), 3–36.

10   Ikenberrry, *After Victory*, 23.

laws that shaped domestic regulation. They created new domestic institutions that incentivized the development of new domestic professions, including for corporate, commercial, intellectual property, and import relief law. Norms regarding the benefits of economic integration, cross-border transactions, the legal means to provide import relief, and the role of intellectual property for innovation changed. These processes often triggered intensive contestation, but the contestation oriented around trade law norms, which framed debates. Litigation over trade barriers became normalized and disputes resolved before a third-party dispute resolution mechanism with an Appellate Body at its pinnacle. The Appellate Body's rulings became increasingly authoritative regarding disputes over the meaning of the rules. In parallel, investor–state arbitration proliferated.

This book showed how Brazil, India, and China transformed themselves through engaging with the WTO. The result was a multilateral legal order for trade, one created and driven largely by the United States and European Union. Yet, by creating such rules and institutions, the United States and European Union made it possible for others to harness them. When emerging powers built legal capacity and adapted themselves in relation to international trade and investment law, they positioned themselves to take on the United States and European Union in shaping the international trade legal order through exercising veto rights, molding the meaning of legal norms through litigation, and developing their own initiatives. After recapitulating the book's argument in light of the case studies, this chapter addresses the book's contribution to theorizing transnational legal orders, and the transportability of trade law capacity going forward.

I. RECAPITULATING THE ARGUMENT IN LIGHT OF THE CASE STUDIES

A. *Investing in Trade Law Capacity: Comparing the Three Cases*

During the 2000s, trade law capacity became a key part of state capacity because of the growing importance of law in governing trade relations. One can build an *ideal type* of trade law capacity by comparing and contrasting what Brazil, India, and China did. As an ideal type, developing trade law capacity involves changes both in state institutions and in the relationship of the state to the private sector. To start, the state created new divisions and units in ministries that specialized in trade law. It needed to ensure continuity of that expertise, potentially involving new career paths for officials. The state also diffused this expertise across ministries that WTO law implicated, both to implement commitments in light of state objectives and to defend and advance its positions at the WTO. In parallel, the state needed to create coordinative mechanisms across ministries to ensure coherence and develop strategies in light of state goals, whether to advance negotiating positions, to defend its own policies, or to challenge others' policies in litigation and before peer review processes. In some cases, the state created entirely new institutions to address new issues, such as in the areas of intellectual property and the WTO's three legalized forms of import relief – antidumping, countervailing duty, and safeguard law. It also needed to enhance expertise in its mission in Geneva and provide sustained, ongoing support to that mission from the capital. In addition, to be effective, states cultivated, incentivized, and induced broader-based trade law capacity outside state institutions in business associations, think tanks, academia, the private bar, and civil society. In combination, individuals and groups harnessed the opportunities provided in a bottom-up manner such that trade-related capacity expanded in new ways. These public and private institutions and networks, in turn, competed and coordinated to advance state and constituent interests and goals.

In building trade law capacity, however, countries worked within their institutional legacies to adapt to the transnational legal order for trade. Through comparing these three countries' experiences, we see how, in their different ways, trade law capacity developed and unfolded within them. Each country had its own institutional heritage and path dependencies, creating opportunities and constraints. Each country would adapt to a changing international environment, including by transforming its institutions. In doing so, each country could observe what others do and respond in kind. They often borrowed US and European models, in large part because much of WTO law reflected US and European law. Yet, countries also could repurpose these models for their own ends.

There are similarities and differences among China, Brazil, and India. India and Brazil are the regional powers in South Asia and South America, and China has become the regional power in East Asia. As the three largest emerging economies, they epitomize what others call the "rise of the rest." Nonetheless, China has by far the largest economy of the three, and the United States, Europe, and other countries view it as the most significant economic challenge and threat. Most importantly, the makeup of their exports varies significantly, as reflected in their trade with each other. Even among them, their trading relationship has been characterized as "neocolonial" in that China imports raw materials from Brazil and India, and exports manufacturing goods to them.[11] These trading patterns raised consternation within Brazil and India. In May 2017, India refused to join China's signature Belt and Road Initiative and the leading English-language Indian newspaper went so far as to write that "the project is little more than a colonial enterprise, leaving debt and broken communities in its wake."[12]

---

[11] For example, in 2010, 98 percent of China's exports to Brazil were manufactured goods, as were 90 percent of its exports to India. In contrast, 75 percent of Brazil's exports to China in that year were classified as "inedible crude materials (except fuels)" and "animal and vegetable oils fats and waxes," while 57 percent of India's exports to China fell into these two categories. John Whalley and Dana Medianu, "The Deepening China Brazil Economic Relationship," CESifo Working Paper no. 3289, Category 8: Trade Policy (December 2010); 2010 International Trade Statistics Yearbook, UN COMTRADE. The make-up of their exports to China shifted since then (with a significant decline in the percentage of mineral exports such as ores from India), but the concerns remain.

[12] Indrani Bagchi, "India Slams China's One Belt One Road initiative, Says it Violates Sovereignty," *Times of India* 1, May 14, 2017.

The three countries also radically differ politically, which affects how they build legal capacity and organize themselves for trade negotiations and dispute settlement. India and Brazil have democratic parliamentary systems, while China is an autocratic regime, with power increasingly consolidated in its "paramount leader" President Xi. As a result, private stakeholders and lawyers need to be much warier in challenging the Chinese state. For this reason, the interviewees generally remain anonymous in the chapters on China. In contrast, lawyers in Brazil challenged the executive before the Brazilian courts, up to the Supreme Court, which forced the Foreign Ministry to change its practice of hiring only foreign lawyers for WTO cases.

Brazil and India traditionally have more vibrant legal cultures and traditions than China. Their executive branches are subject to judicial oversight and lawyers play greater roles in governance. In parallel, Brazil's law firms had significant experience representing foreign investors and thus had much more cosmopolitan backgrounds at the start. Indian lawyers likewise were more experienced in litigation and judicial maneuvering. Accordingly, Brazilian and Indian lawyers have worked alone with government officials in WTO cases, unlike in China which has always depended on foreign law firms to take the lead. Nonetheless, the legal bar has expanded vastly in China, as has civil litigation, as Chapter 6 showed, such that China now hosts five of the top ten, and seventeen of the world's largest one hundred law firms, as measured by number of attorneys.[13]

Brazil and India also have more active private sectors that have long organized their interests through independent trade associations and think tanks. These organizations are separate from the state so that the state must partner with them. In contrast, the primary Chinese trade associations fall within the Ministry of Commerce and are controlled by the government. Only more recently have ad hoc trade associations emerged in China to handle trade-related matters, such as regarding foreign antidumping investigations. In consequence, in Brazil, companies have paid lawyers to work with the government on WTO cases, and such Brazilian cases have depended on private sector financing. Brazil has thus been closest to adopting an American model in which private companies and trade associations hire private lawyers to offer to work with trade officials in WTO cases and in the shadow of potentially bringing a case. They hire either foreign or Brazilian lawyers depending on the context of the case.

In India, in contrast, while companies became more engaged in trade negotiations, they remained relatively disengaged in dispute settlement, in part because of traditional distrust between the Indian bureaucracy and the private sector. The government thus has hired private lawyers on an ad hoc (though partially institutionalized) basis at government rates. Since India is the poorest of the three countries in terms of per capita GDP, it is relatively more concerned about the costs of WTO litigation in light of other development priorities. This factor, combined with

---

[13] "The 2019 Global 100: Ranked by Head Count," *American Lawyer* (September 24, 2019).

a government culture of self-reliance in foreign affairs, likely explains why it alone has not hired high-priced foreign lawyers, and why it has created think tanks attached to government ministries. While the private sector also is less engaged in China, China is the wealthiest of the three countries and the government has outsourced primary responsibility for WTO cases to the top foreign law firms, which the government pays.

Linguistically India is at a relative advantage since English is the WTO's primary working language. China, in contrast, is most disadvantaged since the Chinese language is so distant from English. Since legal texts and legal argumentation are central to WTO dispute settlement, and the Chinese are at a linguistic disadvantage, this also incentivized the government's hiring of preeminent foreign law firms. Moreover, many of the initial representatives of China in the WTO were selected for their English language skills, and not for their trade background. China's first Ambassador to the WTO, Mr. Sun Zhenyu, was an English major.

Nonetheless, there are significant parallels across all three countries. To defend their interests, Brazil, India, and China each invested significant resources in developing trade law capacity. They reorganized government agencies, and they worked with private law firms, trade associations, think tanks, and academics. They diffused trade-related expertise so that the government could tap into private know-how when needed. They adapted new practices of public–private coordination in light of their legal and institutional contexts and heritages. They did so in different but complementary ways.

In each case, they were first placed on the defensive in highly publicized WTO cases. In each case, the country's engagement with the WTO started as a top-down initiative of the government, where the government engaged with non-state actors to boost its trade law capacity. In each case, government officials and private actors began working in public–private partnerships, involving law firms, companies, trade associations, think tanks, and academia, thereby conveying WTO legal norms more broadly and enabling deeper transnational legal ordering. What started as strategic, top-down initiatives became more organic processes. As a result, these countries developed significant trade law capacity in breadth and depth, which included expertise in related disciplines, and, in particular, intellectual property and investment law.

They learned and borrowed from each other's practices. Brazil was the first among emerging economies to forge successful public–private partnerships for WTO litigation and negotiations, which was followed in Geneva. It did so through the embassy's internship program for academics, private sector representatives, and government officials from other departments, as well as through working with private law firms in high-profile cases to take on the United States and Europe. Others followed its successful example in their unique, path-dependent ways. In each case, these countries helped foster the development of a broader trade and investment law community within them, diffusing expertise.

B. *Trade Law and State Change*

To engage with the WTO regime involved more than just the hiring or training of trade lawyers. The book illustrates the capacious and internally contested nature of these states' development of trade law capacity. These processes catalyzed changes that were broad and diffuse in their impact across multiple dimensions. As a general counsel of a major state-owned enterprise in China stated, "the WTO changed every side of our life. It changed our laws, habits and practices."[14]

Each of these countries, in different ways, was known for its traditional emphasis on self-reliance and its resistance to external influence. Yet, all three transformed themselves in investing in law to engage with the WTO. All three had a heritage in which the state traditionally took a leading role in development strategies. In each case, the state over time provided a much greater role for the market and market mechanisms, even though the United States contests China's reversion to greater state control. Because these countries' bureaucracies felt the need to work with private stakeholders, they also became relatively more transparent regarding their trade policies, although transparency too remains a point of contention.

The engagement of Brazil, India, and China with the WTO led to significant changes not only in their laws, but also in their institutions, professions, the relation of the bureaucracy to the private sector, and their norms and practices – which are the different dimensions of state change that Chapter 2 typologized. Trade law – as law generally – is about much more than legal texts and litigation over them. These governments professionalized their trade administrations, opened those administrations to work with stakeholders (namely business), and retained specialist private lawyers. International trade law unleashed competition for expertise that transformed these governments' relations with business and other stakeholders over international trade policy. These investments in expertise created a new class of professional intermediaries for the conveying of trade law norms. International and national trade and regulatory law and practice became enmeshed, with international trade law permeating national laws and institutions. In the process, corporate, business, and economic law generally rose in prominence across these three countries, to the benefit of an emerging profession of corporate lawyers servicing cross-border transactions and strategies.[15]

Rather than viewing the state as weakening because of market forces, or oriented predominantly to support markets, this book showed these states' ongoing significant

[14] Telephone interview, March 30, 2020.
[15] Compare Sida Liu, David Trubek, and David Wilkins, "Mapping the Ecology of China's Corporate Legal Sector: Globalization and its Impact on Lawyers and Society," *Asian Journal of Law and Society* 3 (2016): 2273–2297; *The Indian Legal Profession in the Age of Globalization: The Rise of the Corporate Legal Sector and Its Impact on Lawyers and Society*, eds. David Wilkins, Vikramaditya Khanna, and David Trubek (Cambridge: Cambridge University Press, 2017); and *The Brazilian Legal Profession in the Age of Globalization: The Rise of the Corporate Legal Sector and its Impact on Lawyers and Society*, eds. Luciana Gross Cunha, Daniela Monteiro Gabbay, José Garcez Ghirardi, David M. Trubek, and David B. Wilkins (Cambridge: Cambridge University Press, 2018).

role in trade law and policy. These countries, in transforming themselves as part of the trade legal order, did not simply import the rules in ways the United States hoped. They did not simply follow a "Washington Consensus" model of market liberalization and shrink the state. Through investing in trade law capacity, the state was strengthened to mediate between market liberalization and other state development goals. Through their investments in law, they aimed to participate in and shape the international trade regime itself, both to preserve policy space in line with their development strategies and to enhance access to foreign markets for their products.

These transformations did not occur seamlessly. Rather, different factions and constituencies within the state used and resisted international trade law to advance and curtail domestic policy initiatives. The relative roles of the state and other constituencies in their economic development, trade, and broader economic policies should not be viewed as autonomous, but rather as dynamic and contested responses to the transnational legal ordering of trade. Counterfactually, these countries' laws, institutions, and professions would not have developed as they did without the WTO and the broader trade regime.

C. *Shaping the International Trade Legal Order*

The outcome of contests within these states, in turn, impacted other countries and their constituencies. It did so directly through shaping trade law and legal interpretation at the WTO and indirectly through spurring reactions in other states, and, in particular, the United States. Just as this book showed how state and private actors in Brazil, India, and China adapted to international trade norms and institutions, it illustrated how, recursively, they worked to shape these institutions and norms through negotiation, litigation, interpretation, and domestic practice. Private professionals and other actors engaged with these governments to press for foreign market access, while also helping them mediate between developmental policies and the opportunities and constraints of international trade law. The resulting public–private partnerships significantly enhanced these countries' ability to advance their interests in international trade negotiations and dispute settlement, and, in the process, fundamentally affected the international trade regime. In each case, these collaborations helped shape the meaning and understanding of international trade rules. As a leader of the WTO secretariat summarized, "in the GATT there was the Quad, they came up with a deal and sold it to the rest of the world. Brazil and India were in the second or third tier. China was not a member. Now they are all at the center of the WTO. Nothing can move forward in the WTO without them."[16]

---

[16]   Interview, Geneva, June 28, 2017.

Rules are two-sided. They are tools for the exercise of power and tools for constraining such exercise. They reflect power and create constraints on it. At the time of the WTO's creation, the United States and European Union were economically dominant. They successfully pressed first Brazil and India, and then China, to adopt requirements that aimed to transform their economies and governance of trade. Over time, however, by investing in human capital to build capacity in trade law and policy, these countries took on the United States and Europe in WTO negotiations and dispute settlement and in other trade and investment fora. The WTO is no longer a US and EU liberal hegemonic order. As Kristen Hopewell writes, "the emerging powers have imperiled the existing international order not because they sought to bring about its collapse but precisely the opposite – because they bought into the system and sought to lay claim to its benefits."[17] They did not reject the system; they rather challenged US and EU dominance within it. They demanded "an equal right to intervene in the internal trade and economic policies of the US and other states of the Global North and pressure them to open their markets."[18] Having gained confidence and clout, they no longer label the WTO a neocolonial project. Rather, Chinese commentators view the US attempt to retain its dominance and thwart China's development model as a doomed neocolonial attempt of a declining hegemon.[19]

The United States is no longer in control of WTO agendas. There is now a vacuum of leadership – what Ian Bremmer called a "G-zero world" where no single country or group of countries can drive a global agenda.[20] When he published his book in 2012, commentators critiqued his analysis because soon after, China and the United States worked together to forge and sign the Paris Agreement on climate change, and the United States, European Union, Russia, and China cooperated to reach an agreement with Iran on its nuclear program. But as China continued to rise and the United States, after electing President Trump, responded belligerently by launching a trade war, his analysis appears increasingly astute.

---

[17] Kristen Hopewell, *Breaking the WTO: How Emerging Powers Disrupted the Neoliberal Project* (Stanford: Stanford University Press, 2016), 6–7.

[18] Ibid., 14–15.

[19] Kevin Rudd, "U.S.-China 21: The Future of U.S.-China Relations Under Xi Jinping. Toward a New Framework of Constructive Realism for a Common Purpose," *A Summary Report for the Harvard Kennedy School's Belfer Center for Science and International Affairs*, 12–15; " Yin yilun 'Zhongguo weixie lun' juyou san da tedian," 新一轮"中国威胁论"具有三大特点 (The New "China Threat Theory" Has Three Characteristics), *Beijing Daily News*, February 18, 2019, http://bjrb.bjd.com.cn /html/2019–02/18/content_6359317.htm; Kong Qingjiang, Meiou dui Shijie Maoyi Zuzhi Gaige de Shexiang yu Zhongguo Fangan Bijiao 美欧对世界贸易组织改革的设想与中国方案比较 (A Comparison of the WTO Reform Proposals of the US & EU and China's Proposal), in *Ouzhou Yanjiu* 欧洲研究 (*Chinese Journal of European Studies*), 2019, 3: 38–56, www.cssn.cn/gjgxx/gj_gjzz/ 202002/t20200227_5094029.shtml.

[20] Ian Bremmer, *Every Nation for Itself: Winners and Losers in a G-Zero World* (New York: Penguin Group, 2012).

By tracing the processes through which these countries developed legal capacity to constrain US options against them and, in turn, shape the international trade legal order, this book highlights the link between these countries' legal capacity-building efforts and US disenchantment with the WTO. It is the mismatch between the US vision of the WTO and what it came to be, combined with a structural change in economic competitiveness and power, which spurred the United States to undermine the authoritativeness of the WTO and initiate new competitive lawmaking through bilateral and regional trade negotiations. Counterfactually, why else would the United States have extinguished the WTO Appellate Body, threatened to withhold its contributions to the WTO budget, and even leave the WTO?

As a result, the transnational legal order for trade splintered. Such fragmentation is manifested in not only US and EU initiatives but also those of Brazil, India, and China, such as China's Belt and Road Initiative. Because no one can dictate rules in the WTO, incumbent and emerging powers are developing new strategies in a decentralized, pluralistic trade legal order. As a leading WTO official says, "during the first five years of the Doha round, the WTO absorbed countries' trade personnel and most of the oxygen for trade negotiations. Since 2008, other parts of the trading system have received that oxygen."[21] Brazil long resisted this turn away from multilateralism, but even it is now promoting plurilateral agreements in the WTO and signing new trade and investment agreements outside of it. China, in turn, is developing a new Sino-centric order as an increasingly important part of the ecology of the transnational legal ordering of trade, while both India and Brazil are working to build a nexus of trade and investment agreements based on their own models. New alliances are forming, often on an ad hoc basis as a function of the issue. Brazil and India are wary of China's rise, with India in particular concerned about the implications of the Belt and Road Initiative given its fraught northern border with China and its tense relations with Pakistan. Yet, Brazil and India also have benefitted from Chinese trade and investment, and China became their largest trading partner. These three emerging powers will be critical players in the trade legal order's emerging ecology, whatever the WTO's future place may be within it. As another high-level WTO official remarks, "The WTO has the word 'world' in its name, but the world has changed. We cannot pretend that the WTO will be what the world is not."[22]

II. ELABORATING TRANSNATIONAL LEGAL ORDER THEORY

This book makes five contributions to theorizing the interface between global governance and national law and practice. First, the book *exemplifies* both the demands and the payoffs of applying the theoretical framework of transnational

[21] Interview, Geneva, June 28, 2017.
[22] Interview, Geneva, July 9, 2019.

legal orders by placing international and domestic law and institutions within a single analytic frame and tracing the reciprocal and recursive impacts of each on the other. Applying this theoretical framework is a major endeavor, as it requires sustained field work over time in multiple sites, preferably in multiple countries. This book documents the *reciprocal internal and external aspects of transnational legal ordering*. It illustrates the theoretical framework's power in explaining the mutually constitutive impact of global governance and state development projects through the mediums of law and legal capacity within a field – that of international trade law. Traditionally, scholars' and commentators' terminology and imaginaries tend to distinguish national from international levels of governance as distinct spheres of action – reflective of formal legal distinctions, such as regards jurisdiction and legal sources. This book, in contrast, shows how the linkages between states and international governance institutions are more continuous than discrete for law and legal practice.

Second, the book focuses not on Europe or the United States where much work on multilevel governance and the interaction of national and international law and policy has been done, but rather on *emerging powers*. As Henry Farrell and Abraham Newman write regarding the application of an analogous theoretical framework in international relations called "the new interdependence,"

> scholars of the new interdependence have focused almost exclusively on the US and the EU. This focus is perhaps justifiable to the extent that the EU and US, both separately and together, are the major drivers of regulatory politics in the world economy. But it means that we know very little about the mechanisms (other than more traditional power dynamics) that shape relations between the EU and US, on the one hand, and other countries, especially countries in the global South, on the other.[23]

This book applies transnational legal order theory to the world's three most important emerging powers, China, India, and Brazil. In each case, the project assessed not only these countries' actions at the WTO in Geneva (as done in other books), but also their internal development of legal capacity in their capitals and major cities across the range of issues that the transnational legal ordering of trade implicates. This project overcame the challenge of access to key participants and of language in these countries. Other authors have covered these countries separately, but not in combination involving sustained field work and close collaborations over time. By theorizing transnational legal ordering processes, the book does not solely address these countries' "relations" with the United States and European Union – a traditional international relations issue – but also the rich and contingent contests and developments within them that shape such "relations."

---

[23] Henry Farrell and Abraham Newman, "Domestic Institutions beyond the Nation-State: Charting the New Interdependence Approach," *World Politics* 66 (April 2014): 331–363, 354.

Third, the book illustrates how transnational legal ordering affects developments in one country that impacts constituencies in others in *indirect* ways. Emerging powers both directly and indirectly shaped the international trade legal order. Directly, they ended the longstanding dominance of the United States and European Union in multilateral trade negotiations. Also directly, they shaped the interpretation of WTO rules that were of political importance to the United States – such as regarding US import relief law and agricultural subsidies. These interpretations determined both the meaning of the rules and affected bargaining leverage in negotiations. Critically, for transnational legal order theory, their development of trade law capacity also indirectly shaped the regime through its impact on US politics and strategies. Because of their successes, the United States began working outside of the multilateral system, undermining the WTO's authority and spawning new competitive webs of bilateral and regional agreements that are fundamentally reshaping the ecology of the transnational legal order for trade and broader economic governance.

In practice, these indirect effects – through shaping US politics and strategies – were more important than their direct impact on the legal order. The reactions they spurred in the United States recursively eroded WTO legal authority and splintered the trade order. It is these recursive, indirect effects that transnational legal order theorizing and empirical work must also address. Developments in one state affect constituencies in third states that can create new challenges to the legitimacy and effectiveness of international institutions.

Fourth, the book illustrates how recursive interactions lead not only to the construction and institutionalization of a transnational legal order, but also to its *unsettling*, fragmentation, and potential collapse. The book shows what is at stake with the transnational legal ordering of trade, which implicates the state-market interface, institutional authority within the state, and state professions, norms, and practices. It shows the integral role of an array of state and non-state actors in institutionalizing, resisting, and transforming a transnational legal order. It is a misconception to view transnational processes as moving only unidirectionally toward more order. Transnational legal order theory addresses both processes of settlement and unsettlement, ordering and disordering, institutionalization and collapse. This book shows how the institutionalization of a transnational legal order can have *unintended consequences* that spur its unraveling, including through fragmentation and the rise of competing legal orders, including regional ones.

Fifth, this book applies transnational legal order theory to *a major challenge of our time*: to understand and respond to the implications of China's rise and the relative decline of the United States as a hegemon. Conventionally scholars have assessed whether China as a rising power will be "revisionist" in undermining the legal order that the United States and Europe created.[24] Through tracing transnational legal

---

[24] Jacques deLisle, "China's Rise, the U.S., and the WTO: Perspectives from International Relations Theory," *Illinois Law Review Online* 2018 (2018): 57–71; Aaron L. Friedberg, *A Contest for Supremacy: China, America, and the Struggle for Mastery in Asia* (New York: W.W. Norton & Company, 2012);

processes within China and assessing their recursive direct and indirect impact on international trade law and institutions, this book resolves the seeming *paradox* regarding why the United States – and not China, Brazil, and India – appears to be the revisionist power, unsettling and working to change the rules of the game for trade.[25] As this book explains, while the multilateral system erodes, these countries – but China in particular – simultaneously are developing new options, which, in turn, affect the future of international economic law.

III. GOING FORWARD

A. *The Role of Trade Law Capacity Going Forward*

With the authoritativeness of the WTO unraveling, some may question whether emerging powers' investment in trade law expertise will be for naught.[26] What then would be the relevance of their investments in legal capacity to shape the transnational legal order for trade other than sparking a backlash in a politically polarized United States that could lead to the multilateral trading system's demise? What role will these countries' investments play going forward? How should we conceive of trade law capacity in such a new context?

This is an open question involving considerable uncertainty. The answer will, in part, be a function of the outcome of domestic contests in key countries and their implications for the transnational legal ordering of trade. Yet, given the multiple ways in which trade law capacity matters as a form of capital (or power) and thus an instrumental tool to advance countries' and stakeholders' interests in the highly contested transnational legal field of trade, combined with law's partial autonomy as a field (domestically, internationally, and transnationally), it seems unlikely that the capacity that these countries developed will become irrelevant. Trade law capacity should continue to be deployed in negotiations, dispute settlement, and in domestic policy, and it should be transportable to related areas, such as investment law and international arbitration, as under China's Belt and Road Initiative. However, trade law's role and predominant logic may shift, especially in governing trade relations between the United States, China, and other emerging powers.

First, trade negotiations are continuing in multiple fora. Textual analysis of such free trade agreements shows both borrowing from and references to the WTO,

---

Edward S. Steinfeld, "Playing Our Game: Why China's Rise Doesn't Threaten the West," *Journal of East Asian Studies* 11 (2010): 331.

[25] As Chapter 8 noted, Europe has continued to support the WTO arguably because it has a stronger social safety net and adjustment programs than the United States such that inequality has been less gaping. Moreover, the United States (not Europe) has been the hegemon and is thus more implicated by a hegemonic transition that has been supported by shifts in the relative gains from trade.

[26] William Davey, "Comment on Shaffer/Gao," *Illinois Law Review* 2018 (2018): 36.

which has increased over time.[27] Under the Obama administration, the United States signed the Trans-Pacific Partnership and negotiated with Europe over a Transatlantic Trade and Investment Partnership. Although the Trump administration abandoned the TPP, many of its provisions served as a template for US bilateral negotiations and agreements, including for the revision of NAFTA under the United States-Mexico-Canada Agreement, while new provisions are also being introduced. China, India, and Brazil, in turn, engage in major trade and investment negotiations. China ambitiously aims to construct a Sino-centric trade legal order. India is developing trade networks in South Asia and beyond as part of its "Look East" and "Act East" policies. Brazil remains the dominant economic power in Latin America, and it is negotiating trade and investment agreements in the region and with the world's major economies, while continuing to work to build bridges in WTO negotiations. As trade law expanded and continues to expand beyond the WTO, the demands on legal capacity intensified and should continue.

Moreover, negotiations and deliberations, including attempts at soft law-oriented forms of ordering, will continue at the WTO, such as over fisheries subsidies, electronic commerce, investment facilitation, the domestic regulation of services, agriculture, subsidy notifications, and transparency. If plurilateral agreements are reached, the system could revert to a GATT-like order with side codes.[28] The WTO committee system of monitoring and deliberations will likewise continue and there are calls for making it more active, building from the OECD as a peer-review model of governance.[29]

Second, these countries continue to engage in trade disputes. Even if the WTO's dispute settlement system reverts to what it was under the GATT – where countries held a veto over the adoption of judicial decisions – that system was active, much more so than any other judicial process at the multilateral level.[30] Effective participation in that system can continue to shape the normative understanding of obligations. Meanwhile, China, Brazil, the European Union, and others devised an "interim" WTO appellate mechanism that others will likely join if the WTO Appellate Body is not restored. In addition, regional and bilateral trade and investment negotiations will continue in a competitive environment, and they will contain binding dispute settlement provisions, which may be more frequently

---

[27] Todd Allee, Manfred Elsig, and Andrew Lugg, "The Ties between the World Trade Organization and Preferential Trade Agreements: A Textual Analysis," *Journal of International Economic Law* 20, no. 2 (2017): 333–363.

[28] There already is a plurilateral WTO Agreement on Government Procurement – although it was rumored in 2020 that the Trump administration considered withdrawing from it. New plurilateral agreements could be "open" in being nondiscriminatory against non-members, although they could be conditional, such as requiring a finding of regulatory equivalence.

[29] Interviews, WTO Secretariat Officials and Ambassadors and other officials of different members to the WTO, Geneva, July 2019.

[30] Robert E. Hudec, *Enforcing International Trade Law: The Evolution of the Modern GATT Legal System* (Charlottesville: Lexis Law Publishing, 1993).

used if the WTO system erodes. Bargaining in the shadow of the law and the threat of litigation should continue.

Third, legal know-how initially developed for WTO law is, in part, transportable to related fields. The same domestic lawyers engaged in WTO law have and will partner with government and businesses regarding dispute settlement in other fora. For example, many of the professionals in China that work on negotiations over bilateral investment treaties are the same who work on trade matters, and they build from their trade law experiences, exemplifying the interpenetration of these fields in China. Those in MOFCOM who work on the investment treaty negotiations come from the WTO department, and they work with outside Chinese law firms with significant experience on WTO disputes.[31] The government has harnessed their knowledge to form public-private partnerships in the negotiation of bilateral investment agreements with the United States, European Union, and others.[32] If agreements are reached, these same private law firms hope to work on investor–state cases under the resulting rules. As one lawyer noted, "these law firms can help with the drafting of BIT language because they understand how judicial interpretation works before an international tribunal."[33] Once more, WTO legal knowledge practices diffuse.

Governments' selection of law firms for consultation on international investment matters confirms these links. When in October 2018, China's Ministry of Foreign Affairs announced the law firms selected for its law firm database, it included four subcategories: dispute settlement under the WTO and regional trade agreements; trade barrier investigation and response; trade remedies; and international investment law.[34] Although it is not surprising to see significant overlap in the law firms selected for the first three subcategories given the common subject matter of trade, there was also substantial overlap in the firms listed in the investment law subcategory. The leading Beijing law firms for WTO work, such as King and Wood, Jincheng Tongda & Neal, Zhonglun, and Allbright also are listed in the data base for investment law. Likewise, India's Department of Economic Affairs in the Ministry of Finance, which is responsible for investment negotiation and dispute settlement, considers a law firm's prior representation of the government in international trade disputes as an important attribute in its selection process.

To shape investment law, these countries tapped into the legal capacity that they had built for international trade law. While investment law expertise is distinct in its

---

[31] Interviews with lawyer, Beijing, June 11, 2014, with former MOFCOM official, July 22, 2016, and senior partner, Beijing law firm, July 25, 2016.

[32] Most of China's negotiating team for a bilateral investment treaty with the European Union "came from the WTO sector in MOFCOM." Telephone interview with Chinese lawyer, March 20, 2020.

[33] Interview with senior partner, Beijing law firm, July 25, 2016.

[34] Xie Shanjuan, Zhang Yifei, Shangwubu Lvsuo Shujuku Zaidu Gengxing! Zhexie Lvsuo Ruhe bei Xuanzhong? (MOFCOM Law Firm Database Updated Again! How did These Firms Get Selected?), Lvxinshe, November 7, 2018, available at www.jtnfa.com/cn/news_content.aspx?KeyID=00000000000000003745&MenuID=05003&Lan=CN&PageUrl=news.

technical details, the lawyers in these countries often overlap. This trend is also seen in academia in emerging economies. My coauthors for the chapters on Brazil and India (Michelle Ratton Sanchez Badin and James Nedumpara) exemplify this overlap. Sanchez Badin started as an international trade law academic, consulting with the government, and then turned to investment law, once more consulting with the government while editing a major book entitled *Reconceptualizng International Investment Law from the Global South*.[35] Nedumpara, who worked in India's major trade capacity-building project in the 2000s, now directs the Department of Commerce's Centre on Trade and Investment Law within its Centre for Research in International Trade (or CRIT). Government officials likewise consulted with him on India's development of its model Bilateral Investment Treaty, and he wrote the chapter on India's approach to investment law for Sanchez Badin's book, as well as editing a special issue on India's model BIT.

Such trade law capacity also has helped China build its Belt and Road Initiative, which includes networks of infrastructure contracts, special economic zones, and bilateral trade agreements and memoranda of understanding that, collectively, potentially form a new Sino-centric trade order. When China established the China International Commercial Court in 2018 for disputes under its Belt and Road Initiative, it created an International Commercial Expert Committee to oversee it. The first group of experts included leading Chinese trade law professors such as Shen Sibao and Shi Jingxia, as well as two former WTO Appellate Body Members Zhang Yuejiao from China and David Unterhalter from South Africa, illustrating the links.[36] In 2017, Liu Jingdong, a judge at the Supreme People's Court of China, even suggested using the dispute settlement systems under the WTO or regional trade agreements to handle BRI disputes, signaling Chinese officials' views of the relation of China's experience with the WTO to disputes under its new initiatives.[37] While private lawyers may have separate specialties (especially when it comes to private commercial arbitration), they too provide consulting advice on BRI-related matters. That is the case of the lawyer Peng Jun of the law firm Jincheng Tongda and Neal in Beijing, cited in this book's epigraph.[38] As a lawyer from Huawei stated, "there are skill sets that the young lawyers learned about rule making, about how to create strategy, the importance of thinking ahead; about how to use dispute settlement which was not in the Chinese mindset. Lots of young lawyers will

---

[35]   Fabio Morosini and Michelle Ratton Sanchez Badin, *Reconceptualizng International Investment Law from the Global South* (Cambridge: Cambridge University Press, 2018).

[36]   The two law professors are from the University of International Business and Economics School of Law in Beijing (known as UIBE). Supreme People's Court, The Decision on Appointment of the First Group of Members for the International Commercial Expert Committee, August 24, 2018, at http://cicc.court.gov.cn/html/1/219/235/245/index.html.

[37]   Liu Jingdong, Yidai Yilu Fazhihua Tixi Goujian Yanjiu (A Study on the Establishment of the BRI Legal Governance System), Zhengfa Luntan (Tribune of Political Science and Law), 2017, No. 5, at www.iolaw.org.cn/showArticle.aspx?id=5280.

[38]   Interview, Beijing, 2018.

be affected for the next thirty years. The Chinese legal community has grown leaps and bounds."[39]

Fourth, legal capacity should remain critical for the implementation of state commitments under trade agreements, which trigger domestic contests among stakeholders that attempt to harness international law where helpful to press for domestic change. Trade law should continue to affect multiple areas of domestic law, including customs, intellectual property, and import relief law, as well as procedural approaches applied to all regulation that can implicate trade and investment. Such policymaking involves contestation not only between countries, but also within them.

Yet, the context in which states and other actors develop and deploy trade law capacity has changed. The ordering of trade relations through great power coercion, rather than third-party legal rulings, has reemerged sharply as the US reverted to unilateral measures, others responded in kind, and the WTO's authority declined. Arguably the United States is attempting to compel a revision of the rules of the game to curtail the role of the state in China's economy. It has raised tariffs, in contravention of WTO rules, to compel bilateral negotiations that, in its view, will attain greater "balance." How successful it will be is another question. In a changing global context where geoeconomic strategizing has become more salient, what will be the predominant role and logic for deploying legal capacity?

From this book's legal realist approach to international law, international trade law has both instrumental "lawfare" and "public goods" aspects. In a heightened geoeconomic context, trade law will likely assume a more instrumental, lawfare-type role and logic, especially in relations between the United States and China. In such case, each side can deploy legal arguments to justify and legitimize its actions by harnessing law's normative authority, while avoiding the constraints of neutral, third-party dispute settlement. In parallel, the public goods side of international trade law, involving public reason before and by a neutral third-party institution to resolve disputes and help resolve common problems is declining. Law can still play a public goods role in translating political contests into legal terms to address coordination and cooperation challenges. Yet, international trade law and institutions likely will play more constrained and instrumental roles compared to the WTO multilateral system at the height of its authority. In the context of geoeconomic rivalry, transnational legal ordering should continue to serve as an instrumental tool, and legal ordering should shift from a centralized multilateral system to a pluralist ecology of overlapping and competing trade legal orders of which the WTO forms just a part.

B. *Final Words*

Political fault lines over trade are not just between states, but also within them so that analysis must disaggregate the state. Such politics shape legal ordering transnationally.

---

[39] Telephone interview, March 23, 2020.

Developments in China implicate companies and workers in the United States; the rise of US economic nationalism implicates companies and workers in China. International law and institutions such as the WTO can provide an interface that helps to shape those interactions, but international law and institutions are also reciprocally shaped by them. International law and institutions are both medium and outcome.

For trade liberals, this book has the arc of a tragedy. International trade law rose in prominence and trade law norms permeated deeply within emerging powers' laws, institutions, and professions. Yet, the very success of such transnational legal ordering triggered unintended consequences. As these countries rose in economic importance and built legal capacity to wield WTO law to defend and advance their positions, the United States became disenchanted with the legal order it had created. It elected an economic nationalist who became "a wrecking ball," unsettling the transnational legal order for trade and broader economic governance.

Effective transnational legal orders must be grounded in common perceptions of problems that law can address. If perceptions of underlying problems shift in radically divergent ways within the United States, European Union, and these emerging powers, then the WTO as a multilateral institution based on common rules that permeate domestic laws and institutions becomes unsettled. There is no end of history, no unidirectional force toward a particular manifestation, breadth, or depth of transnational legal ordering. Norms settle and unsettle, internationally and domestically, often in parallel. Will the centralized WTO legal order for trade decline with no replacement? Will it adapt to new challenges? Will the trade legal order fragment into overlapping and competing regional and other transnational legal orders?

The challenge for states will be how to maintain and adapt the international trade legal order to changing political and economic contexts. To maintain the international trading system to foster economic order, sustainable and inclusive growth, and the pacific settlement of disputes through law, the United States, European Union, China, India, and Brazil will need to collaborate to define rules governing the interface of their economies. International trade law and institutions are no nirvana, but the alternative to them could be dire. To paraphrase Peng from this book's epigraph, we are in the history and make the history with the choices we make today.

Acknowledgments

All books are coproductions and originals at the same time. They build on what one has seen, read, and heard, and they synthesize, conceptualize, and analyze in new ways. To paraphrase the great American poet of democracy Walt Whitman, this book contains multitudes.[1] It is a coproduction with those from whom I have learned in diverse ways, including from those interviewed over two decades.

The research spans my employment at four universities, the University of Wisconsin, Loyola University Chicago, the University of Minnesota, and the University of California, Irvine, which I thank for their support. I also thank the National Science Foundation Law and Social Science Program for its research grant for the study of "WTO Dispute Settlement and Legal Capacity" (Grant SES0351192). I thank the World Trade Organization for accepting me as a visiting scholar, and the International Centre on Trade and Sustainable Development for its logistical and research support. I thank David Trubek for first encouraging me to go to Brazil, launching the first case study for this book.

This book builds from earlier work that I published as articles, and, in this sense, it represents a career's worth of empirical and theoretical work. Four of its chapters build from and substantially update, expand, and adapt case studies that I earlier wrote with coauthors Michelle Ratton Sanchez Badin (on Brazil), James Nedumpara and Aseema Sinha (on India), and Henry Gao (on China).[2]

---

[1] Walt Whitman, "Song of Myself," #51, *Leaves of Grass* ("I am large. I contain multitudes.").
[2] In particular, " The Trials of Winning at the WTO: What Lies behind Brazil's Success," *Cornell International Law Journal* 41, no. 2 (2008): 383–501 (with Michelle Ratton Sanchez and Barbara Rosenberg) (relating to Chapter 4); "State Transformation and the Rise of Lawyers: The WTO, India, and Transnational Legal Ordering," *Law & Society Review* 49, no. 3 (2015): 595–629 (with James Nedumpara and Aseema Sinha) (relating to Chapter 5); "China's Rise: How it Took on the U.S. at the WTO," *University of Illinois Law Review* 2018, no. 1 (2018): 115–184 (with Henry Gao) (relating to Chapter 6); and "A New Chinese Economic Order?," *Journal of International Economic Law* 23, no. 3 (2020): 1–29 (with Henry Gao) (relating to Chapter 7); as well as "The Challenges of WTO Law: Strategies for Developing Country Adaptation," *World Trade Review* 5, no. 2 (2006): 177–198 (relating to Chapter 3).

Many people commented on this manuscript at different stages; I hope that I have captured all of them, but surely I have missed some. Commenting on all or a significant part of the manuscript were Claude Barfield, Rachel Brewster Kathleen Claussen, Joseph Conti, Christina Davis, Manfred Elsig, Bryant Garth, Tom Ginsburg, Terry Halliday, Jennifer Hillman, Bernard Hoekman, Kristen Hopewell, Ji Li, Jacques deLisle, Nicolas Lamp, Simon Lester, George Marcus, Tim Meyer, Krzysztof Pelc, Anthea Roberts, Dani Rodrik, Wayne Sandholtz, Alvaro Santos, Alec Stone Sweet, Mark Wu, and two members of the WTO secretariat.

Commenting on early versions of individual chapters were William Alford, Karen Alter, José Alvarez, Juilian Arato, Welber Barral, Chad Bown, Sungjoon Cho, Henrique Choer Moraes, Juscelino Colares, Seth Davis, Mathew Erie, Kevin Davis, Christine Harrington, Alexandra Huneeus, Rob Howse, Benedict Kingsbury, Wei Liang, Robert Lutz, Stephen Marks, Jide Nzelibe, John Odell, John Ohnesorge, Gustavo Oliveira, Margaret Pearson, Nancy Reichman, Benjamin van Rooij, Ben Ross Schneider, Ken Shadlen, Debra Steger, Matt Taylor, Vera Thorstensen, Chris Whytock, Robert Wolfe, Claire Wright, and Peter Yu.

Early versions of the work were presented at workshops at the American Bar Foundation, Australia National University, Brooklyn Law School, CATO Institute, China Center on WTO Studies (Beijing), Columbia University, European University Institute, FGV Direito (São Paulo), Harvard Law School, IDC Herzliya (Israel), Indian School of Business (Hyderabad), ITAM (Mexico City), Jawaharlal Nehru University (JNU, New Delhi), Jiao Tong University (Shanghai), Law and Society Association annual meetings, National Law University Delhi, National Law University Jodphur, Northwestern University, Pontificia Universidad Católica de Chile, Princeton University, Stanford Law School, University of Amsterdam, University of California, Irvine, University of California, Los Angeles, University of Chicago, University of New South Wales, University of Oslo (Pluricourts), University of Southern California, University of Wisconsin, Vanderbilt Law School, World Trade Institute (Berne), World Trade Organization, and Yale Law School.

I am humbled and immensely grateful for these friends' and colleagues' generosity. As one participant at a workshop on the manuscript wrote afterward, "these rare gatherings are a highlight of the profession." The book would not be the same without such exchanges. They are indelibly woven into the manuscript.

I likewise thank numerous excellent research assistants. Those helping me with different aspects of the manuscript at the University of California, Irvine include Erin Costigliolo, Joshua Himmelstern, Allyson Myers, Lauren Navarro, Isaac Ramsey, Benjamin Raynor, Paul Strickland, Chris Valentino, Stephanie Vancil De Olveira, and Carolyn Wang. I also thank the librarians at UCI and the University of Minnesota, and in particular Jessica Pierucci and Mary Rumsey.

Finally, I thank my wife Michele and children Brooks and Sage for their love and support. They are part of me and are in this book. Sage applied her artistic talent to help design the cover for the book.

I close with lines from *"L'Art Poetique"* by the French poet Nicolas Boileau (1636 – 1711), which Sonia Rolland brought to my attention at the book workshop.

> *Hâtez-vous lentement, et, sans perdre courage,*
> *Vingt fois sur le métier remettez votre ouvrage:*
> *Polissez-le sans cesse et le repolissez;*
> *Ajoutez quelquefois, et souvent effacez.*

Here is a rough English translation:

> *Hasten slowly, and without losing courage,*
> *Twenty times put your work back on the loom;*
> *Polish endlessly, and then repolish;*
> *Add sometimes, and often remove.*

I hope I have polished, added, and removed with the right balance. If only the trade legal order could do so.

Abbreviations

ACWL – Advisory Centre on WTO Law
AIIB – Asian Infrastructure Investment Bank
ASEAN – Association of Southeast Asian Nations
ASSOCHAM – Associated Chambers of Commerce and Industry of India
BIT – Bilateral Investment Treaty
BNDES – Brazilian National Development Bank
BRI – Belt and Road Initiative
BRICS – Brazil, Russia, India, China, and South Africa
CAMEX – Brazil's Interministerial Chamber of Foreign Trade
CII – Confederation of Indian Industry
CNI – Brazil's National Confederation of Industries
CRIT – India's Centre for Research in International Trade
DSU – WTO Dispute Settlement Understanding, which is an abbreviation of the
    WTO Understanding on Rules and Procedures Governing the Settlement of
    Disputes
DTL – Department of Treaty and Law
EFTA – European Free Trade Area
FDI – Foreign direct investment
FGV – Fundação Getulio Vargas in Brazil
FICCI – Federation of Indian Chamber of Commerce and Industry
FIESP – Industry Federation of São Paulo
FTA – Free Trade Agreement
GATT – General Agreement on Tariffs and Trade
GDP – Gross domestic product
GSP – General System of Preferences
ICSID – International Centre for Settlement of Investment Disputes
IMF – International Monetary Fund
INMETRO – Brazil's National Institute of Metrology, Standardization and
    Industrial Quality

ISDS – Investor-State Dispute Settlement
MOFCOM – Ministry of Commerce of the People's Republic of China
MOFTEC – Ministry of Foreign Trade and Economic Cooperation
NAFTA – North American Free Trade Agreement
NGO – Non-governmental organization
OECD – Organisation for Economic Co-operation and Development
PPP – Purchasing power parity
RCEP – Regional Comprehensive Economic Partnership
SOE – State-owned enterprise
TLO – Transnational legal order
TPP – Trans-Pacific Partnership
TRIPS – WTO Agreement on Trade-Related Aspects of Intellectual Property Rights
TTIP – Transatlantic Trade and Investment Partnership
UN – United Nations
UNCITRAL – United Nations Commission on International Trade Law
UNCTAD – United Nations Conference on Trade and Development
USMCA – United States-Mexico-Canada Agreement
USTR – United States Trade Representative
WIPO – World Intellectual Property Organization
WTO – World Trade Organization

CPSIA information can be obtained
at www.ICGtesting.com
Printed in the USA
FSHW021657200521
81658FS